THE DRINK DIRECTORY

1,025 Recipes for the Home and Professional Bartender

by Lionel Braun and Marion Gorman

The Bobbs-Merrill Company, Inc.
Indianapolis/New York

COPYRIGHT© 1982 by Lionel Braun and Marion Gorman

All rights reserved.
No part of this publication may be reproduced, stored in a retrieval system or transmitted in any form or by any means, mechanical, electronic, photocopying, recording or otherwise without the prior written permission of the publisher. For information, address The Bobbs-Merrill Co., Inc., 630 Third Avenue, New York, NY 10017

Library of Congress Cataloging in Publication Data
Braun, Lionel
  The drink directory.
  Includes index.
  1. Alcoholic beverages.   2. Beverages.
I. Gorman, Marion.   II. Title.
TX951.B774   641.8'74   82-4239
ISBN 0-672-52705-7   AACR2

Published by The Bobbs-Merrill Company, Inc.
Indianapolis/New York
Manufactured in the United States of America

Designed by Sheila Lynch

Cover design by Mary McKenna Ridge

Many thanks to Libbey Glass for the use of their glassware art.
(Libbey Glass, Div. of Owens-Illinois, Toledo, Ohio)

FIRST EDITION
FOURTH PRINTING — 1984

Contents

The Changing World of Having a Drink	v
About Modern Mixology	1
What to Drink When	1
Bar Equipment	4
Preparation Equipment	8
Ingredient Supplies	9
Prepared Cocktail Mixes	13
Bar Snacks	14
Measurements	15
Shapes of Wine Bottles	17
Calorie Measures	18
Basic Bartending Techniques	19
Drink Chemistry	23
Classic Types of Drinks and Basic Recipes	24
Wines	34
About Wine	34
White Wine Recipes	55
Red Wine Recipes	58
Sparkling Wine Recipes	62
Sherry Recipes	71
Aperitifs	74
About Aperitifs, Vermouth, and Bitters	74
Aperitif Recipes	78

Spirits	89
About Spirits	89
Aquavit Recipes	105
Brandy Recipes	108
Gin Recipes	130
Liqueur Recipes	168
Rum Recipes	211
Tequila Recipes	245
Vodka Recipes	260
Whiskey Recipes	282
Blended	282
Bourbon	296
Canadian	306
Irish	311
Scotch	315
Other Spirit Recipes	323
Beer, Ale, and Sake	324
About Beer, Ale, and Sake	324
Beer, Ale, and Sake Recipes	330
Punches	333
Hot Drinks	350
Non-Alcoholic Drinks	364
Index	369

The Changing World of Having a Drink

A postulate of human progress is surely that the freedom to drink alcohol has brought much of our great advance. Samuel Johnson was his wise self when he said: "There is nothing yet which has been contrived by man by which so much happiness is produced as by a good tavern or inn."

Along with many standard preparations, there are many new drinks which reflect America's more "open" break with traditional ideas. The names of today's drinks are more inventive, more topical, and getting somewhat sweeter. It is estimated that there are around 8,000 different drink recipes being poured today.

Putting this book together had its difficulties. For one, the assistance of so many friends helped put us in good spirits, and put good spirits in us! Marion Gorman and I welcomed contributions from suppliers and bartenders in the United States as well as the United Kingdom, Italy, Mexico, and France who made it possible to understand so much. We absorbed comments and criticisms from liquor-store owners and salesmen, as well as such disparate individuals as lawyers, athletes, and theatre people. Along with the contributions of many distillers, there was the good counsel of A. Buchman for *American Beverage Alcohol Association*.

There is a special admiration and love for A. R., who turned on the light when I was very young a long time ago; and J. C., who kept the light bright; L. S., who complained about the big electric bill; and "Duke," whose sense of theatre played more to humor than tragedy. During the research for this book, I saw too many glasses, too many versions of the same drink, but always, thankfully, a good-sized crowd of contemporary young who embraced the seductive new drinks, and combinations of spirits, that keep the wine and spirit industry from obsolescing.

I am now in full belief that there exists a conspiracy by the younger consumer who, long before the world is blown away, will create a space age cocktail in a new video-game tavern, a Miami disco, or a Beverly Hills bistro, that will dazzle dining and dancing habitúes, as well as the professional bartender trying hard not to be seductive with his assortment of spirits, creams, herbs, and sleight of hand.

The accomplished bartender, which you will learn to be with this book, is a good entertainer. He can shake your drink and stir your emotions! Like any good performer, he can divert you from yourself. You'll experience mixing techniques that may be deliberate or flamboyant, but always with a reassuring face to help you invest a measure of trust in his show. The bartender's performance is sometimes new and sometimes startling, but always to please an audience.

In this book of 1,025 drinks, I have for the most part had to taste most of them with little enough company. I believe my real enjoyment and the social niceties proffered by many of the products was completely lost in selfishness. The pleasure of the mixed drink is sharing it with another! And, now that I can see the finished arrangement and great variety available, it is my intention to restore some sweetness to my soul by having one different drink each night with at least one different friend. "A woman drove me to drink," said W. C. Fields, "and I never wrote to thank her!" More than one lady got me this far and this book is for all of them. Let us move to the bar and permit me to toast them with a drink for 1,025 nights!

Lionel Braun
New York, 1982

About Modern Mixology

WHAT TO DRINK WHEN

A long time ago there existed for most of us a listing of rules for the "before and after" types of drinks that were considered most appropriate during those occasions calling for alcoholic beverages at a social occasion.

This what-and-when of preprandial and postprandial drinks was like a doctor's prescription: exacting, definitive, sweet or sour to the taste, geared to a confining lifestyle and never varying! However, as these are more imaginative times, we are finding more occasions to drink (although consuming a bit less during the occasion), with more leisure time providing reasons to try new tastes.

The word *cocktail* originally meant the drink that preceded the meal, ideally a more or less dry libation to encourage the appetite. Today, when wine has become an anytime drink and liqueurs are soaring to unheard of popularity in variety and mixtures—also for anytime—perhaps any drink interlude can be called a cocktail. (In Great Britain, however, for a cocktail to be called a cocktail, it must have a minimum of three ingredients, exclusive of ice and garnish, by law!)

The traditionalist's after-dinner drink was and is cognac, brandy, Drambuie, Benedictine, or a singular potion accompanied by good black coffee. The more outgoing called for a Stinger, a Scorpion, or a Grasshopper. It was these combinations of liqueurs that inspired Grand Marnier from "neat and straight" to one of the most versatile liqueurs on the bar. "Vodka and" was another building block for the mixed-drink revolution now taking place. The standard and favorite Irish Coffee spawned another list of new after-dinner inspirations. The really inventive consumers are mixing liqueurs and spirits faster than all of the spirit houses can release their new taste thrills. There is Amaretto di Saronno, with its host of copiers, and Pistacha, Frangelico, Lemonier, Midori, the incredible Bailey's Irish Cream, and now peppermint schnapps (already represented by brands from almost every major supplier).

I believe this means that the formality that once pervaded our drinking styles is being relaxed, in much the same way that ethnic foods were once known as "gourmet" foods, only to become a part of today's normal eating environment (e.g., tacos, paella, quiche, frittata, shish kebab, bagels, sushi, mu shu pork). Only two summers ago I was shocked to see tourists (not Americans) in Aix-en-Provence drinking Piña Coladas with salade niçoise!

When it comes to modern mixing, a word of caution: If you choose to go a "long way" with the pleasures of social drinking, keep the number of drinks you consume to half of what you think you can handle. The fun is getting "there" and back!

Current Trends

Starters
Dry sparkling wine. Wine, aperitif wine, or spirit mixed drinks with substantial fruit juice, vegetable juice, broth, or club soda (not too sweet); examples: Kir, Bloody Mary, Bloody Bull, Sangrita Highball, Salty Dog, sherry—dry or medium dry, Campari.

Morning-After and Eye Openers
Shot of straight spirit or Coca Cola neat. Bloody Mary with raw egg. Milk-based mixed drink (not sweet), such as flips.

Brunch
Dry or medium-dry white, rosé, or sparkling wine. Sherry. Aperitif, vermouth, or bitters-based drinks. Any wine or spirit mixed with substantial fruit juice, vegetable juice, broth, or club soda.

Cocktail, Aperitif, Before Meals, Happy Hour
Anything goes!
Dry white, red, or sparkling wine—plain, with ice, spritzer, or mixed drinks. Sherry—dry or sweet. Aperitif, vermouth, or bitters-based drinks. Spirits—straight, on the rocks, with chasers, mixed—all types (traditionally, not too sweet, but with the younger crowd—wine, vodka, rum, tequila, fruit-based drinks, liqueur concoctions).

With Meals
Wine: Wine romances food and accounts for as many good eating marriages as there are specialties chosen by people who savor the art of eating. Wine can be a digestive aid. **Beer:** Many people enjoy beer with their meals, especially with foods that are hot, spicy, or Oriental in nature. **Spirits:** Some people are determined to stay with their favorite Martini or favorite cocktail throughout the meal. If this is your style, you're boss of your own stomach—but when dining starts, you'll be better "off" the hard stuff!

After Meals
For a grand finalé to any good meal, a fine sauterne with dessert or a fortified wine, brandy, or liqueur to be served straight for sipping. If you like postprandial potions, you have a big selection to choose from—other than pousse cafés, frappés, or coffees laced with spirits.

For Nights on the Town
New drinks are like new hit tunes. Ask any bartender who serves a mixed crowd in a club or disco. Classic brandy drinks (with liqueur or fruit mixes) still have their constituency, and there are those who will never veer from their guiding spirit, be it gin, whiskey, or vodka, by day or by night. But if it's a younger crowd, have plenty of rum, tequila, vodka, fruit juices, liqueurs, and wine on hand.

Parties and Holidays
Bar service for a party may range anywhere from a few bottles of

chilled wine and/or basic spirits and mixes, depending on the preferences of the crowd, to a wider selection when the bar is attended by a caterer. Today small receptions often offer dry white wine and sparkling wine only.

When the occasion is ceremonial and festive, such as a wedding, reunion, or holiday get-together, a bowl of punch always enhances the celebration. In warm weather, wine and fruit punches with floats of fresh fruit provide refreshment and tingle for the assembled guests. During winter holidays and celebrations, eggnog, milk punches, or sturdy brandy-bourbon-fruit punches enhance the spirit of camaraderie. In ski lodges, country houses, and other pleasure palaces, hot wine and spirit drinks can add extra warmth!

Nightcap

Alone or together, in these days of stress and strain, a smooth, cushiony bedtime drink helps to bring on sweet dreams. Egg or cream-coated mixed drinks or just a glass of red wine are certainly more pleasurable than pills and other palliatives.

BAR EQUIPMENT

Glassware

Clear, uncolored glassware is preferred for all drinks. Thin glass (budget permitting) seems to make wine, especially, taste better.

Home All-Purpose Supply

10- to 14-oz. Stem Wine Glass

Pat della Monica, long-time head bartender at Windows on the World in New York, recommends this as the ideal all-purpose glass for the home bar. In his home, he keeps a supply in the freezer at all times (top down) and uses them to serve any kind of drink, from a 2-oz. brandy or whiskey, to a 4-oz. cocktail, to a big 14-oz. cooler or foam-capped beer. It is festive, too.

Professional Basic Assortment

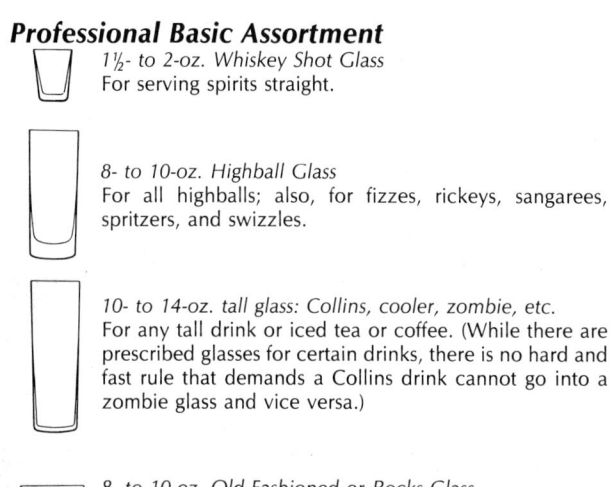

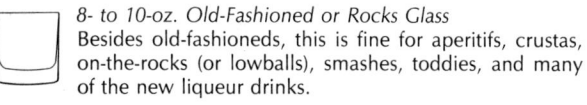

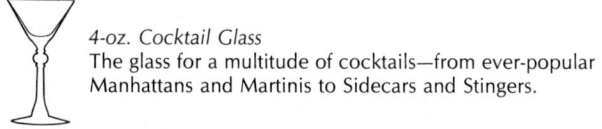

1½- to 2-oz. *Whiskey Shot Glass*
For serving spirits straight.

8- to 10-oz. *Highball Glass*
For all highballs; also, for fizzes, rickeys, sangarees, spritzers, and swizzles.

10- to 14-oz. *tall glass: Collins, cooler, zombie, etc.*
For any tall drink or iced tea or coffee. (While there are prescribed glasses for certain drinks, there is no hard and fast rule that demands a Collins drink cannot go into a zombie glass and vice versa.)

8- to 10-oz. *Old-Fashioned or Rocks Glass*
Besides old-fashioneds, this is fine for aperitifs, crustas, on-the-rocks (or lowballs), smashes, toddies, and many of the new liqueur drinks.

4-oz. *Cocktail Glass*
The glass for a multitude of cocktails—from ever-popular Manhattans and Martinis to Sidecars and Stingers.

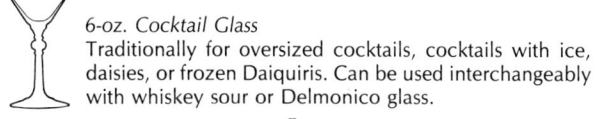

6-oz. *Cocktail Glass*
Traditionally for oversized cocktails, cocktails with ice, daisies, or frozen Daiquiris. Can be used interchangeably with whiskey sour or Delmonico glass.

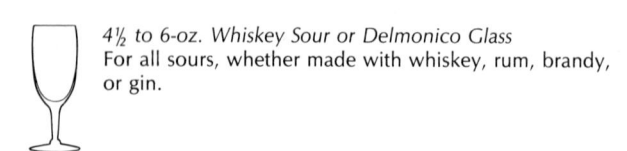

4½ to 6-oz. Whiskey Sour or Delmonico Glass
For all sours, whether made with whiskey, rum, brandy, or gin.

10- to 14-oz. All Purpose Wine Glass
While wine drinks may range in quantity from 4 or more oz., the 10- to 14-oz. all-purpose balloon glass has become increasingly popular as the utilitarian glass for wine, cocktails, highballs, or even a glass of beer. *Note:* The standard 8-oz. glass may, of course, be used for drinks of this capacity.

6- to 8-oz. Tulip Champagne Glass
Today we properly drink sparkling wine in tall, narrow glasses (tulip or flute shapes) to capture the bubbles that are the purpose and reason for the price of champagne. It's a shame to lose them in the wide champagne saucers.

6-, 12-, 16-oz. Brandy Snifter
Choose your preference. The larger the bowl, the more aroma to sniff. In addition to brandy, these glasses are used for liqueurs.

2- to 3-oz. Sherry Glass
For sherry; also for sipping liqueurs.

2-oz Brandy, Pony, or Pousse Café Glass
For straight brandy and liqueurs and for the popular pousse café—a drink constructed of multiple layers of different liquids.

12-oz. Pilsner Glass
Frosted cold, the classiest, most inviting way to drink a glass of beer.

6- to 8-oz. Punch Cup
These usually accompany a large punch bowl. Punch cups, as well as the bowl, should be prechilled.

8- to 10-oz. Heatproof Mug
For all hot drinks and coffee, except after-dinner coffee, when an 8-oz. coffee cup and saucer or demitasse is used.

Specialty Glasses

7½-oz. Parfait Glass
Often used for drinks containing fruit and/or ice cream.

22- to 24-oz. Hurricane Glass, 12- to 15-oz. Squall, 8-oz. Breeze
For tall fruit drinks.

PREPARATION EQUIPMENT

16-oz. mixing glass

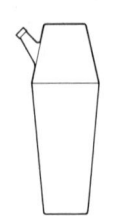

16-oz. shaker

Bar spoon (long handle)
Blender, electric
Citrus juicer
Coasters
Cocktail napkins
Cocktail picks
Cutting board, small

Egg beater
Funnel
Ice bucket (insulated) and tongs
Ice scoop
Jigger measure, double-ended 1-oz. and 1½-oz.

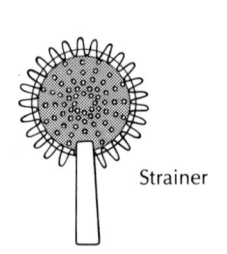

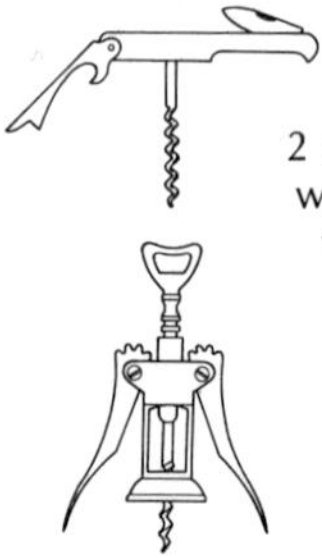

2 corkscrews:
waiter's type
wing type

Strainer

Lemon/lime squeezer
Martini pitcher and stirring rod
Measuring cup
Measuring spoons

Muddler (for crushing mint), sugar cubes, etc.
Paring knife
Stirrers (for serving glasses)
Towels

INGREDIENT SUPPLIES

Alcoholic Stock

Buying Policies

Wine: When you are not familiar with a wine, buy two 750 ml. bottles before buying a case (two, because even one bottle of the greatest wine could be off). For everyday drinking there is a variety of jug wines (domestic and imported) from which to choose. The familiar 1.5 liter (magnum) size is available in a wide selection of brands and price ranges, both domestic and imported.

Spirits: It is sensible to buy known brands for entertaining. There really is a difference in quality from the cheap no-name bottle to the advertised national or regional brand, even in neutral vodkas. In some states, spirits can be purchased in jug sizes, and there is a price advantage. These large containers, however, are not conducive to easy handling, and a decanter is useful to facilitate pouring.

Prepared cocktails, containing spirit base and mixer ingredients, are sold in cans and bottles, in individual servings and larger sizes. For the most part, these premixed drinks are lower in proof than you might normally expect of a cocktail fashioned in a bar or by yourself.

Storing Alcoholic Beverages

Wine: Unopened bottles of nonvintage, jug, and fortified wines can be stored without refrigeration. A safer consideration is to always keep whites cooler than reds. Once opened, nonvintage and jug wines should be refrigerated. Fortified wines, which are higher in alcohol content, can be recorked and will survive for an extended time, even at room temperature.

Spirits: Can be stored at room temperature, even after they are opened. For high-demand drinks, especially those using vodka and gin, it is a good idea to keep a supply of these spirits in the refrigerator.

Beer: The American preference is well chilled.

Minimum Supply

- **1** 1.75 liters vodka
- **1** 1.75 liters Scotch whisky
- **1** 1.75 liters gin
- **1** 1.75 liters rum
- **1** 750 ml. dry vermouth
- **1** 750 ml. sweet vermouth
- **1** 750 ml. coffee liqueur
- **1** 750 ml. amaretto (almond flavor) or Frangelico (hazelnut) liqueur
- **1** 750 ml. B & B (Benedictine and brandy)
- **1** 750 ml. Grand Marnier
- **1** 750 ml. cream liqueur (e.g., Bailey's Irish Cream)
- **2** 750 ml. dry sparkling wine
- **1** 750 ml. spumante
- **4** 750 ml. dry red wine
- **8** 750 ml. dry white wine
- **6** 750 ml. lambrusco type wine
- **2** 6-packs beer

Connoisseur Basic Supply

Vodka:
- **1** 750 ml. American (for mixed drinks)
- **1** 750 ml. Absolut or Finlandia imported (for clean vodka Martini)

Whiskey:
- 1 750 ml. American blended
- 1 750 ml. Bourbon
- 1 750 ml. Sour mash or Tennessee
- 1 750 ml. Canadian
- 1 750 ml. Irish
- 1 750 ml. Scotch (light)
- 1 750 ml. Scotch (heavier or 12-year-old)

Gin:
- 1 750 ml. English
- 1 750 ml. American

Rum:
- 1 750 ml. light
- 1 750 ml. gold
- 1 750 ml. dark
- 1 350 ml. overproof (130+)

Tequila:
- 1 750 ml. white

Brandies:
- 1 750 ml. V.S.O.P. Cognac
- 1 750 ml. California
- 1 500 ml. kirsch
- 1 500 ml. framboise
- 1 500 ml. calvados

Liqueurs:
- 1 750 ml. or 500 ml. bottle of each of following:
    Amaretto
    Benedictine
    Coffee
    Cream liqueur (e.g., Bailey's Irish)
    Drambuie
    Grand Marnier
    Sambuca Romana (anisette)

1 375 ml. bottle of each of following:
   Apricot
   Banana
   Cointreau
   Crème de cacao (dark)
   Crème de cacao (white)
   Crème de menthe (white)
   Maraschino
   Peppermint schnapps
   Strawberry

Aperitifs, Vermouth, Bitters:
1 750 ml. dry vermouth
1 750 ml. sweet vermouth
1 750 ml. Campari
1 375 ml. Angostura bitters
1 375 ml. orange bitters

Bar wine:
2 750 ml. dry sparkling wine
1 750 ml. spumante
4 750 ml. dry red wine
6 750 ml. lambrusco type
8 750 ml. dry white wine

Beer:
2 6-packs (premium or imported)
1 6-pack (light)

Other Basic Drink Ingredients

Carbonated beverages:
   club soda, cola, ginger ale, 7-Up, tonic water
Citrus fruits:
   lemons, limes, oranges—for peel, wedge, juice, or slice
Coconut cream or Piña Colada mix
Cocktail onions
Grenadine syrup
Ice cubes

Maraschino cherries
Mint sprigs
Nutmeg (whole) and grater
Olives, green and black
Rose's lime juice
Salt
Sugar Syrup (see Index)
Superfine sugar
Tabasco sauce
Worcestershire sauce

Special Ingredients

The compleat bartender and host will review favorite drink recipes for special ingredients—certain spirits, liqueurs, vermouths, bitters, and such nonalcoholic accoutrements as cream, eggs, fresh fruit, tomato juice, syrups, nutmeg, pepper mill, cinnamon sticks, etc.

PREPARED COCKTAIL MIXES

Packaged mixes, to which all you need add is the spirit, are available in both dry and liquid forms. They should not be confused with "prepared cocktails," which already have varied amounts of spirit in the preparation. Prepared mixes are convenient for inventorying ingredients for drinks that may not be readily available or are used infrequently. They are easily transportable. Many people use these mixes and find them quite satisfactory, assured of consistency in drink tastes when used according to manufacturer's instructions. Most good bartenders, however, prefer to use fresh ingredients, which afford better taste and always an element of creativity in drink preparation.

BAR SNACKS

Since snack foods have become a major American industry, there is no excuse for the host not to have an arsenal of tasty tidbits to serve with a drink. If it is a party occasion, most likely special trays of festive hors d'oeuvres will be prepared. But a thoughtful bartender or host also maintains a supply of storable snacks for casual and impromptu occasions. The following are some categories of snack foods that can be stored for reasonably long periods of time:

PANTRY
Artichoke hearts
Beans, canned Mexican
Breads, crisp
Capers
Catsup
Chips, potato, corn, banana
Crackers (variety)
Curry Powder
Dressings (cheese flavored and vinaigrette—for dips)
Fish, canned (anchovies sardines, tuna, etc.)
Ham, canned
Mustards
Olives, green, ripe, stuffed
Pâté
Pickles
Pimiento
Popcorn
Raisins
Trail Mix

REFRIGERATOR
Avocado (for dip mixture)
Butter
Cheeses
Frankfurters
Fruit
Horseradish
Italian peppers, pickled
Mayonnaise
Onions
Pâté
Sausages
Sour cream
Tomatoes, cherry
Vegetables (for crudités)— scallions, zucchini, carrots, peppers, celery, cauliflower, broccoli, etc.

FREEZER
Bacon
French bread (baguettes)
Frozen hors d'oeuvres (various—e.g., egg rolls, bouchèes)
Nuts (variety)
Pizza mini-size
Quiche
Ratatouille

MEASUREMENTS

Mixing Measures
1 pinch = ⅛ tsp.
1 dash = ⅙ tsp.
1 tsp. = ⅙ fl. oz.
1 tbs. = ½ fl. oz.
1 pony = 1 fl. oz.
1 jigger = 1½ fl. oz.
2 tbs. = 1 fl. oz.
4 tbs. = ¼ cup = 2 fl. oz.
8 tbs. = ½ cup = 4 fl. oz.
1 cup = ½ pint = 8 fl. oz.
2 cups = 1 pint = 16 fl. oz.
4 cups = 1 qt. = 32 fl. oz.
16 cups = 4 qt. = 1 fl. gal.

Distilled Spirit Bottle Measures

New Metric Measures

Metric Bottle Size	Fluid Ounces	Bottles Per Case
50 ml.	1.7	120
200 ml.	6.8	48
500 ml.	16.9	24
750 ml.	25.4	12
1 liter	33.8	12
1.75 liters	59.2	6

Former U.S. Measures (Approx.)

U.S. Bottle Size	Fluid Ounces
Miniature	1.6
½ pint	8
1 pint	16
⅘ quart ("fifth")	25.6
1 quart	32
½ gallon	64

Wine Bottle Measures

Metric Bottle Size	Fluid Ounces	Name of Bottle	Bottles Per Case
187 ml.	6.3	Split	48
375 ml.	12.7	Tenth	24
750 ml.	25.4	Fifth	12
1 liter	33.8	Quart	12
1.5 liters	50.7	Magnum	6
3 liters	101.4	Double Magnum	4

Today jug wines are marketed in various large-volume containers (glass and cartons), from 1.5 liters to 4 liters, or "wine-in-box," which may contain up to 18 liters.

Servings per Bottle

Spirits:	750 ml. (25.4-oz.)	16 to 24 servings
Wine:	" " " "	6 servings
Sparkling wine:	" " " "	6 to 8 servings

SHAPES OF WINE BOTTLES

Time was when one could tell a wine by the shape of its bottle—the sloping shoulders of the Burgundy, the high shoulders of the Bordeaux, or the slender silhouette for Moselle. Merchandising has taken over, and every producer is seeking some unique product identification. Other than the traditionalists, today's negociant or industrial winemaker uses whatever shape seems to strike a fancy. The more objective, of course, use the bottle shape best related to the original tradition of the wine, e.g., a California Cabernet Sauvignon is usually bottled in a Bordeaux-style bottle, because Cabernet Sauvignon is associated with Bordeaux wine. Still, the principal bottle shapes referred to in the industry are these:

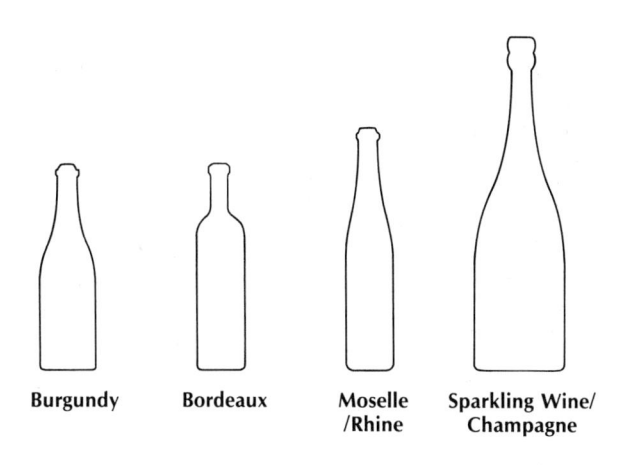

Burgundy **Bordeaux** **Moselle /Rhine** **Sparkling Wine/ Champagne**

CALORIE MEASURES

Beverage	Calories In 1 fl. oz.	Calories in Average Serving — Serving Size	Calories
BEER	13	12 fl. oz. (can)	151
DISTILLED SPIRITS:*			
Gin, Rum, Whiskey, Vodka			
80-proof	64	1½ fl. oz.	97
86-proof	70	" " "	105
90-proof	74	" " "	110
94-proof	78	" " "	116
100-proof	82	" " "	124
LIQUEURS:			
Vary according to content of sugar and fruit added to basic spirit.			
Examples: Crème de menthe and crème de cacao	100	1½ fl. oz.	150
WINE: Dry (Table)	25	3½ fl. oz.	87
WINE: Sweet (Dessert)	50	" " "	141
WINE: Sherry	41	2 fl. oz.	81
MIXERS:			
Cream (heavy)	106	1 tbs.	53
Club Soda	0		0
Cola	17	12 fl. oz. (can)	144
Diet Soda	0		0
Ginger Ale	9	12 fl. oz. (can)	113
Tonic Water	9	12 fl. oz. (can)	113
Lemon Juice (Fresh)	8	1 tbs.	4
Lime Juice (Fresh)	8	" "	4
Orange Juice (Fresh)	14	2 fl. oz. (¼ cup)	28
Pineapple Juice (can, unsweetened)	17	" " " "	34

Source: U. S. Dept. of Agriculture Handbook No. 456; Liqueur: Rodale Press, *Spring* Magazine.

*Brandy, tequila and other spirits not measured but may be presumed to be close to figures given for Distilled Spirits group above.

BASIC BARTENDING TECHNIQUES

Ice: Cubes, Crushed, Block

Ice cube ingredients given in the recipes in this book refer to the standard 1½ × 1 × 1-inch cubes. Three to four of these cubes approximate ½ cup of ice. To obtain crushed ice, process ice cubes in manual or electric ice crusher or blender. Or, wrap ice cubes in sturdy towel and crush with heavy cleaver or mallet. Remember that ice takes on food odors; so, store ice for drink use in separate freezer compartment or in a heavy plastic bag, securely closed. In punch bowls, a large block of ice will keep the mixture cold longer with less dilution than small ice cubes.

Chilled Glasses

The first requirement for a good, cold drink is a chilled glass. If space permits, the best method is to keep a supply of glasses in the freezer, but be sure to stand them on the rim. (If frost drops form on the base, the glass will not stand steady.) Or, glasses may be chilled by twirling them in crushed ice or filling them with ice and letting stand a few minutes.

Washing Glasses

Wash glasses with salt and water and examine them carefully before storing to be sure there are no lipstick or other marks. Soap or detergent has a tendency to remain on glasses unless they are rinsed very, very carefully in hot and then cold water. Avoidance of soap residue is especially important when washing beer glasses as soap will cause the beer to flatten.

Sugar-Frost

To sugar-frost glass (actually, only the rim), chill glass first. Then moisten inside and top of rim by rubbing area with strip (or wedge) or lemon or lime peel or a few drops of spirit that will be used in the drink (or colored spirit—if you are being fancy). Dip moistened rim in bowl of superfine sugar and tap gently with finger to shake off excess sugar. Stand prepared glass in freezer or refrigerator for a moment to set frosting.

Salt-Frost
To coat rim of glass with salt, as for Margarita or Salty Dog, follow procedure for sugar-frost (above), dipping moistened rim in bowl of salt (fine or coarse) instead of sugar.

Warm Cups and Mugs
Just as cold drinks should be really cold, so a hot drink should be properly hot. For a hot drink, warm cup or mug by rinsing in hot water just before adding drink.

Sugar
Superfine (fine granulated) sugar is preferred in mixing drinks. It dissolves more quickly than either confectioners' (powdered) sugar or regular granulated sugar. After superfine sugar is dissolved, the liquid is clear. With confectioners' sugar, the liquid is clouded.

Sugar Syrup
To sweeten a drink, sugar syrup is easiest to use because it mixes instantly. You can cook a supply of sugar syrup and store it in the refrigerator indefinitely.

Recipe for Sugar Syrup
2⅔ cups (1 pound) granulated sugar   **1 cup water**

Combine sugar and water in saucepan and stir over moderate heat until mixture boils. Stop stirring and let syrup boil until it forms a thin thread between the finger and thumb (or registers 225°F. on a candy thermometer). Cool. Pour into screwtop bottle.

Yield 2 cups

Flavored Syrups
Besides sugar syrup for a simple sweetener, there are other commercially prepared syrups for sweetening, flavoring, and/or color-

ing. Some do not contain alcohol; others do. Nonalcoholic syrups include grenadine (rosy red; made with pomegranate juice), cassis syrup (currant), strawberry, blackberry, and other fruit syrups. Gomme is primarily a sugar syrup with a neutral taste. *Because nonalcoholic sweeteners ferment quickly, add 10 percent vodka to them as a preservative.* Those that contain alcohol and are usually classed as liqueurs, even though they are used mainly as flavored syrups, include crème de cassis (currant), Falernum syrup (almond and lime flavor), maraschino liqueur (marasca cherry), orgeat syrup (almond), and crème de noyaux (almond).

Use of Bitters

As mixers and for flavor accents, bitters are used in very small quantities. They are important for adding tang to a great many mixed drinks. Bitters are made from complex combinations of herbs, barks, roots, petals, leaves and peels; usually secret formulas, and all characterized by their own special tastes, usually amplified with the addition of wine and/or spirit. (For types of bitters, see Index under Aperitifs, Vermouths, Bitters.)

Adding Egg or Egg White

To separate the white from the yolk, tap center of egg shell firmly on edge of mixing glass or shaker. Carefully pass egg from one half shell to the other, letting the white slip out and into the container below. The egg ingredient should go into the mixing glass or shaker before adding the liquor to be certain that the egg is fresh (and avoid wasting good spirit).

Shake or Stir?

It's simple to decide which method to use. Cold cocktails become colder quicker when shaken with ice. Stirring takes longer. But there is an important consideration in the look of the finished drink: The stirred drink will remain clear. This "window of clarity" is most evident when a wine-based ingredient (many vermouths and aperitifs) is used. Of course, the clouded appearance of a shaken mixture will recede but not completely disappear. Therefore, if biting cold is more important than the appearance of the drink, shake, rattle, and roll! (Of course, the more ice that is used, whichever the method of preparation, the quicker it will chill.)

About stirring: Stir only in a circular motion, not up and down. In a tall drink, use a long spoon or stirrer and plenty of ice. Stir quickly (in and out), especially when sparkling wine and carbonated beverages are used. Too much movement will leave the drink flat.

Twists of Citrus Peels

For a strip of lemon, lime, orange, or grapefruit peel to be used as a "twist," shave off only the colored surface of the peel; there should be no white membrane included. Unless otherwise specified by the recipe, a strip of peel for a twist should be approximately 1-inch long by ¼-inch wide.

Fruit Garnishes

Unless otherwise noted, all fruit added to drinks should be fresh, if at all possible. Citrus fruits keep well in the refrigerator for four to six weeks. Wedges and slices of lemon, lime, and orange should be neatly cut with a sharp knife. Slices should be thin. For other fruit uses, plan drinks when prescribed fruit is in season. (A delicious garnish for wine drinks: Freeze Thompson seedless grapes and drop a few into the drink. The frozen grapes are like chewy fruit candy.)

Floats

The pousse café, with three to six separate layers of spirits and syrups is the classic demonstration of the "float." Many other drinks are topped with a float of cream or another spirit or a few drops of grenadine, cassis, or some other touch for color and/or flavor accent.

Various spirits, especially liqueurs, float because of different weights of density, with the heaviest liqueur remaining on the bottom, then the next heaviest on top of it. For a general guide, the higher the alcoholic content of a spirit, the lower will be its density. Unfortunately, this isn't true 100 percent of the time. Practicing with the ingredients on hand is the best way of preparing a perfect float.

Procedure: Floating spirits or cream is not as difficult as it looks. The secret rests with using your two hands properly. First pour the bottom layer of the drink into the glass. To float another liquid on top of it, tilt the glass slightly and insert either a teaspoon or a long mixing spoon so that the bottom of the spoon is face up, towards you. Pour the liquid very slowly over the rounded surface of the spoon. The master recipe for pousse café (see Index) includes some layered drink combinations.

DRINK CHEMISTRY

Each ingredient in a drink has a specific function or is a building block that, when blended with something else in the drink, gives a more harmonious end product.

First, there is a base/or primary ingredient, accompanied by either an aromatic agent or a mellowing functionary. There may also be a special flavoring agent or coloring ingredient.

Usually the base of a drink or primary ingredient is a spirit, i.e., brandy, gin, liqueur, rum, tequila, whiskey, or vodka. The enhancing ingredient may be bitters or vermouth. The recipe may include a sweetening agent, fruit or fruit juice. The coating in some drinks may be sugar, egg, or cream.

A safe rule to follow in any drink preparation is to practice first. Some points to remember: (1) Generally limit use of sugar to 1 tsp. per drink; 1 tbs. heavy cream per drink. (2) Use sparingly such ingredients as Falernum syrup, grenadine, and such liqueurs as maraschino, crème de menthe, and apricot. These ingredients should be measured in dashes or teaspoonfuls, if you don't want them to dominate the flavor base. (3) Squeeze fresh juices as needed. Within an hour, juices begin to separate from pulp; and fermentation begins as soon as juice is exposed to air. (4) When mixing fruit flavors in rum drinks, you will find that light rum blends best with fruit liqueurs; fruit brandy with heavier rums.

Alcoholic Content; Proof: Wine labels identify alcoholic volume as "Alcohol (amount) % by volume." For example, a bottle of white wine might show "alcohol 11% by volume." Spirits identify alcoholic strength as "proof." Each degree of proof is equivalent to ½ of 1 percent of alcohol at 60° F. Therefore, a spirit of 80 proof contains 40 percent alcohol, a spirit of 100 proof—50 percent alcohol, etc.

CLASSIC TYPES OF DRINKS AND BASIC RECIPES

There are basic types of drinks from which modern mixology proliferates. From these you can spawn more drink creations than you'll ever drink. Basic formulas have been fairly well systematized, and if you understand the structures, you will be able to prepare a good drink, regardless of what you call it or in what kind of glass it is served.

Aperitif

An aperitif can refer to a bottled mixture of bitters or vermouth with spirit or wine base, which often purports to have certain digestive qualities or appetite stimulus. *In broader usage,* especially in Europe, an aperitif is a drink consumed before a meal ostensibly to open up the appetite. Popular libations for this purpose are not only bottled aperitif mixtures, per se, but also dry white wine, dry sparkling wine, sherry, the kir drink, vermouths, Scotch whisky—straight or with club soda.

Chaser

Not usually an alcoholic drink, but an accompaniment with a

straight spirit drink. The chaser is served in a separate glass. Usually it is plain water or club soda. With some spirits, it can be beer, juice, or soft drink. A special chaser mixture traditionally served with tequila is Sangrita.

Cobbler

A tall drink, either a goblet or other 8- to 10-oz. glass filled with crushed ice, to which any spirit or wine is added. It is garnished with any fresh fruit, and served with a straw.

Basic recipe

 4 to 6 oz. crushed ice
 1 to 2 tsp. superfine sugar
 2½ oz. wine or spirit
 Fresh fruit garnish (mint optional)

Fill glass with ice. Add wine or spirit and sugar, and stir slowly. After glass becomes frosted, garnish with fruit.

Cocktail

The cocktail has long been the classic before-lunch or before-dinner drink. It is the drink that "whets the whistle." Basically, the cocktail drink is about 5 parts spirit to 1 part additive (usually aperitif, vermouth, bitters, or fruit juice), shaken or stirred with ice and strained into a serving glass.

Collins

A tall drink—ice, sugar, citrus juice, and spirit combined in a serving glass and stirred; the glass is then filled with club soda and garnished with lemon and orange slices and cherry. The Tom Collins specifically calls for dry gin; the John Collins for Holland gin.

Basic recipe

 4 to 5 ice cubes
 1 tsp. sugar syrup
 2 tsp. lemon juice
 2 to 2½ oz. spirit
 4 to 6 oz. club soda, chilled
 1 slice lemon
 1 slice orange
 1 maraschino cherry

Combine ice cubes, sugar syrup, lemon juice, and spirit in tall glass and stir until mixture is chilled. Add club soda and stir briefly. Add fruit garnish.

Cooler
A first cousin to the punch but with little or no fruit juice. The formula calls for wine or spirit with plenty of ice and carbonated beverage and a garnish of citrus slice or peel. The original cooler was made with Scotch whisky, and its decoration was one continuous spiral of lemon or orange peel—the Horse's Neck.

Crusta
A drink served in a wine glass with a sugar-frosted rim; inside the glass is a long spiral of orange or lemon peel and an ice cube. A shaker mixture of crushed ice, Angostura bitters, maraschino liqueur, lemon juice, and liquor is strained into the glass.

Cup
A punch mixture *when served from a pitcher*. A liquor or wine-based drink, usually fortified with brandy, sometimes using a sparkling wine or cider, stirred in a pitcher with plenty of ice. Today's fashion serves cups in wine glasses as well as in punch cups.

Daisy
The daisy is an oversize cocktail (usually 5 to 6 ounces), and some drinks prepared in its proportion are called "daisy." The spirit base may be that of any cocktail recipe but more of it, and it is usually sweetened with syrup or liqueur. It is usually served in a 6-oz. stem cocktail glass, but a whiskey sour glass or wine glass can be substituted. Daisies are popular in southern California, especially the Margarita, an example of an oversize cocktail.

Eggnog
A cold, sweet, creamy mixture of egg yolk, sugar, milk, and spirit, which is then folded with stiffly beaten egg white. It is the modern

version of the syllabub. Eggnog is always made in large quantity and served well chilled in a pitcher or punch bowl. Ice is never added to the drink. Any spirit or combination of spirits can be used, although the inclusion of rum is traditional. Nutmeg is usually grated on top of the drink. Today, nonalcoholic eggnog mixes are sold in supermarkets, to which spirit can be added. (The Princeton Reunion Recovery Punch is an eggnog type of drink that is less sweet.) The eggnog is usually served in winter months.

Fix

A small cobbler—a little sugar, lemon juice, crushed ice, and spirit in a small tumbler or highball glass, stirred briefly, and served with a straw. No mix is added.

Basic Recipe

1 tsp. superfine sugar	2½ to 3 oz. spirit
1 tsp. water (to dissolve sugar)	Crushed ice to fill glass
1 to 2 tbs. lemon juice	1 slice lemon

In any type 8- to 10-oz. glass, combine sugar and water, and stir until dissolved. Add lemon juice and spirit, and stir again. Fill glass with ice and stir again. Garnish with lemon slice. Serve with straw.

Fizz

In England, the late morning libation is referred to as "elevenses." There the fizz is popular at eleven as well as midafternoon and evening. A shaker mixture of citrus juice, sugar, spirit, and ice is strained into a highball or other 8- to 10-oz. glass. Sometimes a whole egg, or white only, is added to the shaker. The fizz is always topped with club soda or sparkling wine.

Flip

A whole egg or white only, any choice of wine or spirit, sugar, and crushed ice are shaken and strained into an old-fashioned or other 8- to 10-oz. glass. It is always topped with a sprinkle of nutmeg. Originally, flips were served hot or warm by inserting a red-hot iron into the mixture. Flips are a very soothing drink and are finding new popularity as a morning or bedtime tonic.

Basic recipe

1 egg
1 tsp. superfine sugar
Optional: 1 to 2 tbs. cream

2½ to 3 oz. spirit or combination
Freshly grated nutmeg

Combine all ingredients except nutmeg in shaker and shake vigorously. Strain into whiskey sour glass. Top with sprinkle of nutmeg.

Frappé

Pack cocktail glass with finely crushed ice and pour in liqueur and/or spirit. Insert short straw. A refreshing after-dinner drink.

Highball

Basically the highball consists of 3 to 5 ice cubes, 2 oz. of spirit, and a topping of water or carbonated beverage. Obviously, this simple drink composition has prompted many combinations of spirit and nonalcoholic mixes.

Hot Drinks

Hot drinks of spirit or wine add coziness and warmth on a cold winter day or night. Brandy, rum, whiskey, and wine are the most popular bases. See Index for listing of hot drinks. In a separate category are the after-dinner coffees, Café Royale and Café Grande, elegant any time of the year. See special section on Hot Drinks.

Low Ball

Another term for straight spirits served on-the-rocks or with just a splash of mix, usually in an old-fashioned glass.

Julep

This wonderful refresher is a native American. The julep originated in Kentucky and traditionally is made with Kentucky Bourbon. The concept is to crush fresh mint leaves with sugar in the bottom of the glass; then fill the glass with crushed ice, add the spirit, and stir until the glass is well frosted. As to the authentic formula, the julep is as controversial as the Martini, but here is the general idea as it comes from Steve Wynn, chairman of the Golden Nugget Casino Hotel in Las Vegas, who remembered his grandfather's original recipe:

Original Kentucky Mint Julep—Basic Recipe

10 to 12 mint leaves plus 2 mint sprigs
1 tbs. Sugar Syrup
2 oz. bourbon (Kentucky only!)
Optional: 2 dashes Angostura bitters
6 to 8 oz. crushed ice

Combine mint leaves and sugar syrup in mixing glass and bruise leaves until well macerated with syrup. Add Bourbon and bitters and stir well. Fill 8- to 10-oz. serving glass with crushed ice and strain Bourbon mixture into glass. Stir gently until glass is well frosted. Garnish with mint sprigs (which can be dusted with sugar).

Mist

A mist is similar to a frappé in that spirit is poured into a glass filled with crushed ice. For the mist, fill an old-fashioned glass with crushed ice, pour in spirit, and serve with short straw. Originally mists meant Bourbon or whiskey in crushed ice. Today a variety of spirits, particularly amaretto, Kahlua, and peppermint schnapps are being drunk mist style.

Neat

Any spirit served straight in a whiskey shot glass. Tequila Neat calls for a time-honored ritual (see Index). Neat drinks may be accompanied by a chaser.

On-the-Rocks
Straight spirit poured over ice cubes in an old-fashioned glass. Sometimes a twist of lemon is added. On the rocks drinks may be accompanied with a chaser.

Puff
This is a good before-lunch pick-me-up that can be made with any spirit mixed with equal parts of milk and club soda, over ice.

Basic Recipe
2 ice cubes	2 oz. milk
2 oz. spirit	2 oz. club soda

Place ice cubes in old-fashioned glass. Add spirit and milk, and stir. Add club soda and stir 2 turns.

Punch
A drink mixture prepared in large quantity, which can be made with various combinations of wines, spirits, fruit juices, and carbonated beverages. A punch mixture might be light or hearty, cold or warm, refreshing or rich. Punches were very popular in bygone days in England and the American colonies. Today the popularity of Sangria and wine drinks in general have prompted a revival of punch popularity. It is usually served in a large bowl. If it is served from a pitcher, the drink is called a cup.

Rickey
A simple summertime favorite: Squeeze half a lime or wedge of lemon over a highball glass and drop it in. Add ice cubes and liquor and fill glass with club soda or other mix. If desired, a sweetener, such as grenadine or sugar syrup can be included.

Sangaree
A sweet, tall drink, served with ice that is always topped with a sprinkle of nutmeg and may include a float of port wine. The alcohol can be spirit or wine, even ale or stout.

Basic recipe
- ½ tsp. superfine sugar, or more—to taste
- 1 tsp. water
- 1½ to 2 oz. spirit or wine
- 3 to 4 ice cubes
- Optional: 1 to 2 tbs. port wine
- Freshly grated nutmeg

Combine sugar and water in highball glass and stir until sugar is dissolved. Add spirit or wine and ice cubes, and stir well. If desired, float port wine on top of drink. Top with sprinkle of nutmeg.

Shooter
Contemporary expression for shot of straight spirit with beer chaser.

Shrub
Fruit, fruit juice, sugar, and spirit mixture allowed to stand a few days. Some shrub mixtures are commercially bottled. Shrub can be served hot or cold. Hot—pour shrub into warm mug and top with hot water. Cold—pour shrub into highball glass with ice; top, if desired, with club soda; garnish with fruit.

Smash
A junior julep, served in an old-fashioned glass.

Basic recipe
- 2 sprigs mint
- 1 tsp. sugar syrup
- 1 dash Angostura bitters
- 3 to 4 oz. crushed ice
- 2½ to 3 oz. spirit
- Optional: 1 to 2 oz. club soda

Muddle 1 mint sprig with sugar syrup in old-fashioned glass until well macerated. Add bitters, crushed ice, and spirit. Add club soda, if desired, and garnish with mint.

Sour
A tart drink, garnished with fruit, usually served in a whiskey sour (Delmonico) or old-fashioned glass. A whiskey sour is the most

popular, but the idea is also made with brandy (grape, apple, or apricot).

Basic recipe

   1 tsp. superfine sugar, or more—to taste
   2 tbs. lemon juice
   2⅓ to 3 oz. spirit
   3 to 4 ice cubes
   Garnish: 1 slice of fruit or citrus peel and 1 maraschino cherry

Combine all ingredients except garnish in shaker, and shake vigorously. Strain drink into chilled glass, and add garnish.

Straight

Straight spirit is usually served in a whiskey shot glass, with or without accompanying chaser.

Swizzle

Originally, a tall drink with ice that was stirred with a twig. The idea originated in the West Indies where a 6-inch long twig with three, four, or five short branches was twirled in the pitcher or glass. Today, any long rod with fingers or paddle bottom can be used. The twig or rod is rotated between the hands at the top until the glass is very frosted. Any tall drink filled with crushed ice can be "swizzled" until the glass is frosty and the drink is foamy, which is then called a swizzle.

Syllabub

A milk punch. Beat together sugar syrup, milk, heavy cream, and fortified wine (sherry, port, or Madeira) or spirit. Serve in a bowl and float puffs of beaten egg white on top.

Toddy

The toddy originated as a *hot* drink, a mixture of any sweetened spirit and hot water served in a warm mug. Properly, a toddy contains a slice of lemon or peel, *no* fruit juice, and one or more spices (e.g., cinnamon, clove, nutmeg). The *cold* toddy is distinguished from a sling by the use of plain water instead of club soda (over ice, of course). It is garnished with lemon slice or peel and topped with a sprinkle of spice. The drink is properly served in an old-fashioned glass or one that is taller.

Tonic

A simple tall drink with ice, spirit, and tonic water.

Basic recipe

Ice to fill tall glass to ¾ level	4 to 6 oz. tonic water (or bitter lemon soda)
1½ to 3 oz. gin, light rum, or vodka	1 slice lime or lemon

Pour liquor over ice. Fill glass with tonic water or bitter lemon and garnish with lime or lemon slice.

Wines

ABOUT WINE

What is wine, other than being one of the most pleasant subjects in the world because it relates to contentment? Wine helps reflect the experiences of people at their best and produce a free flow of ideas. The subject of wine is poetry, history, science, humanity itself. In our terms, however, it is the fermented juice of any fruit. Aside from specialty wines, such as elderberry and dandelion, wine is the fermented juice of the grape, the fruit of the *vitis vinifera* plant.

Wine is essentially a natural product as opposed to distilled and malt beverages, which are manufactured. The grape is just about the only fruit that can preserve itself quite naturally; this is due to its content of fermentable sugars plus a "bloom" or haze on its skin, which is a collection of natural yeasts that ferment the grape sugar into alcohol when crushed. Unlike manufactured spirits, there is more to wine than alcohol. Wine is a healthy food, exceeded in nutritive value only by milk and fruit juices; and physicians since Hippocrates have prescribed its gentle stimulus.

In this age of great expectations of technological and industrial products, wine has traveled far in a short period of time, because industrial producers have made use of the same technology that is applied to other food processing. Of course, wines from grapes of a specific year's harvest are still bottled in areas blessed with a special combination of soil, climate, grape varieties, and winemaking art; these are the *vintage wines*. The bulk of wines marketed, however, are *nonvintage,* and quality ranges from very good to very bad, depending on the talents of winemaking and available resources. The only ways to know how good are these wines are to learn the reputations of shippers and retailers and to taste them.

Jug wines, so popular today, are, of course, nonvintage, blended wines and also can range in quality from very good to very bad. Good jug wines are excellent buys for cocktail use, since their character is consistent from bottle to bottle, month after month; and once a large bottle is opened, it will keep well in refrigeration for several days. By definition, jug wine is any wine that is easily purchasable, comes in a container size not less than 1.5 liters, and may be served without too much concern for its price.

Choosing Wine

In each decade of this century, the spectrum of wine sources has changed drastically. In the fifties and sixties, choice of wine for a dinner party would have been a French selection. Today, the California wine market has come of age (there had to be time for the fledgling post-Prohibition vines to grow and mature), and technological advances in production know-how have changed winemaking the world over, including the processing of the French greats.

If you are "into" wine, you have probably embarked on a progressive learning program, mastering the "Appellation Controllée" of the French classified regions, the varietals and prize-winning boutique wineries of California, and the D.O.C. wines of Italy. If you are an adventurer, there are good wines being developed in New York, Washington, Idaho, Michigan, Australia, Yugoslavia, South Africa, and Mexico. Spain and Portugal have long produced great table and fortified wines indigenous to their soil and sun, and German wines demonstrate the dramatic difference of the effect of soil, sun, and technique in another latitude.

The point is that the whole world has become wine conscious. Even the experts cannot individually keep up with tasting all of the new wines and vintages coming into the market. This is the time to stop being a "label and vintage snob" and assume the sophisticated stance of the explorer. Never apologize for a disappointing wine choice. How else will you know whether you have discovered a delightful or less than good wine? And even with great wines, if they are old enough, the chances are fifty/fifty whether they will be drinkable or drainable.

Perhaps for our own benefit we would do well to remember that some of those wine labels that read simply "French table wine" or "Italian table wine," with no identification other than the fact that the wines have been blended and bottled in a plant much like a Coca Cola plant, are respectable beverage wines recognized for what they are. Wine shippers are using proprietary wine names in increasing numbers, and some of the better known names such as Mouton Cadet, Bolla, Chateau La Salle, which are certainly among the better qualities, go as far as to tell you in addition to the name of the wine or brand, the specific region where the wine comes from. For example, the label on the French brand Sommeliere states "Vin de Pays de Bouche du Rhone" (from the Rhone region).

This effort to identify or detail more than just the name of the brand itself is very often a statement from the grower and shipper that these wines are produced within their own strict quality standards from a selected area, as opposed to those wines carrying labels designed to create the impression that they are one of the prestige wines of France or Italy or Germany. When the wine shipper identifies the growing area, he is backing his own taste and offering something that he is not ashamed of, rather than wines which list only the location of a bottling plant or the statement "blended and bottled by" and a lettered or numbered code.

In the past year or so there has been a dizzying proliferation of new wine products, and the list not only includes wine in cans or "bota" bags like the traditional wineskins in Spain, but wines are available in six-packs, in smaller bottles with screw caps, in 18-liter boxes, and, at long last, there is low-calorie light wine. An exciting discovery is the fine quality champagne-type sparkling wine of Spain.

Dry to Sweet Wines

While many Americans say, "I prefer wines that are dry," they have been fooling themselves and those of us who cater to the needs of retailers and restaurants throughout the United States. When they taste a truly dry wine, their reaction, more often than not, is that the wine "tastes sour." "Sour" is more aptly applied to the taste of a lemon, although it is possible for a wine to be sour, if it is a spoiled wine. Depending on the balance of acid and sugar in the wines, there are varying degrees of wine sweetness, which are usually expressed in these terms:

Table wine (still), white and red:
   Dry
   Medium Dry
   Sweet
   Very Sweet

Sparkling wine (champagne):
   Natural (no sweetness at all)
   Brut (little or no sweetness)
   Extra Dry (faintly sweet)
   Sec (dry) (more sweet than extra dry)
   Demi-Sec (sweet)

Information on Wine Labels

Your first confrontation in choosing wine is the label on the bottle. What does it mean? The terms on wine labels are defined by federal regulations and the country of origin.

Wine name: There are three categories of wine names: *generic*, indicating the general type of wine with no restrictions on grapes used; *trademarked proprietary name*, also with no restrictions as to grape content; and *varietal*, which must contain at least 51 percent of the named grape.

Vintage date: Indicates that 95 percent or more of the grapes used to make the wine were harvested in the year stated.

Geographic origin: Where the grapes came from. This identification may range from a precise area, e.g., Napa Valley, to "American," or "French."

Business name and address of bottler: This may or may not be the same as the name and location of the winery.

Percentage of alcoholic content.

Generic Wines

Generic wines have no legal requirement as to grapes used to make them. The generic name relates to the character of wines as made in the region from which the names are drawn. In the United States the following names are regarded as generic:

- Champagne (white and pink sparkling)
- Burgundy (white and red)
- Chablis
- Chianti
- Claret
- Marsala
- Mountain Red
- Mountain White
- Port
- Rhine
- Sauterne (dry and sweet)
- Sherry
- Vin Rosé
- Vino Rosso

Varietal Wines

The better qualities of wine offered today are labeled by the varietal name of the principal or forming grape from which they are made (which must account for at least 51 percent). California producers began the trend of naming wines for the predominant grape used. Grapes may vary significantly from producer to producer, according to the style of the winemaker and his overview of the market. (In the following descriptions of grape varietals, the phonetic pronunciations are linguistically correct, although commercial pronunciations in advertising may vary.)

White Grape Varieties

Aligote *(ah-lee-goh-teh)*. Grown in the Burgundy district of France; produces a light white wine usually called Bourgogne Aligote.

Aurora. Grown in the eastern United States, predominantly in the Finger Lakes region; also in France. A hybrid grape; makes light, fragrant white wines.

Catawba. Grown in the eastern United States. American grape of the species labrusca; gives a good, sweet wine.

Chardonnay *(shar-doh-nay).* Grown in the Burgundy and Champagne districts of France, California, eastern Europe, and South America. This classic white grape produces the best dry white wines of France and California; also gives the *blanc de blancs* of Champagne. Yields fine, luscious wines; dry with great scent and class in California and France.

Chasselas *(shah-seh-lah).* Grown in central Europe, chiefly as a table grape. Only gives good white wines in cool districts, such as Vaud and Valais in Switzerland and Crepy and Pouilly sur-Loire in France.

Chenin Blanc *(she-nah-blanc).* Popular white wine grape from Vouvray in the Loire Valley; also grown in California and South America. Gives soft, scented wines, generally with a slight sweetness.

Colombard *(coh-lom-bar).* Grown in the Cognac region of France and in California. Called French Colombard in California; usually produced for blends of inexpensive chablis, but also sold as a varietal.

Delaware. Grown in the eastern United States. Native white grape of the species *labrusca;* gives scented white wines with a characteristic flavor.

Emerald Riesling. Grown in California. Developed there in 1946 by crossing Johannisberg Riesling with Muscat; similar to Riesling.

Gewurztraminer *(geh-vurtz-tra-mee-nair).* Grown in Alsace, France; Germany; Austria; northern Italy; and California. A superior selection of Traminer which gives full-bodied wines with a characteristic spicy flavor. A white grape with full flavor and aroma.

Grey Riesling. Grown chiefly in California; also in France. Its real name is Chauce Gris. Produces medium dry wines.

Johannisberg Riesling. Grown in central Europe, Australia, and California. Used for the great wines of the Rhine and Mosel regions of Germany; also gives good results in California. Best when not too dry.

Malvasia. Grown in California and in the Mediterranean area. A popular table grape that produces good dessert wines, which are also fine as an aperitif.

Müller-Thurgau *(miller-tur-gou)*. Grown in central Europe, particularly Germany and Austria. Has good yield; gives soft, scented wines.

Muscat (Moscato). Grown in the Mediterranean area, also in northern Italy, France and California. Excellent sweet grape used for Asti Spumante, the famous Italian sparkling wine. Produces outstanding sweet dessert wines in Italy and California.

Pinot Blanc *(pee-noh blanc)*. Grown in the Alsatian, Burgundy, and Champagne districts of France; Germany; Italy; and California. Produces wines of similar class to Chardonnay. In California, where it is well suited, it finds its way into most sparkling wines.

Pinot Gris *(pee-noh gree)*. Grown in Alsace, France; Germany; Switzerland; and northern Italy. A cousin of the Pinot Noir; not well known in the United States. Called *Pinot Grigio* in Italy, *Rulander* in Germany, and *Malvoisie* in Switzerland. Gives fine, full-bodied white wines ranging in color from pale straw to copper.

Riesling *(Rees-ling)*. The distinguished grape of the wines of Alsace, Mosel, and Rhine regions; also grown in Austria, California, Chile, and Switzerland. California-labeled Riesling wines are regarded as semi-varietal because they are generally a blend of various grapes of the Riesling family, of which the base is usually Sylvaner. Riesling wines are characteristically light, fruity, and faintly sweet.

Sauvignon Blanc *(soh-ven-yonh blanc)*. Grown in the upper Loire Valley and Bordeaux, France; California; Chile; Australia. Very fine grape; makes Sancerre and Pouilly-Fumé in the Loire, Graves and Sauternes in Bordeaux. Gives equally good dry or sweet wines.

Semillon *(seh-mee-yoh)*. Grown in Bordeaux, France; California; South America. The second most important white grape in Graves and Sauternes from Bordeaux; excellent for sweet wines. Often blended with Sauvignon Blanc.

Seyval Blanc *(say-val blanc)*. Grown in the eastern United States and Canada; also in France. A hybrid grape developed in France; gives some of the best dry white wines produced in the eastern United States.

Sylvaner. Grown in central Europe; Alsace, France; Germany; and California. Makes agreeable wine but sometimes lacks significant distinction.

Trebbiano. Grown in Italy and France; some acreage in California. Known as *Ugni Blanc* in France where it is grown for brandy production. A chief grape for Soavé, Orvieto, Frascati, and other Italian whites. Also known as the Saint-Emilion grape.

Red Grape Varieties

Baco Noir *(bah-co-nwahr)*. Grown principally in the eastern United States; also in France. A hybrid grape developed in France, named for the botanist who developed it; also called *Baco No. 1*.

Brunello *(broo-nel-lo)*. Grown only in Tuscany, Italy, at present. Combined with selection of Sangiovese grapes, it makes the best and most expensive Italian red wine, the Brunello di Montalcino.

Cabernet Franc *(cah-behr-nay franc)*. Grown in Bordeaux and the middle Loire Valley, France; Italy; and recently, California. Related to Cabernet Sauvignon and very similar. Also called *Breton* in France. In Bordeaux, it is usually blended with Cabernet Sauvignon or Merlot.

Cabernet Sauvignon *(cah-behr-nay soh-ven-yonh)*. Grown in Bordeaux and Provence, France; California; Chile; Australia; South Africa. A very fine red wine grape, responsible for the great Bordeaux reds, particularly Médocs. Usually gives the best red wine of California, with great body and long life.

Carignane *(cahr-ee-nyan)*. Grown in southern France—the Côtes du Rhone area and in the warm climate regions of California, where it is blended and sold as "burgundy" although occasionally as a varietal. Standard quality.

Chancellor Noir *(shan-cel-lor nwahr)*. Grown in the eastern United States and southern France. A hybrid grape, giving medium-bodied wines; well suited to cool, North American climate.

Charbono *(shar-bo-no)*. Grown in California. Gives extremely dark and full-bodied red wines, but relatively rare.

Concord. Grown in the eastern United States and Canada. Native American grape of the species *labrusca;* not ideal for wine. Better suited for juice, jams, and jellies.

De Chaunac *(de sho-ynac)*. Grown in Canada and the eastern United States. A hybrid grape, giving rich wines with plenty of color and substance.

Dolcetto *(dol-chet-to)*. Grown in Piemonte, northern Italy. An agreeable, fruity red grape, giving light, rather soft red wines.

Gamay. Grown in Burgundy, Beaujolais, and the Loire Valley areas of France; Switzerland; and California. Very important in Burgundy but not used for the best wines; sometimes blended with Pinot Noir. Gives good, medium-bodied wines, with plenty of fruit; fairly short lived.

Gamay Beaujolais *(ga-may bo-zho-lay)*. Grown only in California. Originally thought to be the "true" Gamay of the Beaujolais district; now identified as a strain of Pinot Noir; will be gradually phased out in the future. Its wines, however, are generally quite fruity and good.

Grenache *(greh-naash)*. Grown in the southern Rhone area of France, Spain, and California. Used for Tavel and Lirac, among the best rosé wines of France; also gives excellent rosé wines in California. Generally has insufficient color for red wines and is blended with other grapes, as in Chateauneuf-du-Pape.

Malbec. Grown in Bordeaux, France; Argentina; tiny quantities in California. Fine red wine grape; used for wines of Cahors; blended with Cabernet in Bordeaux. Gives rich, full red wines. Should be more widely planted.

Merlot *(mehr-lo)*. Grown in Bordeaux, France; northern Italy; Switzerland; California (increasingly popular); South America. Excellent red wine grape. In Bordeaux, generally blended with other grape varieties. Softens Cabernet Sauvignon and found to improve many California Cabernets.

Nebbiolo. Grown in Lombardi, Italy; small acreage in California. Used in all of the great northern Italian reds—Barolo, Barbaresco, Ghemme, Gattinara, and Valtellina. Very fine wines—rich, slow to mature.

Petite Sirah *(peh-teet see-rah).* Grown in California, also parts of France. Originally thought to be a strain of Syrah; actually a different grape, known as *Duriff.* Gives excellent, very rich red wines; increasingly popular as a varietal.

Pinot Noir *(pee-no nwahr).* Grown in the French Champagne district, Burgundy, Switzerland, Germany, eastern Europe, California, and South America. Excellent red wine grape but not always easy to grow. Vinified as *blanc de noirs,* away from the skins, to make champagne. Traditionally, California Pinot Noir wines have tended to be too light in color, but there has been tremendous improvement recently.

Ruby Cabernet *(roo-bee ca-behr-nay).* Grown only in California. New grape developed in California in 1948 by crossing Carignane with Cabernet Sauvignon. Best suited to warm climate regions; has good color and flavor, but not always sold as a varietal.

Sangiovese *(san-jeeo-vay-seh).* Grown in Tuscany and Emilia-Romagna, Italy. Important grape used for Chianti, but blended with as many as four other grapes for this purpose. Elsewhere, usually sold as a varietal.

Syrah *(see-rah).* Grown in the Rhone area of France. Produces the great Rhone reds—Côte Rotie, Hermitage, and Chateauneuf-du-Pape. Recently introduced in California; not to be confused with Petite Sirah. Gives very rich, robust red wines.

Zinfandel. Grown chiefly in California, at least under this name. America's truly unique red grape; of uncertain origin, probably near Mediterranean or Italy. Gives excellent deep red wine with a characteristic spicy flavor in a multitude of different styles and strengths. Best are from California's North Coast counties.

Basic Types of Wine

The alcoholic beverage industry in America classifies all wines into four basic types, grouped by common characteristics: table wine, sparkling wine, dessert wine, and vermouth.

Table Wine

Technically, table wine means all wine that contains 14 percent or less alcohol. They are mainly dry, nonsweet wines, but nonfortified sweet wines such as sauternes are also included in this classification. Table wines are also called natural or still wines. The following Vintage and Wine Character charts show the range of variety of table wines from dry to sweet and can be helpful in choosing wines.

Light table wines. Since 1981 some wineries have been marketing "lighter" wines. They come in two basic types—soft and light. The light wines are much lower in alcoholic content than regular wines and consequently lower in calorie content—an appeal to diet-conscious Americans. There is little difference between light and soft wines. Both are made by an arrested fermentation process, which causes the wine to have less alcohol but leaves high levels of residual sugar, which explains why these wines tend toward the sweeter side.

(Another way to reduce calories in wine: Some people drop ice cubes into regular wine, white or red. Since regular wines have more taste, one or two clean ice cubes will sustain their style. The 7 or 8 percent light wines will not hold up as well. Or, if you must have low-calorie (low alcohol) wine, try a regular Italian spumante or German wine.)

Wine Character Chart

This chart and the Red Wine chart represent groupings of the most popular wines organized on the basis of their body—light to full—and their degree of sweetness—dry (without sweetness) to off-dry, semi-sweet and very sweet. To help you select the wine you prefer, begin at the top of the chart and read down as sweetness or fullness increases. Each wine is listed in terms of the general characteristics typical of the wines of the region or the grape variety. When ''(var.)'' is encountered, this means that the name of the wine indicates the grape variety from which it is made, rather than its place of origin.

WHITE WINES

	Name of Wine *May be red or white	Country of Origin & Region	Grape Varieties Used
Light-bodied dry	Vinho Verde*	Portugal, Minho River	various
	Chablis	France, Burgundy	Chardonnay
	Aligote	France, Burgundy	(var.)
	Muscadet	France, Loire	(var.)
	French Colombard	various	(var.)
	Pouilly-Fume	France, Loire	Sauvignon Blanc
	Sancerre	" "	" "
	Bordeaux*	France, Gironde	Sauvignon Blanc, Semillon
	Entre-Deux-Mers	France, Bordeaux	" "
	Graves	" "	" "
	Sauvignon Blanc	various	(var.)
	Soave	Italy, Veneto	Garganega, Trebbiano
Medium-bodied dry	Est! Est! Est!	Italy, Lazio	Trebbiano, Malvasia
	Verdicchio	Italy, Marche	(var.)
	Orvieto	Italy, Umbria	Trebbiano, Verdicchio
	Frascati	Italy, Lazio	Malvasia, Trebbiano
	Lacrima Christi*	Italy, Campania	various
	Pinot Blanc	various	(var.)
	Semillon	USA, California	(var.)
	Seyval Blanc	USA, New York State	(var.)
	Pinot Chardonnay	various	(var.)
	Macon*	France, Burgundy	Chardonnay
	Saint-Veran	" "	" "
	Pouilly-Fuisse	" "	" "
	Meursault	" "	" "
Full-bodied dry	Puligny-Montrachet	" "	" "
	Chassagne-Montrachet*	" "	" "
	Corton-Charlemagne	" "	" "
	Montrachet	" "	" "

	Name of Wine	Country of Origin & Region	Grape Varieties Used
Light bodied off dry	Riesling	France, Alsace	(var.)
	Emerald Riesling	USA, California	(var.)
	Johannisberg Riesling	" "	(var.)
	Mosel Riesling	Germany, Mosel-Saar-Ruwer	(var.)
	Rhine Riesling	Germany, Rhine	(var.)
	Sylvaner	France, Alsace	(var.)
	Sylvaner	USA, California	(var.)
	Silvaner	Germany, Rhine	(var.)
	Chenin Blanc	USA, California	(var.)
Medium-bodied semi-sweet	Liebfraumilch	Germany, Rhine	various
	Gewurztraminer	France, Alsace	(var.)
	Gewurztraminer	USA, California	(var.)
	Gewurztraminer	Germany, Rhine	(var.)
	Moscato di Canelli	Italy, Piemonte	Muscat
	Saumur*	France, Loire	Chenin Blanc
	Vouvray	" "	"
Full-bodied very sweet	Auslese	Germany, Mosel Rhine	various
	Barsac	France, Bordeaux	Semillon, Sauvignon Blanc
	Sauternes	" "	Semillon
	Tokay Aszu	Hungary, Carpathian Mts.	Furmint
ROSÉ WINES			
Light-bodied dry	Rosé de Marsannay	France, Burgundy	Pinot Noiir
	Grenache Rosé	USA, California	(var.)
	Rosé of Cabernet	" "	Cabernet Sauvignon
	Grignolino Rosé	" "	(var.)
	Lirac	France, Rhone	Grenache, Cinsault
	Tavel	" "	" "
Full-bodied semi-dry	Cotes de Provence*	France, Provence	" "
	Catawba Rosé	USA, NY State, Ohio	(var.)
	Rosé d' Anjou	France, Anjou	Groslot, Cabernet

© by Beverage Media, 1982.

RED WINES

	Name of Wine	Country of Origin & Region	Grape Varieties Used
Light-bodied dry	Bardolino	Italy, Veneto	Corvina, Molinara
	Valpolicella	" "	" "
	Gamay Beaujolais	USA, California	(var.)
	Beaujolais	France, Burgundy	Gamay
	Chiroubles	" "	"
	Brouilly	" "	"
	St. Amour	" "	"
	Fleurie	" "	"
	Julienas	" "	"
	Chenas	" "	"
	Morgon	" "	"
	Moulin-a-Vent	" "	"
	Cotes-du Rhone*	France, Rhone	Syrah, Grenache
	Corbieres*	France, Languedoc	Carignane, Grenache
	Rioja*	Spain, Navarre	Garnacha, Tempranillo
Medium-bodied dry	Bordeaux*	France, Gironde	Cabernet Sauvignon, Merlot
	Medoc	France, Brodeaux	"
	Margaux	France, Medoc	"
	St. Julien	" "	"
	Pauillac	" "	"
	St. Estephe	" "	"
	Graves	France, Graves	"
	St. Emillon	France, Dordogne	Merlot, Cabernet Franc
	Pomerol	" "	" "
	Chianti	Italy, Tuscany	Sangioveto, Canaiolo
	Zinfandel	USA, California	(var.)
	Chelois	USA, New York State	(var.)
	Cabernet Sauvignon	various	(var.)
	Chancellor Noir	USA, New York State	(var.)
	Pinot Noir	various	(var.)
Full-bodied dry	Burgundy	France, Cote d'Or	Pinot Noir
	Cote de Beaune-Villages	" "	" "
	Beaune	" "	" "
	Chambolle-Musigny	" "	" "
	Pommard	" "	" "
	Nuits-St. Georges	" "	" "
	Vosne-Romanee	" "	" "
	Gevrey-Chambertin	" "	" "
	Chambertin	" "	" "
	Cotes de Provence*	France, Provence	Cinsault, Carignan
	Barbera	Italy, Piemonte	(var.)
	Nebbiolo	" "	(var.)
	Gattinara	" "	Nebbiolo
	Cote Rotie	France, Rhone	Syrah

	Name of Wine	Country of Origin & Region	Grape Varieties Used
Robust, dry	Hermitage	France, Rhone	Syrah
	Chateauneuf-du Pape	" "	Syrah, Grenache
	Petite Sirah	USA, California	(var.)
Robust, sweet	Barbaresco	Italy, Piemonte	Nebbiolo
	Barolo	" "	"
	Mavrodaphne	Greece, Peloponnesus	various
	Passover Wine	USA, New York State	Concord

© by Beverage Media, 1982

Sparkling Wine (including Champagne)

Sparkling wines have bubbles that are induced by a process of two fermentations. First the juice of the grapes is fermented to become still wine. Then sugar and yeast are added, which causes a second fermentation. The wine is bottled and corked, and carbon dioxide gas, a product of the second fermentation, develops. When the bottle is eventually opened, the gas escapes, causing foam and bubbles to rush out of the bottle. There are five degrees of dry to sweet in sparkling wine (see Index, Wines, dry to sweet).

Champagne is sparkling wine produced within the delimited Champagne area in France, and its name is protected by law in many countries but not in the United States. In the U.S. any sparkling wine can be called champagne, but the designation must be preceded with the identification of the source, such as "California champagne," "New York State champagne," etc. Most non-vintage champagne is made from a blend of black and white grapes. *Blanc de blanc* is a wine made exclusively from white grapes. Pink champagne is obtained by adding to the blend a small proportion of the champagne wine that has been vinified as red wine. (Pink champagne is again becoming fashionable for festive events.)

Excellent sparkling wine also comes from the Loire Valley in France, from Spain (made by the *champenoise* method), from Italy (called brut spumante—dry, and Asti spumante—sweet), and Germany (called sekt).

Vintage Chart

Vintage Year	71	72	73	74	75	76	77	78	79	80	81
Red Bordeaux	8	5	6	6	10	8	6	9	8	6	9
White Bordeaux	9*	4*	6*	6*	10*	7	6	7	8	7	8
Red Burgundy	9	8	5	6	2	10	5	9	7	5	5
White Burgundy	9*	4*	8*	6*	7*	8	5	9	8	6	7
Rhone	9	8	7	6	5	10	5	10	7	6	8
Loire Red	9	3	6	5	6	8	5	7	6	5	6
Loire White	9	3	6	5	7	9	6	7	8	6	7
Champagne	9	—	8	—	9	9	—	6	7	6	—
Mosel	10*	3	7	5	9	10	6	5	8	5	7
Rhine	10*	4	7	5	8	10	5	5	8	5	8
Italy: Piemonte	9	3	6	8	7	6	7	10	8	7	8
Italy: Chiante	9	4	5	6	9	3	9	9	8	7	8
Italy: Veneto	9*	5*	8*	7*	8*	6	7	9	8	8	7
California: Napa & Sonoma Valleys	6	5	8	9	7	8	8	10	8	10	8
Port (Vintage)	—	7	—	—	8	—	10	—	—	7	—

No vintage chart can be more than a general guide to a wine's quality. Weather conditions can vary even within a specific region, and winemakers' skills also vary.

*Some dry wines from this vintage may be too old.

10 very great
9 great
8 very good
7 very good

6 good
5 fair
4 fair
3 poor

2 very poor
1 very poor
0 useless

© by Beverage Media, 1982.

Dessert Wine (Fortified Wine)

This is the industry classification for a specific group of fortified wines—Madeira, Marsala, port, and sherry,. The term "fortified" refers to wines that have brandy or other spirit added for the purpose of increasing the alcoholic content or arresting fermentation. (Although "fortified" is a long-established processing term in winemaking, it cannot be used legally in the United States in labeling or advertising.) Dessert wines contain between 16 and 23 percent alcohol. Although they are characteristically sweet in taste, there are varying degrees of dry versions of each type, which are favored as cocktail or aperitif drinks as well as for dessert or after dinner.

Madeira: Wine produced by the unique winemaking customs and climate of the island of Madeira and fortified with brandy made from Madeira wine. The wines range from light and dry to heavier and sweet: *Sercial* compares to fino sherry—light and dry (also called "rainwater"). *Verdelho* is similar to sercial but now is quite rare. *Bual* is the golden sweet Madeira. *Malmsey* is deep gold and very sweet.

Marsala: The wine and the Sicilian city of the same name are derived from the Arabic *Marsh-el-Allah* (harbor of God). These wines are generous and warm with golden yellow color and caramel aroma. Marsala was first created and developed by John and William Woodhouse, Englishmen who saw the need in the 1800s for a wine similar to sherry or Madeira that would satisfy their countrymen's thirst and be less costly. The major styles are: *fine*—17 percent minimum alcohol and four months' aging; *superiore*—18 percent minimum alcohol and two years' aging, sweet and dry; *vergine*—18 percent minimum alcohol and five years' aging, bone dry; *speciale*—18 percent minimum alcohol and six months' aging, made with eggs and other flavorings.

Port: Port wine is generally red, although some white is available. All ports are sweet, if they are true ports. *Vintage port* is usually London-bottled two years after harvest. Vintage port will show two dates on the label—the vintage date and the bottling date. *Ruby port* is young port with a more fruity nose. *Tawny* is paler port that has been held longer in wood, where some color is blanched out. A tawny will be less sweet than a ruby port and somewhat softer.

Sherry: True sherry comes from Spain, although sherry-type wine is also made in Australia, California, Cyprus, and South Africa. Dry to sweet sherries are the following: *manzanilla*—very dry, very pale; *fino*—dry and quite pale: *amontillado*—pale gold, but less dry than fino; *amoroso*—golden color, medium sweet; *cream*—rich, deep gold, sweet.

Vermouth

The alcoholic beverage industry classifies vermouths as wine because many have a wine base and have long been called aperitif wines. Vermouths, together with aperitifs and bitters, are a related and complex group of mixtures and are described in a separate section (see Index under Aperitifs, Vermouths, Bitters.

Types of Wine by Use

For Bar, Cocktail, Aperitif

Wine as a social drink has become as much in demand as spirits, for every occasion. For cocktail drinking, white, rosé, and sparkling wine should be well chilled; red wine may be slightly chilled. Wine ought to be served in stem wineglasses, not in tumblers.

Bar wine, or open stock: Today most cocktail lounges and restaurants have a "house wine" for ordering by the glass, eliminating the need to order a bottle when only a glass or two is desired. The quality of house wine is relative to the establishment. It is appropriate to ask to see the label and know what you are ordering. A recent innovation is the wine bar offering an expanded selection of open-stock wines. These places offer a list of 18 to 24 white and red wines by the "half glass" and "glass."

Wine with Food

It is not the function of this book to muse on the myriad connoisseur combinations of wines with food. But even here there is a new, more liberal attitude toward what goes with what in a meal. After all, there is no physiological rule that says that sweet tastes must come at the end of the meal. (The Chinese serve sweets—dumplings and pastries—in the middle of the meal, followed by more savories.) It is the harmony or compatibility of tastes that is important; then the opportunities for surprising and new taste excitements are endless. Generally, the following guidelines, relating to the intensity of flavor characteristics to the progress of the menu, will help in choosing companionable wines:

Soup: When the soup course is part of a large menu, wine is often not served unless it is a fortified wine (usually sherry or Madeira), whose flavor complements the soup or can be poured into it. With main-dish soups, program the wine to the character of the soup, e.g., onion soup with dry white wine or sparkling wine; pistou or bouillabaisse with a spicier wine or even a light-bodied red.

Seafood: Take a signal from innovative young chefs who are serving red-wine sauces with fish and seafood. If the dish is delicate and light, a light—probably white—wine is appropriate. But a rich seafood like salmon or lobster can be enjoyed with red wine.

Poultry and Red Meat: When these meats are the main course, the excitements of selections represent a wine lover's holiday. Plain-cooked or simply sauced, these foods are fine foils against which to savor the varying complexities of vintage wines. In general, do not be cowed by old rules. Today there are so many wines to choose; be a confident explorer, inquire about the characteristics of various wines, and do not hesitate to drink what interests you, whether it be white or red.

Vegetables and Salads: Today many people enjoy a light meal, at lunch or dinner, of vegetables or a salad. A glass of wine is very enjoyable with these foods, usually a chilled white or a slightly cooled light red wine.

Cheese: Wine and cheese are a marriage made in heaven! It is said that cheese makes any wine taste better and vice versa. Cheese is a perfect appetizer with any wine served as an aperitif. When cheese is served as a separate course within the meal, usually following the main course, the wine selected to accompany it is part of the progression to bigger, fuller flavors. This is the moment to show off your best wine. (If the wine is a masterpiece, don't even serve cheese with it. Truly great wines should be served solo, at the beginning of the meal, to be enjoyed in absolute perfection, when taste buds and attention are fresh and most alive.)

Fruit and Nuts: Fresh and dried fruit and nuts partner amiably with all wines.

Dessert: At this stage of the meal, the wine offering may be ambivalent. Any good sweet wine—sauterne, trockenbeerenauslese, tokay, or any sparkling wine—may accompany dessert. If coffee is served simultaneously, a fortified wine (sherry, port, Madeira, or Marsala), brandy, or liqueur may be offered. With today's preference for just a touch of sweet instead of an elaborate, prepared dessert, a rising fashion is to offer simply an innovative liqueur libation, such as a Toasted Almond or Fire 'n' Ice, with coffee, taking advantage of the many new liqueur flavors and mixing ideas.

How to Open, Pour and Serve Wine

Table wine (with meal)
1. Cut capsule directly below ridge or bulge.
2. Wipe top of cork and area surrounding it.
3. Place corkscrew directly in center of cork. Lever or wing-type corkscrew is preferred.
4. Move screw downward through cork until tip of corkscrew is at bottom of cork.
5. Draw cork straight upward. Do not jerk or pull.

6. Smell cork. The test is not foolproof, but if cork has a corky smell, the wine could be unsatisfactory. Replace bottle, if necessary.
7. Service is clockwise. Fill glass only two-thirds full.
8. Do not wrap napkin around bottle.
9. Keep glasses properly filled.

Sparkling Wine

To open a bottle of sparkling wine, the following procedure prevents bystanders from being hit by a flying cork and assures minimum spillage of good bubbly: Hold bottle slightly inclined, at a 45-degree angle. Unwind and remove wire basket around cork. Firmly grasp bottle with left hand and cork with right hand. Slowly twist bottle (not cork), as cork eases and pops out of bottle. Continue to hold bottle at an angle for about five seconds, until the pressure has equalized itself with that outside the bottle.

To pour sparkling wine, pour wine until foam almost reaches the rim of the glass. Stop for a moment while foam subsides a little. Then pour until glass is two-thirds full.

WHITE WINE RECIPES

CHABLIS COOLER
A highball glass, chilled

1 oz. vodka
2 tsp. grenadine
2 tsp. lemon juice
A few drops vanilla extract
5 to 6 ice cubes
3 to 4 oz. chablis, chilled

Sugar-frost highball glass. Combine all ingredients except ice and chablis in prepared glass, and stir well. Add ice cubes and fill with chablis. *Paul Star, Wine Director, Mullen & Gunn, Buffalo, N.Y.*

FROZEN SOMMELIÈRE
A wine glass (8-oz. or larger), chilled

3 oz. Sommelière dry white wine, chilled
2 tsp. curaçao
1 tsp. lemon juice
½ tsp. orgeat syrup
8 oz. crushed ice
2 dashes Grand Marnier

Combine wine, curaçao, lemon juice, orgeat syrup, and 4 oz. crushed ice in blender at low speed for 10 seconds. Place remaining ice in glass and strain mixture into glass. Top with Grand Marnier. *Sommelière Wines, Great Vintners International, Syosset, N.Y.*

HOLLYWOOD AND WINE

A 10- to 14-oz. tall glass, chilled

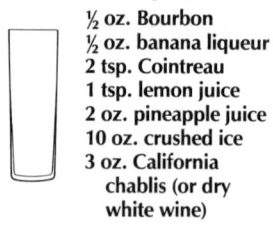

½ oz. Bourbon
½ oz. banana liqueur
2 tsp. Cointreau
1 tsp. lemon juice
2 oz. pineapple juice
10 oz. crushed ice
3 oz. California chablis (or dry white wine)

Combine all ingredients except 6 oz. ice in blender, and blend at low speed 10 to 15 seconds. Use remaining ice to fill glass to ½ level, and strain mixture into glass. Add wine.

KIR

A wine glass (6-oz. or larger), chilled

2 tsp. Guyot crème de cassis
3 to 4 oz. dry white wine, chilled

Slowly pour crème de cassis into glass, rotating glass to coat sides. (If slightest measure of cassis is preferred, pour out excess.) Add wine and stir slowly. *Guyot Crème de Cassis, Korbrand Corp., New York, N.Y.*

MARQUISE

A 4½-oz. cocktail glass, chilled

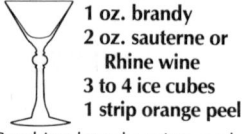

1 oz. brandy
2 oz. sauterne or Rhine wine
3 to 4 ice cubes
1 strip orange peel

Combine brandy, wine, and ice cubes in shaker, and shake vigorously. Strain mixture into glass. Light match. Squeeze orange peel over drink against flame to create blue burst of flame, and drop peel into drink.

RASPBERRY COCKTAIL

4 wine glasses (10- to 14-oz.), chilled

1 cup fresh ripe raspberries
4 oz. vodka or light rum
8 oz. dry white wine, chilled
2 oz. kirsch
12 to 16 ice cubes

Set 4 raspberries aside for garnish. Rub remaining raspberries through fine sieve. Combine strained raspberries with vodka or rum and refrigerate until chilled. At serving time, add wine and kirsch to mixture and stir well. Place 3 to 4 ice cubes in each glass and add drink mixture. Garnish each serving with raspberry.

SAUTERNE COCKTAIL

An old-fashioned glass, chilled

3 to 4 ice cubes
2 oz. Taylor New York State sauterne, chilled
1 teaspoon lemon juice
3 oz. Sprite soda, chilled
1 strip lemon peel

Combine all ingredients except lemon peel in glass and stir. Twist lemon peel over drink to release oil, and drop it in. *The Taylor Wine Co. of The Wine Spectrum, Atlanta, Ga.*

SPRITZER

A highball glass, chilled

2 to 3 ice cubes
4 to 5 oz. dry white wine, chilled
About 4 oz. club soda, chilled
Spiral of lemon peel or slice of fruit

Place ice in glass. Add wine and fill with soda. Garnish with lemon peel or fruit slice.

STAB IN THE BACK
(Pousse Rapier)

A highball glass, chilled

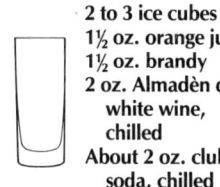

2 to 3 ice cubes
1½ oz. orange juice
1½ oz. brandy
2 oz. Almadèn dry white wine, chilled
About 2 oz. club soda, chilled
1 thin slice orange

Place ice cubes in glass. Add orange juice, brandy, and wine, and stir. Fill glass with soda. Garnish with orange slice. *Almadén Vineyards, San José, Calif.*

WINE CHILLER

A whiskey sour glass, chilled

2 oz. Sommelière dry white wine
3 oz. orange sherbet
2 dashes Southern Comfort
1 fresh cherry

Combine white wine, orange sherbet, and Southern Comfort in blender, and blend at low speed until smooth. Pour mixture into glass. Garnish with cherry and serve with straw. *Sommelière Wines, Great Vintners International, Syosset, N.Y.*

RED WINE RECIPES

BUFFALO SOUR

An 8 oz. wine glass, chilled

1 oz. Canadian whisky
1½ oz. lemon juice
1½ tsp. sugar syrup
3 to 4 ice cubes
2 oz. dry red wine
Lemon slice or maraschino cherry

Combine whisky, lemon juice, sugar syrup, and ice cubes in shaker, and shake well. Strain mixture into glass. Slowly pour wine on top. Drop lemon or cherry into drink.

COLD WINE FLIP

A wine glass (8 oz. or larger), chilled

3 oz. dry red wine or tawny port
1 egg
1 tsp. superfine sugar
6 to 7 ice cubes
Freshly grated nutmeg

Combine wine, egg, sugar, and 3 to 4 ice cubes in shaker, and shake vigorously. Place 3 ice cubes in glass, and strain drink into glass. Top with sprinkle of nutmeg.

DOUBLE DERBY
A highball glass, chilled

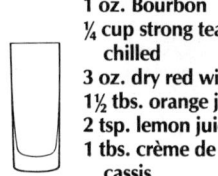

1 oz. Bourbon
¼ cup strong tea, chilled
3 oz. dry red wine
1½ tbs. orange juice
2 tsp. lemon juice
1 tbs. crème de cassis
2 to 3 ice cubes
1 thin slice orange

Combine all ingredients except ice and orange slice in glass, and stir well. Add ice and garnish with orange slice.

FRENCH FLAG
A wine glass (8 oz. or larger), chilled

1½ oz. apricot liqueur
2 to 3 dashes curaçao
3 ice cubes
1 tsp. crème de violette
4 oz. dry red wine

Combine apricot liqueur, curaçao, and ice in shaker, and shake well. Pour crème de violette into wine glass. Slowly strain shaker mixture into glass so that it floats on top of crème de violette. Slowly add red wine so that it floats on top of apricot liqueur mixture.

FROSTED VINES
A whiskey sour glass, chilled

½ oz. brandy
1 oz. Sommelière dry red wine
½ oz. crème de fraise (strawberry liqueur)
2 oz. vanilla ice cream
Freshly grated nutmeg

Combine brandy, red wine, crème de fraises, and ice cream in blender, and blend at low speed 10 to 14 seconds. Pour into glass and top with sprinkle of nutmeg. *Sommelière Wines, Great Vintners International, Syosset, New York, N.Y.*

FRUITY WINE COOLER
A 10-oz. or larger wine glass, chilled

2 tbs. cranberry juice, chilled
2 tbs. Hi-C Wild Berry Fruit Drink, chilled
¼ cup Taylor New York State Lake Country red wine, chilled
3 to 4 ice cubes

Combine all ingredients in glass and stir until glass is frosted. *The Taylor Wine Co. of The Wine Spectrum, Atlanta, Ga.*

ITALIAN RED WINE COCKTAIL

A wine glass (10- to 14-oz.), chilled

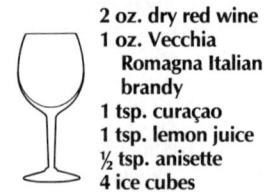

2 oz. dry red wine
1 oz. Vecchia Romagna Italian brandy
1 tsp. curaçao
1 tsp. lemon juice
½ tsp. anisette
4 ice cubes
1 strip orange peel

Combine all ingredients except 2 ice cubes and orange peel in shaker, and shake well. Place 2 ice cubes in glass, and strain drink into glass. Twist orange peel over drink to release oil, and drop it in.

RED WINE COBBLER

A highball glass, chilled

1 tsp. superfine sugar
1 tsp. lemon juice
A few drops maraschino liqueur
Crushed ice to fill glass
About 8 oz. dry red wine
1 pineapple spear

Combine sugar, lemon juice, and maraschino liqueur in glass, and stir until sugar is dissolved. Fill glass with ice. Add red wine to top of glass, and stir. Garnish with pineapple spear.

RED WINE COOLER

A highball glass, chilled

2 to 3 ice cubes
4 oz. dry red wine
1 oz. orange juice
2 tsp. lemon juice
2 tsp. brandy
3 oz. club soda, chilled
1 long spiral of orange rind
1 strip lemon peel

Place ice cubes in glass. Add wine, orange juice, lemon juice, brandy, and club soda, and stir well. Drop orange rind in glass. Twist lemon peel over drink to release oil, and drop it in.

RED WINE RUM COOLER

A highball glass, chilled

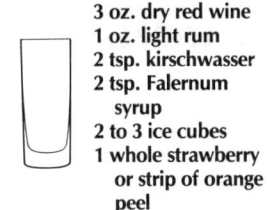

3 oz. dry red wine
1 oz. light rum
2 tsp. kirschwasser
2 tsp. Falernum syrup
2 to 3 ice cubes
1 whole strawberry or strip of orange peel

Combine wine, rum, kirschwasser, Falernum syrup, and ice in glass, and stir well. Drop strawberry or orange peel into drink.

ROSÉ WINE DAIQUIRI

A 4-oz. cocktail glass, chilled

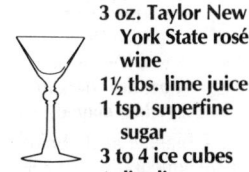

3 oz. Taylor New York State rosé wine
1½ tbs. lime juice
1 tsp. superfine sugar
3 to 4 ice cubes
1 slice lime

Combine all ingredients except lime slice in shaker, and shake vigorously. Strain into glass and garnish with lime slice. *The Taylor Wine Co. of The Wine Spectrum, Atlanta, Ga.*

SOMMELIÈRE FRAPPÉ

A wine glass (8-oz. or larger), chilled

5 to 6 oz. finely crushed ice
4 oz. Sommelière dry red wine
1 tsp. crème de cassis
1 strip lemon peel

Place ice in glass. Pour red wine slowly over ice. Add crème de cassis. Twist lemon peel over drink to release oil, and drop it in. *Sommelière Wines, Great Vintners International, Syosset, New York, N.Y.*

DUC d'AIX en PROVENCE

Follow recipe for Sommelière Frappé, using 2 tsp. strawberry liqueur instead of crème de cassis.

SPARKLING WINE RECIPES

ALTO PARLARE
(Al-toe Par-lar-ay; Tall Talk)
An 8-oz. wine glass, chilled

2 tbs. orange sherbet
½ oz. Cointreau
3 to 4 oz. Folio Spumante Nobile (Italian dry sparkling wine), chilled
1 dash grenadine

Combine orange sherbet and Cointreau in glass. Add sparkling wine and stir until ingredients are well mixed. Top drink with dash of grenadine. *Folio Spumante Nobile, V. Pozzi, Salvalai; Brescia, Italy*

AMBROSIA for TWO
2 whiskey sour glasses, chilled

3 oz. brandy
3 oz. apple brandy
2 dashes raspberry liqueur
5 to 6 ice cubes
4 oz. dry sparkling wine, chilled

Combine brandy, apple brandy, raspberry liqueur, and ice cubes in shaker, and shake vigorously. Strain mixture into 2 glasses. Fill glasses with sparkling wine and stir gently.

AMERICANA
A champagne glass, chilled

- 1 tsp. Bourbon
- 1 dash orange bitters
- ½ tsp. superfine sugar
- 4 oz. dry sparkling wine, chilled
- 1 slice brandied peach

Combine Bourbon, bitters, and sugar in mixing glass, and stir well. Pour in glass. Add sparkling wine (do not stir). Drop in peach slice.

APRIL in PARIS BALL
A champagne glass, chilled

- 1 tsp. Grand Marnier
- 4 oz. dry sparkling wine, chilled
- 1 fresh miniature rose bud

Pour Grand Marnier into glass. Tilt and turn glass to coat inside with the liqueur. Add sparkling wine. Float miniature rose bud.

BELLINI PUNCH
A wine glass (10-to 14-oz.), chilled

- ½ cup sliced peaches
- ¼ tsp. lemon juice
- ¼ tsp. maraschino liqueur
- 1 tsp. superfine sugar
- 6 oz. dry sparkling wine, chilled
- 3 ice cubes

Combine peaches and lemon juice in blender and puree. Add maraschino liqueur and sugar, and blend again. Place ice cubes in glass. Add blender mixture and sparkling wine. Stir 2 or 3 turns. *Windows on the World Restaurant, New York, N.Y.*

BLACK VELVET
A 10- to 14-oz. tall glass, chilled

- 4 to 6 oz. dry sparkling wine, chilled
- 4 to 6 oz. stout, chilled

Combine equal parts of sparkling wine and stout in glass. Stir gently.

CHARTREUSE SPARKLING WINE

A champagne glass, chilled

- 3 to 4 drops green Chartreuse
- 3 to 4 drops Hennessey Cognac
- 4 oz. dry sparkling wine, chilled
- 1 strip lemon peel

Combine all ingredients except lemon peel in glass and stir gently. Twist lemon peel over drink to release oil, and drop it in. *Schieffelin & Co., New York, N.Y.*

CORDIAL MÉDOC CUP

A champagne glass, chilled

- 1 oz. Cordial Médoc liqueur
- ½ oz. cognac
- 1½ tbs. lemon juice
- 1 tsp. sugar syrup
- 3 to 4 ice cubes
- 2 oz. crushed ice
- 2 to 3 oz. dry sparkling wine, chilled
- 1 thin slice orange

Combine Cordial Médoc liqueur, cognac, lemon juice, sugar syrup, and ice cubes in shaker, and shake well. Place crushed ice in glass, and strain mixture into glass. Fill with sparkling wine and garnish with orange slice.

CHICAGO

An old-fashioned glass, chilled

- 1½ oz. brandy
- 3 to 4 drops triple sec
- 1 to 2 dashes Angostura bitters
- 3 to 4 ice cubes
- 4 to 6 oz. dry sparkling wine, chilled

Sugar-frost glass. Combine all ingredients except sparkling wine in shaker, and shake well. Strain mixture into prepared glass. Fill glass with sparkling wine.

CUCUMBER SPARKLING WINE

A champagne glass or wine glass, chilled

- 1 long, narrow cucumber peel
- ½ oz. Benedictine
- 1 tsp. lemon juice
- 4 oz. dry sparkling wine, chilled

Place cucumber peel in glass and add Benedictine and lemon juice. Add sparkling wine and stir gently. Let stand 1 minute before serving.

ELKE SUMMER
A champagne glass, chilled

- 1 tbs. Minttu Peppermint Schnaapps
- 1 dash Grand Marnier
- 4 oz. sparkling wine
- 3 fresh raspberries

Combine peppermint schnapps and Grand Marnier in glass and stir. Add champagne. Float raspberries on top. *Minttu Peppermint Schnaapps, Great Vintners International, Syosset, N.Y.*

EVE
A 10- to 14-oz. wine glass, chilled

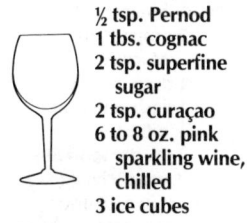

- ½ tsp. Pernod
- 1 tbs. cognac
- 2 tsp. superfine sugar
- 2 tsp. curaçao
- 6 to 8 oz. pink sparkling wine, chilled
- 3 ice cubes

Pour Pernod into glass and turn glass to coat sides. Add cognac. In separate small container, soak sugar with curaçao until sugar is dissolved. Add to glass and stir mixture. Add ice and fill with pink sparkling wine.

FRENCH FOAM
A highball glass, chilled

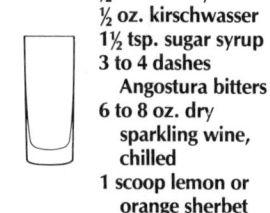

- ½ oz. brandy
- ½ oz. kirschwasser
- 1½ tsp. sugar syrup
- 3 to 4 dashes Angostura bitters
- 6 to 8 oz. dry sparkling wine, chilled
- 1 scoop lemon or orange sherbet

Combine brandy, kirschwasser, sugar syrup, and bitters in glass, and stir well. Fill glass to *half level* with sparkling wine. Float scoop of sherbet on top. Add more sparkling wine to top.

FRENCH LIFT
A champagne glass, chilled

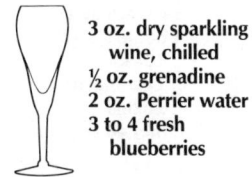

- 3 oz. dry sparkling wine, chilled
- ½ oz. grenadine
- 2 oz. Perrier water
- 3 to 4 fresh blueberries

Fill glass to half level with sparkling wine. Add grenadine. Fill with Perrier. Drop blueberries (which will float up and down in glass) into drink. *Lapogee Lounge, Biltmore Plaza Hotel, Providence, R.I.*

FROBISHER

A highball glass, chilled

2 oz. gin
3 to 4 dashes Angostura bitters
3 to 4 ice cubes
6 to 8 oz. dry sparkling wine, chilled
1 strip lemon peel

Combine gin and bitters in glass and stir. Add ice cubes. Add sparkling wine. Twist lemon peel over drink to release oil, and drop it in.

LANSON COCKTAIL

6 champagne glasses, chilled

6 sugar cubes
1 tsp. Angostura bitters
3 oz. armagnac
1 bottle (750 ml.) Lanson champagne, chilled
6 thin slices orange

Place sugar cube in each glass and sprinkle with 1 or 2 drops Angostura bitters. Trickle ½ oz. armagnac into each glass so that sugar is afloat. Fill with champagne, and garnish with orange slices. *Lanson Champagne, Park Benziger & Co., Inc., Scarsdale, N.Y.*

KIR ROYALE

A champagne glass, chilled

2 tsp. crème de cassis
3 to 4 oz. dry sparkling wine, chilled

Combine crème de cassis and 1 oz. sparkling wine in glass and stir until blended. Add remaining sparkling wine. *Bouvet Brut, Kobrand Corp., New York, N.Y.*

LE COQ HARDY

A champagne glass, chilled

1 sugar cube
1 drop Fernet Branca bitters
1 drop Grand Marnier
1 drop cognac
1 dash Angostura bitters
3 oz. dry sparkling wine, chilled
1 thin slice orange
1 maraschino cherry

Place sugar cube in glass. Add Fernet Branca bitters, Grand Marnier, cognac, and Angostura bitters. Fill with sparkling wine. Garnish with orange slice and cherry.

LEMON MONTSERRAT
8 champagne glasses, chilled

> 3 oz. superfine sugar
> 2 oz. lemon juice
> 4 oz. strawberry liqueur
> 5 to 6 ice cubes
> 2 bottles Montserrat dry sparkling wine, chilled

Combine sugar, lemon juice, strawberry liqueur, and ice cubes in small pitcher or shaker, and stir until sugar is dissolved. Strain mixture, dividing it among 8 glasses. Top each serving with sparkling wine. *Montserrat Sparkling Wines, Great Vintners International, Syosset, N.Y.*

LONDON SPECIAL
An old-fashioned glass, chilled

> 1 sugar cube
> 3 to 4 dashes Peychaud's bitters
> 3 to 4 ice cubes
> 4 oz. dry sparkling wine, chilled
> 1 strip orange peel

Place sugar cube in glass. Add bitters and ice cubes. Then add wine. Twist orange peel over drink to release oil, and drop it in.

PATRIARCA
A champagne glass, chilled

> ½ oz. lime juice
> ½ oz. crème de framboises (raspberry liqueur)
> 3 ice cubes
> 3 to 4 oz. Folio Spumante Nobile (Italian dry sparkling wine), chilled

Combine all ingredients except sparkling wine in mixing glass, and stir well. Strain mixture into champagne glass. Add sparkling wine. *Folio Spumante Nobile, V. Pozzi, Salvalai; Brescia, Italy*

PINK CALIFORNIA SUNSHINE
2 10- to 14-oz. wine glasses, chilled

> 4 ice cubes
> 1 to 2 dashes crème de cassis
> 4 oz. orange juice, chilled
> 4 oz. pink sparkling wine, chilled

Combine all ingredients except sparkling wine in mixing glass, and stir well. Strain mixture, dividing it into 2 wine glasses. Add 2 oz. sparkling wine to each glass.

POINSETTIA
A wine glass (10- to 14-oz.), chilled

3 to 4 ice cubes, optional
½ oz. triple sec or Cointreau
3 oz. cranberry juice, chilled
3 to 4 oz. dry sparkling wine, chilled

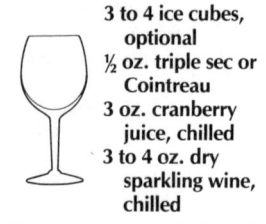

Place ice cubes, if desired, in glass. Add triple sec or Cointreau and cranberry juice. Add sparkling wine. *Windows on the World Restaurant, New York, N.Y.*

SOYER au CHAMPAGNE
A wine glass (10- to 14-oz.), chilled

2 tbs. vanilla ice cream
3 to 4 drops brandy
3 to 4 drops maraschino liqueur
3 to 4 drops cognac
4 oz. dry sparkling wine, chilled
1 thin slice orange
1 maraschino cherry

Combine ice cream, brandy, maraschino liqueur, and cognac in glass, and mix well. Add sparkling wine and stir briefly. Garnish with orange and cherry.

SPANISH DANCER
A champagne glass, chilled

Peel of ½ orange in spiral
1 tsp. triple sec
4 oz. Montserrat dry sparkling wine, chilled

Place orange peel in glass. Add triple sec. Add sparkling wine and stir gently 2 or 3 turns. *Montserrat Sparkling Wine, Great Vintners International, Syosset, N.Y.*

SPARKLING CARIB COCKTAIL
A 10- to 14-oz. tall glass, chilled

½ oz. light rum
1 oz. lime juice
1 oz. pineapple juice
½ tsp. banana or coconut liqueur
6 to 8 ice cubes
4 oz. dry sparkling wine, chilled

Combine rum, lime juice, pineapple juice, liqueur, and 3 to 4 ice cubes in shaker, and shake well. Place remaining ice in glass and strain mixture into glass. Add sparkling wine.

SPARKLING WINE COOLER

A 10- to 14-oz. wine glass, chilled

Crushed ice to fill wine glass
1 oz. brandy
1 oz. Cointreau
6 oz. dry sparkling wine, chilled
1 mint sprig

Fill glass with crushed ice. Add brandy and Cointreau. Fill glass with sparkling wine, and stir gently. Garnish with mint.

SPARKLING WINE JULEP

A champagne or whiskey sour glass, chilled

2 mint sprigs
1 tbs. sugar syrup
Crushed ice to fill champagne glass
1½ oz. brandy
3 oz. dry sparkling wine, chilled

Put 1 mint sprig and sugar syrup in serving glass and crush mint in syrup. Fill glass with crushed ice. Add brandy. Add sparkling wine and stir gently. Garnish with remaining mint.

SPARKLING WINE POLONAISE

A champagne glass, chilled

1 tsp. blackberry liqueur
1 tsp. blackberry brandy
½ tsp. cognac
3 oz. dry sparkling wine, chilled

Sugar-frost rim of glass, moistening rim with blackberry liqueur. Combine blackberry brandy, cognac, and sparkling wine in prepared glass, and stir 2 or 3 turns.

SPIAGGIA PRIVATA

(Spee-ad-jia Pree-vata; Private Beach)
A wine glass (8- to 14-oz.), chilled

3 to 4 ice cubes
2 tbs. lemon juice
1 tsp. melon liqueur
3 to 4 oz. Folio Spumante Nobile (Italian dry sparkling wine), chilled
1 sprig of mint

Put ice cubes in glass. Add melon liqueur and sparkling wine, and stir slowly. Garnish with mint sprig. *Folio Spumante Nobile, V. Pozzi, Salvalai; Brescia, Italy*

SPINNING PEACH
A wine glass (12- to 14-oz.), or large goblet, chilled

1 small fresh ripe peach
6 oz. dry sparkling wine, chilled

Rub a small peach with a paper towel to remove all fuzz. Pierce peach 15 to 20 times with fork and place in glass. Add sparkling wine. (Peach should float and spin in glass.)

SPUMANTE GRANADE
A champagne glass, chilled

1 oz. pomegrante juice (or 1 tsp. grenadine)
4 oz. dry sparkling wine, chilled

Put pomegranate juice or grenadine in glass, then fill with dry sparkling wine. *Loriano Papini, Hotel Principe & Savoia (Ciga), Milan, Italy*

VERO, VERO VERDE
(Vay-ro Vay-ro Vayr-day; Truly, Truly Green)
An old-fashioned glass, chilled

2 tbs. lemon sherbet
2 tsp. green crème de menthe
3 to 4 oz. Folio Spumante Nobile (Italian dry sparkling wine), chilled

Combine lemon sherbet and crème de menthe in glass. Add sparkling wine, and stir until ingredients are well mixed. *Folio Spumante Nobile, V. Pozzi, Salvalai; Brescia, Italy*

SHERRY RECIPES

FARMER'S DAUGHTER

A whiskey sour glass, chilled

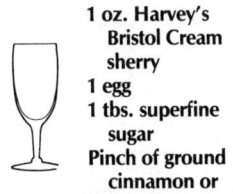

- 1 oz. Harvey's Bristol Cream sherry
- 1 egg
- 1 tbs. superfine sugar
- Pinch of ground cinnamon or cocoa

Separate egg, putting yolk and white in separate small bowls. To yolk, add sugar, and beat until creamy. Continue beating, while slowly adding sherry. Set mixture aside for a moment. With rotary beater, beat egg white to soft peaks. Pour yolk mixture into beaten egg white and stir until well blended. Spoon froth into glass. Sprinkle cinnamon or cocoa on top of drink. *Harvey's Bristol Cream, Heublein, Inc., Hartford, Conn.*

ALMOND COOKIE

Follow recipe for Farmer's Daughter, adding 2 tsp. amaretto and 2 tsp. crème de noyaux to egg yolk mixture.

CREAMY THIGHS

Follow recipe for Farmer's Daughter, adding ½ oz. white crème de cacao to egg yolk mixture.

GREEN HORNET

A 4-oz. cocktail glass, chilled

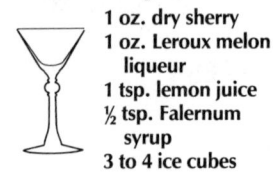

1 oz. dry sherry
1 oz. Leroux melon liqueur
1 tsp. lemon juice
½ tsp. Falernum syrup
3 to 4 ice cubes

Combine all ingredients in shaker, and shake vigorously. Strain drink into glass. *Leroux & Co., Relay, Md.*

O'TOOLE'S COOLER

A highball glass, chilled

4 to 5 ice cubes
1½ oz. Irish whiskey
1 oz. dry sherry
1 tbs. crème de noyaux
1 tbs. lemon juice
4 oz. club soda, chilled

Fill glass with ice cubes to half level. Add Irish whiskey, sherry, crème de noyaux, and lemon juice, and stir. Fill glass to top with soda.

IBIZA

A highball glass, chilled

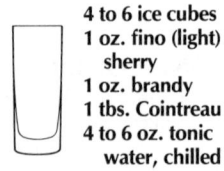

4 to 6 ice cubes
1 oz. fino (light) sherry
1 oz. brandy
1 tbs. Cointreau
4 to 6 oz. tonic water, chilled

Fill glass to half level with ice cubes. Add sherry, brandy, and Cointreau, and stir. Fill glass with tonic.

RENAISSANCE MAN

A 4-oz. cocktail glass, chilled

1½ oz. Jamaica dark rum
½ oz. dry sherry
½ oz. heavy cream
3 to 4 ice cubes
3 oz. crushed ice

Combine all ingredients except *crushed* ice in shaker, and shake vigorously. Put crushed ice in glass, and strain drink into glass.

SPANISH MILKMAID

A 4-oz. cocktail glass, chilled

    1 oz. Harvey's Bristol Cream sherry
1 oz. orange juice
1 tsp. brandy
2 tsp. heavy cream
3 oz. crushed ice

Combine all ingredients in shaker, and shake vigorously. Strain drink into glass. *Harvey's Bristol Cream, Heublein, Inc., Hartford, Conn.*

STRAIGHT LAW

A 4-oz. cocktail glass, chilled

2 oz. dry sherry
1 oz. gin
3 to 4 ice cubes
1 strip lemon peel

Combine all ingredients except lemon peel in mixing glass, and stir until well mixed and chilled. Strain drink into cocktail glass. Twist lemon peel over drink to release oil, and drop it in.

TUXEDO

A 4-oz. cocktail glass, chilled

2 oz. dry sherry
½ oz. anisette
1 dash maraschino liqueur
1 dash Angostura bitters
3 to 4 ice cubes

Combine all ingredients in mixing glass, and stir well. Strain drink into glass.

Aperitifs

ABOUT APERITIFS, VERMOUTHS, AND BITTERS

What They Have in Common

The word *aperitif* originally and still basically means a drink that is intended to open up the appetite—a before-meal drink. But in the drink world there is a group of particular bottled products that are also called aperitifs or aperitif wines, which includes vermouths and bitters. There is a good deal of difference among them and confusion about the definition of many of these products. Their common denominator seems to be that they all have a distinctively bitter characteristic (even underlying those that are sweet), which may be said to whet the appetite. Most also claim to have stomachic or digestive values and some . . . the power of an elixir!

For today's liberated drinking fashions, aperitifs, vermouths, and bitters are more popular than ever, providing an accent or topnote to many new drink concoctions, as well as such classics as the Manhattan and Rob Roy (sweet vermouth) and the Martini (dry vermouth). Many Americans are also enjoying these specialties as drinks in their own right—sipping them straight, on-the-rocks, with club soda—as the French and Italians have done for generations or as the base in mixed drinks, such as the popular Negroni and Puntegroni.

Individual product compositions and marketing descriptions are so diverse that it is difficult to pin down basic definitions of "aperitifs, vermouths, bitters." The following generally represent the interpretations of the alcoholic beverage industry:

Aperitif

Besides the broad meaning of aperitif as a before-meal drink, many in the industry refer to vermouths and *wine*-based bitters as *aperitif wines*. But, some are also fortified with spirit.

Vermouth

Alexis Lichine's New Encyclopedia of Wine and Spirits declares, "Vermouth is not a wine. It is wine-based, but it undergoes so many additions and manipulations that it ceases to be recognizable as the product of the vine. It is, however, a popular and excellent aperitif and is indispensable in some cocktails."

Vermouth is a processed beverage of wine, sugar additive, flavorings from assorted herbs and plants, and alcohol. Originally the French specialized in dry vermouth, and the Italians, sweet. Today, both French and Italian vermouths come in dry and sweet versions, and several brands produce red, rosé, and white vermouths.

Bitters

Bitters seem even less standardized. Generally they are sweet-to-dry flavored liquids with a distinctly bitter topnote. Most of the formulas are secret and include some composition of aromatic plants—seeds, roots, herbs, barks, flowers, and fruits, and often quinine. Most are spirit based, but not all.

There are two legal classes of bitters: medicinal and nonmedicinal. Those classified as medicinal have satisfied severe tests of the Federal Alcohol Tax Unit of the Internal Revenue Service that the regular alcohol tax should not be applied. If these bitters are imported, however, they must still pay the regular duty. Medicinal bitters are under the jurisdiction of the Pure Food Act and in many states are prohibited from sale in liquor stores, even though they may have an alcohol base; they will be found in grocery, drug, or department stores. Fernet Branca is such an example. Most bitters are classified as nonmedicinal and are subject to alcoholic beverage taxes.

Prominent Aperitifs, Vermouths, Bitters

Amer Picon (France) Called "bitter aperitif"; based on orange, quinine, and gentian roots.

Abbott's Aged Bitters (U.S.A.) Aromatic blend; made in Baltimore for over a century.

Angostura Bitters (Trinidad) Originally an appetite stimulant and stomachic compounded of rare plants and herbs by Dr. Johann Gottlieb Siegert in 1830 at Angostura, Venezuela. Still produced by the Siegert family, now in Trinidad. Today Angostura is popularly used as a flavoring agent in drinks and cooking (especially sauces and gravies), although the firm still recommends it as a tonic.

Boonekamp Bitters (Holland) Very strong and bitter digestive. Now distributed by Buton of Italy.

Byrrh Aperitif (France) A wine-based aperitif not too appealing to American tastes. Supposedly developed by a French Pyrenees shepherd.

Campari (Italy) On the label identified as "aperitivo," containing "bitters and liqueur." Gaspare Campari decided this formulation was best of many bitters compounded by his firm in Milan around 1860. The taste is bitter yet aromatic with a faint underlying sweetness; bright red color; 96 proof alcohol base.

Cinzano Vermouth (Italy) A brand of dry and sweet vermouths more and more produced in the United States for American distribution.

Chambery Vermouth (France) A fine French vermouth flavored with strawberry juice; pinkish color.

Dubonnet Aperitif Wine (France and U.S.) Red (rouge), sweet, and white (blanc), dry. That which is sold in America is manufactured from domestic wine with a variety of flavorings added.

Fernet Branca Bitters (Italy) A taste like the ruins of Pompeii. Some say it is made with rhubarb. Sold at 80 proof almost everywhere in the world.

Lillet Aperitif (France) Wine base with delicate herbal and dominant orange flavoring; white and red types.

Martini & Rossi Vermouth (France and Italy) The largest selling vermouths in the world. Available in dry and sweet; red, rosé, white.

Noilly Prat Vermouth (France) A fine-tasting dry vermouth.

Orange Bitters (England) Orange concentrate with light aromatic accent.

Peach Bitters (England) Sharp peach essence with light aromatic accent.

Peychaud's Bitters (U.S.) Slightly more pungent than Angostura; like a catalyst, it opens up flavors. Made in Louisiana.

Punt E Mes Bitters (Italy) Wine base with quinine; very sweet and at same time very bitter; remarkably appetizing.

Rosso Antico (Italy) Italy's most popular aperitif, produced with base and 39 exotic herbs; not called a vermouth.

Unicum Bitters (Hungarian; now produced by Zwack, Italy) Balanced bittersweet flavor, made from more than 40 herbs; 84 proof.

APERITIF RECIPES

ADDINGTON
An old-fashioned glass, chilled

1 oz. dry vermouth
1 oz. sweet vermouth
3 ice cubes
1 tsp. lemon juice
2 to 3 oz. club soda, chilled
1 strip lemon peel

Combine dry and sweet vermouths, ice, and lemon juice in shaker, and shake vigorously. Strain mixture into glass. Add soda. Twist lemon peel over drink to release oil, and drop it in.

ADONIS
An old-fashioned glass, chilled

1 oz. sweet vermouth
3 oz. dry sherry
1 dash orange bitters
5 ice cubes

Combine all ingredients except 2 ice cubes in shaker, and shake vigorously. Put remaining ice in glass and strain drink into glass.

ALGONQUIN

A 4-oz. cocktail glass, chilled

1½ oz. American blended whiskey
1 oz. dry vermouth
1 oz. pineapple juice
3 ice cubes

Combine all ingredients in shaker, and shake vigorously. Strain drink into glass.

ALLIANCE

An old-fashioned glass, chilled

1 oz. English gin
1 oz. dry French vermouth
2 dashes aquavit
5 ice cubes

Combine all ingredients except 2 ice cubes in shaker, and shake vigorously. Place remaining ice in glass and strain into glass.

ALMOND COCKTAIL

An old-fashioned glass, chilled

2 oz. gin
1 oz. dry vermouth
½ tsp. superfine sugar
½ tsp. slivered almonds
½ oz. peach liqueur
1 dash kirsch
2 ice cubes

Combine gin, vermouth, sugar, and slivered almond in small saucepan, and stir over low heat until sugar is dissolved. Pour mixture into mixing glass and let stand for a minute. Add peach liqueur and kirsch, and stir. Put ice in old-fashioned glass and strain drink into glass.

AMERICAN BEAUTY ROSE

A 4-oz. cocktail glass, chilled

¾ oz. dry vermouth
¾ oz. orange juice
½ oz. peppermint schnapps
1 dash strawberry liqueur
3 ice cubes
¾ oz. port wine

Combine all ingredients except port wine in shaker, and shake vigorously. Strain mixture into glass. Tip glass a little and slowly pour in port wine so that it floats.

AMERICANO

A 10- to 14-oz. tall glass, chilled

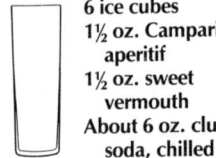

6 ice cubes
1½ oz. Campari aperitif
1½ oz. sweet vermouth
About 6 oz. club soda, chilled

Place ice in tall glass. Add Campari and sweet vermouth, and stir. Fill glass with soda. *Campari, Austin Nichols & Co., Inc., New York, N.Y.*

BITTER BIKINI

An old-fashioned glass, chilled

1½ oz. Campari aperitif
1 oz. dry vermouth
½ oz. triple sec
3 to 4 ice cubes
6 oz. crushed ice

Combine all ingredients except crushed ice in shaker, and shake vigorously. Put crushed ice in glass. Strain into glass. *Campari, Austin Nichols & Co., Inc., New York, N.Y.*

BEAUTY MARK

A 4-oz. cocktail glass, chilled

¾ oz. sweet vermouth
¾ oz. dry vermouth
1 oz. gin
1 tbs. orange juice
3 ice cubes
1 drop grenadine

Combine all ingredients except grenadine in shaker, and shake vigorously. Strain drink into glass. Add drop of grenadine so that it is only a dot on surface of drink.

BLACK TIE

An 8-oz. or larger wine glass, chilled

4 oz. Reynac Pineau des Charentis (aperitif wine from Cognac), chilled
2 oz. dry sparkling wine, chilled
1 black grape

Combine aperitif wine and sparkling wine in glass. Garnish with grape. *La Caravelle Restaurant and Peartree Imports, Inc., New York, N.Y.*

BLOODHOUND
A 4-oz. cocktail glass, chilled

¾ oz. sweet vermouth
¾ oz. dry vermouth
1 oz. gin
1 tsp. strawberry liqueur
3 ice cubes
3 oz. crushed ice
1 fresh strawberry

Combine all ingredients except *crushed* ice and strawberry in shaker, and shake vigorously. Put crushed ice in glass, and strain drink into glass. Garnish with strawberry.

BLOODSTONE
A 4-oz. cocktail glass, chilled

1½ oz. Rosso Antico aperitif
1 oz. gin
3 to 4 ice cubes
1 strip lemon peel

Combine all ingredients except lemon peel in shaker, and shake vigorously. Strain drink into glass. Twist lemon peel over drink to release oil, and drop it in. *Rosso Antico, Bologna, Italy*

BLUE DENIM
An old-fashioned glass, chilled

½ oz. dry vermouth
½ oz. Bourbon
2 dashes Angostura bitters
1 dash blue curaçao
5 ice cubes
1 strip lemon peel

Combine all ingredients except 2 ice cubes and lemon peel in shaker, and shake well. Put remaining ice cubes in glass, and strain drink into glass. Twist lemon peel over drink to release oil, and drop it in.

BLUE MOON
A 4-oz. cocktail glass, chilled

½ oz. dry vermouth
1½ oz. gin
1 tsp. parfait amour (or crème de violette or blue curaçao)
1 dash orange bitters
3 ice cubes
3 oz. crushed ice

Combine all ingredients except *crushed* ice in shaker, and shake well. Place crushed ice in glass, and strain drink into glass.

BOMBAY
A 4-oz. cocktail glass, chilled

1 oz. sweet vermouth
½ oz. dry vermouth
1 oz. cognac
2 dashes Pernod
2 dashes curaçao
4 ice cubes

Combine all ingredients except ice cubes in shaker, and shake vigorously. Place remaining ice cubes in glass, and strain drink into glass.

BRAZIL
A 4-oz. cocktail glass, chilled

1 oz. dry vermouth
1 oz. dry sherry
2 to 3 dashes Ricard
1 dash Angostura bitters
1 strip lemon peel

Combine all ingredients except lemon peel in shaker, and shake vigorously. Strain drink into glass. Twist lemon peel over drink to release oil, and drop it in. For a less dry drink, substitute sweet vermouth in place of dry vermouth, or oloroso (sweet) sherry in place of dry sherry.

CINZANO
A 4-oz. cocktail glass, chilled

3 oz. Cinzano dry vermouth
2 to 3 dashes orange bitters
2 to 3 dashes Angostura bitters
3 ice cubes
1 strip orange peel

Combine all ingredients except orange peel in mixing glass, and stir well. Strain drink into glass. Twist orange peel near surface of drink to cover with oil, and drop in peel. *Cinzano, Turin, Italy*

DIPLOMAT
A 4-oz. cocktail glass, chilled

2 oz. dry vermouth
1 oz. sweet vermouth
2 dashes maraschino liqueur
3 ice cubes
1 strip orange peel

Combine all ingredients except orange peel in mixing glass, and stir well. Strain drink into glass. Twist orange peel over drink to release oil, and drop it in.

DRY DECK
An old-fashioned glass, chilled

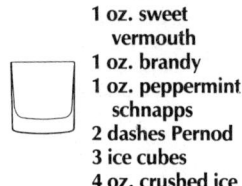

1 oz. sweet vermouth
1 oz. brandy
1 oz. peppermint schnapps
2 dashes Pernod
3 ice cubes
4 oz. crushed ice

Combine all ingredients except ice in shaker, and shake vigorously. Place crushed ice in glass, and strain drink into glass.

FIRST STRIKE
A 4-oz. cocktail glass, chilled

1½ oz. dry vermouth
¾ oz. curaçao
3 to 4 ice cubes
1 oz. club soda
Ground cinnamon

Combine vermouth, curaçao, and ice in mixing glass, and stir well. Strain drink into glass and add club soda. Top with sprinkle of cinnamon.

DUCHESS OF DENVER
A 4-oz. cocktail glass, chilled

¾ oz. dry vermouth
¾ oz. sweet vermouth
1 tsp. lemon juice
1 tbs. amaretto
3 to 4 ice cubes

Combine all ingredients in shaker, and shake vigorously. Strain drink into glass.

GOLD STRIPE
A 4-oz. cocktail glass, chilled

2 oz. dry vermouth
½ oz. yellow Chartreuse
2 dashes orange bitters
3 to 4 ice cubes

Combine all ingredients in shaker, and shake well. Strain drink into glass.

GREEN ROOM
A 4-oz. cocktail glass, chilled

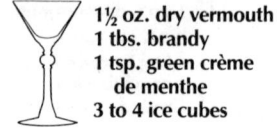

1½ oz. dry vermouth
1 tbs. brandy
1 tsp. green crème de menthe
3 to 4 ice cubes

Combine all ingredients in shaker, and shake vigorously. Strain drink into glass.

HOOPLA
A 4-oz. cocktail glass, chilled

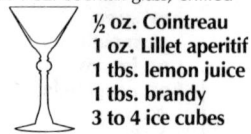

½ oz. Cointreau
1 oz. Lillet aperitif
1 tbs. lemon juice
1 tbs. brandy
3 to 4 ice cubes

Combine all ingredients in shaker, and shake vigorously. Strain drink into glass. *Cointreau Ltd., Lawrenceville, N.J.*

HARPER'S FERRY
A 4-oz. cocktail glass, chilled

1½ oz. dry vermouth
1 tbs. Southern Comfort
1 tbs. light rum
1 tbs. curaçao
3 to 4 ice cubes

Combine all ingredients in shaker, and shake well. Strain drink into glass.

ITALIAN
A 4-oz. cocktail glass, chilled

2 oz. sweet vermouth
1 oz. Fernet Branca bitters
1 tsp. sugar syrup
1 dash Angostura bitters
3 ice cubes

Combine all ingredients in mixing glass, and stir well. Strain drink into cocktail glass.

KINGDOM COME
An old-fashioned glass, chilled

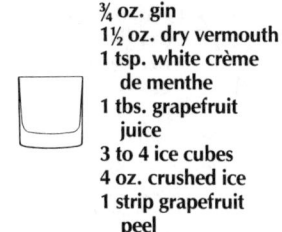

¾ oz. gin
1½ oz. dry vermouth
1 tsp. white crème de menthe
1 tbs. grapefruit juice
3 to 4 ice cubes
4 oz. crushed ice
1 strip grapefruit peel

Combine all ingredients except ice and grapefruit peel in shaker, and shake vigorously. Place ice in glass, and strain drink into glass. Garnish with grapefruit peel.

LILLET COCKTAIL
A 4-oz. cocktail glass, chilled

½ oz. gin
1½ oz. Lillet aperitif
3 to 4 ice cubes
1 strip lemon peel

In shaker, combine gin, Lillet, and ice, and shake vigorously. Strain into glass. Light match. Squeeze lemon peel over drink against flame to create burst of blue flame, and drop peel into drink. *Lillet, Schenley World T. & I. Co., New York, N.Y.*

LEMON COOLER
A 4-oz. cocktail glass, chilled

1½ oz. dry vermouth
½ oz. gin
1 tsp. lemon juice
1 tsp. raspberry liqueur or crème de cassis
3 ice cubes
1 tbs. crushed ice
About 2 oz. 7-Up or Schweppes bitter lemon soda, chilled

Combine dry vermouth, gin, lemon juice, liqueur and ice in shaker, and shake vigorously. Put crushed ice in glass, and strain shaker mixture into glass. Fill to top with 7-Up or bitter lemon soda.

MORNING BECOMES ELECTRIC
An old-fashioned glass, chilled

2 oz. dry vermouth
1 oz. brandy
2 tsp. port wine
1 dash curaçao
5 to 6 ice cubes

Combine all ingredients except 2 or 3 ice cubes in mixing glass, and stir well. Place remaining ice cubes in glass, and strain drink into glass.

NEGRONI

An old-fashioned glass, chilled

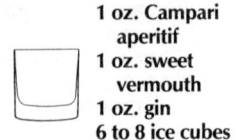

1 oz. Campari aperitif
1 oz. sweet vermouth
1 oz. gin
6 to 8 ice cubes
1 strip lemon peel

Combine Campari, vermouth, gin, and 3 to 4 ice cubes in mixing glass and stir well. Put remaining ice cubes in glass, and strain drink into glass. Twist lemon peel over drink to release oil, and drop it in. *Campari, Austin Nichols & Co., Inc., New York, N.Y.*

PALE MOON

A 4-oz. cocktail glass, chilled

1½ oz. sweet vermouth
1 oz. pineapple juice
2 tsp. gin
1 to 2 dashes curaçao
3 to 4 ice cubes

Combine all ingredients in shaker, and shake vigorously. Strain drink into glass.

PARTY GIRL

A 4-oz. cocktail glass, chilled

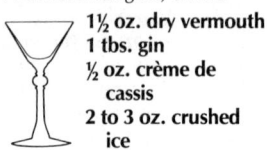

1½ oz. dry vermouth
1 tbs. gin
½ oz. crème de cassis
2 to 3 oz. crushed ice

Combine vermouth, gin, and crème de cassis in mixing glass, and stir briefly. Place crushed ice in glass, and pour drink into glass.

PERFECT COCKTAIL

A 4-oz. cocktail glass, chilled

1 oz. sweet vermouth
1 oz. dry vermouth
1 oz. gin
3 ice cubes
1 strip lemon peel

Combine all ingredients except lemon peel in mixing glass, and stir well. Strain drink into glass. Twist lemon peel over drink to release oil, and drop it in.

PERPETUAL

An old-fashioned glass, chilled

1½ oz. sweet vermouth
1½ oz. dry vermouth
2 to 3 dashes white crème de cacao
1 tsp. crème de violette
5 ice cubes

Combine all ingredients except 2 ice cubes in shaker, and shake vigorously. Put remaining ice cubes in glass, and strain drink into glass.

PUNTEGRONI

A 4-oz. cocktail glass, chilled

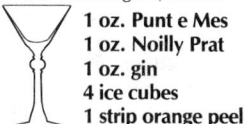

1 oz. Punt e Mes
1 oz. Noilly Prat
1 oz. gin
4 ice cubes
1 strip orange peel

Combine all ingredients except peel in mixing glass, and stir well. Strain drink into glass. Twist orange peel over drink to release oil, and drop it in. *Pen & Pencil Restaurant, New York, N.Y.*

PINK PUSSY*

A 10- to 14-oz. tall glass, chilled

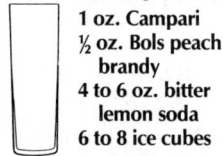

1 oz. Campari
½ oz. Bols peach brandy
4 to 6 oz. bitter lemon soda
6 to 8 ice cubes

Combine all ingredients except soda in glass and stir well. Add soda, and stir briefly. *Winner of Campari Competition, London, 1982, by Geoffrey Glockler, Ritz Casino, Picadilly*

RUBINO

An old-fashioned glass, chilled

1 oz. vodka
2 tbs. red Dubonnet aperitif
1 tbs. Campari
6 to 7 ice cubes

Combine all ingredients except 2 to 3 ice cubes in mixing glass, and stir well. Place remaining ice cubes in glass, and strain drink into glass. *Loriano Papini, Hotel Principe & Savoia (Ciga), Milan, Italy*

SOUR BOWL
An old-fashioned glass, chilled

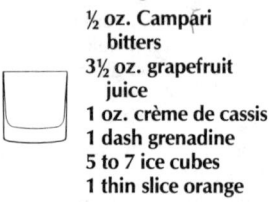

½ oz. Campari bitters
3½ oz. grapefruit juice
1 oz. crème de cassis
1 dash grenadine
5 to 7 ice cubes
1 thin slice orange

Combine all ingredients except 2 or 3 ice cubes and orange slice in shaker, and shake vigorously. Place remaining ice cubes in glass, and strain drink into glass. Garnish with orange slice.

TANGO of LOVE
An old-fashioned glass, chilled

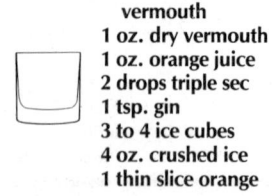

1 oz. sweet vermouth
1 oz. dry vermouth
1 oz. orange juice
2 drops triple sec
1 tsp. gin
3 to 4 ice cubes
4 oz. crushed ice
1 thin slice orange

Combine all ingredients except crushed ice and orange slice in mixing glass, and stir well. Place crushed ice in glass, and strain drink into glass. Garnish with orange slice.

UP the ACADEMY
A 4-oz. cocktail glass, chilled

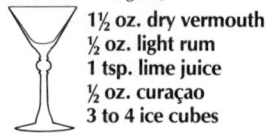

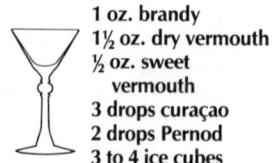

1½ oz. dry vermouth
½ oz. light rum
1 tsp. lime juice
½ oz. curaçao
3 to 4 ice cubes

Combine all ingredients in shaker, and shake vigorously. Strain drink into glass.

VERMOUTH CASSIS
A highball glass, chilled

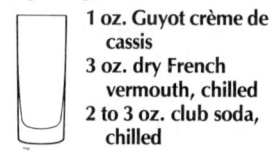

1 oz. Guyot crème de cassis
3 oz. dry French vermouth, chilled
2 to 3 oz. club soda, chilled

Combine crème de cassis and vermouth in glass and stir well. Add soda and stir once. *Guyot Creme de Cassis, Kobrand Corp., New York, N.Y.*

WHIP
A 4-oz. cocktail glass, chilled

1 oz. brandy
1½ oz. dry vermouth
½ oz. sweet vermouth
3 drops curaçao
2 drops Pernod
3 to 4 ice cubes

Combine all ingredients in shaker, and shake vigorously. Strain drink into glass.

Spirits

ABOUT SPIRITS

The Spirit World

More than what we eat, we are what we drink. Water is the most essential element of life, and much of it is imbibed in strange and mysterious ways. The social drink may be mainly water, but the magic ingredient is a touch of alcohol, fermented as beer or wine or distilled as spirits. With spirit beverages (distilled from mashes of grains, roots, fruits, stems, and leaves), the proof is higher and the potions more diverse.

This section is about spirits which for our purposes means any distilled alcoholic beverage. The word *spirit* comes from the observation that during the manufacturing process one can see vapors . . . like ghosts, rising from the fermenting mashes of Bourbon, Scotch, gin, rum, etc.

A spirit is an alcoholic beverage that is manufactured through the process of cooking alcohol-containing plant material, letting it ferment, and then passing the ferment through a distillation chamber where it is heated to 176°F. to vaporize. The vapors are cooled to condense into liquid. Of course, there are intervening steps affecting flavor and proof, but that is the general difference between spirits and wine and beer, which are never distilled. Basically, the distilled product achieves a much higher concentration of alcohol, up to 95 percent, or 190 proof. Other liquid, usually water, is added to the distillate to reduce the proof. Spirits can be bottled as soon as they are processed or they can be aged.

Types of Spirits

Aquavit

The white spirit of the north. Norway, Sweden, and Denmark are the host countries of this strong and pungent potion, which is made similarly to gin, e.g., a grain neutral spirit that is redistilled in the company of caraway seeds instead of juniper berries (the main flavoring of gin).

Aquavit is not popularly known for its mixability but rather for its spectacular "down the hatch" consumption. Aquavit is not sipped but swallowed very cold, often with beer chaser. For best enjoyment, place bottle of aquavit in a freezer for several hours, until the liquid becomes slightly viscous (it won't freeze). Remove and cover with a towel and pour. Don't add ice unless you really want to thin out that rye-bread taste. If you feel adventuresome, you may substitute aquavit in drink recipes calling for kummel liqueurs, using half as much.

Brandy

Brandy is the oldest of spirits, the first distillations recorded in the thirteenth century. It is obtained solely from the fermented juice, mash, or wine of fruit, bottled at not less than 80 proof. The product simply called *brandy* is distilled from *wine* of grapes or other fruits. When a *mash* of fruit is allowed to ferment and be distilled without the intermediate step of becoming wine, the result is called *fruit brandy*. Some of the best fruit brandies are produced in France, those called *eau de vie*, which are described below. The character and quality of all brandies are dependent on soil, fruit, primary wine product, distillation method, and blending.

Wine Brandy

Cognac: The most famous of wine brandies is Cognac. Only brandy made from grapes grown in the delimited district of Charentes, France, clustering around the town of Cognac, may be called Cognac by French law. Today much Cognac is a blend called "fine champagne," a term that refers not to the bubbly wine but to brandy from the Cognac region, which must be a mixture of at least 50 percent from the Grand Champagne zone and the Petite Champagne zone, the two main geographical divisions of the Cognac grape-growing area. There are several types of Cognac: S—Superior or Special; V.S.—Very Superior or Very Special; X—Extra; O—Old; P—Pale (e.g., V.S.O.P.—Very Superior Old Pale). The name Napoleon on a label is pure merchandising and has no significance.

American brandies: American-produced brandies are somewhat sweeter than European counterparts. Well-known products are Christian Bros. X.O., Korbell, Coronet, E & J Gallo.

Armagnac: Made in southwest France, outside the delimited Cognac area but from the same grape. Compared to Cognac, Armagnac is bigger bodied, with a somewhat severe style. Because it is not well known, it is often a better value than many Cognacs.

Asbach Uralt: Rich, smooth, almost liqueur-like German brandy, made from imported, not German, wines.

Grappa: Italian brandy made from wine must, stems, and pips; quite strong.

Marc: French brandy made from the residue of winemaking—skins, stems, pips; produced mainly but not exclusively in the Burgundy area. The enjoyment of its earthy taste is acquired.

Mexican brandy: Brandy is the top selling spirit south of the border, of which El Presidente (Pedro Domecq) is by far the leading brand.

Spanish brandy: Produced in the sherry region; some of excellent quality, such as Fundador and Carlos Segundo.

Pisco brandy: Produced in Peru from muscat grapes and matured in clay casks. Pisco sour is its best-known drink.

Vecchia Romagna Italian brandy: Fine quality classical grape brandy produced in Italy; sold throughout the world.

Fruit Brandy

Apple brandy: American apple brandy is called *apple jack;* lighter than French apple brandy; Laird's is the best known brand. *Calva-*

dos is apple brandy from Normandy, France; aged in wood five to ten years.

Coffee brandy: Less sweet than coffee liqueur.

Slivovitz: Plum brandy produced in Hungary, Poland, Romania, Yugoslavia.

Van der Hum: South African brandy flavored with Seville orange peel and native tangerines.

Other popular fruit brandies include apricot, blackberry, and peach.

Eau de Vie (Water of Life)

A particular type of fruit brandy, distinguished as clear white distlllate, usually made from pits and pulp, and not aged; very fruity fragrance, because it is generally bottled at less than 100 proof. The following are the most popular eaux de vie:

Fraises de Bois: French term for "wild strawberry."

Framboise: French for "raspberries."

Kirsch; Kirschwasser: "Cherry water"; produced in France, Germany, and Switzerland.

Mirabelle: From small yellow Mirabelle plums; made in France and Germany.

Quetsch: From Quetsch plums.

Pear; Poire: The most distinguished is made from the Williams pear, which sometimes has a whole pear in the bottle; produced in France, Germany, and Italy.

Gin

A spirit obtained by redistilling grain spirits with flavoring agents, especially aromatics, which include primarily juniper berries and usually anise, caraway, coriander seed, cacao, cassia bark, lemon peel, licorice, orange peel, orris root. Gin was invented in the seventeenth century at the University of Leyden in Holland to be used as a diuretic. The Dutch liked the medicine. It was discovered by the English in the eighteenth century, and gin was on its way as tonic and spirit. The first distillation for gin is from a fermented mash of grain (barley malt, corn and rye). This distillation is then redistilled with the aromatic mixture. Generally gin is not aged. It is marketed in 80 to 90 proofs. *English and American gins* are light bodied. *Holland gin* has more juniper-berry flavor.

Liqueur (Cordial)

One hundred thirty-five recipes in the Liqueur section, many of which defy basic drink definitions, are testament to the versatility and skyrocketing popularity of these sweet spirits of many flavors and colors. According to the *Oxford* dictionary, the words *liqueur* and *cordial* are synonymous: an alcoholic distilled spirit that has been flavored with aromatic substances and sweetened. Thus, a distillate spirit, usually brandy, has flavoring and sugar syrup added to it to become a liqueur. By law liqueurs must contain at least 2.5 percent sugar additive for sweetening. (This type of fruit spirit with less sweetening is called fruit brandy.) Synthetic or imitation flavorings cannot be used, but vegetable colorings are approved. Liqueurs range in alcoholic content from 36 to 110 proof.

The varieties of liqueurs are legion. Fruit liqueurs are those in which whole fruit is mixed with brandy or spirit until it is infused with the aroma, flavor, and color of the fruit. The mixture is then distilled and the process is completed. Other liqueurs use parts of the plant, seed, skin, root, leaf, bark, and maybe some fruit pulp, too. These may be an herb bouquet combined with distilled spirit and sugar; the flavor combination is brewed and then redistilled. This group is usually colorless, although the producer may add color (e.g., green crème de menthe).

Popular Liqueurs

Abricotine: Apricot liqueur.

Advocaat: Dutch mixture of sweetened egg yolks, brandy, and other ingredients; precursor to the eggnog.

Almond: Almond flavored liqueurs include crème de royaux, orgeat (alcohol-base syrup), and the various brands of Amaretto.

Amaretto: One of the most popular liqueurs in America; generally described as having an almond flavor, although it is made from crushed apricot pits. Amaretto di Saronno was the first.

Anisette (Anis): Worldwide, one of the most popular flavors in liqueurs. Available in 50 to 100 proof, under many names, although Marie Brizard allegedly produced the first in the eighteenth century. Also anisette: Sambuca Romana (Italy), Anis del Mono (Spain), Ouzo (Greece), Raki (Turkey), Escarchado (Portugal), La Tintaine (France).

Aurum: Orange-flavor; made in Italy.

Bailey's Original Irish Cream: A sinfully delicious liqueur imported from Ireland, made with Irish whiskey, Irish cream, and chocolate. It is probably the best-selling liqueur in the U.S. (early eighties) and has inspired many imitators.

Benedictine: A blend of aromatics and Cognac, created at the Benedictine Abbey in Fecamp, France, around 1500. It is available in its original sweetish formula and, in response to popular demand, also bottled as B & B (half Benedictine and half brandy), which is drier.

Blackberry: Blackberry liqueur, containing the legal requirement of sugar additive, and blackberry brandy (less sweet) are probably the most popular fruit-flavored spirits in America.

Chambord: A red berry-flavored liqueur.

Chartreuse: Spice aromatic liqueur on brandy base; produced by the Cistercian monks from an original recipe by Carthusian monks in 1600, containing more than 100 herbs and flowers. Today Yellow (86 proof) and Green (110 proof) are produced in monasteries in Grenoble, France, and Tarragona, Spain.

Cherry Heering: Excellent cherry liqueur from Denmark; 49 proof.

Chocolate: Worldwide, a very popular liqueur. Some of the brands and types available in the U.S., other than the basic white and dark crème de cacao include: Choclair (Swiss), Chococo (with coconut; Virgin Islands), Chokalu (Mexico), Hallgarten's (seven types—lemon, grape, raspberry, cherry, ginger, banana, mint; London), Leroux (a varied list with Chocolate Amaretto the most popular; U.S.A.), Sabra (with orange; Israel), Vandermint (with mint;

Holland), Hiram Walker (a varied list with a splendid Chocolate Cherry and Swiss Chocolate Almond; U.S.A.).

Coconut: Produced by Marie Brizard, France; 60 proof.

Cocoribe: Made from wild coconuts and Virgin Islands rum.

Coffee: Almost all American liquor distributors have a brand; among the most prominent are Kahlua and Kamora, both made in Mexico, and Tia Maria from Jamaica.

Cointreau: See *Orange.*

Cordial Médoc: A reddish, rather sweet liqueur from Bordeaux, made with aged Bordeaux wines blended with curaçao and crème de cacao plus a touch of brandy and fruit liqueur.

Cranberry: Both Boggs and Cranberria have good cranberry taste and color. Good also for basting turkey.

Crème de bananes: Banana liqueur, usually yellow colored but sometimes white or green—from Holland and Indonesia, where it is called *Pisang Ambon.*

Crème de Cacao: A soft, sweet chocolate liqueur blended with vanilla; usually 50 to 54 proof. Available in white and dark colors.

Crème de Cassis: Black currant liqueur; low proof and quite sweet. The best is from Dijon, France. Used essentially in the Kir, popular white wine drink.

Crème de Menthe: Peppermint flavor; green and white (less sweet) versions.

Crème de Noyaux: Originated in Holland and France; made from apricot pits (predecessor of amaretto).

Crème de Violette: Flavor combination of violet and vanilla essences.

Cream Liqueur: As opposed to "crème de" or "cream of" various fruit, nuts, etc., the term "cream liqueurs" refers to liqueurs that have a substantial addition of fresh cream to the spirit base, plus other flavorings. Bailey's Original Irish Cream led the idea and inspired many imitators: Emmet's, Waterford's, Dunphy's, O'Darby—all from Ireland; Baitz (New Zealand); Venetian cream with brandy base from Italy; Quincy Market (U.S.A.).

Crème Yvette: Violet liqueur; strong, sweet, violet flavor and color. Made in U.S.A.

Curaçao: See *Orange*.

Drambuie: Produced in Scotland. It tastes of Scotch whisky and honey but also has an infusion of herbs.

Forbidden Fruit: American liqueur; flavor bouquet of grapefruit, apple, orange, and honey.

Frangelico: Sweet Italian liqueur with hazelnut flavor and some herbs; almost clear color; 56 proof.

Galliano: Yellow herbal and anisette liqueur from Italy.

Glayva: A Scottish liqueur similar to but sweeter than Drambuie. It is made with Scotch whisky and has a slightly stronger taste of the whisky.

Goldwasser: A light sweet liqueur with flavor bouquet of anise, caraway, and orange peel and with tiny flakes of 22-carat gold leaf suspended in the liquid. The gold, once thought to be a curative, is actually for display.

Grand Marnier: Top quality liqueur—combination of Curaçao orange with Cognac base; 80 proof.

Irish Mist: Liqueur based on old Irish whiskey and heather honey.

Izarra: Similar to Chartreuse with armagnac base; in yellow and green; from Basque region of Spain.

Jagermeister: German liqueur known for its digestive properties.

Kahlua: Popular coffee liqueur from Mexico.

Kummel: German and Dutch liqueur; primarily caraway flavor with coriander, cummin, and anise in the bouquet. Available in dry and sweet versions.

Lamoka: Mocha-flavored liqueur; from Mexico.

Lemonier: Lemon-flavored Italian liqueur; 74 proof.

Liqueur 43: White, sweet, vanilla-flavored liqueur from Spain.

Lochan Ora: Scotch whisky based liqueur.

Mandarine: "Napoleon Mandarine" tangerine-flavored liqueur from Belgium. Its copper color is due to steeping tangerines in brandy base.

Maraschino: Made from marasca cherry, near Padua, Italy. Clear spirit with good cherry aroma. Best known brand is Luxardo which is triple distilled and aged.

Marron: Sweet 50-proof liqueur with taste of chestnut puree, from Italy.

Midori: Sweet green melon-flavored liqueur from Japan; 46 proof.

Minttu: Peppermint schnapps, 100-proof, with soft, clean "breath of fresh air" taste; from Finland.

Orange: Curaçao, triple sec, and Cointreau are popular orange-flavored liqueurs in drink recipes. The differences may be explained as follows: Curaçao is an off-white liqueur made from the dried peels of green oranges grown on the Dutch island of Curaçao. Triple sec is a clear orange-flavored liqueur, made more or less like curaçao, not necessarily exclusively of Curaçao oranges, depending on the maker. There are many brands of curaçao and triple sec. Cointreau was at one time called a curaçao. When triple sec made its entre, the name was changed to that of the family Cointreau. It is produced in Angers, France, as well as in the United States. Cointreau, particularly the imported version, is somewhat drier and will produce a better Sidecar. Curaçao is also available with blue or green coloring, to use when special drink effects are desired.

Ouzo: Anise-flavored liqueur from Greece; similar flavor and characteristics of Pernod.

Parfait Amour: French version of Crème Yvette; a very sweet purple-colored liqueur made with violets and other additives such as vanilla and citrus.

Paso Fino: Puerto Rican rum liqueur; 60 proof.

Pastis: French slang term for liqueurs designed to simulate absinthe. (See Index, *Absinthe*.)

Peppermint Schnapps: While schnapps is a spirit similar to aquavit, peppermint schnapps (flavored, of course, with peppermint) with some sweetening added is considered a liqueur. It is characteristically cleaner and lighter than crème de menthe. A fashionable new liqueur; leading brands include Minttu (Finland), Rumpleminze (Germany), and Steel (U.S.A.).

Pernod: Anise and licorice-flavored liqueur designed to simulate absinthe, as described under *Absinthe* (see Index).

Pisang Ambon: Banana liqueur from Holland and Indonesia.

Pistacha: Pistachio-flavored liqueur produced by Cointreau in U.S.A.

Praline: Good praline taste and only 40 proof. Wonderful in souffles as well as drinks.

Punsch: Spicy liqueur with base of arak; specialty of Sweden.

Ricard: France's best known anise and licorice-flavored liqueur designed to simulate absinthe, as described under *Absinthe*.

Sabra: Israeli liqueur with orange-chocolate flavor.

Sloe Gin: Liqueur made of grain spirits with sloe berries (small wild plums). The original English formula was gin based.

Southern Comfort: Smooth and powerful blend of fine bourbon, peach liqueur, and fresh peaches, produced by the Southern Comfort Corp., St. Louis, Missouri. Bottled at 100 proof.

Strega: Anise and herb-flavored Italian liqueur.

Swiss Chocolate Almond: Tastes like a Toblerone chocolate bar; 56 proof.

Tia Maria: Coffee-flavored liqueur from Jamaica, with neutral spirit distilled from molasses.

Triple Sec: See *Orange*.

Tuaca: From Italy, a melange of vanilla, almond, orange, coconut, and citrus makes this 84-proof liqueur quite unusual. A taste treat that should be more popular.

Vandermint: Tastes like chocolate after-dinner mint. From Holland, at 52 proof.

Vielle Curé: From the Bordeaux region; a blend of herbs, Cognac, and Armagnac.

Yukon Jack: Canadian whisky based liqueur.

Rum

The spirit obtained by distilling the fermented products of sugar cane, which is technically a member of the grass family. Wherever cane is grown, rum is usually manufactured. It was first produced on a commercial basis in Jamaica. Today it is produced throughout the Carribean area and in the United States. Rums range from white in color and light in body to dark brown and full bodied.

Since 1976 rum consumption in the United States has risen to the point where it closely follows vodka as the leading spirit, due in large part to the promotion of its compatibility with all kinds of mixes. Rums may or may not be aged. Most are 80 proof.

Types of Rum

Light rum: Also called white rum; rum much the way it comes from the still, with little flavor and color. For a long time it was drunk only locally where rum is made, used to perk up soft drinks and fruit mixtures in the tropical heat. Now it has become popular worldwide, aided by its addition to Coke in the Cuba Libre and by Bacardi's promotion of its discreet quality in all manner of drinks. It is marketed as a light-bodied rum; its color (in different brands) may range from white to the pale gold of whiskey. Rums produced in Puerto Rico, Virgin Islands, Haiti, Mexico, and Santo Domingo are characteristically light.

Dark rum: Usually means full-bodied rum, unless otherwise specified. Since rum comes through distillation almost flavorless, it is made full-bodied by the addition of concentrated flavoring and coloring. The result is aromatic and slightly sweet. This processing step results in distinctly different styles of dark rum by individual producers; descriptions for some are given below. Rums usually characterized as full bodied are Barbados, Jamaica, Demerara, New England, Trinidad, Egypt, and Navy.

Note: While certain rum-producing areas are characterized as specializing in light or dark rums, many of today's producers, wherever they are located, offer a full line of types—light, gold, dark.

Gold rum: Identifies a medium-bodied rum.

Añejo: The Spanish word for old, as applied to aged rum. Añejo rum is usually darker and is identified as añejo on the label—because not all darker-colored rums are aged.

Barbados rum: Unique, somewhat smokey style, because it is flavored with coconut shell, or Madeira, or almonds. Its taste is between light Virgin Islands and full-bodied Jamaica. Barbados rums are best sipped, like brandy.

Demerara rum: Rum specialty of Guyana; one of the darkest rums made, although lighter in flavor than Jamaica; pleasant, rich style.

Haitian rhum: Medium to light body; not much U.S. distribution; best known brand is Barbancourt.

Jamaica rum: Characteristically known as dark and generally full bodied with good flavor. Other types are also produced: over-proof at 151 proof, light gold and aged.

Hawaiian: Light in body and color; similar to Virgin Islands style.

Puerto Rico: The home of Bacardi after the company exiled itself from Cuba. Puerto Rico rums traditionally have been light bodied, but gold, dark, and aged are also produced.

Navy rum: Old-style rum as once issued to the British Navy; still produced; strong and pungent.

Martinique rhum: French West Indies rum either from Martinique or Guadaloupe. Full bodied and very dark with good flavor.

New England rum: While most rums are blends of several rums, New England is a straight rum produced in the U.S. from molasses. It is full bodied but not as rich and flavorful as others.

Over-proof rum: Rum that exceeds 100 proof or 50 percent alcohol. Usually bottled from 130 to 151 proof. Used in drink mixture for overdrive.

Tequila

By Mexican law, the beverage labeled *tequila* must be the distilled spirit of the fermented juice of a specific agave (cactus-type plant), called *Tequilana Weber Amaryllidacaease,* Blue Variety, which has been found to grow and mature best in an area encompassing the state of Jalisco (where the tequila center of Guadalajara and the town of Tequila are located) and parts of the states of Michoacan and Nayarit in Mexico. According to Mexican and United States governmental agreement, tequila must contain at least 51 percent juice from the agave head (fruit) to be called tequila. The rest of it is usually distilled from the juice of sugar cane, which may be why tequila has been likened to rum. And like rum, tequila is unusually compatible when mixed with other ingredients, especially citrus and other fruit while adding its own essence—an intriguing, rather earthy bouquet. Contrary to legend, tequila marketed at 80 to 100 proof is no more powerful than spirits of comparable proofs.

Types of Tequila

White tequila: Bottled as distilled; not aged.

Gold tequila: It may simply have caramel added for coloring or it may have been aged. There is no regulation; check the description on the label.

Tequila añejo: Tequila that has been aged for a minimum of seven years (Mexican Government regulation). *Añejo* is the Spanish word for aged liquor.

Because tequila is strictly controlled by government regulations every step of the process and tank cars destined for the U.S.A. are checked and sealed by government inspectors; one may be sure that there is never a worm in a bottle of tequila. (Sometimes an agave worm is inserted in a bottle of mezcal as a merchandising gimmick.)

Mezcal is the distillate from agave plants which does not meet the requirements of tequila on some point or other, being either from another variety of agave or grown outside the delimited area or processed differently. *Pulque* is not a spirit at all; rather, it is a viscous fermented juice from a very large agave plant that grows in the central regions of Mexico. In these areas, there are pulque taverns, where it is served like beer.

Vodka

According to the Federal Alcoholic Administration Act, vodka produced in the United States is "neutral spirits distilled from any material (grain or cane) at or above 190 proof, reduced to not more than 100 and not less than 80 proof, and after such reduction in proof, so treated . . . as to be without distinctive character, aroma or taste." Vodka brands with flavor, which are on the market, are a result of a distilling formulation in which a touch of the mash is allowed to combine with the neutral spirit. Vodka is not aged. Vodka in Eastern Europe, where it originated, is generally flavored. There, in addition to traditional vodkas, there are herbal, fruit, dessert, and spicy vodkas.

Whiskey

An alcoholic distillate from a fermented mash of grain (e.g., barley, corn, rye, wheat) distilled at less than 190 proof in such manner that the distillate possesses the taste, aroma, and characteristics generally attributed to whiskey, and withdrawn from the distillery at not more than 110 proof and not less than 80 proof.

Basic Types of Whiskies

American blended whiskey: Whiskeys that contain at least 20 percent of 100 proof two-year-old whiskey of any legal type; the remainder may be neutral spirit (absolute alcohol); blended with sherry or fruit juices for a lighter flavor.

Bourbon: Whiskey with a base of at least 51 percent corn. (Southern Comfort is bourbon blended with peach liqueur and peaches and is classified as a liqueur.) Bourbon originated in Kentucky. *Bourbon made in Tennessee is called Tennessee whiskey.*

Canadian whisky: Grain whiskey, similar to American types but usually lighter—a function of individual producer methods. For Canadian (and Scotch), it is always spelled *whisky.*

Irish whiskey: Barley malt whiskey, usually following the same grain formula as Scotch whisky but not smoke cured. It is triple distilled, making it a strong but particularly smooth whiskey.

Scotch whisky: Primarily a distillate of malted barley but may be a combination of barley malts from different soils and types. Characteristically, Scotch whisky is a blend of many different malts, which may include other grains such as corn and rye, with an inherent smoky flavor caused by smoke curing with peat.

Explanations of other types and terms of whiskey:

Corn whiskey: Straight corn whiskey must be made from at least 80 percent corn mash. No aging is required, and it comes in at 80 to 100 proof.

The Glenlivet: The oldest and most famous Highland unblended malt whisky; available in 12- to 25-year-old.

Bottled in Bond: Strictly a federal regulation affecting bookkeeping, with absolutely no bearing on quality. Instead of paying excise tax as soon as the spirit is bottled, the producer may bottle and warehouse *straight* whiskey that is *100 proof and at least 4 years old* without paying the tax. When the whiskey is removed from the bonded warehouse, the tax must then be paid.

Rye: Whiskey made with rye instead of corn; but today rye whiskey is usually part of a blend.

Sour mash: A full-flavored, superior, and costly whiskey. The initial fermentation is from a mixture of malt barley, corn, and rye. Jack Daniels is a foremost brand.

Other Spirits

Absinthe

A powerful licorice-flavored spirit composed of aromatics, wormwood, and highproof spirit or brandy. When mixed with water, absinthe changes into a sequence of colors—from pastel pink to green and finally to opalescent or milky white. Because the ingestion of wormwood can have serious effects on the brain, today the sale of absinthe is forbidden in the United States and most other countries.

There are a number of anise/licorice-flavored liqueurs that have been created to resemble the flavor and characteristics of absinthe, without the wormwood ingredient and of lower proof. Around Marseilles, where this type of liqueur is popular, they are called *pastis*. The foremost absinthe-type liqueurs sold in the United States are Pernod and Ricard.

Arak
A rather rough type spirit from the fermented juice of dates; a type of rum. Batavia arak comes from Indonesia and Yousef from California.

Okoleayo
A colorless distillate of cane molasses blended with base of baked ti roots and rice lees.

Schnapps
Throughout northern Europe (Holland, Germany, and the Scandinavian countries), schnapps is the colloquial expression for "a bit of the strong stuff." As a marketed spirit, differentiated from others, schnapps is a colorless liquor, distilled from potatoes or corn or other grains and highly flavored (from dry to sweet). Flavorings may be from herbs, barks, flowers, and/or roots, often with sugar added. Schnapps, which contains 2.5 percent or more sugar additive, must be identified as a liqueur in America. The higher-proof schnapps has less sugar than American brands, and being drier and lighter, is more like vodka in consistency than the syrupy American-produced schnapps.

AQUAVIT RECIPES

ARCTIC TRICK
A whiskey sour glass, chilled

1½ oz. aquavit
2 tsp. lemon juice
2 tsp. sugar syrup
1 tsp. kirsch
½ egg white
3 oz. crushed ice

Combine all ingredients in shaker, and shake vigorously. Strain drink into glass.

CHERRY DANISH
An old-fashioned glass, chilled

2 oz. aquavit
½ oz. Cherry Heering
2½ tsp. sugar syrup
2½ tsp. lemon juice
½ egg white
3 to 4 ice cubes
2 to 3 oz. club soda, chilled

Combine all ingredients except soda in shaker, and shake vigorously. Strain mixture into glass. Add soda and stir slowly, about 3 turns.

DANISH MARY
An old-fashioned glass, chilled

1½ oz. aquavit
3 to 4 oz. tomato juice
1 tsp. lemon juice
3 to 4 drops Worcestershire sauce
3 to 4 drops Tabasco sauce
3 to 4 ice cubes

Combine all ingredients in shaker, and shake vigorously. Strain drink into glass.

GREAT DANE
A 4-oz. cocktail glass, chilled

1 oz. aquavit
½ oz. cranberry juice
½ oz. cherry brandy
1 dash orange bitters
3 to 4 ice cubes

Combine all ingredients in shaker, and shake vigorously. Strain drink into glass.

FJORD
A 4-oz. cocktail glass, chilled

1 oz. vodka
2 tbs. aquavit
1 tbs. orange juice
1 tbs. lime juice
1 tsp. grenadine
3 to 4 ice cubes
2 oz. crushed ice

Combine all ingredients except *crushed* ice in shaker, and shake vigorously. Put crushed ice in cocktail glass to half level. Strain drink into glass.

LAST DANSK
A 4-oz. cocktail glass, chilled

1 oz. aquavit
2 tsp. Cherry Heering
1 tsp. lemon juice
3 to 4 ice cubes
About 3 oz. crushed ice

Combine all ingredients except crushed ice in shaker, and shake vigorously. Fill glass ¾ level with crushed ice. Strain drink into glass.

MIDNIGHT SUN

A 4-oz. cocktail glass, chilled

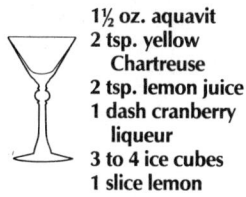

1½ oz. aquavit
2 tsp. yellow Chartreuse
2 tsp. lemon juice
1 dash cranberry liqueur
3 to 4 ice cubes
1 slice lemon

Combine all ingredients except lemon slice in shaker, and shake vigorously. Strain drink into glass. Garnish with lemon slice.

VIKING

An old-fashioned glass, chilled

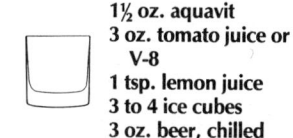

1½ oz. aquavit
3 oz. tomato juice or V-8
1 tsp. lemon juice
3 to 4 ice cubes
3 oz. beer, chilled

Combine all ingredients except beer in mixing glass, and stir well. Strain mixture into glass. Add beer and stir slowly.

SWEDISH SECRET

A 4-oz. cocktail glass, chilled

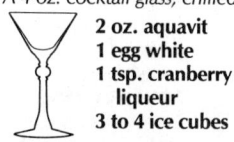

2 oz. aquavit
1 egg white
1 tsp. cranberry liqueur
3 to 4 ice cubes

Combine all ingredients in shaker, and shake vigorously. Strain drink into glass.

BRANDY RECIPES

A.J. COCKTAIL
A 4-oz. cocktail glass, chilled

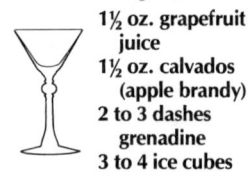

1½ oz. grapefruit juice
1½ oz. calvados (apple brandy)
2 to 3 dashes grenadine
3 to 4 ice cubes

Combine all ingredients in shaker, and shake vigorously. Strain drink into glass.

ALABAMA
A 4-oz. cocktail glass, chilled

1 oz. peach brandy
1 oz. brandy
1 oz. lemon juice
1 tsp. superfine sugar
3 to 4 ice cubes
1 mint sprig

Combine all ingredients except mint sprig in shaker, and shake vigorously. Strain drink into glass. Garnish with mint sprig.

ALEXANDER

A 4-oz. cocktail glass, chilled

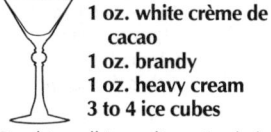

- 1 oz. white crème de cacao
- 1 oz. brandy
- 1 oz. heavy cream
- 3 to 4 ice cubes

Combine all ingredients in shaker, and shake vigorously. Strain drink into glass.

AMERICAN BEAUTY

A 4-oz. cocktail glass, chilled

- ¾ oz. dry vermouth
- ¾ oz. orange juice
- 1 oz. brandy
- 1 dash grenadine
- 1 dash peppermint schnapps
- 3 to 4 ice cubes
- ½ oz. port wine

Combine all ingredients except port wine in shaker, and shake vigorously. Strain mixture into glass. Pour port wine over inverted spoon so that it floats on top of drink.

APHRODITE'S LOVE POTION

A highball glass, chilled

- 4 to 6 ice cubes
- 1½ oz. Metaxa Grand Fine brandy
- 1 to 2 dashes Angostura bitters
- 4 to 6 oz. pineapple juice
- 1 maraschino cherry
- 1 thin slice orange

Place ice cubes in glass. Add brandy and bitters, and stir. Fill glass with pineapple juice. Garnish with cherry and orange slice. *Metaxa Brandies, Fleischmann Distilling Co., New Hyde Park, N.Y*

APPLE BRANDY COCKTAIL

A 4 oz. cocktail glass, chilled

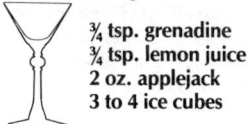

- ¾ tsp. grenadine
- ¾ tsp. lemon juice
- 2 oz. applejack
- 3 to 4 ice cubes

Combine all ingredients in shaker, and shake vigorously. Strain drink into glass.

APPLE BLOW

A highball glass, chilled

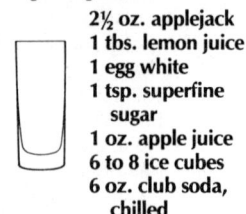

2½ oz. applejack
1 tbs. lemon juice
1 egg white
1 tsp. superfine sugar
1 oz. apple juice
6 to 8 ice cubes
6 oz. club soda, chilled

Combine all ingredients except 3 to 4 ice cubes and soda in shaker, and shake vigorously. Put reserved ice cubes in glass, and strain mixture into glass. Fill with soda.

APPLE CART

An old-fashioned glass, chilled

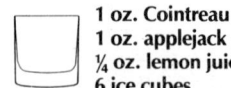

1 oz. Cointreau
1 oz. applejack
¼ oz. lemon juice
6 ice cubes

Combine all ingredients except 3 ice cubes in shaker, and shake vigorously. Put reserved ice cubes in glass, and strain drink into glass.

APPLE LILLET

An old-fashioned glass, chilled

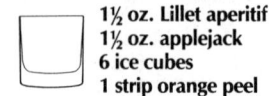

1½ oz. Lillet aperitif
1½ oz. applejack
6 ice cubes
1 strip orange peel

Combine Lillet, applejack, and 3 ice cubes in shaker, and shake vigorously. Put 3 ice cubes in glass. Strain drink into glass. Twist orange peel over drink to release oil, and drop it in. *Lillet, Schenley World T. & I. Co., New York, N.Y.*

APPLE SOUR

A 4-oz. cocktail glass, chilled

¾ tsp. lemon juice
2 oz. applejack
¾ tsp. superfine sugar
3 to 4 ice cubes

Combine all ingredients in shaker, and shake vigorously. Strain drink into glass.

APRICOT BRANDY
A 4-oz. cocktail glass, chilled

2 ice cubes
1½ to 2 oz. apricot brandy
2 to 3 dashes grenadine
1½ oz. club soda, chilled
1 strip lemon peel

Place ice cubes in glass and add apricot brandy. Add grenadine and stir slowly. Add soda to top of glass and stir once. Twist lemon peel over drink to release oil, and drop it in.

APRICOT SOUR
A 4-oz. cocktail glass, chilled

2 tbs. lemon juice
½ tsp. superfine sugar
2 oz. apricot brandy
3 to 4 ice cubes
½ slice lemon

Combine all ingredients except ½ slice lemon in shaker, and shake vigorously. Strain drink into glass. Garnish with ½ slice lemon.

AUNT JEMIMA
A pousse café glass

1 oz. brandy
1 oz. dark crème de cacao
1 oz. Benedictine

In the pousse café, each ingredient should be a separate layer. Hold glass at 45-degree angle and pour brandy slowly against the inside. Add crème de cacao in same manner so that it sits on top of brandy. Add Benedictine in same manner.

BALTIMORE BRACER
A 4-oz. cocktail glass, chilled

1 oz. Sambuca Romana
1 oz. brandy
1 egg white
3 to 4 ice cubes

Combine all ingredients in shaker, and shake vigorously. Strain drink into glass.

BETSY ROSS
A brandy snifter (6-oz. or larger), chilled

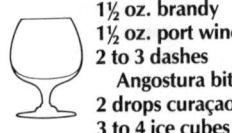

1½ oz. brandy
1½ oz. port wine
2 to 3 dashes Angostura bitters
2 drops curaçao
3 to 4 ice cubes

Combine all ingredients in mixing glass, and stir well. Strain drink into snifter.

BETWEEN the SHEETS
A 4-oz. cocktail glass, chilled

1 oz. Cointreau
1 oz. brandy
1 oz. light rum
1 dash lemon juice
3 to 4 ice cubes

Combine all ingredients in shaker, and shake vigorously. Strain drink into glass. *Cointreau Ltd., Lawrenceville, N.J.*

BETSY ROSSO
A 6-oz. or larger brandy snifter, chilled

1½ oz. brandy
1½ oz. Rosso Antico aperitif
2 to 3 dashes Angostura bitters
2 drops curaçao
3 to 4 ice cubes

Combine all ingredients in mixing glass, and stir well. Strain drink into snifter.

BIG APPLE (KOCH KNOCKER)
An old-fashioned glass, chilled

2 oz. apple juice
2 tbs. applesauce
1½ oz. applejack
½ oz. peppermint schnapps
Ground cinnamon

Combine apple juice and applesauce in small saucepan. Stir mixture, and warm over low heat. Pour into glass. Add applejack and peppermint schnapps, and stir. Dust top with cinnamon.

BLOODY FRENCH DRAGON

A champagne glass, chilled

1½ oz. French brandy or cognac
½ oz. crème de framboises (raspberry liqueur)
3 to 4 ice cubes
3 oz. dry champagne, chilled

Combine all ingredients except champagne in mixing glass, and stir well. Strain mixture into champagne glass. Add champagne.

BOSOM'S CARESS

A 4-oz. cocktail glass, chilled

1 oz. brandy
½ oz. triple sec or curaçao
1 egg yolk
1 tsp. grenadine
3 to 4 ice cubes

Combine all ingredients in shaker, and shake vigorously. Strain drink into glass.

BRANDY BLAZER

A brandy snifter (6-oz. or larger)

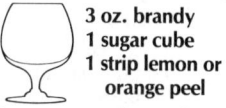

3 oz. brandy
1 sugar cube
1 strip lemon or orange peel

Drop sugar cube on bottom of brandy snifter. Add brandy and mix until cube dissolves. Twist lemon or orange peel over drink to release oil, and drop it in. Tilt glass so brandy is close to rim and ignite. Stand glass straight up. Allow flame to die out. Wait a few seconds before drinking.

BRANDY GUMP

A 4-oz. cocktail glass, chilled

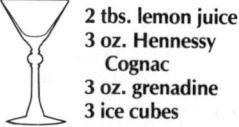

2 tbs. lemon juice
3 oz. Hennessy Cognac
3 oz. grenadine
3 ice cubes

Combine all ingredients in shaker, and shake vigorously. Strain drink into glass. *Schieffelin & Co., New York, N.Y.*

BRANDY OLD-FASHIONED

An old-fashioned glass, chilled

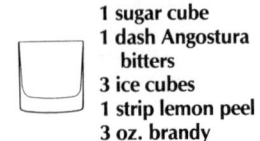

1 sugar cube
1 dash Angostura bitters
3 ice cubes
1 strip lemon peel
3 oz. brandy

Place sugar cube in glass and sprinkle with bitters. Add ice cubes. Twist lemon peel over glass to release oil, and drop it in. Add brandy and stir.

CAVALIERI

A 4-oz. cocktail glass, chilled

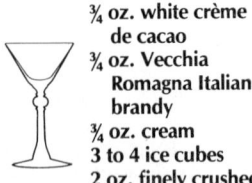

¾ oz. white crème de cacao
¾ oz. Vecchia Romagna Italian brandy
¾ oz. cream
3 to 4 ice cubes
2 oz. finely crushed ice

Combine all ingredients except crushed ice in shaker, and shake vigorously. Put crushed ice in glass and strain drink into glass. *Vecchia Romagna, Buton Distillery, Bologna, Italy.*

CHAMPS ÉLYSÉES

A 4-oz. cocktail glass, chilled

1 dash Angostura bitters
½ tsp. superfine sugar
1 tbs. lemon juice
1½ oz. Hennessy Cognac
¼ oz. yellow Chartreuse
3 to 4 ice cubes

Combine all ingredients in shaker, and shake vigorously. Strain drink into glass. *Schieffelin & Co., New York, N.Y.*

CHERRY BLOSSOM

A 4-oz. cocktail glass, chilled

1 oz. Cherry Marnier
1 tsp. superfine sugar
1½ oz. brandy
3 to 4 dashes triple sec or curaçao
3 to 4 dashes grenadine
½ oz. lemon juice
3 to 4 ice cubes

Moisten rim of cocktail glass with drop of Cherry Marnier and sugar-frost. Combine all ingredients in shaker, and shake vigorously. Strain drink into prepared glass.

CITY SLICKER
A 4-oz. cocktail glass, chilled

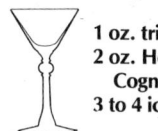

1 oz. triple sec
2 oz. Hennessy Cognac
3 to 4 ice cubes

Combine all ingredients in shaker, and shake vigorously. Strain drink into glass. *Schieffelin & Co., New York, N.Y.*

COLD DECK
A 4-oz. cocktail glass, chilled

1½ oz. brandy
¾ oz. dry vermouth
½ oz. peppermint schnapps
3 to 4 ice cubes

Combine all ingredients in shaker, and shake vigorously. Strain drink into glass.

CLASSIC
A 4-oz. cocktail glass, chilled

¼ oz. Cointreau
¼ oz. maraschino liqueur
1 tsp. lemon juice
1½ oz. brandy
3 to 4 ice cubes

Sugar-frost rim of cocktail glass. Combine all ingredients in shaker, and shake vigorously. Strain drink into prepared glass.

COSTA del SOL
An old-fashioned glass, chilled

1 oz. apricot brandy
2 oz. gin
1 oz. Cointreau
5 to 7 ice cubes

Combine all ingredients except 2 to 3 ice cubes in shaker, and shake vigorously. Put remaining ice cubes in glass, and strain drink into glass. *Cointreau Ltd., Lawrenceville, N.J.*

DANTE'S INFERNO

A 4-oz. cocktail glass

½ oz. apricot liqueur
1½ oz. Vecchia Romagna Italian brandy
½ oz. lemon juice
3 to 4 ice cubes
1 strip orange peel

Sugar-frost rim of cocktail glass. Combine all ingredients except orange peel in shaker, and shake vigorously. Strain drink into prepared glass. Light match over drink, twist orange peel next to flame, and drop peel into drink. *Vecchia Romagna, Buton Distillery, Bologna, Italy.*

DA VINCI

A 4-oz. cocktail glass, chilled

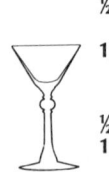

½ oz. Dubonnet Blanc aperitif
1½ oz. Vecchia Romagna Italian brandy
½ oz. lime juice
1 tsp. superfine sugar
3 to 4 ice cubes
1 strip orange peel

In shaker, combine Dubonnet Blanc, brandy, lime juice, sugar, and ice cubes, and shake vigorously. Strain drink into glass. Twist orange peel over drink to release oil, and drop it in. *Vecchia Romagna, Buton Distillery, Bologna, Italy*

DELOS GREEK FIRE
(Metaxa Collins)

A highball glass, chilled

4 to 6 ice cubes
2 oz. Metaxa 7 Star brandy
1 tbs. sugar syrup
1 tsp. lemon or lime juice
About 4 oz. club soda, chilled

Put ice cubes in glass. Add Metaxa brandy, sugar syrup, and lemon or lime juice, and stir. Fill glass to top with club soda. *Metaxa Brandies, Fleischmann Distilling Co., New Hyde Park, N.Y.*

DEMPSEY

A 4-oz. cocktail glass, chilled

1½ oz. applejack
1½ oz. gin
1 to 2 dashes Pernod
1 to 2 dashes grenadine
3 to 4 ice cubes

Combine all ingredients in shaker, and shake vigorously. Strain drink into glass.

DREAM COCKTAIL
A 4-oz. cocktail glass, chilled

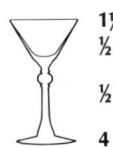

1½ oz. brandy
½ oz. Cointreau liqueur
½ tbs. anisette liqueur
4 ice cubes

Combine all ingredients except 2 ice cubes in shaker, and shake vigorously. Put reserved ice cubes in glass, and strain drink into glass.

EGG SOUR
A 4-oz. cocktail glass, chilled

1 tsp. superfine sugar
1 egg
2 tbs. lemon juice
1½ oz. brandy
1 oz. curaçao
3 to 4 ice cubes

Combine all ingredients in shaker, and shake vigorously. Strain drink into glass.

FANCY BRANDY
A 4-oz. cocktail glass, chilled

¼ tsp. superfine sugar
¼ tsp. curaçao
4 ice cubes
1 dash orange bitters
2 oz. Vecchia Romagna Italian brandy
1 strip lemon peel

Combine all ingredients except lemon peel in shaker, and shake vigorously. Strain drink into glass. Twist lemon peel over drink to release oil, and drop it in. *Buton Distillery, Bologna, Italy*

FATHER SHERMAN
A 4-oz. cocktail glass, chilled

½ oz. orange juice
1½ oz. brandy
½ oz. apricot brandy
3 to 4 ice cubes

Combine all ingredients in shaker, and shake vigorously. Strain drink into glass.

FOXHOUND
An old-fashioned glass, chilled

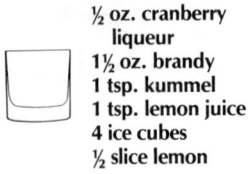

½ oz. cranberry liqueur
1½ oz. brandy
1 tsp. kummel
1 tsp. lemon juice
4 ice cubes
½ slice lemon

Combine all ingredients except 2 ice cubes and lemon slice in shaker, and shake vigorously. Place 2 ice cubes in glass, and strain drink into glass. Garnish with lemon slice.

GAZETTE
An old-fashioned glass, chilled

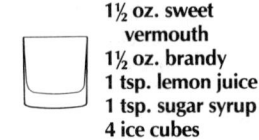

1½ oz. sweet vermouth
1½ oz. brandy
1 tsp. lemon juice
1 tsp. sugar syrup
4 ice cubes

Combine all ingredients except 2 ice cubes in shaker, and shake vigorously. Put reserved ice cubes in glass, and strain drink into glass.

FRENCH LIEUTENANT'S WOMAN
A 4-oz. cocktail glass, chilled

1½ oz. maraschino cherry liqueur
1½ oz. calvados (apple brandy)
1 to 2 dashes crème de noyaux
3 to 4 ice cubes
1 maraschino cherry

Combine all ingredients except cherry in shaker, and shake vigorously. Strain drink into glass. Garnish with cherry.

GRANADA
A highball glass, chilled

1½ oz. Spanish brandy
1 oz. dry sherry
3 to 4 dashes curaçao
4 to 5 ice cubes
6 oz. tonic water

Combine all ingredients except tonic water in glass, and stir. Fill glass with tonic water.

HOT MIKADO
A 4-oz. cocktail glass

½ tsp. crème de noyaux
½ oz. Midori melon liqueur
1½ oz. brandy
3 to 4 ice cubes
2 oz. crushed ice
1 maraschino cherry

Combine cream of almond flavoring, melon liqueur, brandy, and ice cubes in shaker, and shake vigorously. Put crushed ice in glass, and strain drink into glass. Garnish with cherry. *Midori Melon Liqueur, Suntory International, Los Angeles, Calif.*

HUNGARIAN MARTINI
A 4-oz. cocktail glass, chilled

1 oz. Barack (clear apricot brandy)
1 dash dry vermouth
1 dash Tabasco sauce
3 ice cubes
Freshly ground pepper

Combine all ingredients except pepper in shaker, and shake vigorously. Strain drink into glass. Sprinkle top of drink with ground pepper. (Note: This drink can also be served over ice in old-fashioned glass.) *The Bakery Restaurant, Chicago, Ill.*

IL PARADISO
A 4-oz. cocktail glass, chilled

½ oz. Grand Marnier
½ oz. gin
1 oz. brandy
1 to 2 oz. orange juice
3 to 4 ice cubes

Combine all ingredients in shaker, and shake vigorously. Strain drink into glass.

JACKRABBIT
A 4-oz. cocktail glass, chilled

¾ oz. lemon juice
1½ oz. applejack
3 to 4 ice cubes
1 dash grenadine
¼ tsp. superfine sugar

Moisten rim of cocktail glass with extra drop of grenadine and sugar-frost. Combine all ingredients in shaker, and shake vigorously. Strain drink into prepared glass.

KISS 'N' TELL
A 4-oz. cocktail glass, chilled

1 oz. calvados (apple brandy)
1 oz. sloe gin
1 tsp. lemon juice
1 egg white
3 to 4 ice cubes

Combine all ingredients in shaker, and shake vigorously. Strain drink into glass.

JAPANESE
A 4-oz. cocktail glass, chilled

¼ oz. lime juice
¼ oz. orgeat syrup
2 oz. brandy
1 dash Angostura bitters
3 to 4 ice cubes
1 strip lime peel

Combine all ingredients except lime peel in shaker, and shake vigorously. Strain drink into glass. Twist lime peel over drink to release oil, and drop it in.

LA JOLLA
A 4-oz. cocktail glass

½ oz. banana liqueur
2 tsp. lemon juice
1 tsp. orange juice
1½ oz. brandy
3 to 4 ice cubes

Sugar-frost rim of cocktail glass and chill. Combine all ingredients in shaker, and shake vigorously. Strain drink into prepared glass.

LIBERTY

A 4-oz. cocktail glass, chilled

½ oz. light rum
1½ oz. calvados (apple brandy)
½ tsp. sugar syrup
3 to 4 ice cubes
2 oz. finely crushed ice
1 maraschino cherry

Combine rum, calvados, sugar syrup, and ice cubes in shaker, and shake vigorously. Put crushed ice in glass. Strain drink into glass. Garnish with cherry.

MANEATER

A 4-oz. cocktail glass, chilled

½ oz. Southern Comfort
2 dashes orange bitters
1½ oz. brandy
3 to 4 ice cubes
3 oz. finely crushed ice

Combine all ingredients except *crushed* ice in shaker, and shake vigorously. Put crushed ice in glass. Strain drink into glass. *Southern Comfort Corp., St. Louis, Mo.*

MESSALINA

A 4-oz. cocktail glass, chilled

½ tsp. maraschino liqueur
1 oz. pineapple juice
½ tsp. lemon juice
1 dash orange bitters
1½ oz. Vecchia Romagna Italian brandy
3 to 4 ice cubes

In shaker, combine maraschino liqueur, pineapple juice, lemon juice, bitters, brandy, and ice cubes, and shake vigorously. Strain drink into glass. *Buton Distillery, Bologna, Italy.*

METAXA SUNRISE

An old-fashioned glass, chilled

1 oz. Metaxa 7 Star brandy
1 oz. light rum
½ oz. lemon juice
½ oz. Garnier strawberry liqueur
1 tsp. sugar syrup
3 to 4 ice cubes
1 thin slice orange

Combine all ingredients except orange slice in shaker, and shake vigorously. Strain drink into glass. Garnish with orange slice. *Metaxa Brandies, Fleischmann Distilling Co., New Hyde Park, N.Y.*

METROPOLITAN

A 4-oz. cocktail glass, chilled

1 oz. sweet vermouth
1½ to 2 oz. brandy
½ tsp. sugar syrup
2 dashes Angostura bitters
4 to 5 ice cubes

Combine all ingredients except 1 or 2 ice cubes in shaker, and shake vigorously. Put 1 or 2 ice cubes in glass. Strain drink into glass.

MIDNIGHT DELIGHT

A 4-oz. cocktail glass, chilled

½ oz. triple sec
1½ oz. El Presidente Mexican brandy
2 tsp. lime juice
3 to 4 ice cubes

Combine all ingredients in shaker, and shake vigorously. Strain drink into glass. *El Presidente Brandy, Domecq Importers, Inc., Larchmont, N.Y.*

MISSISSIPPI MUD

An old-fashioned glass, chilled

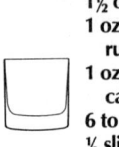

1½ oz. brandy
1 oz. Jamaica dark rum
1 oz. dark crème de cacao
6 to 8 ice cubes
½ slice orange
1 maraschino cherry
1 pineapple cube

Combine brandy, rum, crème de cacao, and 3 or 4 ice cubes in shaker, and shake vigorously. Place 3 or 4 ice cubes in glass, and strain drink into glass. Garnish with orange slice, cherry, and pineapple cube.

MOONLIGHT SERENADE

A highball glass, chilled

1½ oz. applejack
2 tsp. lemon juice
2 tsp. grenadine
3 to 4 ice cubes
2 slices fresh peach
6 oz. club soda, chilled

Combine applejack, lemon juice, grenadine, and ice cubes in shaker, and shake vigorously. Strain into glass. Add peach slices. Fill glass with club soda.

OOM PAUL

A 4-oz. cocktail glass, chilled

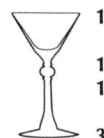

1 oz. Dubonnet Blanc aperitif
1 oz. applejack
1 dash Angostura bitters
3 to 4 ice cubes

Combine all ingredients in mixing glass, and stir briskly. Strain drink into glass. *The Dubonnet Co., Fresno, Calif.*

PANCHO VILLA

A wine glass (8-oz. or larger), chilled

½ oz. gin
½ oz. light rum
1 oz. El Presidente Mexican brandy
1 tsp. Cherry Marnier
4 oz. pineapple juice
4 oz. crushed ice

Combine all ingredients in shaker, and shake vigorously. Strain drink into glass. *El Presidente Brandy, Domecq Importers, Ltd., Larchmont, N.Y.*

JUAREZ COCKTAIL

Follow recipe for Pancho Villa, using 1 oz. white or gold tequila instead of gin.

PEACH VELVET

An old-fashioned glass, chilled

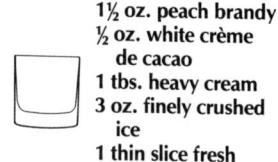

1½ oz. peach brandy
½ oz. white crème de cacao
1 tbs. heavy cream
3 oz. finely crushed ice
1 thin slice fresh peach

Combine all ingredients except peach slice in shaker, and shake vigorously (or these ingredients can be combined in blender and blended until smooth). Pour drink into glass. Garnish with peach slice.

PHOEBE SNOW

A 4-oz. cocktail glass, chilled

1½ oz. Dubonnet Blanc aperitif
1½ oz. brandy
2 to 3 dashes Pernod
3 to 4 ice cubes

Combine all ingredients in shaker, and shake vigorously. Strain drink into glass. *The Dubonnet Co., Fresno, Calif.*

PISCO SOUR
A whiskey sour glass, chilled

1½ oz. Pisco brandy
1 tsp. sugar syrup
1 tsp. lemon or lime juice
1 egg white
3 to 4 ice cubes
2 dashes Angostura bitters

Combine all ingredients except bitters in shaker, and shake vigorously. Strain drink into glass. Top with bitters.

POLARIS
A 4-oz. cocktail glass, chilled

1 oz. applejack
½ oz. brandy
2 dashes Bourbon
3 to 4 ice cubes
2 oz. finely crushed ice

Combine all ingredients except *crushed* ice in shaker, and shake vigorously. Put crushed ice in glass. Strain drink into glass.

RIMINI
A 4-oz. cocktail glass, chilled

1½ oz. Vecchia Romagna Italian brandy
½ oz. lemon juice
1 tsp. mandarin liqueur
3 to 4 ice cubes
1 strip orange peel

Sugar-frost rim of cocktail glass. Combine all ingredients except orange peel in shaker, and shake vigorously. Strain drink into prepared glass. Twist orange peel over drink to release oil, and drop it in. *Vecchia Romagna, Buton Distillery, Bologna, Italy*

SARATOGA
A whiskey sour glass, chilled

2 dashes maraschino liqueur
2 dashes Angostura bitters
1 tbs. crushed pineapple, or 1 tsp. pineapple liqueur
2 oz. brandy
3 to 4 ice cubes

Combine all ingredients in shaker, and shake vigorously. Strain drink into glass.

SICILIAN KISS

A whiskey sour glass, chilled

½ oz. orange juice
¼ oz. lemon juice
1 tsp. superfine sugar
2½ oz. Vecchia Romagna Italian brandy
3 to 4 ice cubes
½ slice lemon

Combine all ingredients except lemon slice in shaker, and shake vigorously. Strain drink into glass. Garnish with ½ slice lemon. *Vecchia Romagna, Buton Distillery, Bologna, Italy*

SIDECAR

A 4-oz. cocktail glass, chilled

½ oz. Cointreau
½ tsp. fresh lemon juice
1 oz. brandy
3 to 4 ice cubes

Combine all ingredients in shaker, and shake vigorously. Strain drink into glass.

SINK or SWIM

A 4-oz. cocktail glass, chilled

1 tbs. sweet vermouth
1½ oz. brandy
1 to 2 dashes Angostura bitters
3 to 4 ice cubes

Combine all ingredients in shaker, and shake vigorously. Strain drink into glass.

SIR WALTER

A 4-oz. cocktail glass, chilld

1 tsp. lemon juice
1 tsp. grenadine
1 tsp. curaçao
¾ oz. light rum
1½ oz. brandy
3 to 4 ice cubes

Combine all ingredients in shaker, and shake vigorously. Strain drink into glass.

SLEEPYHEAD

An old-fashioned glass, chilled

2 to 3 ice cubes
3 oz. brandy
1 strip orange peel
3 to 4 mint leaves
About 3 oz. ginger ale, chilled

Place ice cubes in glass. Add brandy. Twist orange peel over glass to release oil, and drop it in. Add mint leaves and stir mixture slowly. Fill glass with ginger ale.

SLOE BRANDY
A 4-oz. cocktail glass, chilled

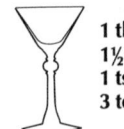

1 tbs. sloe gin
1½ to 2 oz. brandy
1 tsp. lemon juice
3 to 4 ice cubes

Combine all ingredients in shaker, and shake vigorously. Strain drink into glass.

SOURBALL
An old-fashioned glass, chilled

Ice cubes to fill old-fashioned glass
1½ oz. Hiram Walker Apricot-Flavored Brandy
2 tbs. fresh lemon juice
¼ cup fresh orange juice

Fill glass with ice. Pour Hiram Walker Apricot-Flavored Brandy over ice. Add lemon and orange juices, and stir. *Hiram Walker Apricot-Flavored Brandy, Hiram Walker, Inc., Detroit, Mich.*

SOUTH PACIFIC
A whiskey sour glass, chilled

1½ oz. brandy
1½ oz. vodka or gin
1 tbs. lemon juice
3 to 4 oz. grapefruit or pineapple juice
3 to 4 ice cubes

Combine all ingredients in shaker, and shake vigorously. Strain drink into glass. *Note:* A variation of this drink was concocted by American GI's in the Pacific and other tropical outposts. Spirits were poured through punched-in eyes of baby coconuts. Spirit-filled coconuts were allowed to stand and chill for two or three days and POW!

SPECIAL ROUGH
A whiskey sour glass, chilled

1½ oz. calvados (apple brandy)
1½ oz. brandy
3 to 4 drops Pernod
3 to 4 ice cubes
3 oz. finely crushed ice

Combine all ingredients except *crushed* ice in shaker, and shake vigorously. Put crushed ice in glass. Strain drink into glass.

STAR
A 4-oz. cocktail glass, chilled

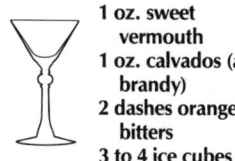

1 oz. sweet vermouth
1 oz. calvados (apple brandy)
2 dashes orange bitters
3 to 4 ice cubes

Combine all ingredients in shaker, and shake vigorously. Strain drink into glass.

STINGER
A 4-oz. cocktail glass, chilled

1½ oz. brandy
1½ oz. white crème de menthe
3 to 4 ice cubes

Combine all ingredients in shaker, and shake vigorously. Strain into glass.

STAR DAISY
A 4-oz. cocktail glass, chilled

1 oz. applejack
1 oz. gin
2 to 3 dashes lemon juice
2 to 3 dashes grenadine
1 tsp. grapefruit juice
3 to 4 ice cubes

Combine all ingredients in shaker, and shake vigorously. Strain drink into glass.

STONE FENCE
An old-fashioned glass, chilled

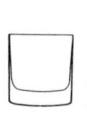

2½ oz. applejack
1 to 2 dashes Angostura bitters
3 to 4 ice cubes
3 to 4 oz. apple juice or cider

Combine all ingredients except apple juice or cider in shaker, and shake vigorously. Strain drink into glass. Add apple juice or cider.

TRE SCALINI

A 4-oz. cocktail glass

½ oz. Cherry Marnier
¼ oz. curaçao
3 to 4 drops grenadine
2 tsp. lemon juice
1½ oz. Vecchia Romagna Italian brandy
3 to 4 ice cubes

Moisten rim of glass with extra drop of Cherry Marnier, and sugar-frost rim. Combine all ingredients in shaker, and shake vigorously. Strain drink into prepared glass. *Buton Distillery, Bologna, Italy*

UNICYCLE

An old-fashioned glass, chilled

1 oz. Cherry Marnier
1 oz. dry vermouth
1 oz. brandy
5 to 6 ice cubes
1 strip lemon peel

Combine Cherry Marnier, dry vermouth, brandy, and 3 or 4 ice cubes in shaker, and shake vigorously. Place 2 ice cubes in glass. Strain drink into glass. Twist lemon peel over drink to release oil, and drop it in.

VIA VENETO

An old-fashioned glass, chilled

2 tsp. Sambuca Romana
2 tsp. lemon juice
1½ oz. Vecchia Romagna Italian brandy
1 egg white
1 tsp. sugar syrup
6 to 7 ice cubes

Combine all ingredients except 3 to 4 ice cubes in shaker, and shake vigorously. (Or these ingredients can be combined in blender and blended at medium speed 15 to 20 seconds.) Place remaining ice cubes in glass, and strain drink into glass. *Sambuca Romana, Palmer & Lord Ltd., Syosset, N.Y.*

WASHINGTON

A 4-oz. cocktail glass, chilled

1½ oz. dry vermouth
1½ oz. brandy
2 dashes Angostura bitters
½ tsp. sugar syrup
3 to 4 ice cubes

Combine all ingredients in shaker, and shake vigorously. Strain drink into glass.

WEEP NO MORE
A 4-oz. cocktail glass, chilled

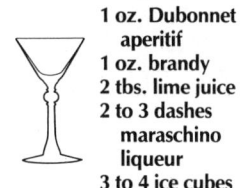

1 oz. Dubonnet aperitif
1 oz. brandy
2 tbs. lime juice
2 to 3 dashes maraschino liqueur
3 to 4 ice cubes

Combine all ingredients in shaker, and shake vigorously. Strain drink into glass. *The Dubonnet Co., Fresno, Calif.*

WIDOW'S KISS
A 4-oz. cocktail glass, chilled

½ oz. Benedictine
½ oz. yellow Chartreuse
1 dash Angostura bitters
1 oz. applejack
3 to 4 ice cubes
½ fresh strawberry

Combine all ingredients except strawberry in shaker, and shake vigorously. Strain drink into glass. Top with strawberry.

WHITE WAY
A 4-oz. cocktail glass, chilled

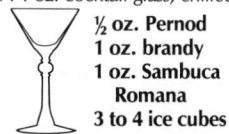

½ oz. Pernod
1 oz. brandy
1 oz. Sambuca Romana
3 to 4 ice cubes

Combine all ingredients in shaker, and shake vigorously. Strain drink into glass. *Sambuca Romana, Palmer & Lord Ltd., Syosset, N.Y.*

ZOOM
A 4-oz. cocktail glass, chilled

1 tsp. honey
1 tbs. hot water
1 tsp. heavy cream
2 oz. brandy
3 to 4 ice cubes

Combine honey and hot water in shaker, and stir until honey is dissolved. Add cream, brandy, and ice cubes, and shake vigorously. Strain drink into glass.

GIN RECIPES

ABBEY
A 4-oz. cocktail glass, chilled

1½ oz. gin
1 oz. orange juice
2 dashes orange bitters
3 to 4 ice cubes
1 maraschino cherry

Combine all ingredients except cherry in shaker, and shake vigorously. Strain into glass. Garnish with cherry.

ACE of SPADES
A 4-oz. cocktail glass, chilled

1½ oz. gin
2 tsp. blackberry liqueur
1 tsp. lime juice
4 to 5 ice cubes

Combine all ingredients in shaker, and shake vigorously. Strain into glass.

ALASKA
A 4-oz. cocktail glass, chilled

1½ oz. gin
¾ oz. yellow Chartreuse
2 dashes orange bitters
3 to 4 ice cubes
2 oz. crushed ice

Combine all ingredients except crushed ice in shaker, and shake vigorously. Put crushed ice in glass. Strain into glass.

ALFONSO SPECIAL
A 4-oz. cocktail glass, chilled

1½ oz. Grand Marnier
½ oz. gin
1 tsp. dry vermouth
1 tsp. sweet vermouth
2 dashes Angostura bitters
3 to 4 ice cubes

Combine all ingredients in shaker, and shake vigorously. Strain into glass.

ALEXANDER'S SISTER
A 4-oz. cocktail glass, chilled

1½ oz. Gordon's gin
½ oz. crème de menthe
½ oz. heavy cream
3 to 4 ice cubes

Combine all ingredients in shaker, shake vigorously, and strain into glass. *Gordon's Dry Gin Co., Ltd., Linden, N.J.*

ARTILLERY
A 4-oz. cocktail glass, chilled

1½ oz. gin
¾ oz. sweet vermouth
3 dashes Angostura bitters
3 to 4 ice cubes

Combine all ingredients in shaker, and shake vigorously. Strain into glass.

BACHELOR and BOBBY SOXER

Two 4-oz. cocktail glasses, chilled

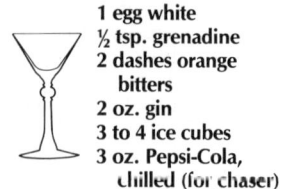

- 1 egg white
- ½ tsp. grenadine
- 2 dashes orange bitters
- 2 oz. gin
- 3 to 4 ice cubes
- 3 oz. Pepsi-Cola, chilled (for chaser)

Combine all ingredients except Pepsi-Cola in shaker, and shake vigorously. Strain into glass. Serve Pepsi-Cola chaser in separate glass.

BARBARY COAST

An old-fashioned glass, chilled

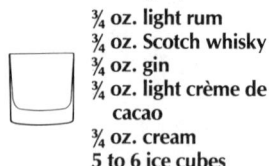

- ¾ oz. light rum
- ¾ oz. Scotch whisky
- ¾ oz. gin
- ¾ oz. light crème de cacao
- ¾ oz. cream
- 5 to 6 ice cubes

Combine all ingredients except 2 to 3 ice cubes in shaker, and shake vigorously. Place remaining ice in glass. Strain into glass.

BARNUM

A 4-oz. cocktail glass, chilled

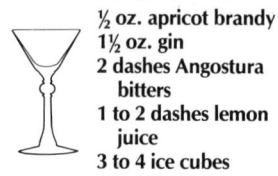

- ½ oz. apricot brandy
- 1½ oz. gin
- 2 dashes Angostura bitters
- 1 to 2 dashes lemon juice
- 3 to 4 ice cubes

Combine all ingredients in shaker, and shake vigorously. Strain into glass.

BEAUTY SPOT

A 4-oz. cocktail glass, chilled

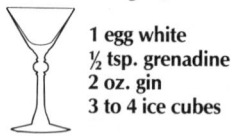

- 1 egg white
- ½ tsp. grenadine
- 2 oz. gin
- 3 to 4 ice cubes

Combine all ingredients except grenadine in shaker, and shake vigorously. *Version 1:* Strain into glass. Top with grenadine. *Version 2:* First place grenadine in glass. Strain over grenadine.

BEE'S KNEES
A 4-oz. cocktail glass, chilled

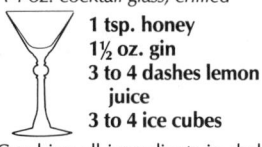

1 tsp. honey
1½ oz. gin
3 to 4 dashes lemon juice
3 to 4 ice cubes

Combine all ingredients in shaker, and shake vigorously. Strain into glass.

BERMUDA ROSE
A 4-oz. cocktail glass, chilled

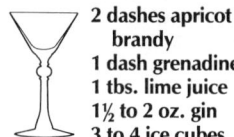

2 dashes apricot brandy
1 dash grenadine
1 tbs. lime juice
1½ to 2 oz. gin
3 to 4 ice cubes

Combine all ingredients in shaker, and shake vigorously. Strain into glass.

BENNETT
A 4-oz. cocktail glass, chilled

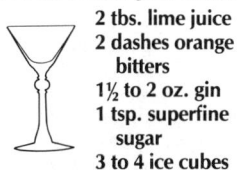

2 tbs. lime juice
2 dashes orange bitters
1½ to 2 oz. gin
1 tsp. superfine sugar
3 to 4 ice cubes

Combine all ingredients in shaker, and shake vigorously. Strain into glass.

BISHOP'S BENEDICTION
A 4-oz. cocktail glass

1 oz. Cointreau ginger liqueur
1½ oz. gin
2 to 3 ice cubes

Combine all ingredients in shaker, and shake vigorously. Strain into glass.

BISHOP'S COCKTAIL

Follow recipe for Bishop's Benediction, using 1 oz. ginger wine instead of ginger liqueur.

BITCH on WHEELS

A 4-oz. cocktail glass, chilled

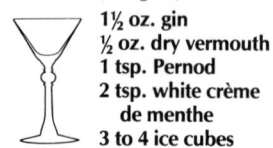

1½ oz. gin
½ oz. dry vermouth
1 tsp. Pernod
2 tsp. white crème de menthe
3 to 4 ice cubes

Combine all ingredients in shaker, and shake vigorously. Strain into glass.

BLOODHOUND

A 4-oz. cocktail glass, chilled

1½ oz. gin
½ oz. dry vermouth (Chambery is ideal.)
½ oz. sweet vermouth
2 dashes strawberry liqueur
2 crushed strawberries
3 to 4 ice cubes

Combine all ingredients in shaker, and shake vigorously. Strain into glass.

BLUEBIRD

A 4-oz. cocktail glass, chilled

3 oz. gin
4 dashes Angostura bitters
4 dashes blue curaçao
3 to 4 ice cubes
1 strip lemon peel
1 maraschino cherry

Combine all ingredients except lemon peel and cherry in shaker, and shake vigorously. Strain into glass. Twist lemon peel over drink to release oil, and drop it in. Garnish with cherry.

BLUE DEVIL
A 4-oz. cocktail glass, chilled

½ oz. blue curaçao
or parfait amour
½ oz. lemon juice
1 oz. gin
2 dashes maraschino
liqueur
3 to 4 ice cubes
½ slice lemon

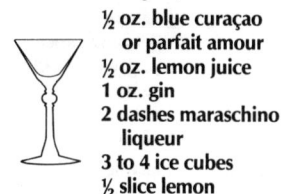

Combine all ingredients except lemon slice in shaker, and shake vigorously. Strain into glass. Garnish with lemon slice.

BONJOUR TRISTESSE
A 4-oz. cocktail glass, chilled

1½ oz. gin
½ oz. Forbidden
Fruit liqueur
2 tsp. triple sec
1 dash orange bitters
3 to 4 ice cubes

Combine all ingredients in mixing glass, and stir briskly. Strain into glass.

BLUE MOON
A 4-oz. cocktail glass, chilled

1½ oz. gin
½ oz. dry vermouth
2 dashes orange
bitters
½ oz. Crême Yvette
3 to 4 ice cubes

Combine all ingredients in shaker, and shake vigorously. Strain into glass.

BOOMERANG
A 4-oz. cocktail glass, chilled

1½ oz. gin
½ oz. dry vermouth
3 to 4 dashes
Angostura bitters
2 dashes maraschino
liqueur
3 to 4 ice cubes

Combine all ingredients in shaker, and shake vigorously. Strain into glass.

Note: The first time I had this drink, kiwi liqueur from New Zealand was used instead of vermouth. The drink was called a "Goolagong," after the Australian tennis player. (L. B.)

BOXCAR No. 1

A whiskey sour glass, chilled

- 1 dash grenadine
- 1½ oz. gin
- 1½ oz. Cointreau
- 1 tsp. lemon or lime juice
- 1 egg white
- 3 to 4 ice cubes

Moisten rim of glass with extra drop of grenadine, and sugar-frost rim. Combine all ingredients in shaker, and shake vigorously. Strain into prepared glass. *Cointreau Ltd., Lawrenceville, N.J.*

BOXCAR No. 2

A 4-oz. cocktail glass, chilled

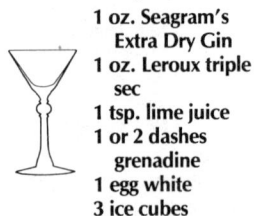

- 1 oz. Seagram's Extra Dry Gin
- 1 oz. Leroux triple sec
- 1 tsp. lime juice
- 1 or 2 dashes grenadine
- 1 egg white
- 3 ice cubes

Sugar-frost rim of cocktail glass. Combine all ingredients in shaker, and shake vigorously. Strain into glass. *Courtesy of Seagram's Complete Party Guide*

BRONX COCKTAIL

A 4-oz. cocktail glass, chilled

- 1½ oz. gin
- ½ oz. orange juice
- 2 tsp. dry vermouth
- 2 tsp. sweet vermouth
- 3 to 4 ice cubes

Combine all ingredients in shaker, and shake vigorously. Strain into glass.

Note: For drier drink, use 2 instead of 1½ oz. gin, and omit sweet vermouth.

BRONX GOLDEN

Follow recipe for above Bronx Cocktail, adding 1 egg yolk to mixture in shaker.

BRONX SILVER

Follow recipe for Bronx Cocktail, adding 1 egg white to mixture in shaker.

B.V.D.
A 4-oz. cocktail glass, chilled

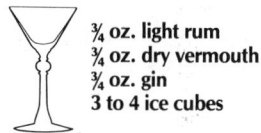

¾ oz. light rum
¾ oz. dry vermouth
¾ oz. gin
3 to 4 ice cubes

Combine all ingredients in shaker, and shake vigorously. Strain into glass.

CAFÉ de PARIS
An old-fashioned glass, chilled

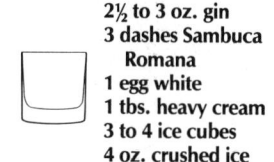

2½ to 3 oz. gin
3 dashes Sambuca Romana
1 egg white
1 tbs. heavy cream
3 to 4 ice cubes
4 oz. crushed ice

Combine all ingredients except crushed ice in shaker, and shake vigorously. Put crushed ice in glass. Strain into glass.

CABARET
A 4-oz. cocktail glass, chilled

1 oz. Dubonnet Blanc aperitif
1 oz. gin
3 to 4 dashes Angostura bitters
2 dashes Pernod
3 to 4 ice cubes
1 maraschino cherry

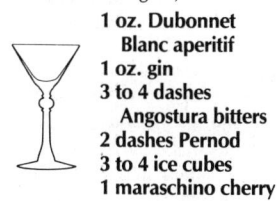

Combine all ingredients in shaker, and shake vigorously. Strain into glass. Garnish with cherry.

CAMPOBELLO
A 4-oz. cocktail glass, chilled

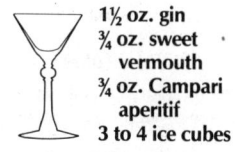

1½ oz. gin
¾ oz. sweet vermouth
¾ oz. Campari aperitif
3 to 4 ice cubes

Combine all ingredients in shaker, and shake vigorously. Strain into glass. *Campari, Austin Nichols & Co., Inc., New York, N.Y.*

CARUSO
A 4-oz. cocktail glass, chilled

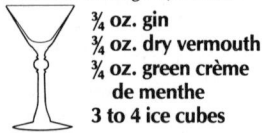

¾ oz. gin
¾ oz. dry vermouth
¾ oz. green crème de menthe
3 to 4 ice cubes

Combine all ingredients in shaker, and shake vigorously. Strain into glass.

CHELSEA MORNING
A 4-oz. cocktail glass, chilled

2 oz. gin
½ oz. Cointreau
1 tbs. lime or lemon juice
3 oz. crushed ice

Combine all ingredients in shaker, and shake vigorously. Strain into glass.

CASINO
A 4-oz. cocktail glass, chilled

2½ oz. gin
2 dashes maraschino cherry liqueur
2 dashes lemon juice
2 dashes orange bitters
3 to 4 ice cubes

Combine all ingredients in shaker, and shake vigorously. Strain into glass.

CHERRY CHASE
A 4-oz. cocktail glass, chilled

1½ oz. gin
½ oz. Cherry Marnier
2 tsp. lemon juice
1 tsp. maraschino liqueur
3 to 4 ice cubes
1 maraschino cherry

Combine all ingredients except cherry in shaker, and shake vigorously. Strain into glass. Garnish with cherry.

COLE PORTER
An old-fashioned glass, chilled

3 small stewed tomatoes, cold (or canned Italian plum tomatoes)
3 ice cubes
1 dash Angostura bitters
1 dash Worcestershire sauce
1½ oz. gin (or vodka)

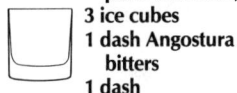

Combine tomatoes, ice cubes, bitters, Worcestershire sauce, and gin (or vodka) in blender, and blend thoroughly. Pour into glass. *The Waldorf-Astoria, New York, N.Y.*

CRIMSON TIDE
A 4-oz. cocktail glass, chilled

2 oz. gin
1 oz. port wine
½ oz. lime juice
3 to 4 ice cubes
1 tsp. grenadine

Combine all ingredients except grenadine in shaker, and shake vigorously. Strain into glass. Float grenadine on top by dripping it slowly over back of teaspoon.

¿CUANTA COSTA?
A 4-oz. cocktail glass, chilled

¾ oz. Cointreau
¾ oz. apricot brandy
¾ oz. gin
3 to 4 ice cubes

Combine all ingredients in shaker, and shake vigorously. Strain into glass.

DEEP SIX
A 4-oz. cocktail glass, chilled

1 oz. gin
1 oz. dry vermouth
1 dash orange bitters
1 dash Pernod
3 to 4 ice cubes
1 black olive

Combine all ingredients except olive in shaker, and shake vigorously. Strain into glass. Garnish with olive.

DERBY
An old-fashioned glass, chilled

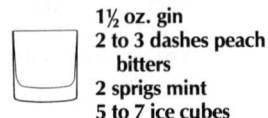

1½ oz. gin
2 to 3 dashes peach bitters
2 sprigs mint
5 to 7 ice cubes

Combine gin, bitters, and 3 to 4 ice cubes in shaker, and shake vigorously. Place 2 to 3 ice cubes in glass. Strain into glass. Garnish with mint sprigs.

EMERALD ISLE
A 4-oz. cocktail glass, chilled

1½ oz. gin
½ oz. green crème de menthe
2 dashes Angostura bitters
3 to 4 ice cubes

Combine all ingredients in shaker, and shake vigorously. Strain into glass.

DIXIE DARLING
An old-fashioned glass, chilled

1 oz. gin
1½ oz. orange juice
2 tsp. dry vermouth
2 tsp. Pernod
2 dashes grenadine
5 to 7 ice cubes

Combine all ingredients except 2 to 3 ice cubes in shaker, and shake vigorously. Place 2 to 3 ice cubes in glass. Strain into glass.

FALKLAND ISLANDS CRUSTA
A wine glass (8-oz. or larger), chilled

1½ tsp. orgeat syrup
1½ oz. gin
1½ oz. brandy or gold rum
1 tsp. lemon juice
3 to 4 ice cubes

Moisten rim of wine glass with a drop of orgeat, and sugar-frost rim. Combine all ingredients in shaker, and shake vigorously. Pour contents, unstrained, into prepared glass.

FALLEN ANGEL

An old-fashioned glass, chilled

2½ to 3 oz. gin
3 to 4 tbs. lemon juice
2 dashes green crème de menthe
1 dash Angostura bitters
6 to 8 ice cubes
1 maraschino cherry

Combine all ingredients except 3 ice cubes and cherry in shaker, and shake vigorously. Place remaining ice in glass, and strain into glass. Garnish with cherry.

FANCY GIN

Follow recipe for Fancy Brandy (p. 117), using 2 oz. gin instead of brandy.

FARMERS' ALMANAC

A 4-oz. cocktail glass, chilled

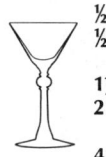

½ oz. dry vermouth
½ oz. sweet vermouth
1½ oz. gin
2 dashes orange bitters
4 oz. crushed ice

Combine all ingredients in shaker, and shake vigorously. Strain into glass.

FINE and DANDY

A 4-oz. cocktail glass, chilled

2 to 3 tsp. lemon juice
½ oz. triple sec
1½ oz. gin
1 dash orange bitters
3 to 4 ice cubes

Combine all ingredients in mixing glass, and stir briskly. Strain into cocktail glass.

FAVORITE BLONDE

A 4-oz. cocktail glass, chilled

½ oz. gin
½ oz. Dubonnet Blanc aperitif
½ oz. apricot brandy
1 dash lemon juice
3 to 4 ice cubes
2 oz. finely crushed ice
1 maraschino cherry

Combine gin, Dubonnet Blanc, apricot brandy, lemon juice, and ice in shaker, and shake vigorously. Put crushed ice in glass, and strain into glass. Garnish with cherry.

FAVORITE

Follow recipe for above Favorite Blonde, using ½ oz. dry vermouth instead of Dubonnet Blanc.

KNOCKOUT

Follow recipe for above Favorite Blonde, with following changes: Use ½ oz. Pernod instead of apricot brandy. Use ½ oz. dry vermouth instead of Dubonnet Blanc.

FERNET BRANCA

A 4-oz. cocktail glass, chilled

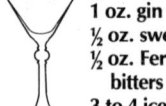

1 oz. gin
½ oz. sweet bitters
½ oz. Fernet Branca bitters
3 to 4 ice cubes

Combine all ingredients in shaker, and shake vigorously. Strain into glass.

GOPHER BALL

Follow recipe for above Fernet Branca, and drop 1 pearl onion into drink.

FIRST NIGHTER
A 4-oz. cocktail glass, chilled

½ oz. gin
1 tsp. Dubonnet Blanc aperitif
1 tsp. maraschino liqueur or kirsch
3 to 4 ice cubes
2 to 3 oz. dry sparkling wine, chilled
1 strip orange peel

Combine gin, Dubonnet Blanc, cherry liqueur or kirsch, and ice in mixing glass, and stir well. Strain into glass. Fill to top with sparkling wine. Twist orange peel over drink to release oil, and drop it in.

50-50
A 4-oz. cocktail glass, chilled

1½ oz. gin
1½ oz. dry vermouth
3 to 4 ice cubes
1 small green olive

Combine all ingredients except olive in shaker, and shake vigorously. Strain into glass. Drop olive into drink.

FRANKENSTEEN
An old-fashioned glass, chilled

1 oz. dry vermouth
1 oz. gin
½ oz. Cointreau
½ oz. apricot brandy
5 to 7 ice cubes
1 green maraschino cherry

Combine vermouth, gin, Cointreau, apricot brandy, and 3 to 4 ice cubes in shaker, and shake vigorously. Place 2 to 3 ice cubes in glass, and strain into glass. Garnish with cherry.

FRITHCO BLOWER

A 4-oz. cocktail glass, chilled

1½ oz. gin
1 tsp. grenadine
1 egg white
3 to 4 ice cubes
1 tsp. California red wine (such as Hearty Mountain Burgundy)

Combine all ingredients except red wine in shaker, and shake vigorously. Strain into glass. Spoon red wine on top of drink.

GIBSON

The Gibson is another name for the extra-dry Martini and is usually garnished with 2 or 3 cocktail onions (although most bartenders stint on the extra onions). Lemon peel is optional.

To prepare a Gibson, follow recipe for 8:1 or 12:1 Martini and garnish with cocktail onions.

ALTHEA GIBSON

Follow recipe for 8:1 or 12:1 Martini (page 154), and garnish with 1 black olive.

GIMLET

A 4-oz. cocktail glass, chilled

2 oz. gin
2 tsp. Rose's lime juice
2 to 3 ice cubes
2 oz. crushed ice

Combine all ingredients except crushed ice in shaker, and shake vigorously. Put crushed ice in glass. Strain into glass.

GIN and IT
A 4-oz. cocktail glass, chilled

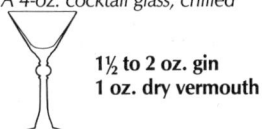

1½ to 2 oz. gin
1 oz. dry vermouth

Combine gin and vermouth in mixing glass, and stir well (*without* ice). Pour into glass.

GIN and TONIC
A highball glass, chilled

4 to 6 ice cubes
2 to 2½ oz. gin
About 6 oz. tonic water, chilled
1 lime or lemon wedge

Put ice in glass. Add gin. Squeeze lime or lemon wedge over glass, and drop it in. Fill to top with tonic.

GIN and SIN
A 4-oz. cocktail glass, chilled

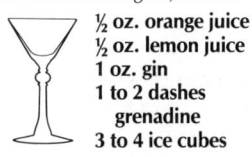

½ oz. orange juice
½ oz. lemon juice
1 oz. gin
1 to 2 dashes grenadine
3 to 4 ice cubes

Combine all ingredients in shaker, and shake vigorously. Strain into glass.

GIN 'N' BITTERS
An old-fashioned glass, chilled

½ tsp. Angostura bitters
3 oz. gin

Traditionally, this drink is made without ice. Use Angostura bitters to coat inside of glass entirely. Pour gin into glass and swirl slightly.

GIN DAIQUIRI

A 4-oz. cocktail glass, chilled

- ¾ oz. light rum
- 1½ oz. gin
- 2 tsp. lime juice
- 1 tsp. superfine sugar
- 3 to 4 ice cubes

Combine all ingredients in shaker, and shake vigorously. Strain into glass.

Note: The original daiquiri was made in Cuba in the early 1900s. Today the daiquiri is made with most white spirits but should always include some rum.

GIN DAISY

A 6-oz. cocktail or wine glass, chilled

- 2 tbs. lemon or lime juice
- ½ tsp. superfine sugar
- 1 tsp. grenadine
- 2 to 2½ oz. gin
- 4 oz. crushed ice
- 2 oz. club soda, chilled
- 1 thin slice orange

Combine lemon or lime juice, sugar, grenadine, gin, and crushed ice in shaker, and shake vigorously. Strain into glass. Add soda. Garnish with orange slice.

GIN FIX

An old-fashioned glass, chilled

- 1 tsp. superfine sugar
- 1 tsp. water
- 2 tbs. lime juice
- 2 to 2½ oz. Tanqueray gin
- 3 to 4 oz. crushed ice

Combine sugar and water in glass, and stir until sugar is dissolved. Continue stirring while adding remaining ingredients one at a time—lime juice, gin, and crushed ice. Serve with short straw.

GIN FIZZ

A highball glass, chilled

2½ to 3 oz. gin
1½ tsp. superfine sugar
½ tsp. lemon juice
7 to 8 ice cubes
4 to 6 oz. club soda, chilled
1 slice lemon

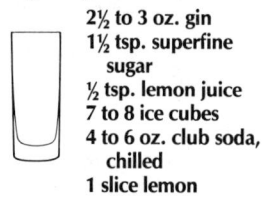

Combine gin, sugar, lemon juice, and 3 to 4 ice cubes in shaker, and shake vigorously. Place 4 to 5 ice cubes in glass. Strain into glass. Add lemon slice. Fill to top with soda.

Note: This popular drink can be made with any spirit, but the gin fizz has been a favorite in British colonies around the world for years. Sparkling wine can be used instead of club soda. Sometimes egg or yolk above is added to the mixture in the shaker.

FIZZOLETTO

Follow recipe for above Gin Fizz, using 4 to 6 oz. spumante wine instead of soda.

GIN MINT FIZZ

Follow recipe for above Gin Fizz, adding 2 dashes white crème de menthe to shaker mixture.

GIN SWIZZLE

A highball glass, chilled

2 to 2½ oz. gin
½ to ¾ oz. lime juice
1 tsp. superfine sugar
½ tsp. Angostura bitters
3 to 4 ice cubes for shaker, plus extra to fill highball glass to half level
About 6 oz. club soda, chilled

Combine gin, lime juice, sugar, bitters, and 3 to 4 ice cubes in shaker, and shake vigorously. Fill glass with extra ice cubes to half level. Strain into glass. Fill to top with soda.

Note: All swizzles are prepared in this manner. Change only the spirit. The name "swizzle" comes from the original use of a 6-inch twig with very small branches. It was swirled between both hands to mix the drink.

GIN ZOOM

A 4-oz. cocktail glass, chilled

1 tsp. honey
1 tbs. boiling water
1 tsp. half and half cream
2½ oz. gin
3 to 4 ice cubes

In separate small container, combine honey and boiling water, and stir until honey is dissolved. Transfer mixture to shaker, and add half and half cream, gin, and ice cubes. Shake vigorously. Strain into glass.

Note: Zooms can be made with other spirit bases, but the procedure always begins with honey.

GOLDEN FIZZ

A highball glass, chilled

2½ oz. gin
1 tbs. superfine sugar
1 tsp. lemon juice
1 egg yolk
6 to 8 ice cubes
3 to 4 oz. club soda, chilled
1 slice lime

Combine gin, sugar, lemon juice, egg yolk, and 3 to 4 ice cubes in shaker, and shake vigorously. Put 3 to 4 ice cubes in glass. Strain into glass. Add lemon slice. Fill to top with soda.

EXORCIST

Follow recipe for above Golden Fizz, with following changes: Use 1 egg white instead of egg yolk. Add ½ oz. Strega liqueur to shaker mixture.

SILVER FIZZ

Follow recipe for above Golden Fizz, using 1 egg white instead of egg yolk.

GOLDEN POND
An old-fashioned glass, chilled

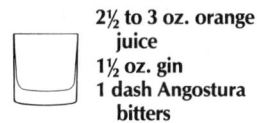

2½ to 3 oz. orange juice
1½ oz. gin
1 dash Angostura bitters
5 to 7 ice cubes

Combine all ingredients except 2 to 3 ice cubes in shaker, and shake vigorously. Place 2 to 3 ice cubes in glass, and strain into glass.

Note: This drink has been called Golden Screw (vodka instead of gin), Golden Date, Golden Spike, Golden Nugget, and Golden Meir. Some even claim it is the recipe for the original Screwdriver.

GYPSY
A 4-oz. cocktail glass, chilled

1¼ oz. sweet vermouth
1¼ oz. gin
3 to 4 ice cubes
1 maraschino cherry

Combine all ingredients except cherry in mixing glass, and stir well. Strain into cocktail glass. Add cherry.

HAARLEM
A 4-oz. cocktail glass, chilled

1 oz. pineapple juice
1 oz. gin
½ tsp. maraschino liqueur or kirsch
3 to 4 ice cubes
2 to 3 pineapple cubes

Combine all ingredients except pineapple cubes in shaker, and shake vigorously. Strain into glass. Spear pineapple with cocktail pick or thin stirrer, and drop into drink.

HASTY PUDDING
A 4-oz. cocktail glass, chilled

1 tsp. grenadine
¼ tsp. Pernod
½ oz. dry vermouth
1½ oz. gin
3 to 4 ice cubes

Combine all ingredients in mixing glass, and stir well. Strain into cocktail glass.

HIT and MISS

An old-fashioned glass, chilled

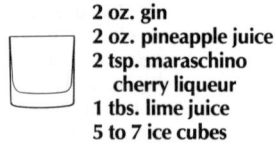

2 oz. gin
2 oz. pineapple juice
2 tsp. maraschino cherry liqueur
1 tbs. lime juice
5 to 7 ice cubes

Combine all ingredients except 2 to 3 ice cubes in blender, and blend at medium speed 10 to 15 seconds. Place remaining ice in glass. Strain into glass.

INVISIBLE MAN

A 10- to 14-oz. tall glass, chilled

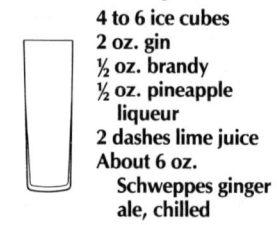

4 to 6 ice cubes
2 oz. gin
½ oz. brandy
½ oz. pineapple liqueur
2 dashes lime juice
About 6 oz. Schweppes ginger ale, chilled

Put ice cubes in glass. Add gin, brandy, pineapple liqueur, and lime juice, and stir slowly until mixed. Top with ginger ale.

I.R.S.

A 4-oz. cocktail glass, chilled. This drink came into being when a U.S. taxpayer prepared his first drink after April 15. It was all he had left on the bar.

½ oz. gin
½ oz. dry vermouth
½ oz. sweet vermouth
½ oz. vodka
2 tbs. orange juice
3 ice cubes

Combine all ingredients in shaker, and shake vigorously. Strain into glass.

JEWEL

A 4-oz. cocktail glass, chilled

¾ oz. green Chartreuse
¾ oz. sweet vermouth
¾ oz. gin
2 dashes orange bitters
3 to 4 ice cubes
1 strip lemon peel

Combine all ingredients except lemon peel in shaker, and shake vigorously. Strain into glass. Twist lemon peel over drink to release oil, and drop it in.

JEWELER'S ROUGE
Follow recipe for above Jewel. Top drink with 2 to 3 dashes strawberry liqueur.

JOCKEY CLUB
An old-fashioned glass, chilled

2 to 3 drops grenadine
2 to 3 drops orange bitters
2 dashes crème de noyaux
2 to 3 drops lemon juice
3 oz. gin
5 to 7 ice cubes
2 to 3 dashes strawberry liqueur

Combine grenadine, orange bitters, crème de noyaux, lemon juice, gin, and 3 to 4 ice cubes in shaker, and shake vigorously. Put 2 to 3 ice cubes in glass, and strain into glass. Top with 2 to 3 dashes strawberry liqueur.

KGB
A 4-oz. cocktail glass, chilled

1 oz. gin
1 oz. Stolichnaya vodka
2 dashes slivovitz
2 dashes kirsch
3 to 4 oz. crushed ice

Combine all ingredients in shaker, and shake vigorously. Strain into glass.

KISS OFF
A 4-oz. cocktail glass, chilled

1 oz. gin
1 oz. Cherry Marnier
1 tsp. dry vermouth
3 to 4 ice cubes

Combine all ingredients in shaker, and shake vigorously. Strain into glass.

LADYFINGER
An old-fashioned glass, chilled

1 oz. gin
1 tbs. kirsch
1 tbs. Cherry Marnier
3 oz. crushed ice

Combine all ingredients in shaker, and shake vigorously. Pour drink, unstrained, into glass.

LEAP YEAR
A 4-oz. cocktail glass, chilled

1½ oz. gin
½ oz. Grand Marnier
½ oz. sweet vermouth
2 to 3 drops lemon juice
3 to 4 ice cubes
1 strip lemon peel

Combine all ingredients except lemon peel in shaker, and shake vigorously. Strain into glass. Twist lemon peel over drink to release oil, and drop it in.

LONDON
A 4-oz. cocktail glass, chilled

1½ oz. gin
2 dashes orange bitters
½ tsp. sugar syrup
2 to 3 drops maraschino liqueur
3 to 4 ice cubes

Combine all ingredients in shaker, and shake vigorously. Strain into glass.

MAIDEN'S BLUSH
A 4-oz. cocktail glass, chilled

2½ oz. gin
1 tsp. curaçao
3 to 4 drops lemon juice
3 to 4 drops grenadine
3 to 4 ice cubes

Combine all ingredients in shaker, and shake vigorously. Strain into glass.

MAIDEN'S PRAYER

A 4-oz. cocktail glass, chilled

- 1½ oz. gin
- 1 oz. Cointreau
- 1 tsp. orange juice
- 1 tsp. lemon juice
- 3 to 4 ice cubes

Combine all ingredients in shaker, and shake vigorously. Strain into glass. *Cointreau Ltd., Lawrenceville, N.J.*

MANHATTAN SOUTH

A 4-oz. cocktail glass, chilled

- 1½ oz. gin
- ¼ oz. dry vermouth
- ¼ oz. Southern Comfort
- 1 to 2 dashes Angostura bitters
- 3 to 4 ice cubes

Combine all ingredients in mixing glass, and stir well. Strain into glass.

MARTINI

The first "original" Martini recipe (from Jerry Thomas of San Francisco) called for half dry vermouth and half gin. From World War II on, however, as we became a nation of "lighter and drier" drinkers, the proportions began to change, with the gin becoming the beneficiary; hence, the "dry Martini." I used to call it "Beefeater-Beefeater" . . . sounding it once for the gin and the second time to announce that I required "Beefeater" again instead of the normal treatment of vermouth. Over the years there have been many versions of the Martini, either through name change or ingredient change, e.g., Dillatini, Tequini, Vodkatini, Gibson, Blenton, etc. The Martini is perceived as a drink of awesome power. Our mixing chart illustrates the history of this popular potion and the choice to live in any age you desire.

Proportions of gin to dry vermouth, from original formula to extra dry on next page.

153

1:1 WORLD WAR I MARTINI

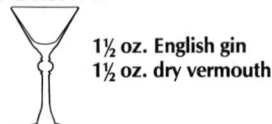

1½ oz. English gin
1½ oz. dry vermouth

2:1 WORLD WAR II (OR ATOMIC AGE) MARTINI

2 oz. English gin
1 oz. dry vermouth

6:1 SPACE AGE (OR SPUTNIK ERA) MARTINI (1960s)

2 oz. English gin
1 tbs. (scant) dry vermouth

8:1 INFLATION MARTINI (1970s) (or Gibson)

2½ oz. gin
1 tbs. (scant) dry vermouth

12:1 LASER AGE MARTINI (1980s) (or Gibson)

2½ oz. English gin
1 tsp. dry vermouth

Serving glass: The Martini or Gibson may be served in a 4-oz. cocktail glass (without ice) or in old-fashioned glass (with ice cubes). Either glass should be chilled to point where it is frosted.

Mixing: Place at least 12 ice cubes in glass pitcher for each drink being prepared. (Ice cubes should be fresh from freezer and dry.) Measure gin first (exact amount for each drink) and pour over ice. The gin will "smoke" as it hits dry, cold ice. Then add vermouth. Stir quickly and with vigor (6 to 8 turns.) Strain into frosted glass:

1. Cocktail glass for "straight up"
2. Old-fashioned glass for "on the rocks"

Garnish with green olive and/or twist of lemon or orange peel, if desired.

MERRY WIDOW

A 4-oz. cocktail glass, chilled

- 1 oz. gin
- 1 oz. dry vermouth
- 2 dashes Benedictine
- 2 dashes Pernod
- 1 dash Angostura bitters
- 3 to 4 ice cubes
- 1 strip lemon peel

Combine all ingredients except lemon peel in shaker, and shake vigorously. Strain into glass. Twist lemon peel over drink to release oil, and drop it in.

MISSISSIPPI MULE

A 4-oz. cocktail glass, chilled

- 1½ oz. gin
- 1 tsp. crème de cassis
- 1 tsp. lemon juice
- 3 to 4 ice cubes

Combine all ingredients in shaker, and shake vigorously. Strain into glass.

MONKEY GLAND

A 4-oz. cocktail glass, chilled

- 1½ oz. gin
- 1½ oz. orange juice
- 3 to 4 drops Benedictine
- 3 to 4 drops grenadine
- 3 to 4 ice cubes

Combine all ingredients in shaker, and shake vigorously. Strain drink into glass.

PETER SELLERS' MINKY

Follow recipe for above Monkey Gland, using 3 to 4 drops Drambuie instead of Benedictine.

MONTMARTRE

A 4-oz. cocktail glass, chilled

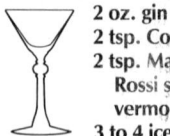

    2 oz. gin
2 tsp. Cointreau
2 tsp. Martini & Rossi sweet vermouth
3 to 4 ice cubes

Combine all ingredients in shaker, and shake vigorously. Strain into glass.

MORNING "MINUTE MAID"

An old-fashioned glass, chilled

    2 oz. gin
1 tbs. Minute Maid frozen grapefruit concentrate
1 tbs. Minute Maid frozen orange juice concentrate
3 to 4 drops grenadine
1 to 2 dashes Angostura bitters
3 to 4 ice cubes

Combine all ingredients in shaker, and shake vigorously. Strain into glass.

MOONSHOT

A whiskey sour glass, chilled

    1½ oz. Gordon's gin
3 oz. clam juice
1 dash Tabasco sauce
4 ice cubes

Combine all ingredients in mixing glass, stir until chilled, and strain into glass. *Gordon's Dry Gin Co., Ltd., Linden, N.J.*

MORRO CASTLE

A 4-oz. cocktail glass, chilled

    1 oz. gin
½ oz. Appleton gold rum
½ oz. pineapple juice
½ oz. lime juice
3 to 4 ice cubes

Sugar-frost rim of cocktail glass. Combine all ingredients in shaker, and shake vigorously. Strain into prepared glass.

Note: A favorite variation in the tropics is to moisten rim of glass with Falernum syrup before coating with sugar.

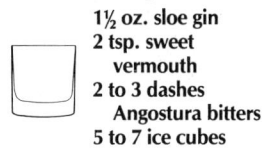

MOULIN ROUGE
An old-fashioned glass, chilled

1½ oz. sloe gin
2 tsp. sweet vermouth
2 to 3 dashes Angostura bitters
5 to 7 ice cubes

Combine all ingredients except 2 to 3 ice cubes in shaker, and shake vigorously. Place reserved ice cubes in glass, and strain into glass.

NAPOLEON
An old-fashioned glass, chilled

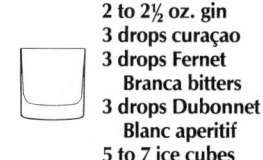

2 to 2½ oz. gin
3 drops curaçao
3 drops Fernet Branca bitters
3 drops Dubonnet Blanc aperitif
5 to 7 ice cubes

Combine all ingredients except 2 to 3 ice cubes in shaker, and shake vigorously. Place reserved ice cubes in glass, and strain into glass.

MULE SHOE
A 4-oz. cocktail glass, chilled

½ oz. gin
½ oz. applejack
½ oz. Southern Comfort
½ oz. maple syrup
3 to 4 ice cubes

Combine all ingredients in shaker, and shake vigorously. Strain into glass.

NAPOLEON III

Follow recipe for above Napoleon, using 3 drops Lillet aperitif instead of Dubonnet Blanc.

NIGHTMARE ALLEY

A 4-oz. cocktail glass, chilled

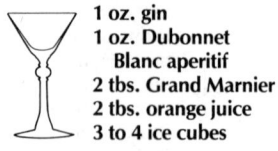

- 1 oz. gin
- 1 oz. Dubonnet Blanc aperitif
- 2 tbs. Grand Marnier
- 2 tbs. orange juice
- 3 to 4 ice cubes

Combine all ingredients in shaker, and shake vigorously. Strain into glass.

NINETEEN

A 4-oz. cocktail glass, chilled

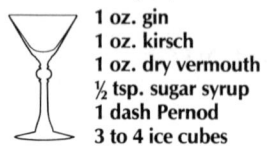

- 1 oz. gin
- 1 oz. kirsch
- 1 oz. dry vermouth
- ½ tsp. sugar syrup
- 1 dash Pernod
- 3 to 4 ice cubes

Combine all ingredients in shaker, and shake vigorously. Strain drink into glass.

1984

Follow recipe for above Nineteen, using ½ oz. Southern Comfort instead of kirsch.

OASIS

A 10- to 14-oz. tall glass, chilled

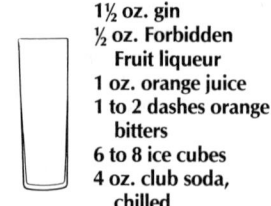

- 1½ oz. gin
- ½ oz. Forbidden Fruit liqueur
- 1 oz. orange juice
- 1 to 2 dashes orange bitters
- 6 to 8 ice cubes
- 4 oz. club soda, chilled
- 1 strip orange peel

In shaker, combine gin, Forbidden Fruit liqueur, orange juice, bitters, and 3 to 4 ice cubes, and shake vigorously. Fill glass with reserved ice cubes to half level. Strain into glass. Fill to top with soda. Twist orange peel over drink to release oil, and drop it in.

OPAL

A 4-oz. cocktail glass, chilled

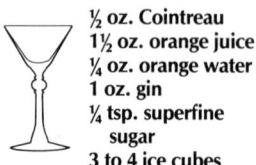

- ½ oz. Cointreau
- 1½ oz. orange juice
- ¼ oz. orange water
- 1 oz. gin
- ¼ tsp. superfine sugar
- 3 to 4 ice cubes

Combine all ingredients in shaker, and shake vigorously. Strain into glass.

OPERA

A 4-oz. cocktail glass, chilled

2 oz. gin
2 tbs. Dubonnet Blanc aperitif
2 tbs. maraschino liqueur or kirsch
3 to 4 ice cubes
1 strip orange peel

Combine all ingredients except orange peel in mixing glass, and stir well. Strain into glass. Twist orange peel over drink to release oil, and drop it in.

ORANGE BLOSSOM

A 4-oz. cocktail glass, chilled

1½ oz. orange juice
1½ oz. gin
½ tsp. superfine sugar
3 to 4 ice cubes
½ slice orange

Sugar-frost rim of cocktail glass. In shaker, combine orange juice, sugar, and ice, and shake vigorously. Add gin, and shake again. Strain into prepared glass. Garnish with orange slice.

ORANGE FIZZ

A highball glass, chilled

2 to 2½ oz. gin
1½ oz. orange juice
½ oz. lemon juice
2 tsp. triple sec
1 tsp. superfine sugar
2 dashes orange bitters
3 to 4 ice cubes plus extra to fill highball glass to half level
4 to 6 oz. club soda, chilled
1 thin slice orange

In shaker, combine gin, orange juice, lemon juice, triple sec, sugar, bitters, and 3 to 4 ice cubes, and shake vigorously. Fill highball glass with extra ice cubes to half level. Strain into glass. Fill to top with soda and stir. Garnish with orange slice.

ORCHID

A 4-oz. cocktail glass, chilled

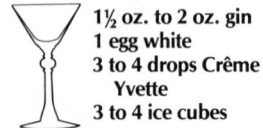

- 1½ oz. to 2 oz. gin
- 1 egg white
- 3 to 4 drops Crême Yvette
- 3 to 4 ice cubes

Combine all ingredients in shaker, and shake vigorously. Strain into glass.

PALM BEACH

A 4-oz. cocktail glass, chilled

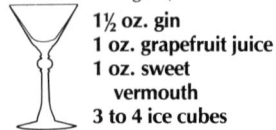

- 1½ oz. gin
- 1 oz. grapefruit juice
- 1 oz. sweet vermouth
- 3 to 4 ice cubes

Combine all ingredients in shaker, and shake vigorously. Strain into glass.

PARADISE ISLAND

A 4-oz. cocktail glass, chilled

- 1 oz. apricot brandy
- 1 oz. gin
- 2 tbs. orange juice
- 3 to 4 ice cubes
- 1 tsp. shredded coconut

Combine all ingredients except coconut in shaker, and shake vigorously. Strain into glass. Sprinkle coconut on top of drink.

PARISIAN

A 4-oz. cocktail glass, chilled

- 1 oz. crème de cassis
- 1 oz. dry vermouth
- 1 oz. gin
- 3 to 4 ice cubes

Combine all ingredients in mixing glass, and stir well. Strain into glass.

PARK and 59TH

A 4-oz. cocktail glass, chilled

- 1 oz. gin
- ½ oz. dry vermouth
- ½ oz. Midori melon liqueur
- 4 oz. crushed ice

Combine all ingredients in shaker, and shake vigorously. Strain into glass.

PINK GIN

A 4-oz. cocktail glass, chilled

- ½ tsp. Angostura bitters
- 3 oz. gin
- 2 to 3 ice cubes

Combine all ingredients in shaker, and shake vigorously. Strain into glass.

PINK LADY
A 4-oz. cocktail glass, chilled

1½ oz. gin
½ oz. applejack
½ oz. lemon juice
1 tsp. grenadine
½ egg white
3 to 4 ice cubes

Combine all ingredients except gin in shaker, and shake until creamy. Then add gin and shake briefly. Strain into glass.

PINK PUSSYCAT
A 4-oz. cocktail glass, chilled

1½ oz. gin
¾ oz. grenadine
1 egg white
3 to 4 ice cubes

Combine all ingredients in shaker, and shake vigorously. Strain into glass.

PINK PANTHER
A 4-oz. cocktail glass, chilled

¾ oz. dry vermouth
¾ oz. gin
1 egg white
2 tbs. orange juice
½ oz. crème de cassis
3 to 4 ice cubes

Combine all ingredients in shaker, and shake vigorously. Strain into glass.

PINK ROSE
A 4-oz. cocktail glass, chilled

1 tsp. strawberry liqueur
1 tsp. lemon juice
1 tsp. cream
1 egg white
1½ oz. gin
3 to 4 ice cubes

Combine all ingredients in shaker, and shake vigorously. Strain into glass.

POODLE
(TV Special)
A highball glass, chilled

- 3 to 4 ice cubes
- 1½ oz. Gordon's gin
- 2 oz. orange juice
- 3 to 4 oz. ginger ale, chilled

Combine ice cubes, gin, and orange juice in glass and stir. Top with ginger ale. *Gordon's Dry Gin Co., Ltd., Linden, N.J.*

PRINCE'S SMILE
A 4-oz. cocktail glass, chilled

- 1 oz. calvados (apple brandy)
- 1 oz. apricot brandy
- 1 oz. gin
- 1 dash lemon juice
- 3 to 4 ice cubes

Combine all ingredients in shaker, and shake vigorously. Strain into glass.

POLYNESIAN CRUSTA
A 4-oz. cocktail glass, chilled

- 2 tsp. lime juice
- 1 to 2 tbs. Cherry Marnier
- 1½ to 2 oz. gin
- 3 to 4 ice cubes

Moisten rim of cocktail glass with drop of lime juice, and sugar-frost rim. Combine all ingredients in shaker, and shake vigorously. Strain into prepared glass.

PRINCETON
A 4-oz. cocktail glass, chilled

- 2 tbs. tawny port wine
- 1½ to 2 oz. gin
- 2 dashes orange bitters
- 3 to 4 ice cubes

Combine port wine, gin, bitters, and ice in shaker, and shake vigorously. Strain into glass.

Q.E.2
A highball glass, chilled

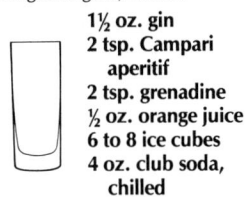

1½ oz. gin
2 tsp. Campari aperitif
2 tsp. grenadine
½ oz. orange juice
6 to 8 ice cubes
4 oz. club soda, chilled

In shaker, combine gin, Campari, grenadine, orange juice, and 3 to 4 ice cubes, and shake vigorously. Place 3 to 4 ice cubes in glass, and strain into glass. Top with soda.

RACQUET CLUB
A 4-oz. cocktail glass, chilled

¾ oz. dry vermouth
2½ oz. gin
2 dashes orange bitters
3 to 4 ice cubes

Combine all ingredients in shaker, and shake vigorously. Strain into glass.

RAMOS GIN FIZZ
A wine glass (6- to 8-oz.), chilled

1 lemon wedge
2 tsp. lemon juice
1 tsp. lime juice
1 egg white
2 tbs. heavy cream
2 oz. gin
½ tsp. superfine sugar
½ tsp. orange water
4 to 6 oz. crushed ice
Optional: A splash of club soda

Moisten rim of wine glass with lemon wedge, and sugar-frost rim. Combine remaining ingredients except soda in shaker, and shake vigorously and continuously until mixture is thick and frothy (or combine in blender at medium speed for 50 to 60 seconds). Strain into prepared glass. If desired, top with splash of soda.

RED SNAPPER

Follow recipe for Bloody Mary using 1½ oz. gin instead of vodka.

ROLLS-ROYCE

A 4-oz. cocktail glass, chilled

- 2 oz. Tanqueray gin
- ½ oz. dry vermouth
- ½ oz. sweet vermouth
- 2 dashes Benedictine
- 3 to 4 ice cubes

Combine all ingredients in shaker, and shake vigorously. Strain into glass.

ROSE COCKTAIL

A 4-oz. cocktail glass, chilled

- 2 oz. gin
- ½ oz. dry vermouth
- ½ oz. apricot brandy
- 1 tsp. Rose's lemon or lime juice
- 3 dashes grenadine
- 3 to 4 ice cubes

Moisten rim of cocktail glass with drop of vermouth, and sugar-frost rim. Combine all ingredients in shaker, and shake vigorously. Strain into prepared glass.

ROSETTA STONE

A 4-oz. cocktail glass, chilled

- 1 tsp. amaretto
- 1 dash grenadine
- 1 tbs. lime juice
- 2½ oz. gin
- 3 to 4 ice cubes

Combine all ingredients in shaker, and shake vigorously. Strain into glass.

SALTY DOG

An old-fashioned glass, chilled

- 1 strip lemon or lime peel
- 3 to 4 ice cubes
- 2½ to 3 oz. grapefruit juice
- 2 oz. gin

Rub lemon or lime peel around rim of old-fashioned glass to moisten, and salt-frost rim of glass. Stand glass in freezer or refrigerator for coating to set. To serve, combine ice, grapefruit juice, and gin in prepared glass and stir.

SEVILLE
A 4-oz. cocktail glass, chilled

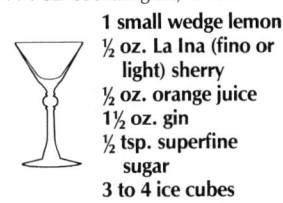

    1 small wedge lemon
    ½ oz. La Ina (fino or light) sherry
    ½ oz. orange juice
    1½ oz. gin
    ½ tsp. superfine sugar
    3 to 4 ice cubes

Moisten rim of cocktail glass with wedge of lemon, and sugar-frost rim. Combine all ingredients in shaker, and shake vigorously. Strain into prepared glass.

SILENCE IS GOLDEN
A 4-oz. cocktail glass, chilled

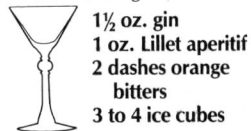

    1½ oz. gin
    1 oz. Lillet aperitif
    2 dashes orange bitters
    3 to 4 ice cubes

Combine all ingredients in shaker, and shake vigorously. Strain into glass.

SINGAPORE SLING
A highball glass, chilled

    1 oz. Cherry Marnier
    2 oz. gin
    2 dashes Angostura bitters
    3 drops Benedictine
    2 tsp. lime or lemon juice
    1 tsp. superfine sugar
    4 to 6 ice cubes

Combine all ingredients except ice in shaker, and shake vigorously. Place ice in glass, and strain into glass.

SNOWBALL
A 4-oz. cocktail glass, chilled

    1 oz. gin
    2 tsp. Crême Yvette
    2 tsp. white crème de menthe
    2 tsp. Sambuca Romana
    2 tsp. cream
    3 to 4 ice cubes

Combine all ingredients in shaker, and shake vigorously. Strain into glass.

STRAWBERRY BLOW FIZZ

An old-fashioned glass, chilled

- 2½ oz. gin
- 2 tsp. Leroux strawberry liqueur
- 1 tsp. superfine sugar
- ¾ oz. cream
- 2 tsp. lemon juice
- 5 to 6 ice cubes
- 4 oz. club soda, chilled
- 1 fresh strawberry

Combine gin, strawberry liqueur, sugar, cream, lemon juice, and 3 or 4 ice cubes in shaker, and shake vigorously. Place remaining ice in glass, and strain into glass. Top with soda and garnish with strawberry.

UNION JACK

A 4-oz. cocktail glass, chilled

- 2½ oz. gin
- ½ oz. Crème Yvette
- 1 tsp. grenadine
- 3 to 4 ice cubes

Combine all ingredients in shaker, and shake vigorously. Strain into glass.

VELVET KISS

A 4-oz. cocktail glass, chilled

- 1 oz. Gordon's gin
- ½ oz. Bols Creme de Banana
- ½ oz. pineapple juice
- 1 oz. heavy cream
- 1 dash grenadine
- 3 to 4 ice cubes

Combine all ingredients in shaker, shake vigorously, and strain into glass. *Gordon's Dry Gin Co., Ltd., Linden, N.J.*

WHITE SALE
A 4-oz. cocktail glass, chilled

- 2 oz. gin
- 2 tbs. Sambuca Romana liqueur
- 2 to 3 drops orange bitters
- 3 to 4 ice cubes

Combine all ingredients in mixing glass, and stir slowly. Strain into glass.

LIQUEUR RECIPES

ABBOT'S DELIGHT
An old-fashioned glass, chilled

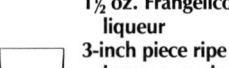

1½ oz. Frangelico liqueur
3-inch piece ripe banana, peeled
2 oz. pineapple juice
3 oz. crushed ice
2 dashes Angostura bitters

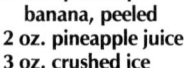

Combine all ingredients in blender, and blend 15 to 20 seconds (until smooth). Pour, unstrained, into glass. *Frangelico, William Grant & Sons, Edison, N.J.*

AFTER-DINNER MINT
A 4-oz. cocktail glass, chilled

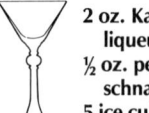

2 oz. Kamora coffee liqueur
½ oz. peppermint schnapps
5 ice cubes

Combine all ingredients except 2 ice cubes in shaker, and shake vigorously. Place reserved ice cubes in glass. Strain into glass. *Kamora Coffee Liqueur, James B. Beam Distilling Co., Chicago, Ill.*

ALMOND FIZZ
An old-fashioned glass, chilled

1 tbs. lemon juice
½ tsp. superfine sugar
1 egg
1 tsp. heavy cream
1½ oz. DuBouchett Crème de Almond
5 ice cubes
3 to 4 oz. club soda, chilled

Combine lemon juice, sugar, egg, cream, crème de almond, and 3 ice cubes in shaker, and shake vigorously. Put 2 ice cubes in glass. Strain into glass. Fill with soda. *DuBouchett Liqueurs, Schenley Distillers Co., New York, N.Y.*

AMARETTO & COGNAC CONTINENTAL STINGER
An old-fashioned glass, chilled

1½ oz. Hiram Walker Amaretto & Cognac
¾ oz. Hiram Walker peppermint schnapps
¼ cup crushed ice
1 mint sprig

Combine Amaretto & Cognac, peppermint schnapps, and ice in blender, and blend until smooth. Pour into glass. Garnish with mint. *Hiram Walker Cordials, Hiram Walker, Inc., Detroit, Mich.*

AMARETTO ICE
A wine glass (8-oz. or larger),

2 scoops French vanilla ice cream
1¼ oz. amaretto

Combine all ingredients in blender, and blend until creamy. Pour into glass. Serve with a spoon. *Tony's Restaurant, St. Louis, Mo.*

APRES SKI
A 4-oz. cocktail glass, chilled

¾ oz. Minttu Peppermint Schnaapps
¾ oz. Kahlua coffee liqueur
¾ oz. white crème de cacao
3 to 4 ice cubes
2 oz. crushed ice

Combine all ingredients except crushed ice in shaker, and shake vigorously. Put crushed ice in glass, and strain into glass. *Minttu Peppermint Schnaapps, Great Vintners International, Syosset, N.Y.*

B-52

A pony glass, chilled

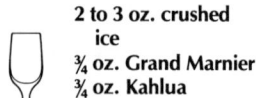

2 to 3 oz. crushed ice
¾ oz. Grand Marnier
¾ oz. Kahlua
½ oz. Bailey's Irish Cream

Put ice in shaker and drain water. Add Grand Marnier, Kahlua, and Bailey's Irish Cream. Shake vigorously, briefly. Strain into glass. *Frank Bernstein, Manager, Tony Roma's Restaurant, New York, N.Y.*

BAILEY'S SHILLELAGH

An old-fashioned glass, chilled

1 oz. Bailey's Irish Cream
½ oz. Jameson's Irish whiskey
4 oz. strong coffee, cold
1 tbs. heavy cream
1 green maraschino cherry

Moisten rim of glass with drop of Irish whiskey, and sugar-frost rim. Pour Bailey's Irish Cream, whiskey, and coffee into prepared glass, and stir well. Top with whipped cream and green cherry. *Grand Hyatt Hotel, New York, N.Y.*

BANANA DAIQUIRI No. 2

A 6-oz. cocktail or wine glass, chilled

½ ripe banana, sliced
1 tsp. superfine sugar
½ oz. lime juice
1½ oz. Cocoribe liqueur
4 oz. crushed ice

Combine banana, sugar, lime juice, Cocoribe, and ice in blender, and blend at high speed 10 to 20 seconds. Strain into glass. *The Forge Restaurant, Miami, Fla.*

BANANAGO

An 8-oz. wine glass, chilled

1½ oz. Lamoka mocha liqueur
1½ oz. cream
¼ banana
3 to 4 oz. crushed ice

Combine all ingredients in blender, and blend until smooth. Pour into glass. Serve with short straw. *Lamoka Liqueur, The Sheldon Marks Co., Los Angeles, Calif.*

BANSHEE
A 4-oz. cocktail glass, chilled

1½ oz. Bols banana liqueur
1 oz. vodka
3 to 4 ice cubes

Combine all ingredients in mixing glass, and stir well. Strain into cocktail glass. *Amsterdam Directors/Erven Lucas Bols Distilling Co., Louisville, Ky.*

BARCLAY
A highball glass, chilled

1 oz. Kahlua coffee liqueur
1 oz. brandy
2½ scoops chocolate ice cream
1 oz. heavy cream
1 tbs. whipped cream
1 tbs. shaved bittersweet chocolate

Combine coffee liqueur, brandy, ice cream, and heavy cream in glass, and stir until mixture is smooth. Top with whipped cream and shaved chocolate. *Philander's, Oak Park, Ill.*

BARBARELLA
A whiskey sour glass, chilled

2 oz. Cointreau
1 oz. Sambuca Romana
3 to 4 oz. crushed ice
1 ice cube

Combine all ingredients except ice in shaker, and shake vigorously. Strain into glass. Add ice. *Cointreau Ltd., Lawrenceville, N.J.*

BARNUM & BAILEY
A 4-oz. cocktail glass, chilled

2 oz. Bailey's Irish Cream
½ oz. apricot brandy
1 tsp. gin
2 to 3 ice cubes
½ maraschino cherry
2 miniature marshmallows

Combine all ingredients except cherry and marshmallows in shaker, and shake vigorously. Strain into glass. Garnish drink with clown face by floating cherry in center (for nose) and one marshmallow on each side of cherry (for eyes). *Bailey's Original Irish Cream, Paddington Corp., New York, N.Y.*

BLUEBERRY SOMBRERO

A wine glass (8-oz. or larger), chilled

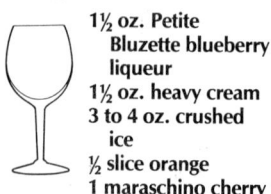

1½ oz. Petite Bluzette blueberry liqueur
1½ oz. heavy cream
3 to 4 oz. crushed ice
½ slice orange
1 maraschino cherry

Combine blueberry liqueur, heavy cream, and ice in blender, and blend until smooth. Pour into glass. Garnish with ½ slice orange and cherry. *Petite Bluzette, David Sherman Corp., St. Louis, Mo.*

BLUEBIRD of HAPPINESS

A brandy snifter (8-oz. or larger), chilled

3 to 4 ice cubes
1½ oz. Petite Bluzette blueberry liqueur
½ oz. amaretto
1½ oz. heavy cream

Place ice in snifter. Add remaining ingredients and stir well. Serve with straw. *Petite Bluzette, David Sherman Corp., St. Louis, Mo.*

THE BLUE HEAVEN

A 4-oz. cocktail glass, chilled (or highball glass filled with ice cubes)

1 oz. blue curaçao
1 oz. light rum
1 oz. pineapple juice
1 tsp. coconut cream
3 ice cubes
1 thin slice orange

Combine all ingredients except orange slice in shaker, and shake vigorously. Strain into glass (or over ice in highball glass). Garnish with orange slice. Or, omit blue curaçao from shaker mixture, and instead, float blue curaçao on top of drink. *Heaven Restaurant, Pittsburgh, Pa.*

BRIGHT FEATHER

An old-fashioned glass, chilled

3 ice cubes
2 oz. Jeremiah Weed Bourbon Liqueur
1 strip lemon peel

Put ice in glass. Add Bourbon liqueur. Twist lemon peel over drink to release oil, and drop it in. *Jeremiah Weed 100 proof Bourbon Liqueur, Heublein, Inc., Hartford, Conn.*

BOLSEYE

A wine glass (8-oz.), chilled

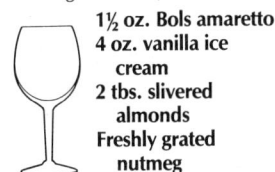

1½ oz. Bols amaretto
4 oz. vanilla ice cream
2 tbs. slivered almonds
Freshly grated nutmeg
1 maraschino cherry

Combine all ingredients except nutmeg and cherry in blender, and blend at low speed 15 to 20 seconds. Pour into glass. Top with sprinkle of nutmeg and garnish with cherry. *Amsterdam Directors/Erven Lucas Bols Distilling Co., Louisville, Ky.*

BROWN CALF BELT

A pony glass

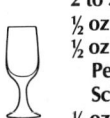

2 to 3 ice cubes
½ oz. coffee liqueur
½ oz. Minttu Peppermint Schnaapps
½ oz. Bailey's Irish Cream

Combine ice, coffee liqueur, and peppermint schnapps in mixing glass and stir until chilled. Strain into glass. Slowly pour Irish cream against inside of glass so that it floats. *Minttu Peppermint Schnaapps, Great Vintners International, Syosset, N.Y.*

BUTTERFLY

A 6-oz. cocktail glass or wine glass, chilled

1½ oz. Bols Advocaat (prepared eggnog)
1½ oz. cherry brandy
3 to 4 ice cubes
3 oz. crushed ice

Combine all ingredients except crushed ice in shaker, and shake vigorously. Put crushed ice in glass, and strain into glass. *Amsterdam Directors/Erven Lucas Bols Distilling Co., Louisville, Ky.*

CABAÑA FRAPPÉ

A 4-oz. cocktail glass, chilled

1 oz. Kamora coffee liqueur
1 oz. banana liqueur
3 ice cubes
2 oz. crushed ice
1 oz. club soda, chilled

Combine coffee liqueur, banana liqueur, and ice cubes in shaker, and shake vigorously. Put crushed ice in glass. Strain into glass. Top with soda. *Kamora Coffee Liqueur, James B. Beam Distilling Co., Chicago, Ill.*

CANDY CANE
(Christmas drink)
A 4-oz. cocktail glass, chilled

1½ oz. Cherry Marnier
1½ oz. Minttu Peppermint Schnaapps
3 ice cubes
1 small candy cane

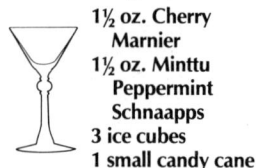

Combine all ingredients in shaker, and shake vigorously. Strain into glass. Garnish with candy cane. *Grand Hyatt Hotel, New York, N.Y.*

CASABLANCA
A 6-oz. cocktail glass or wine glass, chilled

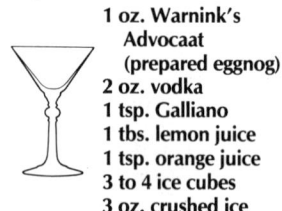

1 oz. Warnink's Advocaat (prepared eggnog)
2 oz. vodka
1 tsp. Galliano
1 tbs. lemon juice
1 tsp. orange juice
3 to 4 ice cubes
3 oz. crushed ice

Combine all ingredients except crushed ice in shaker, and shake vigorously. Put crushed ice in glass and strain into glass. *Warnink's Advocaat, London, England*

CAT'S MEOW
A 4-oz. cocktail glass, chilled

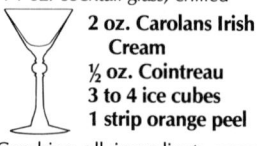

2 oz. Carolans Irish Cream
½ oz. Cointreau
3 to 4 ice cubes
1 strip orange peel

Combine all ingredients except orange peel in shaker, and shake well. Strain into glass. Garnish with orange peel. *Carolans, Cointreau: Renfield Importers Ltd., New York, N.Y.*

CHERRY COLA
A highball glass, chilled

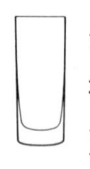

Ice cubes to fill highball glass
1 oz. Cherry Heering liqueur
3 to 4 oz. cola, chilled
1 maraschino cherry
1 lime wedge

Fill highball glass with ice. Add Cherry Heering liqueur. Fill with cola. Garnish with cherry and lime wedge. *Cherry Heering, W.A. Taylor & Co., Miami, Fla.*

CHERRY SPARKLER
A highball glass, chilled

Ice cubes to fill highball glass
1 oz. Cherry Heering liqueur
1 tbs. lemon or lime juice
3 or 4 oz. tonic water, chilled
1 thin slice lemon or lime

Fill glass with ice. Add Cherry Heering liqueur, lemon or lime juice, and tonic and stir. Garnish with lemon or lime slice. *Cherry Heering, W.A. Taylor & Co., Miami, Fla.*

COLD FEET
An old-fashioned glass, chilled

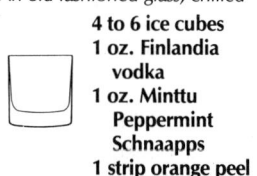

4 to 6 ice cubes
1 oz. Finlandia vodka
1 oz. Minttu Peppermint Schnaapps
1 strip orange peel

Place ice cubes in glass. Add vodka and peppermint schnapps and stir. Twist orange peel over drink to release oil, and drop it in. *Minttu Peppermint Schnaapps, Great Vintners International, Syosset, N.Y.*

CHINCHILLA
A 4-oz. cocktail glass, chilled

¾ oz. Benedictine
¾ oz. triple sec
¾ oz. light cream
4 oz. cracked ice

Combine all ingredients in shaker, shake vigorously, and strain into glass. *Julius Wile Sons & Co., Div. of Beverage Group of Nabisco Products, Inc., Lake Success, N.Y.*

CHOCOLATE MINT SMOOTHIE
A highball glass, chilled

1 oz. Vander Mint liqueur
1 oz. peppermint schnapps
2½ scoops chocolate ice cream
1 tbs. whipped cream
2 chocolate mints
1 tsp. shaved bittersweet chocolate

Combine Vander Mint liqueur, peppermint schnapps, and ice cream in glass, and stir until smooth. Top with whipped cream, mints, and shaved chocolate. *Philander's, Oak Park, Ill.*

CLAIRE'S DELIGHT

A wine glass (12- to 14-oz.), chilled

1½ scoops vanilla ice cream
1½ oz. milk
1 oz. Midori melon liqueur
½ oz. crème de noyaux
1 small slice melon
1 tbs. whipped cream
1 maraschino cherry

Combine ice cream, milk, melon liqueur, and crème de noyaux in blender, and blend until smooth. Pour drink into glass. Garnish with melon slice, whipped cream, and cherry. *Biltmore Plaza, Providence, R.I.*

COOL BANANA

A 4-oz. cocktail glass, chilled

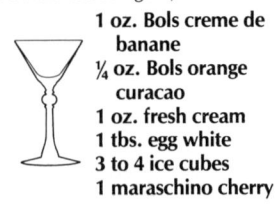

1 oz. Bols creme de banane
¼ oz. Bols orange curacao
1 oz. fresh cream
1 tbs. egg white
3 to 4 ice cubes
1 maraschino cherry

Combine all ingredients except cherry in shaker, and shake vigorously. Strain into glass. Garnish with cherry. *Bob Butaga, Ritz Hotel, Picadilly, London, England*

CREAM of MELON

A 4-oz. cocktail glass, chilled

1 oz. Mikha melon liqueur
½ oz. Taaka vodka
2 oz. half and half cream
3 to 4 ice cubes

Combine all ingredients in shaker, and shake vigorously. Strain into glass. *Mikha Melon Liqueur and Taaka Vodka, The Sazerac Co., Inc., New Orleans, La.*

CREAMSICLE

A 10- to 14-oz. tall glass, chilled

Ice cubes to fill tall glass to ½ level
1½ oz. 43 Liqueur
1½ oz. milk
3 oz. orange juice, chilled

Place ice in glass to ½ level. Add remaining ingredients and stir. *"Creamsicle"® is a registered trademark of Popsicle Industries. Drink by Wellington, Ltd., Lake Success, N.Y.*

CREMA CAFÉ

A 4-oz. cocktail glass, chilled

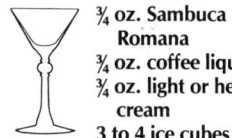

¾ oz. Sambuca Romana
¾ oz. coffee liqueur
¾ oz. light or heavy cream
3 to 4 ice cubes

Combine all ingredients in shaker, and shake vigorously. Strain into glass. *Sambuca Romana, Palmer & Lord Ltd., Syosset, N.Y*

DANISH SNOWBALL

A wine glass (8 oz. or larger), chilled

1 large scoop cherry-vanilla ice cream
4 to 5 drained dark sweet cherries
1½ oz. Cherry Heering liqueur

Place ice cream in glass. In separate small glass, combine cherries and Cherry Heering liqueur. Pour over ice cream. Serve with spoon. *Cherry Heering, W.A. Taylor & Co., Miami, Fla.*

DANDELION

A 4-oz. cocktail glass, chilled

3 oz. Tuaca liqueur
1 egg
½ tsp. superfine sugar
3 to 4 ice cubes
Freshly grated nutmeg

Combine all ingredients except nutmeg in shaker, and shake vigorously. Strain into glass. Top with sprinkle of nutmeg.

ECLIPSE

An old-fashioned glass, chilled

1 maraschino cherry
3 to 4 tsp. grenadine
1 oz. gin
1½ oz. sloe gin
3 to 4 ice cubes
1 strip orange peel

Place cherry in glass and barely cover it with grenadine. Combine gin, sloe gin, and ice in shaker, and shake vigorously. Strain slowly onto inside of glass so that it floats on grenadine. Twist orange peel over drink to release oil, and drop it in.

ERMINE TAIL
A pony glass

1 oz. Sambuca Romana
½ oz. heavy cream
Instant espresso coffee powder

Pour Sambuca Romana into glass. Add cream, pouring it over back of spoon into glass so that cream floats. Sprinkle top of drink with espresso coffee powder. *Sambuca Romana, Palmer & Lord Ltd., Syosset, N.Y.*

FAST TANGO
A 10- to 14-oz. tall glass, chilled

1½ oz. Warnink's Advocaat (prepared eggnog)
¾ oz. orange juice
3 to 4 oz. ginger ale, chilled
About 8 oz. crushed ice
1 maraschino cherry

Fill glass to 2/3 level with ice. Add advocaat and orange juice, and stir. Add ginger ale. Garnish with cherry. *Warnink's Advocaat, London, England*

FINNIAN'S RAINBOW
A pousse café glass

½ oz. Midori melon liqueur
½ oz. yellow Chartreuse
½ oz. Cherry Heering
½ oz. dark crème de cacao
½ oz. Minttu Peppermint Schnaapps

When pouring ingredients into glass, do not jar or jiggle glass. All ingredients must be of equal quantity. Pour melon liqueur into sherry glass, and from sherry glass, pour it slowly down the inside of pousse café glass. Follow same procedure individually in order with remaining ingredients so that each ingredient is a separate layer in the glass. *Minttu Peppermint Schnaapps, Great Vintners International, Syosset, N.Y.*

FINNISH FLYER

A 4-oz. cocktail glass, chilled

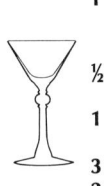

1 oz. Minttu Peppermint Schnaapps
½ oz. Sambuca Romana
1 oz. white crème de cacao
3 to 4 ice cubes
2 oz. crushed ice
1 strip lemon peel

Combine peppermint schnapps, Sambuca Romana, crème de cacao, and ice cubes in shaker, and shake well. Put crushed ice in glass and strain into glass. Twist lemon peel over drink to release oil, and drop it in. *Minttu Peppermint Schnaapps, Great Vintners International, Syosset, N.Y.*

FIRE 'N' ICE

A pony glass

½ oz. cranberry liqueur
1 oz. Minttu Peppermint Schnaapps

Pour cranberry liqueur into glass. Then slowly pour peppermint schnapps against inside of glass so that it will float on top of cranberry liqueur. *Minttu Peppermint Schnaapps, Great Vintners International, Syosset, N.Y.*

FINNISH MINTTINI

A 4-oz. cocktail glass, chilled

1 oz. Minttu Peppermint Schnaapps
1½ oz. gin
3 to 4 ice cubes
1 strip lemon peel

Combine all ingredients except lemon peel in mixing glass and stir well. Strain into glass. Twist lemon peel over drink to release oil, and drop it in. *Minttu Peppermint Schnaapps, Great Vintners International, Syosset, N.Y.*

FIRST SNOW

A 4-oz. cocktail glass, chilled

2 oz. Lakka (cloudberry) liqueur, chilled
2 to 3 tbs. whipped cream

Pour Lakka liqueur into glass. Top with whipped cream. *Lakka Liqueur, Great Vintners International, Syosset, N.Y.*

FLAMINGO ROAD

A 4-oz. cocktail glass, chilled

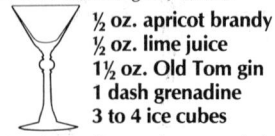

- ½ oz. apricot brandy
- ½ oz. lime juice
- 1½ oz. Old Tom gin
- 1 dash grenadine
- 3 to 4 ice cubes

Combine all ingredients in shaker, and shake vigorously. Strain into glass.

FRENCH SUMMER

A 10- to 14-oz. wine glass, chilled

- ¾ oz. Chambord Liqueur Royale
- 5 to 6 ice cubes
- 1 slice lemon
- 1 slice orange
- 3 oz. Perrier water

Combine liqueur and ice in glass. Drop fruit slices into glass. Add Perrier water and stir briefly. *Charles Jacquin et Cie., Inc., Philadelphia, Pa.*

FOREIGN AFFAIR

A 4-oz. cocktail glass, chilled

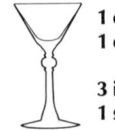

- 1 oz. brandy
- 1 oz. Sambuca Romana
- 3 ice cubes
- 1 strip lemon peel

Combine all ingredients in shaker, and shake vigorously. Strain into glass. Twist lemon peel over drink to release oil, and drop it in. *Sambuca Romana, Palmer & Lord Ltd., Syosset, N.Y.*

FRIAR TUCK

An old-fashioned glass, chilled

- 2 oz. Frangelico liqueur
- 2 oz. lemon juice
- 1 tsp. grenadine
- 5 to 6 ice cubes
- 1 thin slice orange
- 1 maraschino cherry

Combine Frangelico, lemon juice, grenadine, and 3 to 4 ice cubes in shaker, and shake well. Place 2 to 3 ice cubes in glass, and strain into glass. Garnish with orange slice and cherry. *Frangelico, William Grant & Sons, Edison, N.J.*

FROSTBITE
An old-fashioned glass, chilled

Crushed ice to fill old-fashioned glass to ¾ level
1½ oz. white crème de cacao
½ oz. Kahlua coffee liqueur
3 oz. light or heavy cream
½ oz. peppermint schnapps
3 to 4 dashes cola

Fill glass with ice to ¾ level. Add crème de cacao, coffee liqueur, and cream, and stir slowly 1 or 2 turns. Add dashes of cola, slowly, to give soda a float effect. Serve with short straw. *Resorts International Hotel Casino, Atlantic City, N.J.*

GARDEN of SWEDEN
An old-fashioned glass, chilled

1 oz. Swedish punsch liqueur
1 oz. gold rum
1 tsp. lime juice
1 tsp. pineapple juice
1 to 2 dashes grenadine
3 to 4 ice cubes
4 to 5 oz. crushed ice

Combine all ingredients except crushed ice in shaker, and shake vigorously. Fill glass to half level with crushed ice. Strain into glass.

GINNY-GIN SOUTHERN
An old-fashioned glass, chilled

1 oz. gin
1½ oz. Southern Comfort
1 tsp. lemon juice
1 tsp. grapefruit juice
5 to 7 ice cubes

Combine all ingredients except 2 to 3 ice cubes in shaker, and shake vigorously. Place reserved ice in glass, and strain into glass. *Southern Comfort Corp., St. Louis, Mo.*

GOLDEN DREAM
A whiskey sour glass, chilled

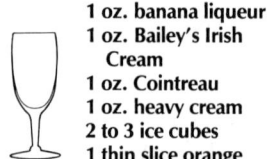

- 1 oz. banana liqueur
- 1 oz. Bailey's Irish Cream
- 1 oz. Cointreau
- 1 oz. heavy cream
- 2 to 3 ice cubes
- 1 thin slice orange
- 1 maraschino cherry

Combine all ingredients except orange slice and cherry in blender, and blend at medium speed 10 to 15 seconds. Strain into glass. Garnish with orange slice and cherry. *Kevin McKinley, Galleria, Western Hotel, Detroit, Mich.*

GRASSHOPPER
A 4-oz. cocktail glass, chilled

- ¾ oz. green crème de menthe
- ¾ oz. white crème de cacao
- 1 oz. light cream
- 3 oz. crushed ice

Combine all ingredients in shaker, and shake vigorously. Strain into glass.

ICEHOPPER

Follow recipe for Grasshopper, using ¾ oz. Minttu Peppermint Schnaapps instead of green crème de menthe. *Minttu Peppermint Schnaapps, Great Vintners International, Syosset, N.Y.*

THE GREAT DANE
A highball glass, chilled

- ½ oz. Cherry Heering liqueur
- 4 oz. orange juice, chilled
- 1½ oz. gin
- Crushed ice to fill highball glass
- 1 to 2 oz. ginger ale, chilled

Combine Cherry Heering liqueur, orange juice, and gin in glass, and stir. Fill with ice. Add ginger ale and stir. *Cherry Heering, W.A. Taylor & Co., Miami, Fla.*

GREEN DEMON
An old-fashioned glass, chilled

- 1½ oz. Pistacha liqueur
- 1½ oz. vodka
- 5 to 7 ice cubes

Combine all ingredients except 2 to 3 ice cubes in shaker, and shake vigorously. Put remaining ice in glass, and strain into glass.

GREEN MACHINE
A 4-oz. cocktail glass, chilled

1 oz. Midori melon liqueur
1 oz. light rum
1 tsp. lemon juice
½ oz. Pisang Ambon liqueur
3 to 4 ice cubes

Combine all ingredients in shaker, and shake vigorously. Strain into glass. *Pisang Ambon, Fleischmann Distilling Co., New Hyde Park, N.Y.*

GROUND ZERO
A whiskey sour glass, chilled

¾ oz. Minttu Peppermint Schnaapps
¾ oz. Bourbon
¾ oz. vodka
½ oz. Kahlua coffee liqueur
3 to 4 ice cubes
3 oz. finely crushed ice

Combine all ingredients except crushed ice in shaker, and shake vigorously. Put crushed ice in glass. Strain into glass. *Minttu Peppermint Schnaapps, Great Vintners International, Syosset, N.Y.*

H. WALKER'S SPARKPLUG
An old-fashioned glass, chilled

Crushed ice to fill old-fashioned glass
1½ oz. Hiram Walker Amaretto & Cognac
2 to 3 oz. cola, chilled
1 lime wedge

Fill glass with crushed ice. Add Amaretto & Cognac. Top glass with cola. Garnish with lime wedge. *Hiram Walker Amaretto & Cognac, Hiram Walker, Inc., Detroit, Mich.*

HARVEY SLY BANGER
A highball glass, chilled

1 oz. Galliano
1 oz. vodka
6 oz. orange juice
2 scoops vanilla ice cream

Combine all ingredients in blender, and blend thoroughly. Pour into glass. *Macchus Sly Fox, Birmingham, Mich.*

HUNGARIAN CREAM FIZZ

A 4-oz. cocktail glass, chilled

- 1 oz. Hungarian pear cordial (or Zwack Viennese)
- 1 oz. brandy
- 2 oz. milk
- 3 ice cubes
- 1 strip lemon peel

Combine all ingredients except lemon peel in shaker, and shake until frothy. Strain into glass. Twist lemon peel over drink to release oil, and drop it in. *The Bakery Restaurant, Chicago, Ill.*

ICEBREAKER

A highball glass, chilled

- 4 to 6 ice cubes
- 1½ oz. Minttu Peppermint Schnaapps
- 6 oz. club soda
- 1 strip lemon peel
- 1 strip orange peel

Place ice in glass. Add peppermint schnapps and soda, and stir slowly. Twist lemon and orange peels over drink to release oils and drop them in. *Minttu Peppermint Schnaapps, Great Vintners International, Syosset, N.Y.*

ITALIAN DREAM

A wine glass (10- to 14-oz.), chilled

- ½ oz. Venetian cream liqueur
- ½ oz. brandy
- ½ oz. Kahlua coffee liqueur
- 2 large scoops vanilla ice cream
- ¼ oz. Galliano
- 1 tbs. whipped cream
- 1 tsp. shaved chocolate

Combine Venetian cream liqueur, brandy, Kahlua coffee liqueur, and vanilla ice cream in blender, and blend until thick and creamy. Pour into glass. Float Galliano on top. Garnish with whipped cream and shaved chocolate. Serve with short straw. *Luis de la Garza, beverage manager, Royal Sonesta Hotel, New Orleans, La.*

JACKHAMMER
An old-fashioned glass, chilled

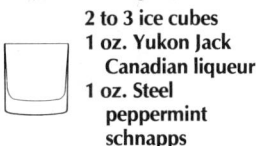

2 to 3 ice cubes
1 oz. Yukon Jack Canadian liqueur
1 oz. Steel peppermint schnapps

Place ice in glass. Add Yukon Jack Canadian liqueur and peppermint schnapps. Stir. *Yukon Jack and Steel, Heublein, Inc., Hartford, Conn.*

JACK 'N' JUICE
A highball glass, chilled

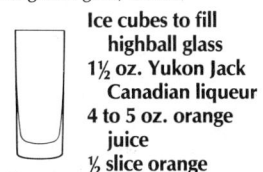

Ice cubes to fill highball glass
1½ oz. Yukon Jack Canadian liqueur
4 to 5 oz. orange juice
½ slice orange

Fill glass with ice. Add Yukon Jack Canadian liqueur. Top with orange juice. Garnish with ½ slice orange. *Yukon Jack 100 proof Imported Canadian Liqueur, Heublein, Inc., Hartford, Conn.*

JACK O'HARA
A 4-oz. cocktail glass, chilled

1½ oz. Yukon Jack Canadian liqueur
1½ oz. cranberry juice
½ tbs. lime juice
3 to 4 ice cubes

Combine all ingredients in shaker, and shake vigorously. Strain into glass. *Yukon Jack 100 proof Imported Canadian Liqueur, Heublein, Inc., Hartford, Conn.*

JELLY BEAN
(Reagan Reverie)
An old-fashioned glass, chilled

1½ oz. Pistacha liqueur
1½ oz. half and half cream
5 ice cubes
6 blanched pistachio nuts, crushed
3 to 4 jelly beans

Combine Pistacha liqueur, half and half, and 3 ice cubes in shaker, and shake vigorously. Put 2 ice cubes in glass, and strain drink into glass. Sprinkle with crushed pistachio nuts. Spear jelly beans on cocktail pick or thin stirrer and stand in drink, letting them rest on rim of glass. *Pistacha Liqueur, Cointreau Ltd., Lawrenceville, N.J.*

KAHLUA HUMMER

An 8- to 10-oz. wine glass, chilled

- 1 oz. Kahlua coffee liqueur
- 1 oz. Bacardi light rum
- 4 oz. vanilla ice cream

Combine all ingredients in blender and blend 5 to 10 seconds, until mixture is smooth. Pour into glass. Serve with short straw. *Kahlua Coffee Liqueur, Maidstone Wine & Spirits, Los Angeles, Calif.*

LADY LUCK

A 6-oz. cocktail glass, chilled

- 2 to 3 ice cubes
- ½ oz. blackberry brandy
- ½ oz. amaretto
- ½ oz. Sambuca Romana
- 2 oz. light cream

Put ice in glass. Add blackberry brandy, amaretto, Sambuca Romana, and cream. Stir slowly. *Resorts International Hotel Casino, Atlantic City, N.J.*

LAST MANGO in TEXAS

A highball glass, chilled

- 1 oz. Grand Marnier
- ½ oz. Swiss chocolate liqueur
- 1 oz. orange juice
- 2 scoops mango ice cream
- 1 thin orange slice
- 1 maraschino cherry

Combine all ingredients except orange slice and cherry in blender, and blend until smooth. Pour into glass. Garnish with orange slice and cherry. *Four Seasons Plaza National Hotel, San Antonio, Tex.*

LATANGO

A champagne glass, chilled

- 1 oz. Lamoka mocha liqueur
- 1 oz. light rum
- 1 tbs. coconut cream
- 1 oz. light or heavy cream
- 3 to 4 oz. crushed ice

Combine all ingredients in blender, and blend until smooth. Pour into glass. Serve with short straw. *Lamoka Liqueur, The Sheldon Marks Co., Los Angeles, Calif.*

LEMON DROPS

A 4-oz. cocktail glass, chilled

1 oz. Lemonier liqueur
1 oz. lemon juice
½ tsp. honey
3 oz. crushed ice
1 thin slice lemon
1 thin slice lime

Combine all ingredients except lemon and lime slices in shaker, and shake vigorously. Strain into glass. Garnish with lemon and lime slices. *Lemonier Liqueur, Bisleri Co., Milan, Italy.*

LIGHT FINNTASTIC

A 10- to 14-oz. wine glass, chilled

2 oz. instant cocoa mix
8 oz. milk
1 scoop vanilla ice cream
1 oz. Minttu Peppermint Schnaapps

Combine cocoa mix, milk, ice cream, and peppermint schnapps in blender and blend until smooth. Pour into glass. Serve with straw or spoon. *Minttu Peppermint Schnaapps, Great Vintners International, Syosset, N.Y.*

M & M COCKTAIL

A 4-oz. cocktail glass, chilled

¾ oz. Hiram Walker Swiss Chocolate Almond
¾ oz. Minttu Peppermint Schnaapps
¾ oz. Hiram Walker white crème de cacao
4 oz. finely crushed ice
2 to 3 M & M chocolate candies

Put ice in blender and drain excess water. Add Swiss Chocolate Almond liqueur, peppermint schnapps, and crème de cacao, and blend until smooth. Pour into glass. Garnish with M & M candies. *Minttu Peppermint Schnaapps, Great Vintners International, Syosset, N.Y.*

MACKENZIE GOLD

An old-fashioned glass, chilled

3 ice cubes
1½ oz. Yukon Jack Canadian liqueur
1 oz. grapefruit juice

Place ice in glass. Add remaining ingredients. *Yukon Jack 100 proof Imported Canadian Liqueur, Heublein, Inc., Hartford, Conn.*

MALIBU BEACH

A 4-oz. cocktail glass, chilled

2 oz. Malibu Coconut Rum liqueur
¾ oz. vodka
1 oz. orange juice
1 dash grenadine
3 to 4 ice cubes
1 maraschino cherry

Combine all ingredients except cherry in shaker, and shake vigorously. Strain into glass and garnish with cherry. *Tony Tighe, U.K. Bartenders Guild, and Twelve islands Shipping Co., London NW1, England*

MAN IN THE MOON

A highball glass, chilled

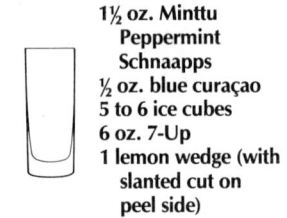

1½ oz. Minttu Peppermint Schnaapps
½ oz. blue curaçao
5 to 6 ice cubes
6 oz. 7-Up
1 lemon wedge (with slanted cut on peel side)

Combine peppermint schnapps, curaçao, and ice in glass and stir well. Add 7-Up and stir briefly. Hook lemon wedge on outside of glass so that it looks like a crescent moon. *Minttu Peppermint Schnaapps, Great Vintners International, Syosset, N.Y.*

MELANCHOLY BABY

An old-fashioned glass, chilled

6 oz. crushed ice
1½ oz. Midori melon liqueur
1 lime wedge

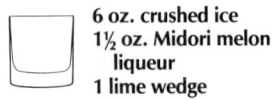

Fill glass with ice to ¾ level. Add melon liqueur. Squeeze lime wedge over drink to release juice, and drop it in. Stir slowly. *Midori Liqueur, Suntory International, Los Angeles, Calif.*

MARDI GRAS FLOAT

A 4-oz. cocktail glass, chilled

2 oz. Praline liqueur
1 oz. vodka
3 ice cubes
1 tbs. whipped cream
1 tsp. chocolate shavings
1 tsp. grated coconut

Combine Praline liqueur, vodka, and ice in mixing glass, and stir well. Strain into glass. Top with whipped cream, and sprinkle with chocolate shavings and grated coconut. *Praline Liqueur, Hiram Walker, Inc., Detroit, Mich.*

MELON BALL

A 6-oz. cocktail glass, chilled

1½ oz. Midori melon liqueur
1½ oz. pineapple juice
1½ oz. vodka
4 oz. crushed ice

Combine all ingredients in shaker, shake vigorously, and strain into glass. (Or, ingredients without crushed ice can be poured over ice cubes in old-fashioned glass.) *Windows on the World, New York, N.Y.*

MELON JAMAICAN

A highball glass, chilled

1½ oz. Kahlua coffee liqueur
1½ oz. Myers's dark rum
1½ oz. Midori melon liqueur
4 oz. piña colada liquid mix
6 ice cubes
1 pineapple spear

Combine all ingredients except 3 ice cubes and pineapple spear in shaker, and shake vigorously. Place reserved ice in glass, and strain drink into glass. Garnish with pineapple spear. *Smokey Mountains' Inn on the Plaza, Asheville, N.C.*

MELON LADY

An old-fashioned glass, chilled

3 to 4 ice cubes
1½ oz. Midori melon liqueur
1½ oz. half and half cream
2 to 3 ice cubes
Freshly grated nutmeg

Put ice in glass. Add melon liqueur and stir. Float half and half on top. Sprinkle with nutmeg. *Midori Liqueur, Suntory International, Los Angeles, Calif.*

MELON PATCH
A highball glass, chilled

4 to 5 ice cubes
½ oz. vodka
1 oz. Midori melon liqueur
½ oz. triple sec
About 4 oz. club soda, chilled
1 thin slice orange
1 slice lime

Place ice in glass. Add vodka, melon liqueur, and triple sec, and stir. Fill with soda. Garnish with orange and lime slices. *Midori Liqueur, Suntory International, Los Angeles, Calif.*

MIDNIGHT SAUNA
A 4-oz. cocktail glass, chilled

1 oz. vodka
¾ oz. Minttu Peppermint Schnaapps
½ oz. cranberry liqueur
1 dash orange bitters
3 to 4 ice cubes
2 oz. crushed ice
1 thin slice orange

Combine vodka, peppermint schnapps, cranberry liqueur, orange bitters, and ice cubes in shaker, and shake well. Put crushed ice in glass and strain into glass. Garnish with orange slice. *Minttu Peppermint Schnaapps, Great Vintners International, Syosset, N.Y.*

MIDORI COOLER
A highball glass, chilled

4 to 5 ice cubes
1½ oz. Midori melon liqueur
About 4 oz. club soda, chilled
1 slice lime

Place ice in glass. Add melon liqueur. Add soda and stir slowly. Garnish with lime slice. *Midori Liqueur, Suntory International, Los Angeles, Calif.*

MIDORI SOUR
A 4-oz. cocktail glass, chilled

2 oz. Midori melon liqueur
2 tsp. lemon juice
1 tsp. sugar syrup
3 to 4 ice cubes

Combine all ingredients in shaker, and shake vigorously. Strain into glass. *Midori Liqueur, Suntory International, Los Angeles, Calif.*

MINTTU PARFAIT
A parfait glass, chilled

- 1 oz. Minttu Peppermint Schnaapps
- ½ oz. dark crème de cacao
- 4 to 5 oz. vanilla ice cream
- 1 tbs. shaved chocolate

Combine peppermint schnapps and créme de cacao in mixing glass and stir well. Place ice cream in parfait glass and pour spirit mixture over ice cream. Top with shaved chocolate. Serve with spoon. *Minttu Peppermint Schnaapps, Great Vintners International, Syosset, N.Y.*

MINTTU SCHNAAPPSICLE®
A champagne glass, chilled

- 4 to 6 oz. fresh snow or finely crushed ice
- 1½ oz. Minttu Peppermint Schnaapps
- 1½ oz. dark crème de cacao

Lightly pack champagne glass with snow or crushed ice. Combine peppermint schnapps and crème de cacao in mixing glass, stir well, and pour over snow or ice. Serve with straw. "Schnaappsicle"® is a registered trademark of *Great Vintners International, Syosset, N.Y.*

MINTTU SHOOTER
A whiskey shot glass and highball glass, chilled

- 1½ oz. Minttu Peppermint Schnaapps
- 6 oz. beer, cold

Pour peppermint schnapps into shot glass. Pour beer into highball glass. Drink schnapps and wash with favorite beer. *Minttu Peppermint Schnaapps, Great Vintners International, Syosset, N.Y.*

MINTY MOOSE

An old-fashioned glass, chilled

> 2 tsp. unflavored gelatin
> 1½ oz. milk
> 1½ oz. Minttu Peppermint Schnaapps
> 2 tsp. dark crème de cacao
> 2 oz. crushed ice

In small saucepan, combine milk and gelatin, and stir over low heat until gelatin is dissolved. Transfer mixture to blender, add peppermint schnapps and crushed ice, and blend at low speed 15 to 20 seconds. Strain into glass, and stand drink in freezer for a few minutes to thicken. *Minttu Peppermint Schnaapps, Great Vintners International, Syosset, N.Y.*

NORTHERN LIGHTS

A 10- to 14-oz. tall glass, chilled

> Ice cubes to fill tall glass
> 1½ oz. Yukon Jack Canadian liqueur
> 3 to 4 oz. cranberry juice
> 3 to 4 oz. orange juice

Fill tall glass with ice. Pour Yukon Jack Canadian liqueur over ice. Add equal parts cranberry juice and orange juice to fill glass, and stir. *Yukon Jack 100 proof Imported Canadian Liqueur, Heublein, Inc., Hartford, Conn.*

NUTHOUSE DELIGHT

A wine glass (8-oz. or larger), chilled

> 1½ oz. Kahlua coffee liqueur
> 3 oz. vanilla ice cream
> 2 oz. milk
> 2 oz. smooth peanut butter

Combine all ingredients in blender, and blend until smooth. Pour into glass. Serve with short straw. *Smokey Mountains Inn on the Plaza, Asheville, N.C.*

NUTTY STINGER

A 4-oz. cocktail glass, chilled

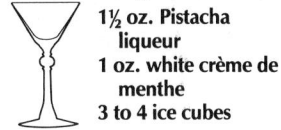

1½ oz. Pistacha liqueur
1 oz. white crème de menthe
3 to 4 ice cubes

Combine all ingredients in shaker, and shake vigorously. Strain into glass. *Pistacha Liqueur, Cointreau Ltd., Lawrenceville, N.J.*

OLD FORGE PUNCH

A highball glass, chilled

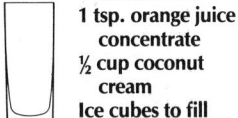

1 oz. CocoRibe liqueur
1 tsp. lemonade concentrate
1 tsp. orange juice concentrate
½ cup coconut cream
Ice cubes to fill highball glass
4 to 5 oz. club soda, chilled
1 thin slice orange
1 thin slice lemon

Combine CocoRibe liqueur, lemonade and orange juice concentrates, and coconut cream in glass, and stir well. Fill glass with ice and soda. Garnish with orange and lemon slices. Serve with straw. *The Forge Restaurant, Miami, Fla.*

143 PERCENT

A 4-oz. cocktail glass, chilled

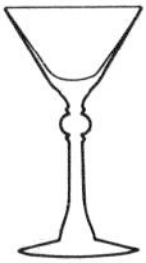

1½ oz. Swedish punsch liqueur
1 oz. 43 liqueur
1 tsp. orange juice
1 dash grenadine
3 to 4 ice cubes

Combine all ingredients in shaker, and shake vigorously. Strain into glass. *43 Liqueur, Wellington Importers, Lake Success, N.Y.*

ORANGE GALLIANT

A 4-oz. cocktail glass, chilled

½ oz. Grand Marnier
½ oz. Galliano
½ oz. grenadine
1½ oz. light or heavy cream
3 to 4 ice cubes

Combine all ingredients in shaker, and shake vigorously. Strain into glass. *Frank, bartender, Friars Club, New York, N.Y.*

ORANGE TONIC
A highball glass, chilled

Ice cubes to fill highball glass
1½ oz. De Kuyper curaçao
3 to 4 oz. tonic water, chilled
1 thin slice orange

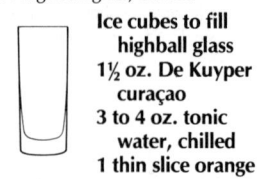

Fill glass with ice. Pour curaçao over ice. Add tonic. Garnish with orange slice. *De Kuyper Curaçao National Distillers Products Co., New York, N.Y.*

ORANGECICLE
A 10- to 14-oz. tall glass, chilled

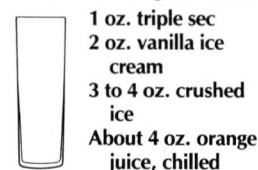

1 oz. triple sec
2 oz. vanilla ice cream
3 to 4 oz. crushed ice
About 4 oz. orange juice, chilled

Combine all ingredients except orange juice in blender, and blend until smooth. Pour into glass. Add orange juice and stir only until mixed. *Smokey Mountains' Inn on the Plaza, Asheville, N.C.*

ORGASM
A 4-oz. cocktail glass, chilled

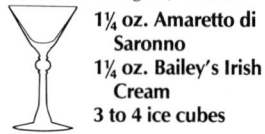

1¼ oz. Amaretto di Saronno
1¼ oz. Bailey's Irish Cream
3 to 4 ice cubes

Combine all ingredients in shaker, and shake vigorously. Strain into glass.

OXBEND BEND
A highball glass, chilled

1 dash grenadine
6 to 8 ice cubes
1 oz. Southern Comfort
½ oz. white or gold tequila
6 oz. orange juice
1 maraschino cherry

Put dash of grenadine in glass, and fill with ice. Add Southern Comfort and tequila. Top with orange juice. Do not stir. Garnish with cherry. *Jackson Lake Lodge, Grand Teton National Park, Moran, Wyo.*

PACIFIC PACIFIER
A whiskey sour glass, chilled

½ oz. light cream or half and half
½ oz. banana liqueur
1 oz. Cointreau
3 to 4 ice cubes
3 oz. finely crushed ice

Combine all ingredients except crushed ice in shaker, and shake vigorously. Put crushed ice in glass. Strain into glass. *Cointreau Ltd., Lawrenceville, N.J.*

PALM SUNDAE
A 10- to 14-oz. brandy snifter, chilled

1 oz. Malibu Coconut Rum liqueur
2 to 3 oz. crushed ice
1 dash fresh lime juice
1 dash grenadine
1 scoop vanilla ice cream
1 maraschino cherry
1 slice orange
2 straws

Combine coconut liqueur, crushed ice, lime juice, and grenadine in blender and blend at low speed 15 to 20 seconds. Strain into snifter. Add ice cream. Decorate with cherry and orange slice. Serve with 2 straws. *Tony Tighe, U.K. Bartenders Guild, and Twelve Islands Shipping Co., London NW1, England*

THE PAPPY McCOY
A highball glass, chilled

Ice cubes to fill highball glass
1 oz. Jeremiah Weed Bourbon liqueur
½ oz. José Cuervo tequila
About 4 oz. orange juice, chilled

Fill glass with ice. Add Bourbon liqueur and tequila. Top with orange juice, and stir. *Jeremiah Weed 100 proof Bourbon Liqueur, Heublein, Inc., Hartford, Conn.*

PAVAROTTI
An old-fashioned glass, chilled

1½ oz. amaretto
½ oz. brandy
2 tsp. white crème de cacao
5 to 6 ice cubes

Combine all ingredients except 2 or 3 ice cubes in shaker, and shake vigorously. Put extra ice in glass, and strain drink into glass.

PEAR SOUR
A whiskey sour glass, chilled

1½ oz. lemon juice
2½ oz. Zwack Viennese pear liqueur
1 tbs. superfine sugar
3 to 4 ice cubes
1 slice fresh or canned pear (If fresh, sprinkle with lemon juice to avoid discoloration.)

Combine lemon juice, pear liqueur, sugar, and ice cubes in shaker, and shake well. Strain into glass. Garnish with pear. *The Four Seasons Restaurant and Peartree Imports, New York, N.Y.*

PEARLS of PRALINE
A highball glass, chilled

1½ oz. Praline liqueur
1½ oz. Coco Lopez coconut cream
3 oz. light or heavy cream
4 oz. crushed ice

Combine Praline liqueur, Coco Lopez, cream, and ice in blender, and blend until smooth. Pour into glass. *Praline Liqueur, Hiram Walker, Inc., Detroit, Mich.*

PEPE LAMOKA
An old-fashioned glass, chilled

3 to 4 ice cubes
1½ oz. Lamoka mocha liqueur
1½ oz. brandy

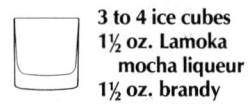

Place ice in glass. Add mocha liqueur and brandy, and stir gently. *Lamoka Liqueur, The Sheldon Marks Co., Los Angeles, Calif.*

PERSIAN MELON
An old-fashioned glass, chilled

2 to 3 ice cubes
1½ oz. Midori melon liqueur
½ oz. Pistacha liqueur
1 tsp. lime juice
3 oz. ginger ale, chilled
3 blanched pistachio nuts

Place ice in glass. Add melon liqueur, Pistacha liqueur, and lime juice, and stir slowly. Add ginger ale. Garnish with pistachio nuts. *Midori Liqueur, Suntory International, Los Angeles, Calif.*

PETE'S BANANA
A highball glass, chilled

1¼ oz. Kahlua coffee liqueur
2 scoops vanilla ice cream
½ banana, peeled and sliced, plus 1 slice for garnish
¼ tsp. fresh grated nutmeg
1 oz. milk
1 maraschino cherry

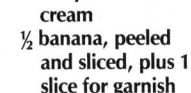

Combine all ingredients except 1 banana slice and cherry in blender, and blend until smooth. Pour into glass. Garnish with banana slice and cherry. *Four Seasons Plaza Nacional Hotel, San Antonio, Tex.*

PEUGEOT à PARIS
A 4-oz. cocktail glass, chilled

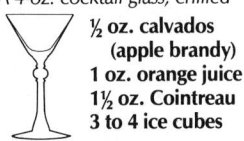

½ oz. calvados (apple brandy)
1 oz. orange juice
1½ oz. Cointreau
3 to 4 ice cubes

Combine all ingredients in shaker, and shake vigorously. Strain into glass. *Cointreau Ltd., Lawrenceville, N.J.*

POLAR BEAR
A whiskey sour glass, chilled

1 oz. banana liqueur
1 oz. Minttu Peppermint Schnaapps
1 oz. light cream
3 oz. crushed ice

Combine all ingredients in shaker, and shake vigorously. Strain into glass. *Minttu Peppermint Schnaapps, Great Vintners International, Syosset, N.Y.*

PRALINE BOURBON STREET
An old-fashioned glass, chilled

Ice cubes to fill old-fashioned glass
2 oz. Praline liqueur
1 oz. Walker's Deluxe Bourbon

Fill glass with ice. Add remaining ingredients. *Praline Liqueur, Hiram Walker, Inc., Detroit, Mich.*

POUSSE CAFÉ

A pousse café glass (not chilled)

- 1 tsp. grenadine
- 1 tsp. dark crème de cacao
- 1 tsp. maraschino liqueur
- 1 tsp. green crème de menthe
- 1 tsp. crème de violette
- 1 tsp. brandy

Because there are so may liquids to be layered, the ingredients are poured over a stirring rod instead of the standard back-of-the-spoon technique.

Pour grenadine into pousse café glass. Insert stirring rod in glass and *slowly* pour each ingredient *over stirring rod* in this order: crème de cacao, maraschino liqueur, crème de menthe, crème de violette, and brandy. Each liquid should show through the glass as a separate layer.

OTHER POUSSE CAFÉ COMBINATIONS

Follow the same technique in composing any of the following pousse café combinations:

- 2 tsp. white crème de cacao
- 2 tsp. cherry liqueur
- 2 tsp. kummel
- Top with whipped cream

or

- 2 tsp. banana liqueur
- 2 tsp. Cherry Heering
- 2 tsp. brandy

or

- 2 tsp. dark crème de cacao
- 2 tsp. coffee brandy
- 2 tsp. Sambuca Romano

or

STARS and STRIPES FOREVER
(Old Glory)
- 2 tsp. grenadine
- 2 tsp. heavy cream
- 2 tsp. Crème Yvette or crème de violette

RED LION

An old-fashioned glass, chilled

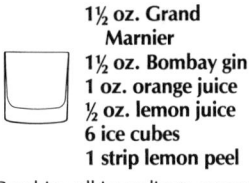

1½ oz. Grand Marnier
1½ oz. Bombay gin
1 oz. orange juice
½ oz. lemon juice
6 ice cubes
1 strip lemon peel

Combine all ingredients except 3 ice cubes and lemon peel in shaker, and shake vigorously. Put reserved ice in glass. Strain into glass. Twist lemon peel over drink to release oil, and drop it in. *Grand Marnier, Carillon Importers, New York, N.Y.*

RED RUSSIAN

An old-fashioned glass, chilled

3 ice cubes
1 oz. Cherry Heering liqueur
2 oz. vodka

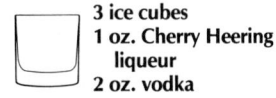

Place ice in glass. Add Cherry Heering liqueur and vodka, and stir. *Cherry Heering, W.A. Taylor & Co., Miami, Fla.*

REINDEER MILK

A 10- to 14-oz. tall glass, chilled

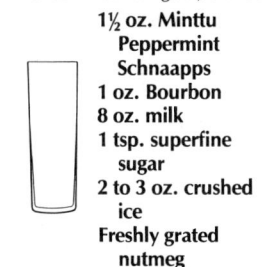

1½ oz. Minttu Peppermint Schnaapps
1 oz. Bourbon
8 oz. milk
1 tsp. superfine sugar
2 to 3 oz. crushed ice
Freshly grated nutmeg

Combine all ingredients except nutmeg in blender and blend until smooth. Pour drink into glass and top with sprinkle of nutmeg. *Minttu Peppermint Schnaapps, Great Vintners International, Syosset, N.Y.*

RHETT BUTLER

A 4-oz. cocktail glass, chilled

1½ oz. Southern Comfort
1 tbs. lime juice
1 tsp. lemon juice
1 tsp. curaçao
1 tsp. sugar syrup
3 to 4 ice cubes

Combine all ingredients in shaker, and shake vigorously. Strain into glass. *Southern Comfort Corp., St. Louis, Mo.*

RIVET

A whiskey shot glass

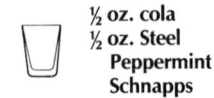

½ oz. cola
½ oz. Steel Peppermint Schnapps

Combine both ingredients in whiskey shot glass. *Steel Peppermint Schnapps, Heublein, Inc., Hartford, Conn.*

ROMAN SNOWBALL

An 8-oz. wine glass, chilled

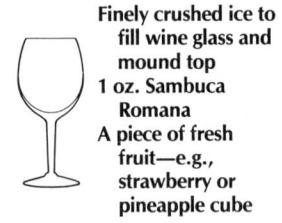

Finely crushed ice to fill wine glass and mound top
1 oz. Sambuca Romana
A piece of fresh fruit—e.g., strawberry or pineapple cube

Fill glass with finely crushed ice and mound top. Add Sambuca Romana. (Drink turns milky white, like snowball.) Garnish with fruit. Serve with short straw. *Sambuca Romana, Palmer & Lord Ltd., Syosset, N.Y.*

ROMAN STINGER

A 4-oz. cocktail glass, chilled

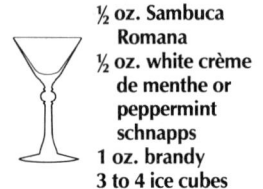

½ oz. Sambuca Romana
½ oz. white crème de menthe or peppermint schnapps
1 oz. brandy
3 to 4 ice cubes

Combine all ingredients in shaker, and shake vigorously. Strain into glass. *Sambuca Romana, Palmer & Lord Ltd., Syosset, N.Y.*

RUSTY NAIL

An old-fashioned glass, chilled

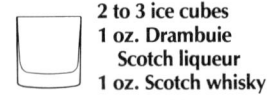

2 to 3 ice cubes
1 oz. Drambuie Scotch liqueur
1 oz. Scotch whisky

Put ice in glass. Add Drambuie and Scotch whisky, and stir. *Drambuie, W. A. Taylor & Co., Miami, Fla.*

SLALOM FRAPPÉ

A 4-oz. cocktail glass, chilled

2 oz. Minttu Peppermint Schnaapps
1 tsp. Cognac or brandy
4 oz. finely crushed ice

Combine peppermint schnapps and cognac or brandy in mixing glass and stir well. Mound crushed ice in glass and pour over ice. *Minttu Peppermint Schnaapps, Great Vintners International, Syosset, N.Y.*

SNAKEBITE

An old-fashioned glass, chilled

4 ice cubes
2 oz. Yukon Jack Canadian liqueur
1 dash lime juice

Put ice in glass. Add remaining ingredients. *Yukon Jack 100 proof Imported Canadian Liqueur, Heublein, Inc., Hartford, Conn.*

SNOWBIRD

Prepare as Slalom Frappé, using only 1 oz. peppermint schnapps and 1 oz. vodka instead of brandy.

SLOE GIN FIZZ

A wine glass (6 oz. or larger), chilled

2½ to 3 oz. sloe gin
2 tsp. lemon juice
1 tsp. superfine sugar
3 to 4 ice cubes
2 to 3 oz. club soda, chilled

Combine all ingredients except soda in shaker, and shake vigorously. Strain into glass. Add soda and stir 2 to 3 turns.

SLOW SCREW

An old-fashioned glass, chilled

Follow recipe for Screwdriver using 1½ oz. sloe gin instead of vodka.

SLOW COMFORTABLE SCREW

An old-fashioned glass, chilled

Follow recipe for Screwdriver (p. 279), using 1½ oz. sloe gin instead of vodka, plus ½ oz. Southern Comfort. *Both screws by Pauline Freelove, Secretary, U.K. Bartenders Guild, London W1R 3PJ, England*

SANTA ANA'S BANDANA

A wine glass (10- to 14-oz.), chilled

- 1¼ oz. amaretto
- ½ oz. Coco Lopez coconut cream
- 3 oz. cream
- 4 oz. crushed ice
- 1 tbs. toasted shredded coconut

Combine all ingredients except shredded coconut in blender, and blend until smooth. Pour into glass. Sprinkle toasted coconut on top. *Four Seasons Plaza Nacional Hotel, San Antonio, Tex.*

SCARLETT O'HARA

An old-fashioned glass, chilled

- ½ fresh peach, peeled, soaked in 1 tbs. Grand Marnier
- 3 tbs. lemon juice
- 1½ oz. Southern Comfort
- 3 to 4 oz. crushed ice

Combine all ingredients in blender, and blend at medium speed 15 to 20 seconds. Strain into glass. *Southern Comfort Corp., St. Louis, Mo.*

SAVOY HOTEL (Pousse Cafe)

A pony glass

- ½ oz. white crème de cacao
- ½ oz. Benedictine
- ½ oz. brandy

Each ingredient should be a separate layer in the glass. Hold glass at angle. Slowly pour crème de cacao down side of glass. Keep glass tilted and slowly pour in Benedictine; then, brandy.

SOMBRERO

An old-fashioned glass, chilled

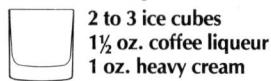

2 to 3 ice cubes
1½ oz. coffee liqueur
1 oz. heavy cream

Place ice cubes in glass and add coffee liqueur. Pour heavy cream over back of spoon into glass so that it floats. *Windows On The World Restaurants, New York, N.Y.*

STAR of BRAZIL

A whiskey sour glass, chilled

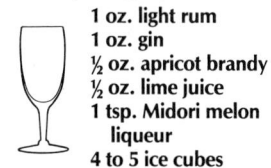

1 oz. light rum
1 oz. gin
½ oz. apricot brandy
½ oz. lime juice
1 tsp. Midori melon liqueur
4 to 5 ice cubes

Combine all ingredients in shaker, and shake vigorously. Strain into glass. *Midori, Suntory International, Los Angeles, Calif.*

STIRRUP CUP

A highball glass, chilled

1½ to 2 oz. Southern Comfort
1 oz. cranberry liqueur
1 tbs. lemon juice
5 to 7 ice cubes
3 oz. grapefruit juice
3 to 4 oz. club soda, chilled
1 or 2 mint sprigs

Combine Southern Comfort, cranberry liqueur, lemon juice, and 3 to 4 ice cubes in shaker, and shake vigorously. Place 2 to 3 ice cubes in glass, and strain mixture into glass. Add grapefruit juice. Top with soda, and stir 2 or 3 turns. Garnish with mint sprigs. *Southern Comfort Corp., St. Louis, Mo.*

STRAWBERRY FIELDS

A wine glass (10-oz. or larger), chilled

> 1¼ oz. strawberry liqueur
> ½ oz. curaçao
> ½ oz. heavy or light cream
> 1 scoop vanilla ice cream
> ½ cup fresh strawberries, plus 1 whole strawberry for garnish

Combine all ingredients in blender except 1 whole strawberry, and blend until creamy. Pour into glass. Garnish with strawberry. *Boca Raton Hotel and Club, Boca Raton, Fla.*

STREGA DAIQUIRI

A 4-oz. cocktail glass, chilled

> 1 oz. Strega liqueur
> 1 oz. light rum
> ½ oz. lemon juice
> ½ oz. orange juice
> ½ tsp. confectioners' sugar
> 4 to 6 oz. crushed ice
> 1 maraschino cherry

Combine all ingredients except cherry in blender, and blend until smooth. Pour into glass. Garnish with cherry. *Liquore Strega, Paterno Imports Ltd., Chicago, Ill.*

STREGA FREEZE

An 8-oz. or larger wine glass, chilled

> 1½ oz. Strega liqueur
> 1 oz. vodka
> 2 oz. orange juice
> 2 scoops vanilla ice cream

Combine all ingredients in blender, and blend until smooth. Pour into glass. Serve with short straw. *Liquore Strega, Paterno Imports Ltd., Chicago, Ill.*

SUISSESSE

A 4-oz. cocktail glass, chilled

> 1½ oz. anisette
> ½ oz. Pernod
> 1 dash brandy
> 1 egg white
> 3 ice cubes

Combine anisette, Pernod, brandy, egg white, and ice in shaker, and shake vigorously. Strain into glass. *The Waldorf-Astoria, New York, N.Y.*

THE SUNSHINE SPECIAL
A highball glass, chilled

- Ice cubes to fill highball glass
- 1 oz. Cherry Heering liqueur
- 1 oz. orange juice
- 1 oz. lemon juice
- 1 tsp. superfine sugar
- 1 oz. club soda, chilled
- 1 maraschino cherry
- ½ slice orange

Fill highball glass with ice. Add Cherry Heering liqueur, orange juice, lemon juice, sugar, and stir. Add soda. Garnish with cherry and orange slice. *Cherry Heering, W.A. Taylor & Co., Miami, Fla.*

SUPER BOWL COCKTAIL (Referee's Revenge)
An old-fashioned glass, chilled

- 1½ oz. Bailey's Irish Cream
- 1¼ oz. Frangelico liqueur
- 3 oz. vanilla ice cream
- 1 oz. orange juice
- 1 Oreo biscuit

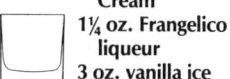

Combine all ingredients in blender, and blend until smooth (20 to 25 seconds). Pour drink, unstrained, into glass. Accompany with biscuit. *Fred Weaver, Summit Lounge, Western Hotel, Detroit, Mich.*

SWEDISH LULLABY
A 4-oz. cocktail glass, chilled

- 1½ oz. Swedish punsch liqueur
- 1 oz. Cherry Marnier
- ½ oz. lemon juice
- 3 to 4 ice cubes

Combine all ingredients in shaker, and shake vigorously. Strain into glass. *Cherry Marnier, Carillon Importers, New York, N.Y.*

TAWNY RUSSIAN
An old-fashioned glass, chilled

- 3 to 4 ice cubes
- 1 oz. De Kuyper Coconut Amaretto liqueur
- 1 oz. Gilbey's vodka

Place ice in glass. Add Coconut Amaretto liqueur and vodka, and stir. *De Kuyper, Gilbey's: National Distillers Products Co., New York, N.Y.*

THIRSTY CAMEL

An old-fashioned glass, chilled

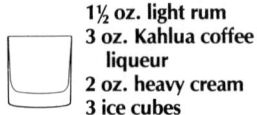

1½ oz. light rum
3 oz. Kahlua coffee liqueur
2 oz. heavy cream
3 ice cubes
1 cinnamon stick

Combine rum, coffee liqueur, heavy cream, and ice in shaker, and shake vigorously. Strain into glass. Garnish with cinnamon stick. *Kahlua, Maidstone Wine & Spirits, Inc., Universal City, Calif.*

TOASTED ALMOND

A 4-oz. cocktail glass, chilled

1½ oz. amaretto
½ oz. coffee liqueur
1 oz. heavy cream.
3 oz. crushed ice
Freshly grated nutmeg

Combine all ingredients except nutmeg in shaker, and shake well. Strain into glass. Top with sprinkle of nutmeg. *Windows On The World Restaurants, New York, N.Y.*

UNCLE MINTY

For 3 to 4 servings

Milton Berle offered this drink at the Friars Club in Los Angeles for those of us who like mint tea with more than a hint of mint. Follow recipe for Island Rum Tea, with following changes: Omit rum. Use 4 oz. Minttu Peppermint Schnaapps.

VEGAS SMILE

Any extra-large glass (20-oz.), chilled

1½ oz. dark rum
3¼ oz. Galliano
1 oz. orange juice
½ oz. pineapple juice
1 dash passion fruit juice
12 oz. crushed ice
1 maraschino cherry
1 pineapple spear

Combine rum, Galliano, orange juice, pineapple juice, passion fruit juice, and 8 oz. crushed ice in blender, and blend until smooth. Put remaining ice in 20-oz. serving glass and add blender mixture, unstrained. Garnish with cherry and pineapple spear. *Caesar's Palace, Las Vegas, Nev.*

VELVET HAMMER
A 4-oz. cocktail glass, chilled

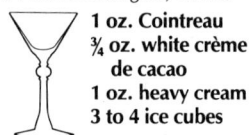

1 oz. Cointreau
¾ oz. white crème de cacao
1 oz. heavy cream
3 to 4 ice cubes

Combine all ingredients in shaker, and shake vigorously. Strain into glass. *Cointreau Ltd., Lawrenceville, N.J.*

VENETIAN BLIND
An old-fashioned glass, chilled

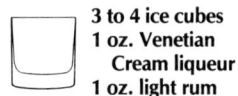

3 to 4 ice cubes
1 oz. Venetian Cream liqueur
1 oz. light rum

Place ice in glass. Add Venetian Cream and rum, and stir. *Venetian Cream, W.A. Taylor & Co., Miami, Fla.*

WALRUS
A highball glass, chilled

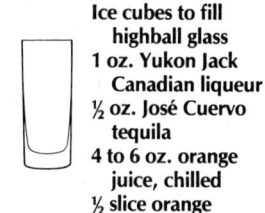

Ice cubes to fill highball glass
1 oz. Yukon Jack Canadian liqueur
½ oz. José Cuervo tequila
4 to 6 oz. orange juice, chilled
½ slice orange

Fill glass with ice. Add Yukon Jack Canadian liqueur and tequila. Top with orange juice and stir. Garnish with ½ slice orange. *Yukon Jack 100 proof Imported Canadian Liqueur, Heublein, Inc., Hartford, Conn.*

WEEKEND
An old-fashioned glass, chilled

1½ oz. Grand Marnier
½ oz. dry vermouth
1½ oz. Bombay gin
2 dashes lemon juice
3 ice cubes
1 strip lemon peel

Combine all ingredients in shaker, and shake vigorously. Strain into glass. Twist lemon peel over drink to release oil, and drop it in. *Grand Marnier; Bombay Gin: Carillon Importers, New York, N.Y.*

WELSH CONNEXION
A 4-oz. cocktail glass, chilled

- 1 oz. Malibu Coconut Rum liqueur
- ¾ oz. Bols blue curaçao
- 2 oz. orange juice
- 1 tbs. egg white
- 4 to 5 ice cubes
- 2 maraschino cherries

Created in honor of H.R.H., The Prince of Wales, in celebration of the royal wedding, 1982. When mixed, the ingredients produce the colors of the Welsh flag—red, white, and green.

Combine all ingredients except cherries in shaker, and shake vigorously. Strain into glass. Poured drink will have peak of white foam. Curaçao, now green, will fall to bottom of glass. Top drink with cherries. *Tony Tighe, Athenaeum Hotel, London, England*

WHITE CLOUD
A highball glass, chilled

- 4 ice cubes
- 1 oz. Sambuca Romana
- 4 to 6 oz. club soda, chilled

Put ice in glass. Add Sambuca Romana. Top with soda. *Sambuca Romana, Palmer & Lord Ltd., Syosset, N.Y.*

WHITE GLOVES
A 4-oz. cocktail glass, chilled

- 1½ oz. Minttu Peppermint Schnaapps
- ½ oz. light rum
- ½ oz. Cointreau
- 3 to 4 ice cubes

Combine all ingredients in shaker, and shake vigorously. Strain into glass. *Minttu Peppermint Schnaapps, Great Vintners International, Syosset, N.Y.*

WHITE LADY
A 4-oz. cocktail glass, chilled

- 2 oz. Cointreau
- 2 tsp. white crème de menthe
- 1 tbs. brandy
- 3 to 4 ice cubes

Combine all ingredients in shaker, and shake vigorously. Strain into cocktail glass. *Cointreau Ltd., Lawrenceville, N.J.*

BLACK LADY

Follow recipe for White Lady, using 2 tsp. Kahlua coffee liqueur instead of white crème de menthe.

WHITE LILY

An old-fashioned glass, chilled

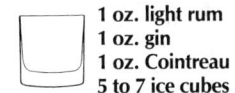

1 oz. light rum
1 oz. gin
1 oz. Cointreau
5 to 7 ice cubes

Combine all ingredients except 2 to 3 ice cubes in shaker, and shake vigorously. Put remaining ice in glass. Strain into glass. *Cointreau Ltd., Lawrenceville, N.J.*

WHITE-OUT

A 4-oz. cocktail glass, chilled

1½ oz. Cointreau
1 oz. Minttu Peppermint Schnaapps
1 tsp. brandy
3 to 4 ice cubes

Combine all ingredients in shaker, and shake well. Strain into glass. *Minttu Peppermint Schnaapps, Great Vintners International, Syosset, N.Y.*

WHITE MOUSE

A whiskey sour glass, chilled

1 oz. Minttu peppermint schnapps
½ oz. white crème de cacao
2 oz. orange juice
½ egg white
3 oz. crushed ice
½ maraschino cherry

Combine all ingredients except cherry in shaker, and shake vigorously. Strain into glass. Garnish with ½ cherry for pink nose. *Minttu Peppermint Schnaapps, Great Vintners International, Syosset, N.Y.*

WHITE VELVET

A 4-oz. cocktail glass, chilled

1½ oz. Sambuca Romana
1 egg white
1 tsp. lemon juice
3 oz. finely crushed ice

Combine all ingredients in blender, and blend at medium speed 15 to 20 seconds (or these ingredients can be combined in shaker and shaken vigorously). Strain into glass. *Sambuca Romana, Palmer & Lord Ltd., Syosset, N.Y.*

WHITE WHISKER

A 4-oz. cocktail glass, chilled

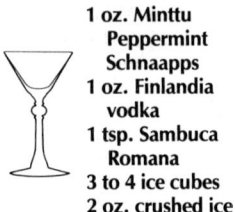

- 1 oz. Minttu Peppermint Schnaapps
- 1 oz. Finlandia vodka
- 1 tsp. Sambuca Romana
- 3 to 4 ice cubes
- 2 oz. crushed ice

Combine all ingredients except crushed ice in shaker, and shake vigorously. Put crushed ice in glass and strain drink into glass. *Minttu Peppermint Schnaapps, Great Vintners International, Syosset, N.Y.*

WIDOW'S DREAM

A 6-oz. cocktail glass, chilled

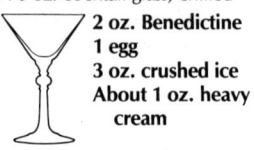

- 2 oz. Benedictine
- 1 egg
- 3 oz. crushed ice
- About 1 oz. heavy cream

Combine Benedictine, egg, and ice in shaker, and shake vigorously. Strain into glass. Top with cream and stir 2 or 3 turns. *Barbara Conwell, Food and Drink Consultant, New York, N.Y.*

RUM RECIPES

ACAPULCO No. 1
A 4-oz. cocktail glass, chilled

- ¾ oz. Meyers's dark Jamaica rum
- ¾ oz. Olmeca white tequila
- 1½ oz. pineapple juice
- 2 tsp. grapefruit juice
- 3 ice cubes
- 1 thin slice orange

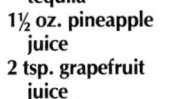

Combine all ingredients in shaker, and shake vigorously. Strain into glass. Garnish with orange slice. *Courtesy of Seagram's Complete Party Guide*

ACAPULCO No. 2
A 4-oz. cocktail glass, chilled

- 1½ oz. light rum
- 1 tbs. triple sec
- 1 tbs. lime juice
- 1 tsp. superfine sugar
- 1 egg white
- 3 to 4 ice cubes
- 3 mint leaves

Combine all ingredients except mint leaves in shaker, and shake vigorously. Strain into glass. Float mint leaves.

ADIÓS, MUCHACHOS
An old-fashioned glass, chilled

- ¾ oz. El Presidente Mexican brandy
- ¼ oz. sweet vermouth
- ¼ oz. white or gold tequila
- 1 oz. light rum
- 2 tsp. lime juice
- 3 to 4 ice cubes

Sugar-frost rim of old-fashioned glass. Combine all ingredients in shaker, and shake vigorously. Strain into prepared glass. *El Presidente Brandy, Domecq Importers, Inc., Larchmont, N.Y.*

ANKLE BREAKER
An old-fashioned glass, chilled

- 1 oz. cherry brandy
- ¾ oz. lemon juice
- 1 to 1½ oz. Jamaica over-proof rum (131-proof)
- 2 tsp. sugar syrup
- 3 to 4 ice cubes

Combine all ingredients in shaker, and shake vigorously. Strain into glass.

ANDALUSIA
A 4-oz. cocktail glass, chilled

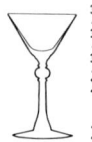

- ¾ oz. brandy
- ¾ oz. dry sherry
- ¾ oz. light rum
- 2 to 3 dashes Angostura bitters
- 3 to 4 ice cubes

Combine all ingredients in mixing glass, and stir well. Strain into glass.

APPLE PIE
A 4-oz. cocktail glass, chilled

- 1½ oz. light rum
- ¾ oz. sweet vermouth
- 2 tbs. calvados (apple brandy)
- 1 dash grenadine
- 1 tsp. lemon juice
- 3 to 4 ice cubes

Combine all ingredients in shaker, and shake vigorously. Strain into glass.

APRICOT PIE

Follow recipe for above Apple Pie, using 2 tbs. apricot brandy instead of calvados.

APRICOT LADY
An old-fashioned glass, chilled

1½ oz. Barbados rum (full-bodied)
½ oz. triple sec
1 egg white
2 to 3 oz. apricot nectar (or 1 oz. apricot liqueur)
4 oz. crushed ice

Combine all ingredients except 2 oz. ice in shaker, and shake vigorously (or these ingredients can be combined in blender; blend at low speed 15 to 20 seconds). Put reserved ice in glass. Strain drink into glass.

ARRIBA
A 4-oz. cocktail glass, chilled

1 oz. coffee brandy
1 oz. light rum
½ oz. light or heavy cream
3 to 4 ice cubes

Combine all ingredients in shaker, and shake vigorously. Strain into glass.

AUNT AGATHA
An old-fashioned glass or 6-oz. cocktail glass, chilled

3 to 4 oz. orange juice, chilled
1½ to 2 oz. light rum
2 to 3 ice cubes
1 dash Angostura bitters
½ slice orange

Combine all ingredients except bitters and orange slice in glass, and stir slowly. Dot surface of drink with bitters. Garnish with orange slice.

BACARDI AMERICAN FLYER

A 4-oz. cocktail glass, chilled

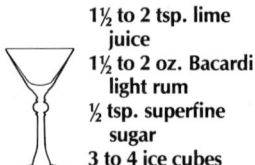

1½ to 2 tsp. lime juice
1½ to 2 oz. Bacardi light rum
½ tsp. superfine sugar
3 to 4 ice cubes
2 oz. dry sparkling wine, chilled

Combine all ingredients except wine in shaker, and shake vigorously. Strain into glass. Add wine. Stir quickly. *Bacardi Imports, Inc., Miami, Fla.*

BACARDI ANCIENT MARINER

An old-fashioned glass, chilled

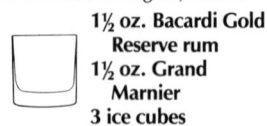

1½ oz. Bacardi Gold Reserve rum
1½ oz. Grand Marnier
3 ice cubes

Place ice in glass. Pour rum and Grand Marnier over ice and stir. *Bacardi Imports, Inc., Miami, Fla.*

BACARDI BANANA DAIQUIRI

A 4-oz. cocktail glass, chilled

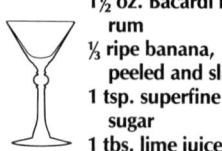

1½ oz. Bacardi light rum
⅓ ripe banana, peeled and sliced
1 tsp. superfine sugar
1 tbs. lime juice
4 oz. crushed ice

Combine all ingredients in blender, and blend 15 to 20 seconds (until smooth but still thick). Pour into glass. *Bacardi Imports, Inc., Miami, Fla.*

BACARDI COCKTAIL

A 4-oz. cocktail glass, chilled

1 tsp. lime juice
2 dashes grenadine
1 to 1½ oz. Bacardi light rum
3 to 4 ice cubes

Combine all ingredients in shaker, and shake vigorously. Strain into glass. *Bacardi Imports, Inc., Miami, Fla.*

BACARDI ORIGINAL DAIQUIRI

A 4-oz. cocktail glass, or old-fashioned glass, chilled

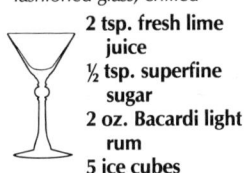

2 tsp. fresh lime juice
½ tsp. superfine sugar
2 oz. Bacardi light rum
5 ice cubes

Sugar-frost cocktail or old-fashioned glass. Combine all ingredients except 2 ice cubes in shaker, and shake vigorously. Place remaining ice in prepared glass, and strain into glass. *Bacardi Imports, Inc., Miami, Fla.*

BACARDI DRIVER

An old-fashioned glass, chilled

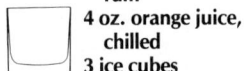

2 oz. Bacardi light rum
4 oz. orange juice, chilled
3 ice cubes
1 lemon or lime wedge

Put ice in glass. Pour rum over ice. Add orange juice and stir. Squeeze lemon or lime wedge over drink, and drop it in. *Bacardi Imports, Inc., Miami, Fla.*

BACARDI FRIO (frappé)

A 4-oz. cocktail glass, chilled

½ oz. banana liqueur
1 tbs. orange juice
1 oz. Bacardi light rum
About 6 oz. finely crushed ice

Combine all ingredients except 3 oz. crushed ice in shaker, and shake vigorously. Fill glass to half level with reserved ice. Strain into glass. *Bacardi Imports, Inc., Miami, Fla.*

BACARDI MONKEY WRENCH

A highball glass, chilled

6 ice cubes
3 oz. Bacardi light rum
4 to 5 oz. grapefruit juice, chilled

Place ice in glass. Pour rum over ice. Add grapefruit juice and stir. *Bacardi Imports, Inc., Miami, Fla.*

BACARDI STRAWBERRY DAIQUIRI

Follow recipe for Bacardi Banana Daiquiri (see pg. 214), using 5 large fresh or frozen strawberries instead of banana ingredient. *Bacardi Imports, Inc., Miami, Fla.*

BATIDA de PIÑA
A 10- to 14-oz. tall glass, chilled

2½ to 3 oz. Jamaica dark rum
4 to 6 oz. crushed pineapple
½ tsp. superfine sugar
4 oz. crushed ice
2 to 3 ice cubes
1 mint sprig

Combine rum, pineapple, sugar, and crushed ice in blender, and blend at high speed 25 to 30 seconds. Place ice cubes in glass and pour in blender mixture, unstrained. Garnish with mint sprig.

BEACH BLANKET
A 4-oz. cocktail glass, chilled

1 oz. light rum
1 oz. Southern Comfort
1 tbs. curaçao
1 tsp. lemon juice
1 to 2 dashes orange bitters
3 to 4 ice cubes

Combine all ingredients in shaker, and shake vigorously. Strain into glass.

BEAUTY AND THE BEACH

Follow recipe for Beach Blanket, using 1 tbs. Grand Marnier instead of curaçao.

BEACH BUM
An old-fashioned glass, chilled

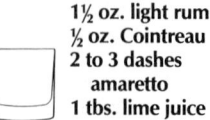

1½ oz. light rum
½ oz. Cointreau
2 to 3 dashes amaretto
1 tbs. lime juice
4 oz. crushed ice
2 to 3 ice cubes

Combine all ingredients except ice cubes in shaker, and shake vigorously. Place ice cubes in glass, and strain into glass.

BEE'S KISS
A 4-oz. cocktail glass, chilled

2 oz. light rum
1 tsp. honey
1 tsp. heavy cream
3 to 4 ice cubes

Combine all ingredients in shaker, and shake vigorously. Strain into glass.

BLACK MAGIC
A 4-oz. cocktail glass, chilled

1½ oz. Jamaica dark rum
1 oz. Tia Maria coffee liqueur
2 tsp. lime juice
3 to 4 ice cubes

Combine all ingredients in shaker, and shake vigorously. Strain into glass.

BLACK MARIA
An old-fashioned glass, chilled

1½ oz. gold rum
1½ oz. Tia Maria coffee liqueur
½ tsp. instant coffee powder
½ tsp. superfine sugar
3 to 4 oz. crushed ice

In glass, combine rum, coffee liqueur, instant coffee powder, and sugar, and stir until coffee and sugar are dissolved. Add ice and stir again—slowly.

BLACK SAPPHIRE
A 4-oz. cocktail glass, chilled

2 oz. Bacardi añejo (aged) rum
1 tsp. apricot brandy
2 to 3 tsp. pineapple juice
1 tsp. Bacardi Gold Reserve rum
3 to 4 ice cubes

Combine all ingredients in shaker, and shake vigorously. Strain into glass.

BLACK STRIPE
An old-fashioned glass, chilled

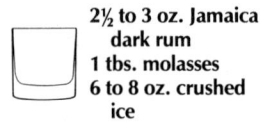

2½ to 3 oz. Jamaica dark rum
1 tbs. molasses
6 to 8 oz. crushed ice

Combine all ingredients in shaker, and shake vigorously (or ingredients can be combined in blender and blended at medium speed 15 to 20 seconds). Pour mixture, unstrained, into glass.

BOLERO
An old-fashioned glass, chilled

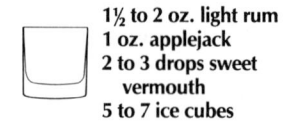

1½ to 2 oz. light rum
1 oz. applejack
2 to 3 drops sweet vermouth
5 to 7 ice cubes

Combine all ingredients except 2 or 3 ice cubes in shaker, and shake vigorously. Place remaining ice in glass. Strain into glass.

BLUE MOUNTAIN
An old-fashioned glass, chilled

1½ oz. Jamaica dark rum
¾ oz. Tia Maria coffee liqueur
½ to ¾ oz. vodka
2 tbs. orange juice
5 to 7 ice cubes

Combine all ingredients except 2 or 3 ice cubes in shaker, and shake vigorously. Place remaining ice in glass. Strain into glass.

BROWN DERBY
An old-fashioned glass, chilled

½ oz. lime juice
1 tsp. maple syrup
1½ oz. Meyers's dark Jamaican rum
5 ice cubes
1 slice lime

Combine all ingredients except 2 ice cubes and lime slice in shaker, and shake vigorously. Place reserved ice in glass. Strain into glass. Garnish with lime slice.
Courtesy of Seagram's Complete Party Guide

BUENAS NOCHES

A 4-oz. cocktail glass, chilled

1½ oz. Jamaica dark rum
½ oz. Kahlua coffee liqueur
2 tsp. heavy cream
3 to 4 ice cubes

Combine all ingredients in shaker, and shake vigorously. Strain into glass.

BUSHRANGER

A 4-oz. cocktail glass, chilled

1 oz. light rum
1 oz. Dubonnet aperitif
2 to 3 dashes Angostura bitters
3 to 4 ice cubes

Combine all ingredients in shaker, and shake vigorously. Strain into glass.

CAFETAL

A highball glass, chilled

1 oz. half and half or light cream
1 tsp. superfine sugar
1½ oz. light rum
1 oz. Tia Maria coffee liqueur
4 oz. crushed ice
Ground cinnamon

Combine all ingredients except cinnamon in shaker, and shake well. Pour mixture, unstrained, into glass. Sprinkle cinnamon on top of drink. *Jorge Pagan, bartender, 1981 Gold Medal winner at Caribe Hilton, San Juan, P.R.*

CANEY

Papaya cup: Cut thin slice off bottom of papaya so that it will stand steady. Cut top third off papaya. Remove seeds and carefully scoop out pulp from bottom ⅔ section, leaving ¼-inch shell. Chill papaya cup while preparing drink mixture.

- 1 yellow-ripe but firm Hawaiian papaya (5 to 6 inches long)
- 2 oz. half and half cream
- 1 tsp. superfine sugar
- 1½ oz. light rum
- ¾ oz. apricot brandy
- 8 oz. crushed ice
- Garnish: fresh flower blossom

In blender, combine 3 to 4 tbs. papaya pulp, half and half, and sugar, and blend. Add rum and apricot brandy, and blend again. Add ice and blend 20 to 30 seconds, or until smooth. Pour, unstrained, into papaya cup. Garnish with fresh flower blossom. Serve with short straw. *Jorge Pagan, Beverage Salon Prix d'Honneur at Caribe Hilton, San Juan, P.R.*

CASA BLANCA

A 4-oz. cocktail glass, chilled

- 2 oz. Appleton gold rum
- ¼ tsp. curaçao
- ¼ tsp. maraschino liqueur
- ¾ tsp. lime juice
- 1 dash Angostura bitters
- 3 to 4 ice cubes

Combine all ingredients in shaker, and shake vigorously. Strain into glass.

CASINO COOLER

A 10- to 14-oz. tall glass, chilled

- 3 to 4 ice cubes
- ½ oz. crème de bananes
- ¼ oz. Rose's lime juice
- 1½ oz. dark rum
- 4 to 5 oz. pineapple juice
- 1 dash grenadine
- ½ slice orange
- 1 maraschino cherry

Place ice in glass. Combine crème de bananes, lime juice, rum, and pineapple juice in shaker, and shake well. Strain into glass. Top with grenadine. Garnish with orange and cherry. *Resorts International Hotel Casino, Atlantic City, N.J.*

CHA-CHA-CHA

An old-fashioned glass, chilled

- 2 to 2½ oz. light rum
- ½ oz. pineapple liqueur
- 1 oz. lime juice
- 1 tbs. triple sec
- 5 to 7 oz. crushed ice
- 1 slice lime

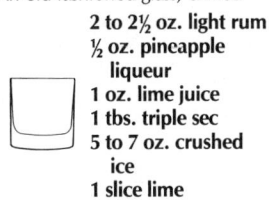

In shaker, combine rum, pineapple liqueur, lime juice, triple sec, and 3 to 4 oz. ice, and shake vigorously. Put remaining ice in glass. Strain into glass. Garnish with lime slice.

CHERRY RUM DAIQUIRI

A 4-oz. cocktail glass, chilled

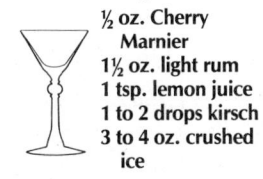

- ½ oz. Cherry Marnier
- 1½ oz. light rum
- 1 tsp. lemon juice
- 1 to 2 drops kirsch
- 3 to 4 oz. crushed ice

Combine all ingredients in shaker, and shake vigorously. Strain into glass.

CHINA

A 4-oz. cocktail glass, chilled

- 2 oz. gold rum
- 1 tsp. curaçao
- 3 to 4 drops grenadine
- 1 tbs. passion fruit juice or syrup
- 2 to 3 dashes Angostura bitters
- 3 to 4 ice cubes

Combine all ingredients in shaker, and shake vigorously. Strain into glass.

CHOCOLATE RUM

An old-fashioned glass, chilled

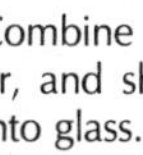

- 1½ oz. light rum
- ¾ oz. white crème de cacao
- ¾ oz. white crème de menthe
- 1 tbs. heavy cream
- 1 tbs. over-proof rum (151-proof)
- 4 to 5 ice cubes

Combine all ingredients in shaker, and shake vigorously. Strain into glass.

CHRISTOPHER COLUMBUS

An old-fashioned glass, chilled

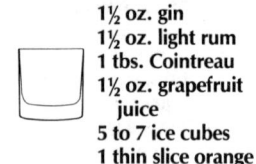

- 1½ oz. gin
- 1½ oz. light rum
- 1 tbs. Cointreau
- 1½ oz. grapefruit juice
- 5 to 7 ice cubes
- 1 thin slice orange

Combine all ingredients except 2 or 3 ice cubes and orange slice in shaker, and shake vigorously. Place remaining ice in glass. Strain into glass. Garnish with orange slice.

CLOCK and DAGGER

An old-fashioned glass, chilled

- 2 oz. Jamaica dark rum
- 1 to 2 dashes orange bitters
- 1 tsp. vodka
- 1 tsp. Bourbon
- 3 to 4 ice cubes
- 3 to 4 oz. cola, chilled
- 1 strip lime peel

In shaker, combine rum, bitters, vodka, Bourbon, and ice cubes, and shake vigorously. Strain into glass. Fill with cola. Twist lime peel over drink to release oil, and drop it in.

COCKATOO

A 4-oz. cocktail glass, chilled

- ¾ oz. banana liqueur
- 1 oz. Appleton gold rum
- ¾ oz. Pernod
- 3 to 4 ice cubes

Combine all ingredients in shaker, and shake vigorously. Strain into glass.

COLUMBIA

A 4-oz. cocktail glass, chilled

- 1½ oz. light rum
- ¾ oz. raspberry liqueur
- 1 tsp. kirsch
- ½ oz. lemon juice
- 3 to 4 ice cubes

First, sugar-frost rim of cocktail glass. Combine all ingredients in shaker, and shake vigorously. Strain into glass.

CORKSCREW
A 4-oz. cocktail glass, chilled

1½ oz. light rum
½ oz. peach liqueur
1 tbs. dry vermouth
3 or 4 ice cubes

Combine all ingredients in shaker, and shake vigorously. Strain into glass.

CREOLE WOMAN
An old-fashioned glass, chilled

2 to 3 ice cubes
1½ oz. light rum
2 dashes Tabasco sauce
1 tsp. lime juice
3 to 4 oz. beef bouillon
1 dash celery salt
1 cucumber spear

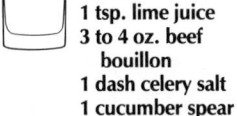

Place ice in glass. Add rum, Tabasco sauce, lime juice, and beef bouillon, and stir. Sprinkle celery salt on top, and garnish with cucumber spear.

CROWN JEWEL
A 10- to 14-oz. wine glass, chilled

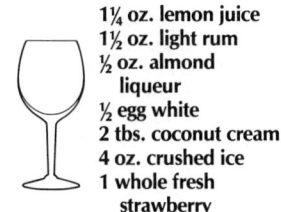

1¼ oz. lemon juice
1½ oz. light rum
½ oz. almond liqueur
½ egg white
2 tbs. coconut cream
4 oz. crushed ice
1 whole fresh strawberry

Combine all ingredients except strawberry in blender, and blend until smooth and creamy. Pour, unstrained, into glass. Float strawberry on top. *Fairmont Hotel, San Francisco, Calif.*

CUBA LIBRE
A highball glass, chilled

4 to 6 ice cubes
1 tbs. lime juice
1½ to 2½ oz. light rum
4 to 5 oz. cola, chilled
1 slice lime

Place ice in glass. Add lime juice and rum. Add cola and stir. Garnish with lime slice.

CUBA LIBRE COCKTAIL

A 4-oz. cocktail glass, chilled

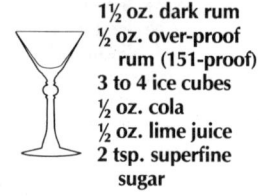

1½ oz. dark rum
½ oz. over-proof rum (151-proof)
3 to 4 ice cubes
½ oz. cola
½ oz. lime juice
2 tsp. superfine sugar

Combine dark and over-proof rums and ice cubes in shaker, and shake well. Add cola, lime juice, and sugar, and stir until sugar is dissolved. Strain into glass. *The Forge Restaurant., Miami, Fla.*

CUBAN COCKTAIL SPECIAL

An old-fashioned glass, chilled

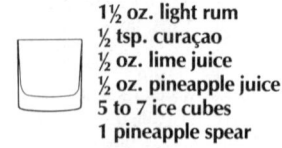

1½ oz. light rum
½ tsp. curaçao
½ oz. lime juice
½ oz. pineapple juice
5 to 7 ice cubes
1 pineapple spear

Combine all ingredients except 3 ice cubes and pineapple spear in shaker, and shake vigorously. Place remaining ice in glass. Strain into glass. Garnish with pineapple spear.

DRY HOLE

A highball glass, chilled

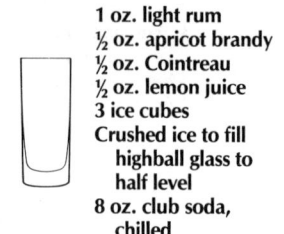

1 oz. light rum
½ oz. apricot brandy
½ oz. Cointreau
½ oz. lemon juice
3 ice cubes
Crushed ice to fill highball glass to half level
8 oz. club soda, chilled

Combine all ingredients except crushed ice and soda in shaker, and shake vigorously. Fill glass with crushed ice to half level. Strain into glass. Top with soda. *Petroleum Club of Houston, Houston, Tex.*

EL COQUI

A highball glass, chilled

- 1 oz. over-proof Jamaica rum (151-proof)
- 1½ oz. Jamaica gold rum
- ½ oz. triple sec
- ½ oz. white crème de cacao
- ½ oz. guava juice
- ½ oz. Mai Tai syrup
- ½ oz. lemon juice
- 2 dashes Angostura bitters
- 6 oz. crushed ice
- 1 thin slice orange
- 1 pineapple spear

Combine all ingredients except orange slice and pineapple spear in blender, and blend 20 to 30 seconds. Pour, unstrained, into glass. Garnish with orange slice and pineapple spear. *Hector Torres, bar manager, Caribe Hilton, San Juan, P.R.*

EL PRESIDENTE

A 4-oz. cocktail glass, chilled

- 1½ to 2 oz. light rum
- ¼ oz. dry vermouth
- ½ tsp. grenadine
- ¼ oz. curaçao
- 3 to 4 ice cubes

Combine all ingredients in shaker, and shake vigorously. Strain into glass.

EYE OPENER

A 4-oz. cocktail glass, chilled

- 1½ oz. light rum
- 1 tsp. triple sec
- 1 tsp. white crème de cacao
- 3 to 4 dashes Ricard (anisette aperitif)
- 1 tsp. Falernum syrup or sugar syrup
- 1 egg yolk
- 3 to 4 ice cubes

Combine all ingredients in shaker, and shake vigorously. Strain into glass.

FAIR and WARMER
A 4-oz. cocktail glass, chilled

2 oz. light rum
½ oz. sweet vermouth
2 to 3 dashes curaçao
3 to 4 ice cubes
1 strip lemon or orange peel

Combine all ingredients except lemon or orange peel in shaker, and shake vigorously. Strain into glass. Twist lemon or orange peel over drink to release oil, and drop it in.

FALERNUM SOUR
An old-fashioned glass, chilled

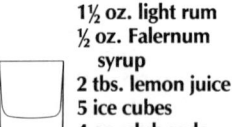

1½ oz. light rum
½ oz. Falernum syrup
2 tbs. lemon juice
5 ice cubes
4 oz. club soda, chilled
1 thin slice orange

In shaker, combine rum, Falernum syrup, lemon juice, and 3 ice cubes, and shake vigorously. Place remaining ice in glass. Strain into glass. Add soda, and garnish with orange slice. *Falernum, The Sazerac Co., New Orleans, La.*

FIG LEAF
A 4-oz. cocktail glass, chilled

1½ oz. sweet vermouth
1½ oz. light rum
1 tbs. lemon juice
2 dashes Angostura bitters
3 to 4 ice cubes
1 maraschino cherry

Combine all ingredients except cherry in shaker, and shake vigorously. Strain into glass. Garnish with cherry.

FIRST LADY
A wine glass (8-oz. or larger), chilled

1½ oz. light rum
½ oz. Minttu Peppermint Schnaapps
1 oz. mango nectar
3 oz. crushed ice
2 drops grenadine

Combine all ingredients except grenadine in shaker, and shake vigorously. Strain into glass. Top with 2 drops grenadine. *Minttu Peppermint Schnaapps, Great Vintners International, Syosset, N.Y.*

FREE SILVER

A highball glass, chilled

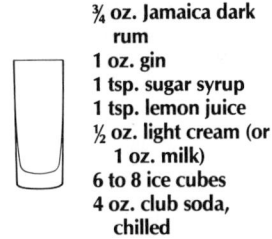

- ¾ oz. Jamaica dark rum
- 1 oz. gin
- 1 tsp. sugar syrup
- 1 tsp. lemon juice
- ½ oz. light cream (or 1 oz. milk)
- 6 to 8 ice cubes
- 4 oz. club soda, chilled

In shaker, combine rum, gin, sugar syrup, lemon juice, cream (or milk), and 3 or 4 ice cubes, and shake vigorously. Place remaining ice in glass. Strain mixture into glass. Top with soda.

FROZEN MINT DAIQUIRI

A wine glass (8-oz. or larger), or old-fashioned glass, chilled

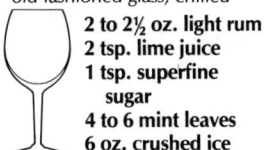

- 2 to 2½ oz. light rum
- 2 tsp. lime juice
- 1 tsp. superfine sugar
- 4 to 6 mint leaves
- 6 oz. crushed ice

Combine all ingredients in blender, and blend at medium speed 15 to 20 seconds. Pour mixture into glass. Serve with straw.

GAUGUIN

A cocktail or wine glass (6-oz. or larger), or old-fashioned glass, chilled

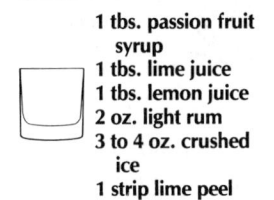

- 1 tbs. passion fruit syrup
- 1 tbs. lime juice
- 1 tbs. lemon juice
- 2 oz. light rum
- 3 to 4 oz. crushed ice
- 1 strip lime peel

Combine all ingredients except lime peel in blender, and blend at medium speed 10 to 15 seconds. Pour, unstrained, into glass. Twist lime peel over drink to release oil, and drop it in.

GILDED CAGE

A 4-oz. cocktail glass, chilled

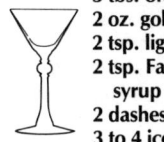

- 3 tbs. orange juice
- 2 oz. gold rum
- 2 tsp. light rum
- 2 tsp. Falernum syrup
- 2 dashes lemon juice
- 3 to 4 ice cubes

Combine all ingredients in shaker, and shake vigorously. Strain into glass.

HAIL CAESAR!
A whole pineapple shell, chilled

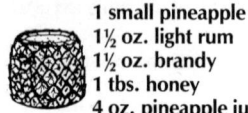

- 1 small pineapple
- 1½ oz. light rum
- 1½ oz. brandy
- 1 tbs. honey
- 4 oz. pineapple juice
- 3 ice cubes

Cut off leaf top of pineapple. Cut out pineapple pulp, leaving hollowed-out fruit container. Crush 4 tbs. pineapple pulp and set aside remaining pulp for other use. In blender, combine crushed pulp plus all remaining ingredients and blend until smooth. Strain mixture into pineapple container. Serve with straw. *Caesar's Palace, Las Vegas, Nev.*

HART BREAKER
A highball glass, chilled

- 8 ice cubes
- 4 oz. bitter lemon soda, chilled
- 1½ oz. Lemon Hart Demerera Rum

Place ice in glass. Add soda and rum, and stir slowly. *Julius Wile Sons, Div. Nabisco Products, Inc., New York, N.Y.*

HAVANA CLUB
A 4-oz. cocktail glass, chilled

- 2½ oz. light rum
- ½ oz. dry vermouth
- 3 to 4 ice cubes

Combine all ingredients in shaker, and shake vigorously. Strain into glass.

HOLY MOLEY
A 4-oz. cocktail glass, chilled

- 1½ oz. light rum
- 2 tbs. Kahlua coffee liqueur
- 1 dash curaçao
- 2 tbs. dark crème de cacao
- 3 to 4 ice cubes

Combine all ingredients in shaker, and shake vigorously. Strain into glass.

HONEY BEE

A 4-oz. cocktail glass, chilled

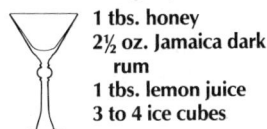

1 tbs. honey
2½ oz. Jamaica dark rum
1 tbs. lemon juice
3 to 4 ice cubes

Combine all ingredients in shaker, and shake vigorously. Strain into glass.

HONEYSUCKLE (Air Mail)

Follow recipe for above Honey Bee, using 1½ oz. Puerto Rico light rum instead of Jamaica dark rum.

HURRICANE

A 4-oz. cocktail glass, chilled

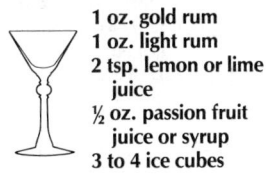

1 oz. gold rum
1 oz. light rum
2 tsp. lemon or lime juice
½ oz. passion fruit juice or syrup
3 to 4 ice cubes

Combine all ingredients in shaker, and shake vigorously. Strain into glass.

ICE CREAM COLADA

A 12- to 14-oz. wine glass, chilled

1½ oz. light rum
½ oz. banana, melon, or strawberry liqueur
2 scoops vanilla ice cream
4 oz. crushed pineapple
3 oz. coconut cream
1 oz. heavy cream
1 tsp. shredded coconut

Combine all ingredients except shredded coconut in blender, and blend until mixture is smooth. Pour into glass. Sprinkle with shredded coconut. *Boca Raton Hotel & Club, Boca Raton, Fla.*

INDIAN PAINTBRUSH

A 14-oz. or larger brandy glass, chilled

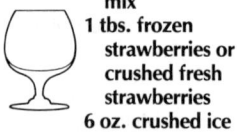

2½ oz. gold rum
5 oz. piña colada mix
1 tbs. frozen strawberries or crushed fresh strawberries
6 oz. crushed ice
1 fresh strawberry
1 pineapple cube

In blender, combine rum, piña colada mix, strawberries, and ice, and blend until smooth. Pour into glass. Garnish with fresh strawberry and pineapple cube on pick. *Strutting Grouse Restaurant, Jackson Hole Golf and Tennis Club, Grand Teton National Park, Moran, Wyo.*

JAMAICA FAREWELL

A 10- to 14-oz. tall glass, chilled

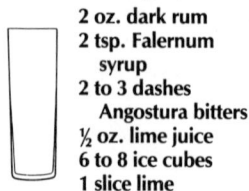

2 oz. dark rum
2 tsp. Falernum syrup
2 to 3 dashes Angostura bitters
½ oz. lime juice
6 to 8 ice cubes
1 slice lime

In glass, combine rum, syrup, bitters, lime juice, and 3 or 4 ice cubes. Stir well to mix and chill ingredients, then add remaining ice. Garnish with lime slice.

JAMAICA GLORY

An old-fashioned glass, chilled

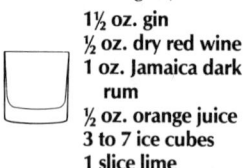

1½ oz. gin
½ oz. dry red wine
1 oz. Jamaica dark rum
½ oz. orange juice
3 to 7 ice cubes
1 slice lime

Combine all ingredients except 2 or 3 ice cubes and lime slice in shaker, and shake vigorously. Place remaining ice in glass, and strain into glass. Garnish with lime slice.

JOLLY ROGER

An 8- to 14-oz. wine glass, chilled

1 oz. Myers's Jamaica dark rum
1 oz. Leroux banana liqueur
2 oz. lemon juice
6 ice cubes

Combine all ingredients except 3 ice cubes in shaker, and shake vigorously. Place reserved ice in glass. Strain into glass. *Courtesy of Seagram's Complete Party Guide*

JELLY BEAN FIX
(Cabinet Cocktail)
An old-fashioned glass, chilled

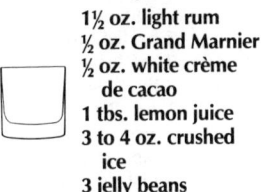

- 1½ oz. light rum
- ½ oz. Grand Marnier
- ½ oz. white crème de cacao
- 1 tbs. lemon juice
- 3 to 4 oz. crushed ice
- 3 jelly beans

Combine all ingredients except ice and jelly beans in mixing glass and stir well. Place ice in glass, add drink, and garnish with jelly beans. *Note:* A fix usually contains sugar. In this drink, the liqueurs provide the sweetening.

JUNTA
A 10- to 14-oz. tall glass, chilled

- 1½ oz. gold rum
- 1 oz. Southern Comfort
- 3 to 4 oz. dark English tea
- 2 tsp. lemon juice
- 2 to 3 tsp. superfine sugar
- 4 to 6 ice cubes
- 3 oz. club soda, chilled

Combine all ingredients except soda in glass, and stir. Add soda, and stir again—slowly.

LIME DAIQUIRI
A 4-oz. cocktail glass, chilled

- 1½ oz. light rum
- 1½ oz. lime juice
- 2 tsp. orgeat syrup
- 3 to 4 ice cubes
- 1 strip lime peel

Combine all ingredients except lime peel in shaker, and shake vigorously. Strain into glass. Twist lime peel over drink to release oil, and drop it in.

LIMEY
A 4-oz. cocktail glass, chilled

- 1 oz. light rum
- 2 tsp. triple sec
- 1 tbs. lime juice
- 2 tsp. lime liqueur
- 3 to 4 oz. crushed ice

Combine all ingredients in blender, and blend at medium speed 10 to 15 seconds. Strain into glass.

LOUISIANA LULLABY
A 4-oz. cocktail glass, chilled

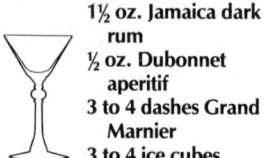

   1½ oz. Jamaica dark rum
   ½ oz. Dubonnet aperitif
   3 to 4 dashes Grand Marnier
   3 to 4 ice cubes
   1 strip lemon peel

Combine all ingredients except lemon peel in shaker, and shake vigorously. Strain into glass. Twist lemon peel over drink to release oil, and drop it in.

MAI TAI
A highball glass, chilled

   2 tbs. lime juice
   ¾ oz. curaçao
   3 dashes orgeat syrup
   2 oz. Trader Vic's Mai Tai rum
   8 to 10 ice cubes
   1 pineapple spear
   1 mint sprig

In shaker, combine lime juice, curaçao, orgeat syrup, rum, and 3 ice cubes, and shake vigorously. Place remaining ice in glass. Strain into glass. Garnish with pineapple spear and mint sprig. *Trader Vic Rums, Park Benziger & Co., Inc., Scarsdale, N.Y.*

MANDEVILLE
A 4-oz. cocktail glass, chilled

   1½ oz. Jamaica dark rum
   1 oz. light rum
   1 tbs. lemon juice
   1 tbs. cola
   ¼ tsp. Ricard (anise-licorice liqueur)
   ¼ tsp. grenadine
   3 to 4 ice cubes

Combine all ingredients in shaker, and shake vigorously. Strain into glass.

MARY PICKFORD
An old-fashioned glass, chilled

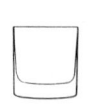

   1½ oz. pineapple juice
   1½ oz. light rum
   ¼ tsp. kirsch
   ¼ tsp. grenadine
   3 to 4 ice cubes

Combine all ingredients in shaker, and shake vigorously. Strain into glass.

MISTRESS MARY

Follow recipe for Mary Pickford, using ¼ tsp. crème de cassis instead of grenadine.

MIAMI WHAMMY

A 4-oz. cocktail glass, chilled

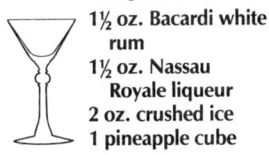

1½ oz. Bacardi white rum
1½ oz. Nassau Royale liqueur
2 oz. crushed ice
1 pineapple cube

Combine rum and liqueur in mixing glass and stir. Put ice in glass and add mixture. Garnish with pineapple cube on pick. *Terrace Room, Omni Hotel, Miami, Fla.*

NUECES AMIGO
(Nuts to You)

An old-fashioned glass, chilled

½ oz. gold rum
1 oz. Hiram Walker Swiss Chocolate Almond liqueur
½ oz. amaretto
1 oz. heavy cream
4 to 5 oz. crushed ice
1 toasted, blanched almond, crushed

Combine all ingredients except 2 or 3 oz. crushed ice and almond in shaker, and shake vigorously. Put remaining ice in glass, and strain into glass. Sprinkle almond on top.

NAVY GROG

An old-fashioned glass, chilled

2 tbs. lime juice
¾ tsp. grenadine
3 dashes orgeat syrup
1 tbs. chocolate syrup
3 oz. Trader Vic's Navy Grog rum
5 ice cubes

Combine all ingredients except 3 ice cubes in shaker, and shake vigorously. Place remaining ice in glass, and strain into glass. *Trader Vic Rums, Park Benziger & Co., Inc., Scarsdale, N.Y.*

OJOS VERDES
(Green Eyes)

An old-fashioned glass, chilled

2 oz. light rum
1 oz. pineapple juice
1 tsp. lime juice
1 tsp. orgeat syrup
4 oz. crushed ice
2 dashes green Passionola (passion fruit syrup)

Combine all ingredients except Passionola in blender, and blend at low speed 15 to 20 seconds. Strain into glass. Dot top with green Passionola.

PAGO PAGO

An old-fashioned glass, chilled

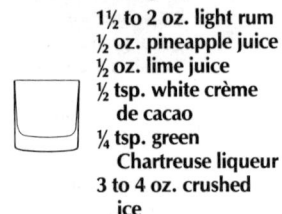

1½ to 2 oz. light rum
½ oz. pineapple juice
½ oz. lime juice
½ tsp. white crème de cacao
¼ tsp. green Chartreuse liqueur
3 to 4 oz. crushed ice

Combine all ingredients in shaker, and shake vigorously. Strain into glass.

PANAMA

A 4-oz. cocktail glass, chilled

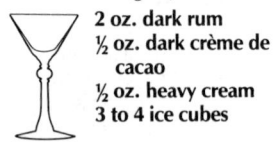

2 oz. dark rum
½ oz. dark crème de cacao
½ oz. heavy cream
3 to 4 ice cubes

Combine all ingredients in shaker, and shake vigorously. Strain into glass.

PARADISE LOST

A large cocktail or wine glass (6-oz. or larger), chilled

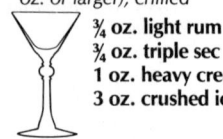

¾ oz. light rum
¾ oz. triple sec
1 oz. heavy cream
3 oz. crushed ice

Combine all ingredients in shaker, and shake vigorously. Strain into glass.

PARISIAN BLONDE

Follow recipe for Paradise Lost, using ¾ oz. dark rum instead of light rum.

PIÑA COLADA

A 10- to 14-oz. tall glass, chilled

4 oz. pineapple juice
1 oz. Coco Lopez mix
2 oz. light rum
4 oz. crushed ice
1 pineapple spear
1 maraschino cherry

Combine all ingredients except pineapple spear and cherry in blender, and blend until creamy and thick—like a shake. Pour drink into glass. Garnish with pineapple spear and cherry. *Caribe Hilton International, San Juan, P.R.*

PINK CREOLE
A 4-oz. cocktail glass, chilled

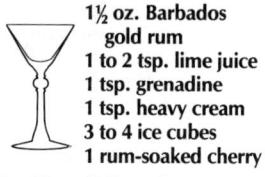

1½ oz. Barbados gold rum
1 to 2 tsp. lime juice
1 tsp. grenadine
1 tsp. heavy cream
3 to 4 ice cubes
1 rum-soaked cherry

Combine all ingredients except cherry in shaker, and shake vigorously. Strain into glass. Garnish with cherry.

PINK VERANDA
An old-fashioned glass, chilled

1 oz. gold rum
½ oz. Jamaica dark rum
½ oz. lime juice
1 tsp. superfine sugar
1½ oz. cranberry juice
½ egg white
4 to 5 ice cubes

Combine all ingredients except 1 or 2 ice cubes in shaker, and shake vigorously. Place remaining ice in glass. Strain into glass.

MAIN CHANCE
Follow recipe for Pink Veranda, using ½ to ¼ oz. cranberry liqueur instead of cranberry juice.

PIRATE of PENZANCE
A 4-oz. cocktail glass, chilled

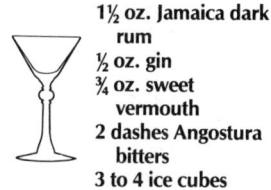

1½ oz. Jamaica dark rum
½ oz. gin
¾ oz. sweet vermouth
2 dashes Angostura bitters
3 to 4 ice cubes

Combine all ingredients in mixing glass, and stir well. Strain into glass.

PLANTER'S COCKTAIL
An 8-oz. mug, chilled

1½ oz. Jamaica dark rum
1 oz. orange juice
1 oz. sugar syrup
1 oz. lime juice
4 to 5 ice cubes
2 to 3 oz. crushed ice
3 to 4 drops grenadine

Combine all ingredients except crushed ice and grenadine in shaker, and shake vigorously. Put crushed ice in mug. Strain drink into mug. Top with grenadine.

PLANTER'S PUNCH
A 10- to 14-oz. tall glass, chilled

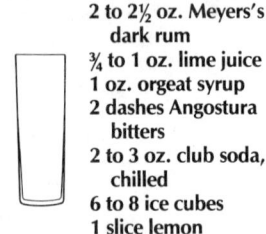

2 to 2½ oz. Meyers's dark rum
¾ to 1 oz. lime juice
1 oz. orgeat syrup
2 dashes Angostura bitters
2 to 3 oz. club soda, chilled
6 to 8 ice cubes
1 slice lemon
1 slice lime

In glass, combine rum, lime juice, orgeat syrup, bitters, and soda, and stir. Add ice until glass is filled. Garnish with lemon and lime slices.

PONCE de LEÓN
A 4-oz. cocktail glass, chilled

2 oz. light rum
½ oz. grapefruit juice
½ oz. mango nectar
1 tsp. lemon juice
¼ tsp. superfine sugar
3 to 4 ice cubes

Sugar-frost rim of cocktail glass. Combine all ingredients in shaker, and shake vigorously. Strain into prepared glass.

PLAZA PLEASER
A highball glass, chilled

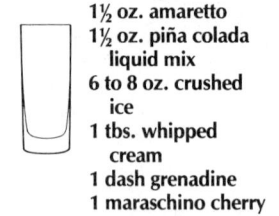

1½ oz. light rum
1½ oz. amaretto
1½ oz. piña colada liquid mix
6 to 8 oz. crushed ice
1 tbs. whipped cream
1 dash grenadine
1 maraschino cherry

In blender, combine rum, amaretto, piña colada mix, and crushed ice, and blend until creamy and thick—like a shake. Pour into glass. Top with whipped cream, grenadine, and cherry. *Smokey Mountains' Inn on the Plaza, Asheville, N.C.*

PRECIOUS LADY
A 4-oz. cocktail glass, chilled

1½ oz. Bacardi Gold Reserve rum
¼ oz. lime juice
1 tsp. heavy cream
½ egg white
3 to 4 ice cubes

Combine all ingredients in shaker, and shake vigorously. Strain into glass.

PUSSER'S PAIN KILLER
A 14-oz. tall glass, chilled

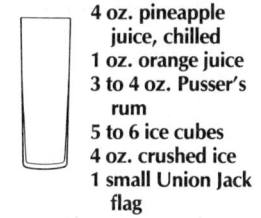

- 1 oz. coconut cream
- 4 oz. pineapple juice, chilled
- 1 oz. orange juice
- 3 to 4 oz. Pusser's rum
- 5 to 6 ice cubes
- 4 oz. crushed ice
- 1 small Union Jack flag

Combine coconut cream, pineapple juice, orange juice, rum, and ice cubes in shaker, and shake vigorously. Put crushed ice in glass and strain drink into glass. Garnish with small Union Jack Flag. *Jules Berman Co., Los Angeles, Ca.*

Note: Pusser's Rum (British Virgin Islands) was the issue of the British Royal Navy from 1667 until July, 1970, when the daily ration was abolished.

QUARTER DECK
A 4-oz. cocktail glass, chilled

- ½ oz. cream sherry
- 1½ oz. light rum
- 1 tsp. lime juice
- 3 to 4 ice cubes

Combine all ingredients in shaker, and shake vigorously. Strain into glass.

REFRESCO
A grapefruit half with pulp and membrane neatly removed

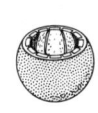

- 1½ oz. light rum
- ¾ oz. triple sec
- 1½ oz. lemon juice
- 2 oz. grapefruit juice
- 1 tsp. superfine sugar
- 4 oz. crushed ice

Combine all ingredients in shaker, and shake vigorously. Strain into grapefruit shell. Serve with short straw. *José Cruz, bartender, Silver Award winner at Caribe Hilton, San Juan, P.R.*

RUBY HUNTER
A 4-oz. cocktail glass, chilled

- 1 oz. light rum
- 1 tbs. Southern Comfort
- 1 tsp. lime juice
- 1½ oz. banana liqueur
- 3 to 4 ice cubes

Combine all ingredients in shaker, and shake vigorously. Strain into glass.

RON COCO
Coconut in husk

> 1 whole coconut in husk
> 1½ oz. light rum
> 1 oz. apricot brandy
> ¾ oz. coconut cream
> 2 oz. fresh coconut water (from coconut)
> 6 oz. crushed ice
> 1 tbs. shredded coconut

With ice pick, poke holes in coconut eyes, drain water, and reserve. Chop off top quarter of coconut. In shaker, combine rum, apricot brandy, coconut cream, coconut water, and ice, and shake vigorously. Pour into coconut. Shred a little of the coconut pulp from the top section that was cut off, and sprinkle shredded coconut on top. Serve with straw. *Efrain Vazquez, Gold Medal winner at Caribe Hilton, San Juan, P.R.*

RUM DANDY
An old-fashioned glass, chilled

> 2 oz. pineapple juice
> 1 oz. orange juice
> 1½ oz. Jamaica dark rum
> 1 tsp. banana liqueur
> 1 tsp. lime juice
> 3 oz. crushed ice

Combine all ingredients in blender, and blend at slow speed 10 to 15 seconds. Strain into glass.

RUM OASIS
An old-fashioned glass, chilled

> 1½ oz. light rum
> 3 to 4 oz. orange juice
> 1 tsp. cherry brandy
> 4 to 5 ice cubes
> 3 to 4 oz. ginger ale, chilled
> 1 strip lime peel

In shaker, combine rum, orange juice, cherry brandy, and 3 to 4 ice cubes, and shake vigorously. Place remaining ice in glass. Strain drink into glass, and add ginger ale. Twist lime peel over drink to release oil, and drop it in. *Peter and Charles Zohos, drink mixologists, New York, N.Y.*

RUMPELSTILTSKIN

A whiskey sour glass, chilled

2 oz. gold rum
1 oz. over-proof rum (151-proof)
1 tbs. orgeat syrup
1 egg
1 tsp. cream
3 to 4 ice cubes
Freshly grated nutmeg

Combine all ingredients in shaker, and shake vigorously. Strain into glass. Top with nutmeg.

SAN JUAN

A 4-oz. cocktail glass, chilled

1½ oz. light rum
¾ oz. brandy
1 tsp. grenadine
½ tsp. lime juice
3 to 4 ice cubes

Combine all ingredients in shaker, and shake vigorously. Strain into glass.

PURO'S PALACE

Follow recipe for above San Juan, using ¾ oz. Frangelico liqueur instead of brandy. *Louis Puro, Palace Hotel, San Juan, P.R.*

SAN JUAN'S BOLERO

A 4-oz. cocktail glass, chilled

1 oz. Puerto Rico rum (light rum)
½ oz. apricot brandy
¼ oz. lime juice
1 oz. orange juice
3 ice cubes
½ slice orange
1 maraschino cherry

Combine all ingredients except orange slice and cherry in shaker, and shake vigorously. Strain into glass. Garnish with ½ slice orange and cherry. *Swiss Chalet Restaurant, San Juan, P.R.*

SAXON LORD

A 4-oz. cocktail glass, chilled

2 tsp. lime juice
½ tsp. orgeat syrup
1½ oz. light rum
2 dashes Grand Marnier
3 to 4 ice cubes

Combine all ingredients in shaker, and shake vigorously. Strain into glass.

SCORPION

A 10-oz. old-fashioned glass, chilled

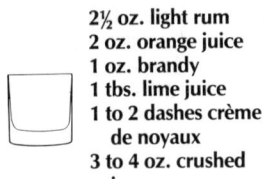

2½ oz. light rum
2 oz. orange juice
1 oz. brandy
1 tbs. lime juice
1 to 2 dashes crème de noyaux
3 to 4 oz. crushed ice
1 thin slice orange

Combine all ingredients except orange slice in blender, and blend at medium speed 10 to 15 seconds. Strain into glass. Garnish with orange slice.

SEPTEMBER MORN

A whiskey sour glass, chilled

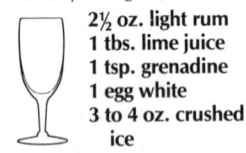

2½ oz. light rum
1 tbs. lime juice
1 tsp. grenadine
1 egg white
3 to 4 oz. crushed ice

Combine all ingredients in shaker, and shake vigorously. Strain into glass.

SEVILLA

A 4-oz. cocktail glass, chilled

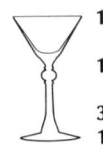

1½ oz. Jamaica dark rum
1 oz. sweet vermouth
3 to 4 ice cubes
1 strip orange peel

Combine all ingredients except orange peel in shaker, and shake vigorously. Strain into glass. Twist orange peel over drink to release its oil, and drop it in.

POKER

Follow recipe for Sevilla, using 1½ oz. light rum instead of Jamaica dark rum.

SHANGHAI

A 4-oz. cocktail glass, chilled

1½ oz. dark rum
1 tbs. lemon juice
2 tbs. Sambuca Romana liqueur
3 to 4 drops grenadine
3 to 4 ice cubes

Combine all ingredients in shaker, and shake vigorously. Strain into glass.

SHARK'S TOOTH

A highball glass, chilled

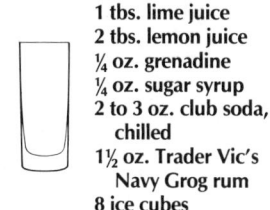

1 tbs. lime juice
2 tbs. lemon juice
¼ oz. grenadine
¼ oz. sugar syrup
2 to 3 oz. club soda, chilled
1½ oz. Trader Vic's Navy Grog rum
8 ice cubes

Combine all ingredients except 5 ice cubes in shaker, and shake vigorously. Place reserved ice in glass. Strain into glass. *Trader Vic Rums, Park Benziger & Co., Inc., Scarsdale, N.Y.*

SLEDGEHAMMER
(Third Rail)

A 4-oz. cocktail glass, chilled

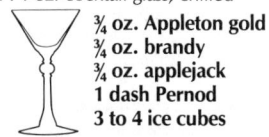

¾ oz. Appleton gold
¾ oz. brandy
¾ oz. applejack
1 dash Pernod
3 to 4 ice cubes

Combine all ingredients in shaker, and shake vigorously. Strain into glass.

Note: A Third Rail is prepared with ¾ oz. light rum instead of dark rum. *Appleton Rum, Schieffelin & Co., New York, N.Y.*

STILETTO

A 4-oz. cocktail glass, chilled

1½ oz. light rum
2 tsp. Amaretto di Saronno liqueur
1 tsp. lime juice
½ tsp. superfine sugar
1 dash orange bitters
3 to 4 ice cubes

Combine all ingredients in shaker, and shake vigorously. Strain into glass.

SPIRITUAL RUBESCENCE

A highball glass, chilled

1½ oz. light rum
2 oz. pineapple juice
½ oz. crème de coconut
½ oz. white crème de cacao
1¼ oz. light cream
1¼ oz. cranberry juice
6 ice cubes

Combine rum, pineapple juice, crème de coconut, crème de cacao, cream, and 3 ice cubes in shaker, and shake vigorously. Put remaining ice in glass. Strain into glass. Add cranberry juice and stir slowly. *Grand Hyatt Hotel, New York, N.Y.*

SUN WORSHIPER
A highball glass, chilled

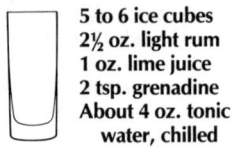

5 to 6 ice cubes
2½ oz. light rum
1 oz. lime juice
2 tsp. grenadine
About 4 oz. tonic water, chilled

Fill glass with ice. Add rum, lime juice, and grenadine, and stir. Top with tonic. Stir briefly, about 2 turns.

SWINGER'S COCKTAIL
A 4-oz. cocktail glass, chilled

1 oz. gold rum
1 oz. amaretto
1 oz. vodka
1 dash Southern Comfort
3 oz. crushed ice

Combine all ingredients in shaker, and shake vigorously. Strain into glass.

SUTTER'S MILL
An old-fashioned glass, chilled

2 to 2½ oz. light rum
1 tsp. coconut cream
1 tsp. lime juice
2 to 3 oz. crushed ice
2 oz. club soda, chilled
½ tsp. crushed almond

In shaker, combine rum, coconut cream, lime juice, and ice, and shake vigorously. Strain into glass. Add soda. Sprinkle almond on top.

TAHITI CLUB
An old-fashioned glass, chilled

2 to 2½ oz. gold rum
2 tsp. lime juice
2 tsp. lemon juice
2 tsp. pineapple juice
½ tsp. kirsch
3 to 4 ice cubes

Combine all ingredients in shaker, and shake vigorously. Strain into glass.

TORRID ZONE

A 4-oz. cocktail glass, chilled

2 oz. gold rum
2 tsp. Tia Maria coffee liqueur
1 tsp. heavy cream
3 to 4 ice cubes
½ tsp. shredded coconut

Combine all ingredients except shredded coconut in shaker, and shake vigorously. Strain into glass. Sprinkle shredded coconut on top.

WHITE LION

An old-fashioned glass, chilled

1½ oz. dark rum
1½ oz. lime juice
1½ tsp. Falernum syrup
3 to 4 drops raspberry syrup
2 to 3 dashes Angostura bitters
3 to 6 ice cubes

Combine all ingredients except 1 or 2 ice cubes in shaker, and shake vigorously. Place remaining ice in glass. Strain into glass.

WITCH'S TWITCH

A highball glass, chilled

4 to 6 ice cubes
1½ oz. Barbados gold rum
2 tsp. white crème de cacao
2 tsp. triple sec
1 tbs. heavy cream
½ small lime
4 oz. club soda, chilled
Ground cinnamon
Freshly grated nutmeg

In glass, put ice, rum, crème de cacao, and triple sec, and stir. Squeeze ½ lime over drink, and drop it in. Add soda and stir. Top with sprinkles of cinnamon and nutmeg.

ZOMBIE

A 10- to 14-oz. tall glass, chilled

- 1 oz. pineapple juice
- 2 tbs. lime juice
- ½ oz. papaya juice
- ¾ oz. light rum
- ¾ oz. 90-proof white Barbados rum
- 1½ oz. gold rum
- 1 tsp. superfine sugar, plus a little extra for topping
- 6 to 8 ice cubes
- 1 pineapple spear
- 1 maraschino cherry
- 1 tbs. over-proof rum (151-proof)

In shaker, combine pineapple juice, lime juice, papaya juice, light rum, Barbados rum, gold rum, 1 tsp. sugar, and 3 to 4 ice cubes, and shake vigorously. Place remaining ice in glass, and strain shaker mixture over ice. Garnish with pineapple spear and cherry. Float over-proof rum on surface. Top with sprinkle of sugar.

TEQUILA RECIPES

BERTHA
A highball glass, chilled

- Crushed ice to fill highball glass
- 1½ oz. Sauza white tequila
- 1½ tsp. superfine sugar
- 1 tbs. fresh lemon or lime juice
- ½ tsp. dry red wine
- 1 strip lemon peel
- 1 maraschino cherry

Fill glass with ice. Add tequila, sugar, lemon or lime juice, and wine, and stir. Twist lemon peel over drink to release oil, and drop it in. Garnish with cherry. *Tequila Sauza, National Distillers Products Co., New York,. N.Y.*

BLOODY MARIA
A 10- to 14-oz. wine glass, chilled

- Ice cubes to fill wine glass
- 1½ oz. José Cuervo white or Cuervo Especial gold tequila
- 3 oz. Snap-E-Tom tomato cocktail, chilled
- 1 lime wedge

Place ice in glass. Add tequila and tomato cocktail, and stir. Garnish with lime wedge. *Cuervo Tequila, Snap-E-Tom: Heublein, Inc., Hartford, Conn.*

BLUE CHIMNEY SMOKE

A 10-oz. or larger wine glass (or tall glass), chilled

> About 6 oz. finely crushed ice
> 1½ oz. white tequila
> 4 oz. orange juice, chilled
> 1 dash blue curaçao

Put ice in glass. Add tequila and orange juice, and stir. Float blue curaçao on top.

CHARRO

An old-fashioned glass, chilled

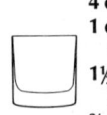

> 4 oz. crushed ice
> 1 oz. Sauza white tequila
> 1⅓ oz. evaporated milk
> ⅔ oz. strong coffee
> 2 ice cubes

Combine all ingredients except ice cubes in shaker, and shake vigorously. Place ice cubes in glass, and strain into glass. *Tequila Sauza, Mexico*

CHANGUIRONGO

A highball glass, chilled

> Crushed ice to fill highball glass to ½ level
> 1½ oz. white or gold tequila
> About 4 oz. carbonated soft drink (any flavor, such as orange crush, bitter lemon, grapefruit, etc.), chilled
> 1 wedge lemon or lime

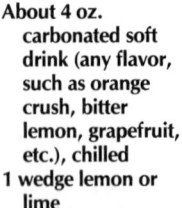

Fill glass with ice to ½ level. Add tequila, and fill glass with soft drink. Garnish with wedge of lemon or lime.

COCO LOCO
(Crazy Coconut)

This drink is traditionally served inside a whole coconut in husk. If that is not available, use a highball glass.

    1 coconut in husk or 1 coconut in shell
    1 oz. white tequila
    1 oz. gin
    1 oz. rum
    ½ oz. grenadine
    3 to 4 ice cubes
    1 wedge lime or lemon

With whole coconut in husk, chop a 2- or 3-inch hole in the top. Leave coconut water inside coconut and add tequila, gin, rum, grenadine, and ice, and stir well. Squeeze lime or lemon wedge over drink, and drop it in. Serve with long straw.

For highball glass, pierce holes through eyes in hard shell of coconut, and drain coconut water into cup. Put ice in glass. Add coconut water, tequila, gin, rum, and grenadine, and stir well. Squeeze lime or lemon wedge over drink, and drop it in. Serve with straw.

COMPADRE

A 4-oz. cocktail glass, chilled

    1 oz. Sauza white tequila
    ⅓ oz. grenadine
    4 drops maraschino liqueur
    4 drops Angostura bitters
    2 oz. crushed ice

Combine all ingredients in shaker, and shake vigorously. Strain into glass. *Tequila Sauza, Mexico*

CONCHITA

A highball glass, chilled

    3 ice cubes
    1½ oz. José Cuervo white tequila
    ½ tsp. lemon juice
    6 to 8 oz. grapefruit juice or grapefruit soda

Combine all ingredients except grapefruit juice or grapefruit soda in glass, and stir. Fill with juice or soda and stir again. *Tequila Cuervo, Mexico*

DEPTH CHARGE (Submarine or Submarino)
A highball glass and a whiskey shot glass, chilled

6 oz. beer, chilled
1½ oz. white or gold tequila

Pour beer into highball glass. Pour tequila into shot glass. Drop shot glass containing tequila into beer and let it sink to bottom.

EL CONEJO
An old-fashioned glass, chilled

¾ oz. white tequila
¾ oz. Rabbit's Punch liqueur
3 to 4 ice cubes
1 carrot stick

Combine tequila, Rabbit's Punch liqueur, and ice in glass. Use carrot stick as stirrer. *Rabbit's Punch, The Black Prince Distillery, Clifton, N.J.*

DUKE'S DAISY
An 8-oz. or larger wine glass, chilled

2 oz. white tequila
2 tsp. lime juice
2 tsp. raspberry liqueur
3 to 4 ice cubes
3 to 4 oz. club soda, chilled

Combine all ingredients except soda in shaker, and shake vigorously. Strain into glass. Add soda.

FIESTA
A 4-oz. cocktail glass, chilled

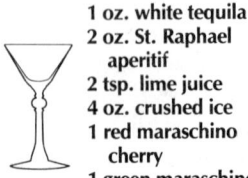

1 oz. white tequila
2 oz. St. Raphael aperitif
2 tsp. lime juice
4 oz. crushed ice
1 red maraschino cherry
1 green maraschino cherry

Combine all ingredients except cherries in shaker, and shake vigorously. Strain into glass. Garnish with red and green cherries. *Estoril Restaurant, Mexico City, Mexico*

FROZEN TEQUILA
A champagne glass, chilled

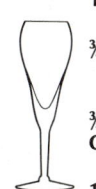

1½ oz. José Cuervo white tequila
¾ oz. sugar syrup, or 1½ tbs. superfine sugar
¾ oz. lime juice
Crushed ice to fill champagne glass
1 thin slice lime
1 maraschino cherry

Combine all ingredients except lime slice and cherry in blender, and blend until smooth slush. Fill glass with mixture. Garnish top with lime slice and cherry. Serve with straw and small spoon. *José Cuervo Tequila, Heublein Inc., Hartford, Conn.*

GAVILAN .45
A highball glass, chilled

Ice cubes to fill highball glass
1½ oz. Gavilan white or gold tequila
4 oz. beer, chilled
Salt

Fill glass with ice. Add tequila. Add beer. Sprinkle salt on top. *Gavilan Tequila, Foreign Vintages, Inc., Louisville, Ky., Great Neck, N.Y.*

GENTLE BULL
An 8-oz. or larger brandy snifter, chilled

1½ oz. white tequila
¾ oz. Kahula coffee liqueur
1 oz. cream
3 or 4 ice cubes
4 oz. crushed ice

Combine all ingredients except crushed ice in shaker, and shake vigorously. Put crushed ice in snifter. Strain into glass.

GOLDEN MARGARITA
An old-fashioned glass, chilled

2 oz. Cuervo Especial gold tequila
1 oz. curaçao
¾ oz. lime juice
2 oz. crushed ice
1 thin slice lime

Combine all ingredients except lime slice in shaker, and shake vigorously. Pour, unstrained, into glass. Garnish with lime slice. *Cuervo Tequila, Heublein, Inc., Hartford, Conn.*

GORDITA

An old-fashioned glass, chilled

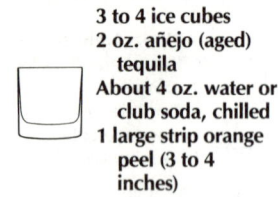

- 3 to 4 ice cubes
- 2 oz. añejo (aged) tequila
- About 4 oz. water or club soda, chilled
- 1 large strip orange peel (3 to 4 inches)

Place ice in glass. Add tequila. Add water or soda in quantity desired. Add orange peel. Stir. *Tlaquepaque Restaurant, Acapulco, Mexico*

HAND GRENADE

A 4-oz. cocktail glass, chilled

- 3 oz. unsweetened cranberry juice
- 1 oz. white tequila
- 3 to 4 ice cubes
- 1 strip orange peel

Combine juice, tequila, and ice in mixing glass, stir well, and strain into glass. Twist orange peel over drink to release oil, and drop it in. *Pen and Pencil Restaurant, New York, N.Y.*

HORNY BULL

A highball glass, chilled

- Ice cubes to fill highball glass
- 1½ oz. Montezuma white tequila
- 4 to 6 oz. orange juice, chilled

Fill glass with ice. Add tequila, and top with orange juice. Stir. *Montezuma Tequila, Barton Brands, Inc., Chicago, Ill.*

MARGARITA No. 1

A 4-oz. cocktail glass, chilled

- 1 strip lime or lemon peel
- 1½ oz. Sauza white tequila
- ½ oz. triple sec
- 1 oz. lime or lemon juice
- 2 oz. crushed ice

Rub lime or lemon peel around rim of glass to moisten and salt-frost rim with coarse salt (see Modern Mixology). In shaker, combine tequila, triple sec, lime or lemon juice, and ice, and shake vigorously. Strain into prepared glass. *Tequila Sauza, National Distillers Products Co., New York, N.Y.*

GRAND MARGARITA

Follow recipe for Margarita No. 1, using ½ oz. Grand Marnier instead of triple sec. *Garcia's of Scottsdale, Las Vegas, Nev.*

MARGARITA No. 2

A 4-oz. cocktail glass, chilled

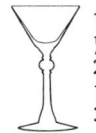

1 lime wedge
½ oz. Cointreau
2 oz. white tequila
1 tbs. lime juice
3 to 4 ice cubes

Rub lime wedge around rim of glass to moisten and salt-frost rim with coarse salt. Combine Cointreau, tequila, lime juice, and ice in shaker, and shake vigorously. Strain into prepared glass. *Cointreau Ltd., Lawrenceville, N.J.*

MATADOR

A champagne glass, chilled

1 oz. white tequila
2 oz. pineapple juice
½ oz. lime juice
2 oz. crushed ice

Combine all ingredients in shaker, and shake vigorously. Pour, unstrained, into glass.

MEXICAN SUNRISE

A highball glass, chilled

Crushed ice to fill highball glass
1½ oz. José Cuervo white tequila
1 tsp. grenadine
⅓ tsp. crème de cassis liqueur
1 tbs. fresh lime juice
About 4 oz. club soda, chilled

Fill glass with ice. Add tequila, grenadine, crème de cassis, lime juice, and soda to fill. Stir gently. *Young's Market Co., Los Angeles, Calif.*

MOCKINGBIRD

A 4-oz. cocktail glass, chilled

1½ oz. Josè Cuervo white tequila
2 tsp. white crème de menthe
1 oz. fresh lime juice
3 to 4 ice cubes

Combine all ingredients in shaker, and shake vigorously. Strain into glass. *José Cuervo Tequila, Heublein, Inc., Hartford, Conn.*

PIÑA
(Pineapple Sunrise)
A 10- to 14-oz. tall glass, chilled

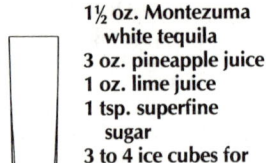

- 1½ oz. Montezuma white tequila
- 3 oz. pineapple juice
- 1 oz. lime juice
- 1 tsp. superfine sugar
- 3 to 4 ice cubes for shaker, plus extra to fill tall glass

Combine all ingredients with 3 to 4 ice cubes in shaker, and shake vigorously. Fill glass with extra ice. Strain into glass. *Montezuma Tequila, Barton Brands, Ltd., Chicago, Ill.*

PIÑATA
A whiskey sour glass, chilled

- 1½ oz. white tequila
- 1 tbs. banana liqueur
- 1 oz. lime juice
- 2 oz. crushed ice

Combine all ingredients in blender, and blend at medium speed until smooth. Pour, unstrained, into glass.

REVOLUTION
An old-fashioned glass, chilled

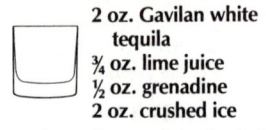

- 2 oz. Gavilan white tequila
- ¾ oz. lime juice
- ½ oz. grenadine
- 2 oz. crushed ice

Combine all ingredients in shaker, and shake vigorously. Pour, unstrained, into glass. *Gavilan Tequila, Foreign Vintages, Inc., Louisville, Ky.*

ROSITA
An old-fashioned glass, chilled

- Crushed ice to fill old-fashioned glass
- 1½ oz. Cuervo Especial gold tequila
- ¾ oz. dry vermouth
- ¾ oz. sweet vermouth
- 1½ oz. Campari aperitif
- 1 strip lemon peel

Fill glass with crushed ice. Add tequila, dry and sweet vermouths and Campari, and stir gently. Twist lemon peel over drink to release oil, and drop it in. Serve with short straw. *Cuervo Tequila, Heublein, Inc., Hartford, Conn.*

SANGRITA HIGHBALL
A highball glass, chilled

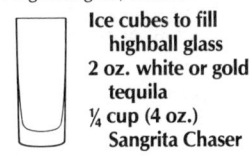

Ice cubes to fill highball glass
2 oz. white or gold tequila
¼ cup (4 oz.) Sangrita Chaser

Fill glass with ice. Add tequila and Sangrita Chaser, and stir.

SAUZA COCKTAIL
A 4-oz. cocktail glass, chilled

½ oz. lemon juice
1 oz. Sauza white tequila
1 tsp. superfine sugar
4 dashes grenadine
2 oz. crushed ice
1 thin slice lemon
1 maraschino cherry

Combine all ingredients except lemon slice and cherry in shaker, and shake vigorously. Pour, unstrained, into glass. Garnish with lemon slice and cherry. *Tequila Sauza, National Distillers Products Co., New York, N.Y.*

SPANISH MOSS
A 4-oz. cocktail glass, chilled

1½ oz. white or gold tequila
2 tbs. Kahlua coffee liqueur
3 to 4 ice cubes
3 drops green crème de menthe

Combine all ingredients except crème de menthe in shaker, and shake vigorously. Strain into glass. Dot top with green crème de menthe.

¡SI!
A highball glass, chilled

1 oz. lemon juice
1 tsp. superfine sugar
1½ oz. white or gold tequila
Crushed ice to fill highball glass to ¾ level
3 to 4 oz. strong coffee, hot

In glass, combine lemon juice and sugar, and stir until sugar is dissolved. Add tequila, and stir again. Fill glass to ½ inch from rim with ice. Pour coffee over ice, and stir. *Yes Restaurant, Acapulco, Mexico.*

SILK STOCKINGS

An 8-oz. or larger wine glass, chilled

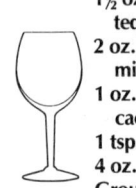

1½ oz. Sauza white tequila
2 oz. evaporated milk
1 oz. white crème de cacao
1 tsp. grenadine
4 oz. crushed ice
Ground cinnamon
1 maraschino cherry

In blender, combine tequila, evaporated milk, crème de cacao, grenadine, and ice, and blend at medium speed until smooth. Pour, unstrained, into glass. Sprinkle with cinnamon and garnish with cherry. *Tequila Sauza, National Distillers Products Co., New York, N.Y.*

SNAKE RIVER STINGER

4 whiskey shot glasses

4 oz. Cuervo Especial gold tequila
½ oz. Pernod
½ oz. white crème de menthe
4 oz. crushed ice

Combine all ingredients in mixing glass, stir, and strain into 4 shot glasses. Serve as a shooter without garnish. *Colter Bay Village, Grand Teton Lodge Co., Grand Teton National Park, Moran, Wyo.*

SPANISH MOSS

A 4-oz. cocktail glass, chilled

1½ oz. white or gold tequila
2 tbs. Kahlua coffee liqueur
3 to 4 ice cubes
3 drops green crème de menthe

Combine all ingredients except crème de menthe in shaker, and shake vigorously. Strain into glass. Dot top with green crème de menthe.

SUNRISE

An 8-oz. wine glass, chilled

1½ oz. Pancho Villa white tequila
1 oz. grenadine
3 oz. orange juice, chilled
4 oz. crushed ice
1 thin slice lime

Combine all ingredients except lime slice in shaker, and shake vigorously. Strain into glass. Garnish with lime slice. *Pancho Villa Tequila, E. Martinoni Co., S. San Francisco, Calif.*

SUNSET

An 8-oz. or larger wine glass, chilled

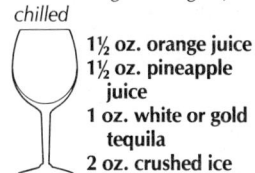

1½ oz. orange juice
1½ oz. pineapple juice
1 oz. white or gold tequila
2 oz. crushed ice

Sugar-frost rim of glass. Combine all ingredients in blender, and blend at medium speed about 30 seconds. Pour, unstrained, into prepared glass. *Su Casa Restaurant, Chicago, Ill.*

TAXCO FIZZ

A 14-oz. tall glass, chilled

4 oz. crushed ice
2 oz. white tequila
2 tbs. fresh lime juice
1 tsp. superfine sugar
2 dashes orange bitters
1 egg white
About 4 oz. club soda, chilled

Combine all ingredients except soda in shaker, and shake vigorously. Pour, unstrained, into glass. Top with soda.

TAPATIO
(Tah-pay-tee-o)

A highball glass, chilled

3 ice cubes
2 oz. Sauza añejo (aged) tequila
5 to 6 oz. ginger ale, chilled
1 strip lemon peel

Place ice in glass. Add tequila and top with ginger ale. Twist lemon peel over drink to release oil, and drop it in. *Tequila Sauza, Mexico*

TEQUILA BLOODY BULL

A 10- to 14-oz. tall glass, chilled

4 oz. crushed ice
2 oz. white tequila
3 oz. tomato juice, chilled
3 oz. beef bouillon, chilled
1 dash Tabasco sauce
1 dash Worcestershire sauce

If desired, salt-frost rim of glass, using celery salt. Combine all ingredients in glass, and stir.

TEQUILA COLLINS
A 14-oz. tall glass, chilled

Crushed ice to fill glass to ¾ level
1½ oz. José Cuervo white or Cuervo Especial gold tequila
1 oz. sugar syrup
1 oz. fresh lime or lemon juice
6 to 8 oz. club soda, chilled
1 maraschino cherry
1 thin orange slice

Fill glass to ¾ level with ice. Add tequila, sugar syrup, and lime or lemon juice. Top with soda, and stir. Garnish with cherry and orange slice. *Cuervo Tequila, Heublein, Inc., Hartford, Conn.*

TEQUILA JULEP
A highball glass, chilled

Crushed ice to fill highball glass
4 sprigs mint
1 tsp. superfine sugar
1½ oz. Sauza white or gold tequila
4 to 6 oz. club soda, chilled

Fill glass with ice. In separate dish, crush 3 mint sprigs with sugar and add to glass. Add tequila and stir. Top with soda. Stir gently until glass is frosted. Garnish with remaining mint spring. *Tequila Sauza, National Distillers Products Co.*

TEQUILA MARTINI
Also called Mexitini or Tequini

Follow recipe for standard Martini (see p. 153), using white tequila in place of gin, and adding a few drops of Pernod. Serve well chilled. *Club Industriales, Mexico City*

TEQUILA 'n' COLA
A highball glass, chilled

Ice cubes to fill highball glass
2 tbs. lemon juice
1 oz. white or gold tequila
4 to 6 oz. cola, chilled
1 strip lemon peel

Combine all ingredients except lemon peel in glass, and stir. Twist lemon peel over drink to release oil, and drop it in.

TEQUILA NEAT
A 2-oz. whiskey shot glass

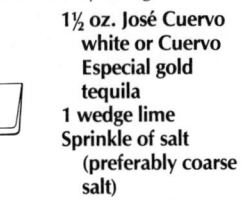

1½ oz. José Cuervo white or Cuervo Especial gold tequila
1 wedge lime
Sprinkle of salt (preferably coarse salt)

This is the traditional Mexican ritual for drinking tequila straight. Lick back of *left* hand between thumb and index finger and sprinkle area with salt. Take shot glass of tequila in same hand. Take wedge of lime in *right* hand. Lick salt from back of hand, drink tequila, and bite into lime wedge—all in one quick sequence. *José Cuervo Tequila, Heublein, Inc., Hartford, Conn.*

TEQUILA with SANGRITA CHASER
2 whiskey shot glasses

Sangrita Chaser mixture:
(makes 1 C. or 8 servings)

1 cup fresh orange juice
¼ tsp. Tabasco sauce, or ½ tsp. Dōna Maria or Bufalo sauce
¼ tsp. Worcestershire sauce
¼ tsp. coarse salt
½ tsp. grenadine
¼ tsp. lime or lemon juice

A traditional way of drinking tequila in Mexico is a shot glass of tequila accompanied by a chaser of Sangrita (approximately 2 oz.).

Combine all chaser ingredients in blender or shaker, and mix well. (Mixture keeps well in refrigerator for several weeks.) Serve in shot glass, as described above.

TEQUILA TROPICAL
A highball glass, chilled

Crushed ice to fill highball glass to ¾ level
1½ oz. José Cuervo white or Cuervo Especial gold tequila
½ oz. grenadine
3 oz. orange juice, chilled
1 tsp. lemon juice
½ slice orange
1 maraschino cherry

Fill highball glass to ¾ level with ice. Add tequila, grenadine, orange juice, and lemon juice, and stir. Garnish with orange slice and cherry. *Cuervo Tequila, Heublein, Inc., Hartford, Conn.*

T'N'T
(Tequila 'n' Tonic)
A highball glass, chilled

Ice cubes to fill highball glass to ¾ level
2 oz. Sauza white tequila
½ oz. lime or lemon juice
About 6 oz. tonic water, chilled
1 strip lime or lemon peel

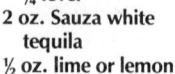

Fill glass to ¾ level with ice. Add tequila and lime or lemon juice. Fill glass to top with tonic, and stir. Twist lime or lemon peel over drink to release oil, and drop it in. *Tequila Sauza, National Distillers Products Co., New York, N.Y.*

TOREADOR
A 4-oz. cocktail glass, chilled

1½ oz. white tequila
½ oz. white crème de cacao
½ oz. cream
2 oz. crushed ice
1 tbs. whipped cream
Pinch of cocoa

Combine all ingredients except whipped cream and cocoa in shaker, and shake vigorously. Strain into glass. Top with whipped cream, and sprinkle sparingly with cocoa.

TROMBONE

A 12- to 14-oz. tall glass, chilled

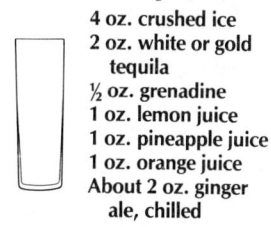

- 4 oz. crushed ice
- 2 oz. white or gold tequila
- ½ oz. grenadine
- 1 oz. lemon juice
- 1 oz. pineapple juice
- 1 oz. orange juice
- About 2 oz. ginger ale, chilled

Combine all ingredients except ginger ale in mixing glass, and stir. Pour, unstrained, into tall glass. Top with ginger ale.

VIVA VILLA

A whiskey sour glass, chilled

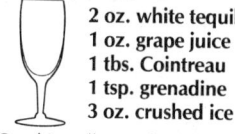

- 2 oz. white tequila
- 1 oz. grape juice
- 1 tbs. Cointreau
- 1 tsp. grenadine
- 3 oz. crushed ice

Combine all ingredients in blender, and blend at low speed 15 to 20 seconds. Strain into glass.

VODKA RECIPES

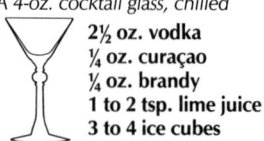

APPLE KNOCKER
A 4-oz. cocktail glass, chilled

- 2½ oz. vodka
- 2 tbs. cider
- 1 tsp. lemon juice
- 1 tsp. strawberry liqueur
- 3 to 4 ice cubes

Combine all ingredients in shaker, and shake vigorously. Strain into glass.

AQUEDUCT
A 4-oz. cocktail glass, chilled

- 2½ oz. vodka
- ¼ oz. curaçao
- ¼ oz. brandy
- 1 to 2 tsp. lime juice
- 3 to 4 ice cubes

Combine all ingredients in shaker, and shake vigorously. Strain into glass.

BANANA BOAT
A whiskey sour glass, chilled

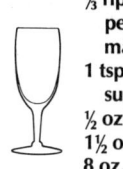

⅓ ripe banana, peeled and mashed
1 tsp. superfine sugar
½ oz. lime juice
1½ oz. Taaka vodka
8 oz. crushed ice
1 slice lime

Combine all ingredients except lime slice in shaker, and shake vigorously (or these ingredients can be combined in blender, and blended). Strain into glass. Garnish with lime slice. *Taaka Vodka, The Sazerac Co., New Orleans, La.*

BLACK MARBLE
An old-fashioned glass, chilled

2 to 3 ice cubes
3 oz. Stolichnaya vodka (chilled in freezer)
1 black olive
1 thin slice orange

Place ice in glass. Add vodka. Drop in olive and orange slice. *Stolichnaya Vodka, Monsieur Henri Wines Ltd., White Plains, N.Y.*

BLOODY BULL
An old-fashioned glass, chilled

1½ oz. V-8 tomato cocktail
1½ oz. beef bouillon
1½ oz. vodka
1 to 2 tsp. fresh lemon juice
1 dash Tabasco sauce
1 dash Worcestershire sauce
Freshly ground pepper, to taste
3 to 4 ice cubes

Combine all ingredients in shaker, and shake vigorously. Strain into glass.

BARNACLE BILL
Follow recipe for Bloody Bull, using 1½ oz. clam juice instead of beef bouillon.

BULL SHOT
Follow recipe for Bloody Bull, with following changes: Omit V-8 tomato cocktail. Use 3 oz. beef bouillon.

GEISHA GIRL
Follow recipe for Bloody Bull, using 1½ oz. Gekkekan sake instead of beef bouillon.

COCK 'n' BULL
Follow recipe for Bloody Bull, using chicken consommé instead of V-8 tomato cocktail. (Also use beef bouillon, as specified in recipe.)

MARIA SANGRE
Follow recipe for Bloody Bull, using Crosse & Blackwell Gazpacho instead of V-8 tomato cocktail, plus 2 tbs. fresh lemon juice.

BLOODY MARY
An old-fashioned glass, chilled

> 3 oz. V-8 tomato cocktail or tomato juice
> 1½ oz. vodka
> 1 to 2 tsp. fresh lemon juice
> 1 dash Tabasco sauce
> 1 dash Worcestershire sauce
> Freshly ground pepper, to taste
> 3 to 4 ice cubes

Combine all ingredients in shaker, and shake vigorously. Strain into glass.

RED FLANNELS

Follow recipe for above Bloody Mary, adding 1 to 2 tsp. prepared horseradish to mixture in shaker.

BLUE LAGOON
A 4-oz. cocktail glass, chilled

> 1½ oz. vodka
> 2 tsp. blue curaçao
> 2 dashes Angostura bitters
> ½ oz. pineapple juice
> 3 to 4 ice cubes
> 1 strip lemon peel

Combine all ingredients except lemon peel in shaker, and shake vigorously. Strain into glass. Twist lemon peel over drink to release oil, and drop it in.

BLUE MONDAY
A 4-oz. cocktail glass, chilled

> 1 oz. Cointreau
> 2 oz. vodka
> Optional: 2 drops blue vegetable coloring
> 3 to 4 ice cubes

Combine all ingredients in shaker, and shake vigorously. Strain into glass.

BLUSHIN' RUSSIAN
A 4-oz. cocktail glass, chilled

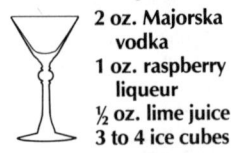

2 oz. Majorska vodka
1 oz. raspberry liqueur
½ oz. lime juice
3 to 4 ice cubes

Combine all ingredients in shaker, and shake vigorously. Strain into glass. *Majorska Vodka, Palmer & Lord Ltd., Syosset, N.Y.*

CAPE CODDER
An old-fashioned glass, chilled

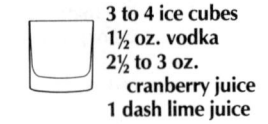

3 to 4 ice cubes
1½ oz. vodka
2½ to 3 oz. cranberry juice
1 dash lime juice

Combine all ingredients in glass, and stir slowly.

BOGGY BAY

Follow recipe for Cape Codder, using 1 oz. Boggs Cranberry Liqueur instead of cranberry juice.

BULLFROG
An old-fashioned glass, chilled

3 ice cubes
1½ oz. Smirnoff vodka
4 oz. limeade (can use reconstituted frozen limeade)
2 slices lime

Place ice in glass. Add vodka and limeade, and stir slowly. Garnish with lime slices. *Smirnoff Vodka, Heublein, Inc., Hartford, Conn.*

CAPE GRAPE
A highball glass, chilled

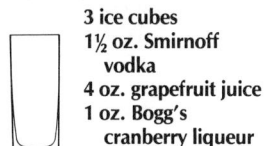

3 ice cubes
1½ oz. Smirnoff vodka
4 oz. grapefruit juice
1 oz. Bogg's cranberry liqueur
1 strip grapefruit peel

Place ice in glass. Add vodka, grapefruit juice, and cranberry liqueur, and stir slowly. Twist grapefruit peel over drink to release oil, and drop it in. *Smirnoff Vodka, Heublein, Inc., Hartford, Conn.*

CARMEN MIRANDA
An old-fashioned glass, chilled

1 oz. vodka
1 oz. gold rum
1 to 2 tsp. lime juice
1 tsp. Falernum syrup
About 3 inches peeled banana, sliced
3 oz. crushed ice

Combine all ingredients in blender, and blend at medium speed 10 to 15 seconds. Strain into glass.

CATNIP
An old-fashioned glass, chilled

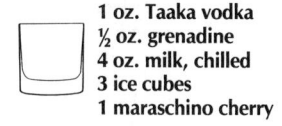

1 oz. Taaka vodka
½ oz. grenadine
4 oz. milk, chilled
3 ice cubes
1 maraschino cherry

Combine all ingredients except cherry in shaker, and shake vigorously. Place cherry in glass. Strain into glass. *Taaka Vodka, The Sazerac Co., New Orleans, La.*

CLAMDIGGER
An old-fashioned glass, chilled

1½ oz. Wolfschmidt vodka
3 oz. tomato juice
3 oz. clam juice
1 dash Tabasco sauce
1 dash Worcestershire sauce
2 to 3 ice cubes
1 strip lemon peel

Combine vodka, tomato juice, clam juice, Tabasco sauce, and Worcestershire sauce in mixing glass, and stir well. Place ice in glass, and strain into glass. Twist lemon peel over drink to release oil, and drop it in. *Wolfschmidt Vodka, Seagram Distillers Co., New York, N.Y.*

DARK EYES

A 6-oz. brandy snifter, chilled

2 tsp. blackberry brandy
1½ oz. vodka
1 to 2 tsp. lime juice
2 to 3 ice cubes
1 slice lime

Combine all ingredients except lime slice in shaker, and shake vigorously. Strain into snifter. Garnish with lime slice.

DUBLIN DELIGHT
(For St. Patrick's Day)

An old-fashioned glass, chilled

1½ oz. vodka
¾ oz. Midori melon liqueur
3 ice cubes
4 to 5 oz. crushed ice
1 green maraschino cherry

In shaker, combine vodka, melon liqueur, and ice cubes, and shake vigorously. Fill glass to ½ level with crushed ice. Strain into glass. Garnish with cherry. *Grandy Hyatt Hotel, New York, N.Y.*

EASY PIECE

A 4-oz. cocktail glass, chilled

1 oz. Cherry Heering
1½ oz. vodka
1 tsp. dry vermouth
1 tbs. orange juice
3 oz. crushed ice

Combine all ingredients in shaker, and shake vigorously. Strain into glass.

EGGHEAD

An old-fashioned glass, chilled

1½ oz. Smirnoff vodka
4 oz. orange juice
1 egg
5 ice cubes

Combine all ingredients except 2 ice cubes in blender, and blend at medium speed until thoroughly mixed. Place reserved ice in glass. Pour into glass. *Smirnoff Vodka, Heublein, Inc., Hartford, Conn.*

FAN-TAN

An old-fashioned glass, chilled

- 3 ice cubes
- 1 oz. Majorska vodka
- ½ oz. gold rum
- ¾ oz. coffee liqueur
- 2 oz. milk

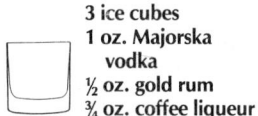

Put ice in glass. Add remaining ingredients and stir. *Majorska Vodka, Palmer & Lord Ltd., Syosset, N.Y.*

FLAME of LOVE

A 10- to 14-oz. wine glass, chilled

- ½ oz. Tio Pepe dry sherry
- 3 oz. vodka
- 2 4-inch strips orange peel
- 3 oz. crushed ice

Pour sherry into glass and swirl to coat inside of glass. Pour out excess. Twist 1 orange peel over glass to release oil, and drop it in. Place ice cubes in glass, and add vodka. Light match and twist remaining orange peel next to flame, and drop into drink. *Chasen's Restaurant, Los Angeles, Calif.*

FRONT-PAGE DYNAMITE

An old-fashioned glass, chilled

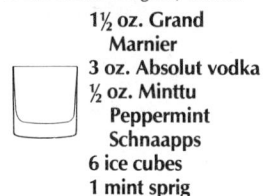

- 1½ oz. Grand Marnier
- 3 oz. Absolut vodka
- ½ oz. Minttu Peppermint Schnaapps
- 6 ice cubes
- 1 mint sprig

Combine all ingredients except 3 ice cubes and mint in shaker, and shake vigorously. Place reserved ice in glass, and strain into glass. Garnish with mint sprig. *Grand Marnier Absolut Vodka, Carillon Importers, New York, N.Y.*

GORKY PARK

A 4-oz. cocktail glass, chilled

- 2½ oz. vodka
- 1 tsp. grenadine
- 3 large fresh strawberries
- 1 dash orange bitters
- 2 to 3 oz. crushed ice

Combine all ingredients except ½ strawberry in shaker, and shake vigorously (or these ingredients can be combined in blender and blended at medium speed 10 to 15 seconds.) Strain into glass. Garnish with reserved ½ strawberry.

GINGERSNAP

A highball glass, chilled

    3 ice cubes
1½ oz. Smirnoff vodka
1 oz. ginger-flavored brandy
2 oz. pineapple juice
4 oz. lemonade (can use reconstituted frozen concentrate)
1 strip lemon peel

Place ice in glass. Add vodka, brandy, pineapple juice, and lemonade, and stir slowly. Twist lemon peel over drink to release oil, and drop it in. *Smirnoff Vodka, Heublein, Inc., Hartford, Conn.*

GOLDA MAJOR
(Ma-yor)

A 4-oz. cocktail glass, chilled

1 oz. Majorska vodka
1 oz. orange juice
1 oz. apricot liqueur
3 to 4 ice cubes

Combine all ingredients in shaker, and shake vigorously. Strain into glass. *Majorska Vodka, Palmer & Lord, Ltd., Syosset, N.Y.*

GRASS SKIRT

½ coconut shell

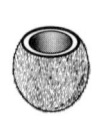

1½ oz. vodka
½ oz. Coco Lopez mix
3 oz. orange juice
4 ice cubes
1 pineapple spear

Combine vodka, Coco Lopez mix, and orange juice in blender, and blend 15 seconds. Pour into ½ coconut shell. Add ice and pineapple spear. Serve with short straw. *Petroleum Club of Houston, Houston, Tex.*

GYPSY MOTH

A 4-oz. cocktail glass, chilled

½ oz. Benedictine
1½ oz. vodka
1 tsp. lemon juice
1 tsp. orange juice
4 ice cubes
1 thin slice orange

Combine all ingredients except orange slice in shaker, and shake vigorously. Strain into glass. Garnish with orage slice.

HARVEY WALLBANGER

A 10- to 14-oz. tall glass, chilled

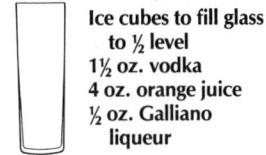

Ice cubes to fill glass to ½ level
1½ oz. vodka
4 oz. orange juice
½ oz. Galliano liqueur

Fill glass with ice to ½ level. Add vodka and orange juice, and stir. Float Galliano on top.

HAWAIIAN EYE

An old-fashioned glass, chilled

1 oz. Kahlua coffee liqueur
1 oz. heavy cream
1½ oz. vodka
½ oz. Bourbon
2 tsp. banana liqueur
1 egg white
3 oz. pineapple juice
3 oz. crushed ice
1 pineapple spear

Combine all ingredients except pineapple spear in blender, and blend at medium speed 15 to 20 seconds. Pour into glass. Garnish with pineapple spear.

HAWAIIAN MINT LIMEADE

A highball glass, chilled

4 ice cubes
1½ oz. Smirnoff vodka
3 oz. limeade (can use reconstituted frozen limeade)
2 oz. pineapple juice
1 tsp. green crème de menthe
1 pineapple spear

Place ice in glass. Add vodka, limeade, and pineapple juice, and stir well. Garnish with pineapple spear. *Smirnoff Vodka, Heublein, Inc., Hartford, Conn.*

HAYRIDE

An old-fashioned glass, chilled

1½ oz. Smirnoff vodka
1 dash grenadine
4 oz. orange juice
5 ice cubes
1 thin slice orange

Combine all ingredients except 2 ice cubes and orange slice in shaker, and shake vigorously. Place reserved ice in glass. Strain into glass. Garnish with orange slice. *Smirnoff Vodka, Heublein, Inc., Hartford, Conn.*

HIGH ROLLER
An old-fashioned glass, chilled

1½ oz. vodka
¾ oz. Grand Marnier
4 oz. orange juice, chilled
3 ice cubes
1 tsp. grenadine

Combine all ingredients in shaker, and shake vigorously. Strain into glass. Dot surface with grenadine. *Resorts International Hotel Casino, Atlantic City, N.J.*

JESSE WHITE
A 4-oz. cocktail glass, chilled

1½ oz. vodka
½ oz. light rum
½ oz. Cointreau
2 tsp. lime juice
1 tsp. superfine sugar
3 to 4 ice cubes

Combine all ingredients in shaker, and shake vigorously. Strain into glass. *Frank, bartender, The Friars Club, New York, N.Y.*

IMPERIAL CZAR
An 8-oz. or larger wine glass, chilled

1 oz. vodka
1 oz. Grand Marnier
½ oz. lime juice
1 dash orange bitters
3 to 4 ice cubes
3 oz. dry sparkling wine, chilled

Combine all ingredients except wine in shaker, and shake vigorously. Strain into glass. Add wine. Stir 1 turn.

JUDGMENT DAY
An old-fashioned glass, chilled

2½ oz. 100-proof vodka
½ oz. brandy
½ oz. cherry brandy
5 to 7 ice cubes

Combine all ingredients except 2 to 3 ice cubes in shaker, and shake vigorously. Place reserved ice in glass, and strain into glass.

KANGAROO

An old-fashioned glass, chilled

1 to 2 oz. vodka
¾ oz. dry vermouth
4 oz. crushed ice
1 strip lemon peel

Combine all ingredients except lemon peel in glass, and stir. Twist lemon peel over drink to release oil, and drop it in.

BOOMERANG

Follow recipe for Kangaroo, adding ½ oz. kiwi fruit liqueur to mixture.

THE KISS
(For Valentine's Day)

A 4-oz. cocktail glass, chilled

1¼ oz. vodka
¾ oz. cherry Suisse (chocolate cherry liqueur)
¾ oz. heavy cream
3 ice cubes
½ fresh strawberry

Combine all ingredients except strawberry in shaker, and shake vigorously. Strain into glass. Garnish with strawberry. *Grand Hyatt Hotel, New York, N.Y*

KREMLIN COLONEL

A 4-oz. cocktail glass, chilled

1½ to 2 oz. vodka
2 tbs. sugar syrup
3 to 4 ice cubes
3 to 4 mint leaves

Combine all ingredients except mint leaves in shaker, and shake vigorously. Strain into glass. Tear mint leaves in halves and drop into glass.

KRETCHMA

An old-fashioned glass, chilled

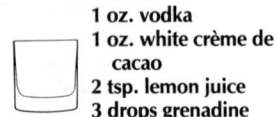

1 oz. vodka
1 oz. white crème de cacao
2 tsp. lemon juice
3 drops grenadine
5 to 7 ice cubes

Combine all ingredients except 2 to 3 ice cubes in shaker, and shake vigorously. Place reserved ice in glass. Strain into glass.

LA BELLE LIZA

An old-fashioned glass, chilled

1 oz. vodka
1 oz. sweet vermouth
1 oz. heavy cream
2 tsp. triple sec
2 tsp. white crème de cacao
3 oz. crushed ice

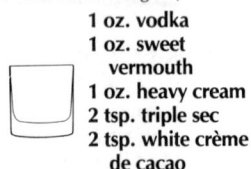

Combine all ingredients in shaker, and shake vigorously. Strain into glass.

MALINKY MALCHIK (Little Russian Kid)

A highball glass, chilled

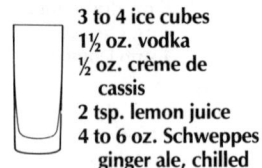

3 to 4 ice cubes
1½ oz. vodka
½ oz. crème de cassis
2 tsp. lemon juice
4 to 6 oz. Schweppes ginger ale, chilled

Place ice in glass. Add vodka, crème de cassis, and lemon juice. Stir slowly while adding ginger ale.

MIDNIGHT SUN

A 4-oz. cocktail glass, chilled

2½ oz. Finlandia vodka
½ oz. grenadine
3 ice cubes
1 small wedge lemon

Combine all ingredients except lemon wedge in mixing glass, and stir slowly. Strain into glass. Garnish with lemon wedge. *Finlandia Vodka, The Buckingham Corp., New York, N.Y.*

MR. LUCKY
A 4-oz. cocktail glass, chilled

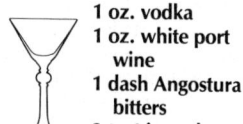

1 oz. vodka
1 oz. white port wine
1 dash Angostura bitters
3 to 4 ice cubes
1 strip lemon peel

Combine all ingredients except lemon peel in shaker, and shake vigorously. Strain into glass. Twist lemon peel over drink to release oil, and drop it in.

MOON over MOSCOW
A 4-oz. cocktail glass, chilled

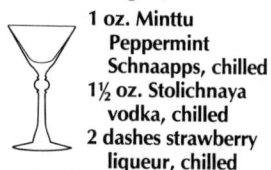

1 oz. Minttu Peppermint Schnaapps, chilled
1½ oz. Stolichnaya vodka, chilled
2 dashes strawberry liqueur, chilled

It is important that all ingredients and glass be chilled before assembling drink. Combine peppermint schnapps, vodka, and strawberry liqueur in mixing glass, and stir well. Pour into cocktail glass. *Minttu Peppermint Schnaapps, Great Vintners International, Syosset, N.Y.*

MOSCOW MULE
A highball glass, chilled

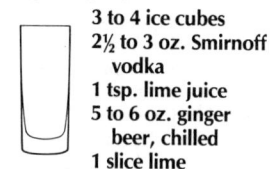

3 to 4 ice cubes
2½ to 3 oz. Smirnoff vodka
1 tsp. lime juice
5 to 6 oz. ginger beer, chilled
1 slice lime

Place ice in glass. Add vodka and lime juice. Stir slowly while adding ginger beer. Garnish with lime slice.

Note: Many people claim credit for this now-famous drink, but the original was the work of Jack Martin of Heublein. Martin concocted it at Cock 'n' Bull Restaurant on La Cienega Boulevard, Los Angels, Calif.

MYSTIC COOLER
A highball glass, chilled

> 1½ oz. vodka
> ½ oz. orange juice
> ½ oz. pineapple juice
> ½ oz. grapefruit juice
> Crushed ice to fill highball glass to ¾ level
> ½ oz. crème de bananes
> 1 tsp. green grenadine
> 1 slice lime

Combine vodka and all 3 juices, in mixing glass, and stir well. Fill glass with ice to ¾ level. Add drink mixture. Float crème de bananes on top. Slowly add grenadine to float. Garnish with lime slice. *Leonard Williams, Royal Sonesta Hotel, New Orleans, La.*

NAKED MAJA
An old-fashioned glass, chilled

> 6 ice cubes
> 2 oz. Majorska vodka
> 1 orange wedge, unpeeled

Combine 3 ice cubes and vodka in mixing glass, and stir until vodka is very cold. Place remaining ice in glass. Strain vodka into glass. Score peel of orange wedge with tines of fork, and drop wedge into drink. *Majorska Vodka, Palmer & Lord Ltd., Syosset, N.Y.*

NINOTCHKA
A 4-oz. cocktail glass, chilled

> 1½ oz. Wolfschmidt vodka
> 1 tsp. lemon juice
> 2 tsp. white crème de cacao
> 4 to 5 ice cubes

Combine all ingredients in shaker, and shake vigorously. Strain into glass. *Wolfschmidt Vodka, Seagram Distillers Co., New York, N.Y.*

ODESSA FILE
A 4-oz. cocktail glass, chilled

> 2 oz. 100-proof vodka
> 1 oz. dry vermouth
> 2 dashes kummel
> 3 to 4 ice cubes

Combine all ingredients in shaker, and shake vigorously. Strain into glass.

OPEN SESAME

A 4-oz. cocktail glass, chilled

1½ oz. vodka
¾ oz. cherry brandy
½ oz. lemon juice
2 dashes dry vermouth
1 dash orange bitters
3 to 4 ice cubes
¼ tsp. sesame seeds

Combine all ingredients except sesame seeds in shaker, and shake vigorously. Strain into glass. Sprinkle seeds on top.

PANZER

A 4-oz. cocktail glass, chilled

1 oz. gin
1 oz. vodka
1 oz. Cointreau
3 to 4 ice cubes

Combine all ingredients in shaker, and shake vigorously. Strain into glass. *Cointreau Ltd., Lawrenceville, N.J.*

PEACHARINO

An 8-oz. or larger wine glass, chilled

1½ oz. vodka
½ peeled peach, fresh or canned
½ oz. lemon juice
1 tbs. peach or apricot preserve
4 oz. crushed ice

Combine all ingredients in blender, and blend at medium speed until almost smooth. Pour, unstrained, into glass.

PINK MINK

A 4-oz. cocktail glass, chilled

2 to 3 tsp. strawberry liqueur
1½ oz. vodka
½ oz. light rum
3 to 4 ice cubes
½ fresh strawberry

Moisten rim of cocktail glass with drop of strawberry liqueur, and sugar-frost rim. Combine all ingredients except strawberry in shaker, and shake vigorously. Strain into prepared glass. Garnish with ½ strawberry.

THE PITTSBURGH SPIRIT

A 4-oz. cocktail glass, chilled

1 oz. vodka
½ oz. amaretto
¼ oz. triple sec
¼ oz. Galliano
2 oz. orange juice
3 ice cubes

Combine all ingredients in shaker, and shake vigorously. Strain into glass. *Created in honor of Pittsburgh Spirit Soccer Club by Heaven Restaurant, Pittsburgh, Pa.*

POLISH SIDECAR

A small glass screwtop jar (5- to 6-oz.)

    1½ oz. Polish vodka
    ¾ oz. lemon juice
    ¾ oz. Polish fruit
        wine
    3 to 4 ice cubes

Combine vodka, lemon juice, fruit wine, and ice cubes in shaker, and shake vigorously. Strain into jar.

PRAIRIE OYSTER

An 8-oz or larger wine glass, chilled

    1 egg yolk
    2 oz. vodka
    2 oz. tomato juice
    1 tsp. lemon juice
    2 dashes
        Worcestershire
        sauce
    Salt and freshly
        ground pepper

Drop unbroken egg yolk on bottom of glass. In separate mixing glass, combine tomato juice, vodka, lemon juice, and Worcestershire sauce, and mix well. Pour over egg yolk. Sprinkle salt and pepper, to taste, on top.

Note: After World War II, this morning pick-me-up was a favorite of the professional military in Panama, Brazil, and Paraguay, where it is still called a "prairie oyster."

PURPLE PASSION

A highball glass, chilled

    1 small cluster
        grapes (garnish)
    3 ice cubes
    1½ oz. Smirnoff
        vodka
    3 oz. grapefruit
        juice, chilled
    3 oz. Concord grape
        juice, chilled

Place cluster of grapes in freezer for 5 minutes to become frosty. Place ice in glass. Add vodka and juices, and stir slowly. Lower grape cluster into glass. *Smirnoff Vodka, Heublein, Inc., Hartford, Conn.*

RED BARON
An old-fashioned glass, chilled

- 1½ oz. vodka
- 2 oz. tomato juice
- 1 oz. sauerkraut juice
- 1 dash Tabasco sauce
- Freshly ground pepper, to taste
- 6 to 8 ice cubes

Combine all ingredients except 3 to 4 ice cubes in shaker, and shake vigorously. Put remaining ice in glass, and strain into glass.

RED ROCK CANYON
A 10- to 14-oz. tall glass, chilled

- 1½ oz. vodka
- ¼ oz. crème de cassis
- ¼ oz. peach brandy
- ¼ oz. Cointreau
- 8 oz. crushed ice
- 2 to 3 dashes Campari aperitif
- 1 maraschino cherry
- 1 slice orange

Combine vodka, crème de cassis, peach brandy, Cointreau, and 4 oz. ice in blender, and blend until smooth. Put remaining ice in glass, and add blender mixture, unstrained. Float Campari on top. Garnish with cherry and orange slice. *Caesar's Palace, Las Vegas, nev.*

RUSSIAN BEAR
An old-fashioned glass, chilled

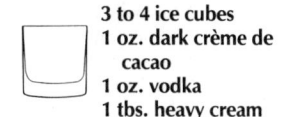

- 3 to 4 ice cubes
- 1 oz. dark crème de cacao
- 1 oz. vodka
- 1 tbs. heavy cream

Place ice in glass. Add remaining ingredients, and stir.

RUSSIAN COCKTAIL
A 4-oz. cocktail glass, chilled

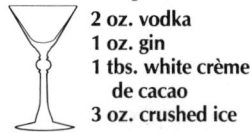

- 2 oz. vodka
- 1 oz. gin
- 1 tbs. white crème de cacao
- 3 oz. crushed ice

Combine all ingredients in shaker, and shake vigorously. Strain into glass.

RUSSIAN COFFEE
A 4-oz. cocktail glass, chilled

- 1¼ oz. vodka
- 1¼ oz. coffee liqueur
- ½ oz. heavy cream
- 3 to 4 oz. crushed ice

Combine all ingredients in blender, and blend at medium speed 10 to 15 seconds. Strain into glass.

RUSSIAN LADY
A whiskey sour glass, chilled

2 oz. vodka
1 oz. lemon juice
1 oz. sugar syrup
½ oz. heavy cream
3 dashes strawberry liqueur
4 to 5 ice cubes

Combine all ingredients in shaker, and shake vigorously. Strain into glass.

RUSSIAN PIPELINE
A highball glass, chilled

Crushed ice to fill highball glass
1 oz. kummel
1½ oz. Stolichnaya vodka

Fill glass with ice. Add kummel and vodka, and stir.

RUSSIAN NAIL
An old-fashioned glass, chilled

3 to 4 ice cubes
1 oz. vodka
¾ oz. Drambuie
1 strip lemon peel

Place ice in glass. Add vodka and Drambuie, and stir. Twist lemon peel over drink to release oil, and drop it in.

SALT LICK
An 8-oz. or larger wine glass, chilled

2 oz. bitter lemon soda, chilled
3 to 4 ice cubes
1½ oz. vodka
2 oz. grapefruit juice

Moisten rim of glass with few drops of bitter lemon soda, and salt-frost rim. Place ice in glass. Add vodka, remaining bitter lemon soda, grapefruit juice, and stir gently.

SCREWDRIVER

An old-fashioned glass, chilled

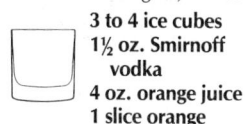

3 to 4 ice cubes
1½ oz. Smirnoff vodka
4 oz. orange juice
1 slice orange

Place ice in glass. Add vodka and orange juice, and stir slowly. Garnish with orange slice. *Smirnoff Vodka, Heublein, Inc., Hartford, Conn.*

SLIM JIM

A highball glass, chilled

Ice cubes to fill highball glass
1 oz. vodka
6 to 8 oz. diet soda (any flavor), chilled
1 slice lemon or lime

Fill glass with ice. Add vodka. Fill glass with diet soda. Garnish with lemon or lime slice.

SLALOM

A 4-oz. cocktail glass, chilled

½ oz. vodka
½ oz. white crème de cacao
1 tsp. heavy cream
½ oz. Sambuca Romana
3 oz. crushed ice

Combine all ingredients in blender, and blend at medium speed 10 to 15 seconds. Strain into glass.

SOLIDARITY

A 4-oz. cocktail glass, chilled

2 oz. Polish vodka
½ oz. Polish blackberry brandy
½ oz. Polish slivovitz
2 dashes orange bitters
3 to 4 ice cubes

Combine all ingredients in shaker, and shake vigorously. Strain into glass.

STOLI FREEZE
A pony glass, chilled

> 2 oz. Stolichnaya vodka
> Freshly ground pepper

About 1 hour before serving, place bottle of vodka and pony glass in freezer. When glass is frosted and vodka is very cold, fill glass to brim with vodka. Top with sprinkle of pepper. *Stolichnaya Vodka, Monsieur Henri Wines Ltd., White Plains, N.Y.*

TINGLE
A 4-oz. cocktail glass, chilled

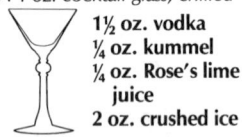

> 1½ oz. vodka
> ¼ oz. kummel
> ¼ oz. Rose's lime juice
> 2 oz. crushed ice

Combine all ingredients in shaker, and shake vigorously. Strain into glass.

VOLGA BOATMAN
A 4-oz. cocktail glass, chilled

> 1 oz. Wolfschmidt vodka
> 1 oz. Leroux cherry-flavored brandy
> 1 oz. orange juice
> 3 ice cubes
> 1 maraschino cherry

Combine all ingredients except cherry in shaker, and shake vigorously. Strain into glass. Add cherry. *Courtesy of Seagram's Complete Party Guide*

VODKA MARTINI
A 4-oz. cocktail glass or old-fashioned glass

Follow recipe for any style Martini, using vodka in place of gin.

WARSAW
A 4-oz. cocktail glass, chilled

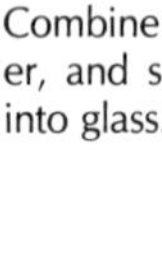

> 2½ oz. Polish vodka
> 1 dash dry vermouth
> ½ oz. blackberry brandy
> 2 dashes lemon juice
> 3 to 4 ice cubes

Combine all ingredients in shaker, and shake vigorously. Strain into glass.

WHISTLER'S MOTHER
An old-fashioned glass, chilled

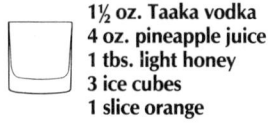

1½ oz. Taaka vodka
4 oz. pineapple juice
1 tbs. light honey
3 ice cubes
1 slice orange

Combine all ingredients except orange slice in shaker, and shake vigorously. Strain into glass. Garnish with orange slice. *Taaka Vodka, The Sazerac Co., New Orleans, La.*

YELLOW FEVER
A highball glass, chilled

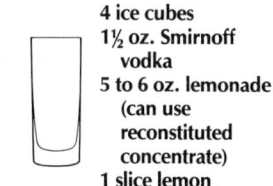

4 ice cubes
1½ oz. Smirnoff vodka
5 to 6 oz. lemonade (can use reconstituted concentrate)
1 slice lemon

Place ice in glass. Add vodka and lemonade, and stir slowly. Garnish with lemon slice. *Smirnoff Vodka, Heublein, Inc., Hartford, Conn.*

WOMBAT
An old-fashioned glass, chilled

1½ oz. Taaka vodka
1 oz. Coco Lopez coconut cream
2 oz. pineapple juice
3 ice cubes
1 pineapple spear

Combine all ingredients except pineapple spear in shaker, and shake vigorously. Strain into glass. Garnish with pineapple spear. *Taaka Vodka, The Sazerac Co., New Orleans, La.*

ZERO OPTION
A 4-oz. cocktail glass, chilled

1 oz. vodka
1 oz. applejack
½ oz. gin
1 tsp. Grand Marnier
1 tsp. lime juice
1 dash grenadine
3 to 4 ice cubes
2 oz. finely crushed ice

Combine all ingredients except crushed ice in shaker, and shake vigorously. Put crushed ice in glass, and strain into glass.

Whiskey

BLENDED WHISKEY RECIPES

ASSASSINO
A 10- to 14-oz. tall glass, chilled

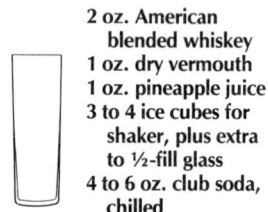

2 oz. American blended whiskey
1 oz. dry vermouth
1 oz. pineapple juice
3 to 4 ice cubes for shaker, plus extra to ½-fill glass
4 to 6 oz. club soda, chilled
2 drops Sambuca Romana

Combine whiskey, vermouth, pineapple juice, and 3 to 4 ice cubes in shaker, and shake vigorously. Fill glass to ½ level with extra ice cubes. Strain mixture into glass. Add soda to top. Add 2 drops Sambuca Romana.

BLACK HAWK
A 4-oz. cocktail glass, chilled

½ oz. lemon juice
1 tsp. superfine sugar
1½ oz. American blended whiskey
½ oz. sloe gin
2 to 3 ice cubes

Combine lemon juice and sugar in mixing glass, and stir well. Add whiskey, sloe gin, and ice cubes, and stir gently. Strain into glass.

BLAZING SADDLE

A highball glass, chilled, and an old-fashioned glass wide enough to stand highball glass inside it

> 1 tsp. superfine sugar
> 2 tsp. lemon juice
> 1½ tbs. orange juice
> 1 oz. American blended whiskey
> ½ oz. Southern Comfort
> 6 to 8 ice cubes
> 6 oz. club soda, chilled
> 1 small piece dry ice

Combine sugar, lemon juice, orange juice, whiskey, Southern Comfort, and 3 to 4 ice cubes in shaker, and shake vigorously. Strain into glass. Add 2 to 3 ice cubes. Fill glass with soda, reserving 1 to 2 tbs. Stand highball glass in wider old-fashioned glass. Place small piece of dry ice in old-fashioned glass, and spoon 1 or 2 tbs. soda over dry ice—which will then puff like smoke.

BLENDED COMFORT

A highball glass, chilled

> 1 oz. Southern Comfort
> 2 oz. American blended whiskey
> 1 oz. orange juice
> ¾ oz. dry vermouth
> 2 tbs. lemon juice
> ¼ fresh peach, peeled
> 4 oz. crushed ice plus extra to fill glass
> ½ slice orange
> ½ slice lemon

Combine Southern Comfort, blended whiskey, orange juice, dry vermouth, lemon juice, peach, and 4 oz. ice in blender, and blend at medium speed 20 to 25 seconds. Fill highball glass with extra ice. Strain into glass. Garnish with orange and lemon. *Southern Comfort Corp., St. Louis, Mo.*

BOOT HILL

A 4-oz. cocktail glass, chilled

> 1½ oz. American blended whiskey
> ½ oz. applejack
> ½ oz. lemon juice
> 1 tsp. sugar syrup
> 3 to 4 ice cubes

Combine all ingredients in shaker, and shake vigorously. Strain into glass.

BOSTON SOUR

A 14-oz. tall glass, chilled

- 1 tsp. superfine sugar
- 2½ tbs. lemon juice
- 1 egg white
- 2 oz. American blended whiskey
- 3 to 4 ice cubes, plus extra to fill highball glass to ⅔ level
- 4 oz. club soda, chilled
- 1 slice lemon
- 1 maraschino cherry

Combine sugar, lemon juice, egg white, whiskey, and 3 to 4 ice cubes in shaker, and shake vigorously. Strain into glass. Add extra ice cubes to ⅔ level of glass. Top with soda. Garnish with lemon slice and cherry.

BRASSY BLONDE

A 10- to 14-oz. tall glass, chilled

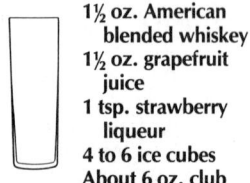

- 1½ oz. American blended whiskey
- 1½ oz. grapefruit juice
- 1 tsp. strawberry liqueur
- 4 to 6 ice cubes
- About 6 oz. club soda, chilled

Combine all ingredients except soda in glass, and stir slowly. Top with soda and stir briefly, about 2 turns.

PEAR BOTTOM

Follow recipe for Brassy Blonde, using 1 tsp. Williams pear brandy instead of strawberry liqueur.

CABLEGRAM

A highball glass, chilled

- 2 tbs. lemon juice
- 1 tsp. superfine sugar
- 2 oz. American blended whiskey
- Ice cubes to fill highball glass to ⅔ level
- About 4 oz. ginger ale, chilled

Combine lemon juice and sugar, and stir until sugar is dissolved. Add whiskey and stir gently. Add ice to ⅔ level of glass. Fill glass to top with ginger ale.

CALIFORNIA GIRL
A 10- to 14-oz. tall glass, chilled

- 1 tbs. lemon juice
- 1 tbs. lime juice
- 1 tbs. superfine sugar
- 2 oz. American blended whiskey
- 2 dashes strawberry liqueur
- 3 to 4 ice cubes
- About 4 oz. crushed ice
- 3 to 4 oz. club soda, chilled

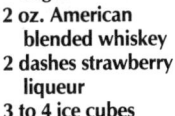

Combine lemon juice, lime juice, sugar, whiskey, strawberry liqueur, and ice cubes in shaker, and shake vigorously. Fill glass to ⅓ level with crushed ice. Strain mixture into glass. Top with soda.

CHAPEL HILL
A 4-oz. cocktail glass, chilled

- 2 oz. American blended whiskey
- ¾ oz. triple sec
- 1 tbs. lemon juice
- 3 to 4 ice cubes
- 1 strip orange peel or thin slice of orange

Combine all ingredients except orange peel or slice in shaker, and shake vigorously. Strain into glass. Twist orange peel over glass to release oil, and drop it in; or garnish with orange slice.

COLD KISS
A 4-oz. cocktail glass, chilled

- 1½ oz. American blended whiskey
- ½ oz. Minttu Peppermint Schnaapps
- 2 tsp. white crème de cacao
- 3 oz. crushed ice

Combine all ingredients in shaker, and shake vigorously. Strain into glass. *Minttu Peppermint Schnaapps, Great Vintners International, Syosset, N.Y.*

CREOLE
A 4-oz. cocktail glass, chilled

- 1½ oz. American blended whiskey
- 1 oz. sweet vermouth
- 1 to 2 dashes Benedictine
- 1 to 2 dashes Amer Picon liqueur
- 3 to 4 ice cubes
- 1 strip lime peel

Combine all ingredients except lime peel in shaker, and shake vigorously. Strain into glass. Twist lime peel over drink to release oil, and drop it in.

COTTON BALE

Follow recipe for Creole, with following changes: Use 6-oz. cocktail glass. Add ½ egg white to ingredients in shaker. Garnish with 1 maraschino cherry instead of lime peel.

DEAR JOHN

A 4-oz. cocktail glass, chilled

1½ oz. American blended whiskey
½ oz. Southern Comfort
1 tsp. orgeat syrup
2 tsp. lime juice
3 to 4 ice cubes
½ strawberry

Combine all ingredients except strawberry in shaker, and shake vigorously. Strain into glass. Garnish with strawberry.

DERBY

A 4-oz. cocktail glass, chilled

1½ oz. American blended whiskey
2 tsp. triple sec
2 tsp. sweet vermouth
1 tbs. lime juice
3 to 4 ice cubes
1 sprig mint

Combine all ingredients except mint in shaker, and shake vigorously. Strain into glass. Garnish with mint sprig.

DE RIGUEUR

A 4-oz. cocktail glass, chilled

1½ oz. American blended whiskey
½ oz. grapefruit juice
2 tsp. honey
3 to 4 ice cubes

Combine all ingredients in shaker, and shake vigorously. Strain into glass.

DINAH

A 4-oz. cocktail glass, chilled

2½ oz. American blended whiskey
½ oz. lemon juice
½ tsp. superfine sugar
3 to 4 ice cubes

Combine all ingredients in shaker, and shake vigorously. Strain into glass.

DIXIE DARLING
A 4-oz. cocktail glass, chilled

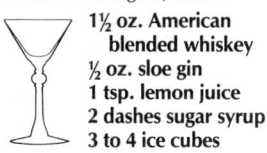

1½ oz. American blended whiskey
½ oz. sloe gin
1 tsp. lemon juice
2 dashes sugar syrup
3 to 4 ice cubes

Combine all ingredients in shaker, and shake vigorously. Strain into glass.

DUBONNET MANHATTAN
A 4-oz. cocktail glass, chilled

1 oz. Dubonnet aperitif
1 oz. American blended whiskey
3 to 4 ice cubes
1 maraschino cherry

Combine all ingredients except cherry in shaker, and shake vigorously. Strain into glass. Garnish with cherry.

DOUBLE STANDARD
A whiskey sour glass, chilled

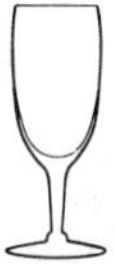

1 oz. gin
1 oz. American blended whiskey
2 tsp. lemon juice
½ tsp. superfine sugar
½ tsp. grenadine
3 to 4 ice cubes

Combine all ingredients in shaker, and shake vigorously. Strain into glass.

FRISCO TROLLEY
A 4-oz. cocktail glass, chilled

1½ oz. American blended whiskey
½ oz. Benedictine
2 tsp. lemon juice
3 to 4 ice cubes

Combine all ingredients in shaker, and shake vigorously. Strain into glass.

CALIFORNIA STREET

Follow recipe for Frisco Trolley, adding 1 tsp. Cointreau to ingredients in shaker.

GLOOM LIFTER

An old-fashioned glass, chilled

1½ oz. American blended whiskey
1 tbs. brandy
1 tsp. sugar syrup
1 tsp. lemon juice
1 tbs. raspberry liqueur
½ egg white
3 to 4 ice cubes

Combine all ingredients in shaker, and shake vigorously. Strain into glass.

HORSE CAR

An old-fashioned glass, chilled

1 oz. dry vermouth
1 oz. sweet vermouth
1 oz. American blended whiskey
2 dashes Angostura bitters
5 to 7 ice cubes
1 tangerine section

Combine dry and sweet vermouths, whiskey, bitters, and 3 to 4 ice cubes in mixing glass, and stir well. Place remaining ice in glass. Strain into glass. Garnish with tangerine section.

HORSE'S NECK

A 10- to 14-oz. tall glass, chilled

1 lemon
3 to 4 ice cubes
2½ to 3 oz. American blended whiskey
About 4 oz. ginger ale, chilled

Carefully peel lemon with peeler in one continuous strip. Place strip in glass. Add ice, whiskey, and squeeze of lemon juice. Top with ginger ale. Stir briefly—2 or 3 turns.

JAPANESE FIZZ No.1

A whiskey sour glass, chilled

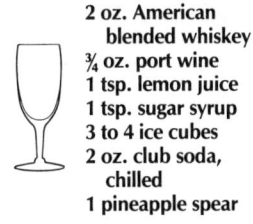

- 2 oz. American blended whiskey
- ¾ oz. port wine
- 1 tsp. lemon juice
- 1 tsp. sugar syrup
- 3 to 4 ice cubes
- 2 oz. club soda, chilled
- 1 pineapple spear

Combine all ingredients except soda and pineapple in shaker, and shake vigorously. Strain mixture into glass. Add soda. Garnish with pineapple spear.

FU MAN-CHU

Follow recipe for Japanese Fizz #1, using ½ oz. mandarin Napoleon liqueur instead of ¾ oz. port wine.

GINZU FIZZ

Follow recipe for Japanese Fizz #1, using ¾ oz. plum wine instead of ¾ oz. port wine.

LADY DAY

A 4-oz. cocktail glass, chilled

- 1½ oz. American blended whiskey
- 2 tsp. banana liqueur
- 1 tsp. lemon juice
- 1 tsp. orange juice
- 3 oz. crushed ice

Combine al ingredients in shaker, and shake vigorously. Strain into glass.

LADY in RED

A 4-oz. cocktail glass, chilled

- 1½ oz. American blended whiskey
- 2 tsp. kirsch
- 2 tsp. Cherry Marnier
- 3 oz. crushed ice

Combine all ingredients in shaker, and shake vigorously. Strain into glass.

LIP BALM

A 4-oz. cocktail glass, chilled

1½ oz. American blended whiskey
½ oz. Jamaica dark rum
1 tsp. coconut cream
1 dash white crème de cacao
3 to 4 ice cubes

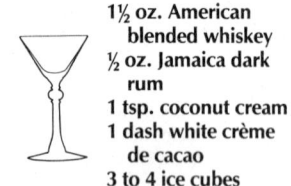

Combine all ingredients in shaker, and shake vigorously. Strain into glass.

MANHASSET

Follow recipe for Manhattan (Dry or Medium), using 2 tsp. lemon juice instead of 1 dash Angostura bitters.

MANHATTAN

A 4-oz. cocktail glass, chilled

The Manhattan, like the Martini, has so many variations that the connoisseur must experiment to determine the favorite formula, so that the taste is always the same. The following are popular preferences for dry, medium, and sweet versions:

DRY MANHATTAN

2 oz. American blended whiskey
¾ oz. dry vermouth
1 dash Angostura bitters
3 to 4 ice cubes

MEDIUM MANHATTAN

2 oz. American blended whiskey
2 tsp. sweet vermouth
2 tsp. dry vermouth
1 dash Angostura bitters
3 to 4 ice cubes

SWEET MANHATTAN

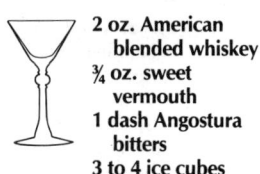

2 oz. American blended whiskey
¾ oz. sweet vermouth
1 dash Angostura bitters
3 to 4 ice cubes

Combine all ingredients in mixing glass, and stir well. Strain into glass.

Note: Any of these versions can also be prepared using Bourbon or Canadian whisky instead of American blended whiskey.

NARRAGANSETT
A 4-oz. cocktail glass, chilled

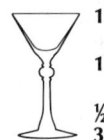

1½ to 2 oz. American blended whiskey
1 tbs. sweet vermouth
½ tsp. anisette
3 to 4 ice cubes

Combine all ingredients in shaker, and shake vigorously. Strain into glass.

NEW YORK COCKTAIL
A 4-oz. cocktail glass, chilled

2½ oz. American blended whiskey
½ tsp. superfine sugar
1 dash grenadine
2 tsp. lime juice
3 to 4 ice cubes
1 strip orange peel

Combine all ingredients except orange peel in shaker, and shake vigorously. Strain into glass. Twist orange peel over drink to release oil, and drop it in.

NEW YORK SOUR
A whiskey sour glass, chilled

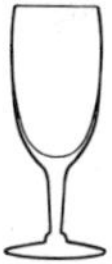

2 oz. American blended whiskey
1 oz. lemon juice
1 tsp. superfine sugar
½ oz. dry red wine
3 to 4 ice cubes
½ slice lemon
1 maraschino cherry

Combine whiskey, lemon juice, sugar, and ice in shaker, and shake vigorously. Strain mixture into glass. Float wine on top. Garnish with ½ lemon slice and cherry.

OPENING NITE
A 4-oz. cocktail glass, chilled

1½ oz. American blended whiskey
½ oz. dry vermouth
½ oz. strawberry liqueur
3 to 4 ice cubes

Combine all ingredients in mixing glass, and stir well. Strain into glass.

PREAKNESS
A 4-oz. cocktail glass, chilled

2½ oz. American blended whiskey
½ tsp. sweet vermouth
½ tsp. Benedictine
1 dash Angostura bitters
3 to 4 ice cubes

Combine all ingredients in mixing glass, and stir gently. Strain into glass.

PALM READER
A 4-oz. cocktail glass, chilled

1½ oz. American blended whiskey
1 oz. orange juice
1 tbs. gold rum
2 to 3 ice cubes

Combine all ingredients in mixing glass, and stir gently. Strain into glass.

SANTA ANITA

Follow recipe for Preakness (above), using ½ tsp. Grand Marnier instead of Benedictine.

RATTLESNAKE

A whiskey sour glass, chilled

2 oz. American blended whiskey
1 tsp. lemon juice
1 tsp. Falernum syrup
1 egg white
1 dash Pernod
3 to 4 ice cubes

Combine all ingredients in shaker, and shake vigorously. Strain into glass.

COPPERHEAD

Follow recipe for Rattlesnake (above), using 1 tsp. Cherry Marnier instead of Falernum syrup.

7 & 7

A highball glass, chilled

6 to 8 ice cubes
1½ oz. Seagram's 7 Crown blended whiskey
Approximately 4 oz. 7-Up soda

Fill highball glass with ice. Add whiskey. Top with 7-Up and stir 2 or 3 turns. *Courtesy "Seagram's Party Guide"*

SOUL KISS

An old-fashioned glass, chilled

1 oz. American blended whiskey
1 oz. dry vermouth
½ oz. orange juice
½ oz. Dubonnet aperitif
5 to 7 ice cubes
½ slice orange

Combine all ingredients except 2 to 3 ice cubes in mixing glass, and stir well. Place extra ice in glass, and strain into glass.

STICK SHIFT
A 4-oz. cocktail glass, chilled

1 oz. American blended whiskey
1 oz. gin
1 oz. sweet vermouth
3 to 4 ice cubes

Combine all ingredients in mixing glass, and stir gently. Strain into glass.

WHEELER DEALER
A 4-oz. cocktail glass, chilled

1½ oz. American blended whiskey
1 oz. dry vermouth
1 tsp. creme de framboises
3 to 4 ice cubes

Combine all ingredients in shaker, and shake vigorously. Strain into glass.

T.L.C.
A 4-oz. cocktail glass, chilled

2 oz. American blended whiskey
2 dashes triple sec
2 dashes Pernod
2 dashes Dubonnet aperitif
3 to 4 ice cubes
1 strip lime peel

Combine all ingredients except lime peel in mixing glass, and stir well. Strain into glass. Twist lime peel over drink to release oil, and drop it in.

WHISKEY SOUR
A whiskey sour glass, chilled

2 oz. American blended (or Bourbon) whiskey
1½ tbs. lemon juice
¾ tsp. superfine sugar
3 to 4 ice cubes
1 thin slice lemon
1 maraschino cherry

Combine all ingredients except lemon slice and cherry in shaker, and shake vigorously. Strain into glass. Garnish with lemon slice and cherry.

WHISKEY T.N.T.

A 4-oz. cocktail glass, chilled

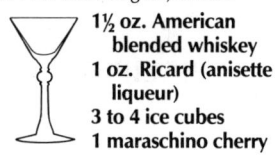

- 1½ oz. American blended whiskey
- 1 oz. Ricard (anisette liqueur)
- 3 to 4 ice cubes
- 1 maraschino cherry

Combine all ingredients except cherry in shaker, and shake vigorously. Strain into glass. Garnish with cherry.

WHITE SHADOW

An old-fashioned glass, chilled

- 1 oz. American blended whiskey
- 1 oz. Pernod
- 1 oz. heavy cream
- 3 oz. crushed ice
- 2 to 3 ice cubes
- Freshly grated nutmeg

Combine whiskey, Pernod, cream, and crushed ice in shaker, and shake vigorously. Place ice cubes in glass, and strain into glass. Top with sprinkle of nutmeg.

DARK SHADOW

Follow recipe for White Shadow, adding 1 tbs. Jamaica dark rum to ingredients in shaker.

FIVE-O'CLOCK SHADOW

Follow recipe for White Shadow with following changes: Prepare drink except for nutmeg. Float 1 tsp. dark crème de cacao on top of drink.

BOURBON WHISKEY RECIPES

BALTIMORE ORIOLE
An old-fashioned glass, chilled

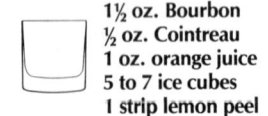

1½ oz. Bourbon
½ oz. Cointreau
1 oz. orange juice
5 to 7 ice cubes
1 strip lemon peel

Combine all ingredients except 2 to 3 ice cubes and lemon peel in shaker, and shake vigorously. Place remaining ice in glass, and strain drink into glass. Twist lemon peel over drink to release oil, and drop it in.

BLACK BIRD
A 4-oz. cocktail glass, chilled

½ oz. lemon juice
1 tsp. superfine sugar
2 to 3 ice cubes
1½ oz. Old Crow Bourbon
½ oz. sloe gin

Combine lemon juice and sugar in mixing glass, and stir well. Add ice, Bourbon, and sloe gin, and stir again. Strain into glass.

BOURBON AND BRANCH
A highball glass, chilled

3 to 4 ice cubes
1½ oz. Benchmark Sour Mash Premium Bourbon
4 to 5 oz. spring water

Place ice cubes in glass and add Bourbon. Fill glass with spring water. *Courtesy of "Seagram's Complete Party Guide"*

BOURBON COWBOY
An old-fashioned glass, chilled

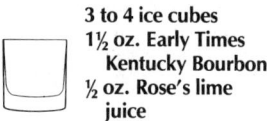

3 to 4 ice cubes
1½ oz. Early Times Kentucky Bourbon
½ oz. Rose's lime juice
½ oz. triple sec

Combine all ingredients in glass and stir. *Early Times Distillery Co., Shively, Ky.*

BOURBON DAISY
An old-fashioned glass, chilled

1 tsp. grenadine
1 tbs. lemon juice
1 tsp. Southern Comfort
1½ oz. Bourbon
3 to 4 ice cubes
4 oz. club soda, chilled
1 pineapple spear

Combine all ingredients except soda and pineapple spear in shaker, and shake vigorously. Strain into glass. Top with soda. Garnish with pineapple spear.

BOURBON ITALIAN
A 4-oz. cocktail glass, chilled

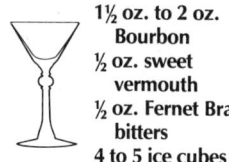

1½ oz. to 2 oz. Bourbon
½ oz. sweet vermouth
½ oz. Fernet Branca bitters
4 to 5 ice cubes

Combine all ingredients in mixing glass, and stir well. Strain into glass.

SPAGHETTI WESTERN

Follow recipe for Bourbon Italian (above), adding 1 to 2 dashes anisette liqueur to ingredients in shaker.

BRENNAN'S MILK PUNCH
An old-fashioned glass, chilled

1½ oz. Bourbon
3 oz. milk or half and half cream
1 tsp. powdered or superfine sugar
1 dash vanilla extract
2 ice cubes
Freshly grated nutmeg

Combine all ingredients except nutmeg in shaker, and shake vigorously. Strain into glass. Sprinkle nutmeg on top. *Brennan's Restaurant, New Orleans, La.*

BUSTED BROWNIE
An old-fashioned glass, chilled

2 oz. Bourbon
1 oz. dark crème de cacao
1 tbs. heavy cream
3 oz. crushed ice
2 to 3 ice cubes
2 blanched almonds

Combine all ingredients except ice cubes and almonds in shaker, and shake vigorously. Place ice cubes in glass, and strain drink into glass. Garnish with almonds.

CHATEAU JULEP
A 14-oz. tall glass, chilled

6 oz. crushed ice
3 to 4 mint sprigs
1 sugar cube, or 1 tsp. superfine sugar
1 tsp. water
3 oz. Bourbon
3 to 4 oz. dry sparkling wine, chilled

Place ice in glass and set aside. In separate glass, combine 2 mint sprigs, sugar, and water, and muddle with stirrer or spoon until sprigs are well macerated. Add Bourbon to mint mixture. Stir and strain into glass. Add wine.

COOL COLONEL
A 10- to 14-oz. tall glass, chilled

Ice cubes to fill glass
1 oz. Southern Comfort
1 oz. Bourbon
3 oz. strong tea, chilled
½ oz. lemon juice
¼ oz. sugar syrup
2 to 4 oz. club soda, chilled
1 strip lemon peel

Fill glass with ice. Add Southern Comfort, Bourbon, tea, lemon juice, and sugar syrup, and stir. Top with soda. Twist lemon peel over drink to release oil, and drop it in. *Southern Comfort Corp., St. Louis, Mo.*

DELTA FLIGHT
A highball glass, chilled

    1½ oz. Bourbon
    ½ oz. Southern Comfort
    2 tsp. lemon juice
    1 tsp. sugar syrup
    6 to 8 ice cubes
    1 slice fresh peach

Combine all ingredients except 4 to 5 ice cubes and peach in shaker, and shake vigorously. Place remaining ice in glass, and strain drink into glass. Garnish with peach slice.

EL RANCHO BRANDY
A 4-oz. cocktail glass, chilled

    1½ oz. Bourbon
    1½ oz. brandy
    1 tsp. lemon juice
    1 tsp. Grand Marnier
    3 to 4 ice cubes

Combine all ingredients in shaker, and shake vigorously. Strain into glass.

EWING, J.R.
An old-fashioned glass, chilled

    2 oz. Bourbon
    2 dashes peach bitters
    2 ice cubes
    1 red grape (Red Emperor), or black cherry

Combine Bourbon, bitters, and ice in glass, and stir gently. Drop grape or cherry into drink.

FANCY TURKEY

Follow recipe for Fancy Brandy (see p. 117), using 2 oz. Wild Turkey Bourbon instead of brandy.

FLINTLOCK
A 4-oz. cocktail glass, chilled

    ½ oz. applejack
    1½ oz. Bourbon
    3 drops grenadine
    1 dash peppermint schnapps
    1 tsp. lemon juice
    3 to 4 ice cubes

Combine all ingredients in shaker, and shake vigorously. Strain into glass.

FORESTER

An old-fashioned glass, chilled

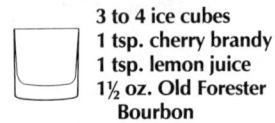

3 to 4 ice cubes
1 tsp. cherry brandy
1 tsp. lemon juice
1½ oz. Old Forester Bourbon

Place ice in glass. Add cherry brandy, lemon juice, and Bourbon, and stir. *Old Forester, Brown-Forman Distilling Co., Louisville, Ky.*

GOLDEN GLOW

A 4-oz. cocktail glass, chilled

½ oz. Jamaica dark rum
1½ oz. Bourbon
¼ oz. orange juice
¼ oz. lemon juice
3 to 4 ice cubes
1 dash grenadine

Combine all ingredients except grenadine in shaker, and shake vigorously. Strain into glass. Top with grenadine.

GLOWWORM

A 4-oz. cocktail glass, chilled

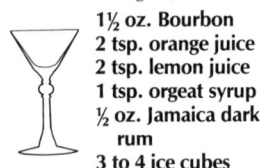

1½ oz. Bourbon
2 tsp. orange juice
2 tsp. lemon juice
1 tsp. orgeat syrup
½ oz. Jamaica dark rum
3 to 4 ice cubes

Combine all ingredients in shaker, and shake vigorously. Strain into glass.

GOLDEN NUGGET

A 10- to 14-oz. tall glass, chilled

1½ oz. Bourbon
1 oz. lemon juice
1 tbs. Galliano
1 tsp. orgeat syrup
7 to 8 ice cubes
3 to 4 oz. club soda or ginger ale, chilled

Combine Bourbon, lemon juice, Galliano, orgeat syrup, and 3 to 4 ice cubes in mixing glass, and stir well. Place remaining ice in glass, and strain drink into glass. Top with soda or ginger ale. *Golden Nugget Casino Hotel, Las Vegas, Nev.*

GRAND CENTRAL STATION

A 4-oz. cocktail glass, chilled

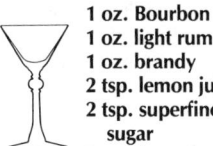

1 oz. Bourbon
1 oz. light rum
1 oz. brandy
2 tsp. lemon juice
2 tsp. superfine sugar
3 to 4 ice cubes

Combine all ingredients in shaker, and shake vigorously. Strain into glass.

HOLLY GOLIGHTLY

A 4-oz. cocktail glass, chilled

1½ oz. Bourbon
½ oz. framboise (raspberry brandy)
½ oz. triple sec
1 tsp. orgeat syrup
1 oz. orange juice
3 to 4 ice cubes

Combine all ingredients in shaker, and shake vigorously. Strain into glass.

GREAT DIVIDE

A highball glass, chilled

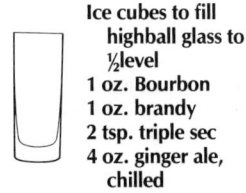

Ice cubes to fill highball glass to ½ level
1 oz. Bourbon
1 oz. brandy
2 tsp. triple sec
4 oz. ginger ale, chilled

Fill glass with ice to ½ level. Add Bourbon, brandy, and triple sec, and stir. Fill with ginger ale.

JULEP I

A 10- to 14-oz. tall glass, chilled

7 to 8 oz. crushed ice
3 to 4 mint sprigs
1 sugar cube, or 1 tsp. superfine sugar
1 tsp. water
3 oz. Bourbon

Put ice in glass and set aside. In separate glass, combine 2 mint sprigs, sugar, and 1 tsp. water, and muddle with stirrer or spoon until sprigs are well macerated. Add Bourbon to mixture. Stir, strain into glass which has been set aside, and stir again. Garnish with remaining mint.

JULEP II
A highball glass, chilled

1 sugar cube or 1 tsp. superfine sugar
8 to 10 mint leaves
1 oz. water
4 to 5 ice cubes
2½ to 3 oz. Bourbon

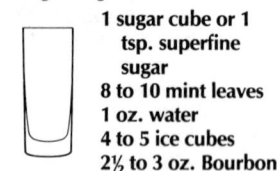

Put sugar, mint leaves, and water in glass. Macerate leaves with stirrer, and let stand about 30 seconds. Add ice. Pour Bourbon into glass, stirring slowly. Let drink stand a few minutes before serving.

LAS VEGAS
A highball glass, chilled

½ oz. Galliano
1 oz. lemon juice
1½ oz. Bourbon
1 tsp. sugar syrup
3 to 4 ice cubes
Finely crushed ice to fill highball glass to ½ level

Combine all ingredients except crushed ice in shaker, and shake vigorously. Fill glass to ½ level with crushed ice. Strain into glass.

KENTUCKY COLONEL
A 4-oz. cocktail glass, chilled

2½ oz. Bourbon
½ oz. Benedictine
4 to 5 ice cubes

Combine all ingredients in shaker, and shake vigorously. Strain into glass.

MASON-DIXON
A 4-oz. cocktail glass, chilled

1 oz. Bourbon
2 tsp. white crème de cacao
1 oz. light rum
2 tsp. white crème de menthe
3 to 4 ice cubes
3 oz. crushed ice

Combine all ingredients except crushed ice in shaker, and shake vigorously. Put crushed ice in glass, and strain into glass.

MIDNIGHT COWBOY
A 4-oz. cocktail glass, chilled

1½ oz. Bourbon
1 oz. Jamaica dark rum
1 tbs. heavy cream
4 oz. crushed ice

Combine all ingredients in shaker, and shake vigorously. Strain into glass.

MOTHER 'N' CALF
An old-fashioned glass, chilled

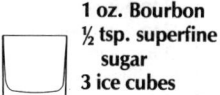

1 oz. Bourbon
½ tsp. superfine sugar
3 ice cubes
4 to 5 oz. milk
Ground cinnamon

Combine Bourbon and sugar in glass, and stir until sugar is dissolved. Add ice and milk, and stir slowly. Sprinkle with cinnamon.

MILLIONAIRE
A whiskey sour glass, chilled

½ oz. curaçao
1 egg white
2 dashes grenadine
1½ oz. Bourbon
3 to 4 ice cubes

Combine all ingredients in blender, and blend at medium speed 20 to 30 seconds. Strain into glass.

OLD DEVIL MOON
An old-fashioned glass, chilled

1½ oz. Bourbon
1 oz. Cointreau
3 oz. orange juice, chilled
5 to 7 ice cubes
1 tsp. grenadine

Combine Bourbon, Cointreau, orange juice, and 3 to 4 ice cubes in shaker, and shake vigorously. Place remaining ice in glass, and strain into glass. Float grenadine on top.

PRESBYTERIAN

A 10- to 14-oz. tall glass, chilled

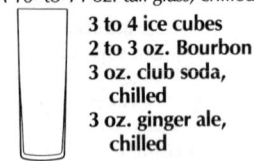

> 3 to 4 ice cubes
> 2 to 3 oz. Bourbon
> 3 oz. club soda, chilled
> 3 oz. ginger ale, chilled

Place ice in glass. Add Bourbon. Then top with equal parts of soda and ginger ale.

RODEO RIDER

An old-fashioned glass, chilled

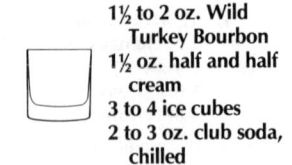

> 1½ to 2 oz. Wild Turkey Bourbon
> 1½ oz. half and half cream
> 3 to 4 ice cubes
> 2 to 3 oz. club soda, chilled

Combine all ingredients except soda in shaker, and shake vigorously. Strain into glass. Add soda. *Wild Turkey, Austin Nichols & Co., New York, N.Y.*

RICHELIEU

A 4-oz. cocktail glass, chilled

> 1 oz. Dubonnet Blanc aperitif
> 1 tsp. Vielle Cure liqueur
> 1½ to 2 oz. Bourbon
> 3 to 4 ice cubes
> 1 strip orange peel

Combine all ingredients except orange peel in shaker, and shake vigorously. Strain into glass. Twist orange peel over drink to release oil, and drop it in. *The Dubonnet Co., Fresno, Calif.*

SAN FRANCISCO TROLLEY

A highball glass, chilled

> 4 ice cubes
> 2½ oz. Bourbon
> 3 oz. pineapple juice
> 3 oz. cranberry juice

Place ice in glass. Add Bourbon, and stir. Add juices, and stir again.

SCARLET LADY
A 4-oz. cocktail glass, chilled

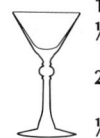

1½ oz. Bourbon
½ oz. cranberry liqueur
2 tbs. grapefruit juice
½ tsp. orgeat syrup
3 to 4 ice cubes

Combine all ingredients in mixing glass, and stir well. Strain into glass.

STONE AGE SOUR
A whiskey sour glass, chilled

1½ oz. Bourbon
1 tbs. lemon juice
3 to 4 dashes Minttu Peppermint Schnaapps (100-proof)
½ tsp. sugar syrup
2 to 3 ice cubes
3 oz. crushed ice

Combine all ingredients except crushed ice in mixing glass, and stir well. Put crushed ice in glass, and strain into glass.

SUB-BOURBON
An old-fashioned glass, chilled

2 to 3 ice cubes
1½ oz. Bourbon
2 tbs. orange juice
2 dashes gold rum

Place ice in glass. Add remaining ingredients, and stir slowly until chilled.

CANADIAN WHISKY RECIPES

BANFF COCKTAIL
A 4-oz. cocktail glass, chilled

1½ oz. Canadian whisky
½ oz. Grand Marnier
2 dashes kirsch
1 dash orange bitters
3 to 4 ice cubes

Combine all ingredients in shaker, and shake vigorously. Strain into glass.

BEAUFORT BLAST
An old-fashioned glass, chilled

1½ oz. Canadian whisky
1 oz. Minttu Peppermint Schnaapps
½ tsp. white crème de cacao
1 egg white
5 to 7 ice cubes
2 to 3 oz. club soda, chilled

Combine all ingredients except 2 to 3 ice cubes and soda in shaker, and shake vigorously. Place remaining ice in glass, and strain mixture into glass. Top with soda.

CANADIAN BLACKBERRY

An old-fashioned glass, chilled

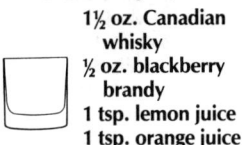

- 1½ oz. Canadian whisky
- ½ oz. blackberry brandy
- 1 tsp. lemon juice
- 1 tsp. orange juice
- 5 to 7 ice cubes

Combine all ingredients except 2 to 3 ice cubes in shaker, and shake vigorously. Place remaining ice in glass, and strain drink into glass.

BAGGY PANTS

Follow recipe for Canadian Blackberry (above), using ½ oz. cranberry liqueur instead of blackberry brandy.

CHERRY PICKER

Follow recipe for Canadian Blackberry (above), using ½ oz. Cherry Marnier instead of blackberry brandy.

CANADIAN McINTOSH

A 4-oz. cocktail glass, chilled

- 1½ oz. Canadian whisky
- 1 tbs. triple sec
- 1 tsp. superfine sugar
- 2 dashes apple juice
- 2 to 3 oz. crushed ice

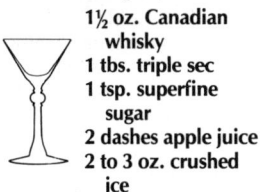

Combine all ingredients in shaker, and shake vigorously. Strain into glass.

CANADIAN MISTY MORNING

A 4-oz. cocktail glass, chilled

- 3 to 4 ice cubes
- 1½ oz. Canadian Mist whisky
- ¾ oz. Cointreau
- 1 tbs. grenadine
- 2 tbs. lemon juice
- 1 strip lemon peel

Combine all ingredients except lemon peel in shaker, and shake vigorously. Strain into glass. Twist lemon peel over drink to release oil, and drop it in. *Canadian Mist Distillers Ltd., Collingwood, Ont.*

CANADIAN REDCOAT

A 4-oz. cocktail glass, chilled

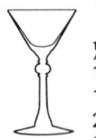

1½ oz. Canadian whisky
½ oz. Scotch whisky
1 tsp. lemon juice
1 tsp. orange juice
2 dashes grenadine
3 to 4 ice cubes

Combine all ingredients in shaker, and shake vigorously. Strain into glass.

DOMINION

A whiskey sour glass, chilled

1½ oz. Canadian whisky
1 oz. Grand Marnier
1 tsp. lemon juice
1 tsp. heavy cream
1 egg
3 to 4 ice cubes
Freshly grated nutmeg

Combine all ingredients except nutmeg in shaker, and shake vigorously. Strain into glass. Sprinkle with nutmeg.

FUR TRAPPER

A 12- to 14-oz. tall glass, chilled

1½ oz. Canadian whisky
3 oz. tomato juice, chilled
1 tsp. Worcestershire sauce
½ tsp. Tabasco sauce
2 to 3 ice cubes
About 6 oz. cold beer
Salt
Freshly ground black pepper

Combine whisky, tomato juice, Worcestershire sauce, Tabasco sauce, and ice in mixing glass, and stir well. Strain into glass. Slowly add beer while slowly stirring. Sprinkle with salt and pepper.

HALIFAX

A 4-oz. cocktail glass, chilled

1½ oz. Canadian whisky
½ oz. amaretto
½ oz. heavy cream
3 to 4 ice cubes

Combine all ingredients in shaker, and shake vigorously. Strain into glass.

KLONDIKE

An old-fashioned glass, chilled

1½ oz. Canadian whisky
½ oz. apple brandy
1 tsp. lemon juice
2 dashes white crème de menthe
2 to 3 drops grenadine
3 to 4 ice cubes
6 oz. crushed ice

Combine all ingredients except crushed ice in shaker, and shake vigorously. Put crushed ice in glass, and strain drink into glass.

NORTHERN LIGHT

A 4-oz. cocktail glass, chilled

1 oz. Canadian whisky
½ oz. dry vermouth
½ oz. Grand Marnier
½ oz. cranberry liqueur
3 to 4 ice cubes

Combine all ingredients in shaker, and shake vigorously. Strain into glass.

NIAGARA FALLS

A 4-oz. cocktail glass, chilled

1½ oz. Canadian whisky
½ oz. Irish Mist liqueur
½ oz. heavy cream
3 to 4 ice cubes
Freshly grated nutmeg

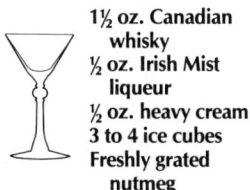

Combine all ingredients except nutmeg in shaker, and shake vigorously. Strain into glass. Sprinkle with nutmeg.

RENFREW

A 4-oz. cocktail glass, chilled

1½ oz. Canadian whisky
½ oz. Drambuie
1 tsp. kirsch
2 to 3 oz. crushed ice

Combine all ingredients in shaker, and shake vigorously. Strain into glass.

THE WESTERN MARTINI

An old-fashioned glass, chilled

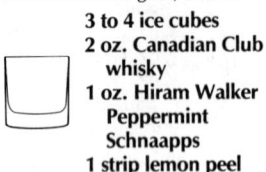

- 3 to 4 ice cubes
- 2 oz. Canadian Club whisky
- 1 oz. Hiram Walker Peppermint Schnaapps
- 1 strip lemon peel

Combine all ingredients except lemon peel in glass and stir briefly. Twist lemon peel to release oil over drink, and drop it in. *Hiram Walker Incorporated, Detroit, Mich.*

TORONTO COCKTAIL

A 4-oz. cocktail glass, chilled

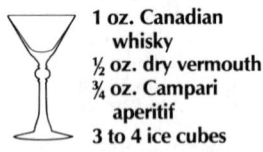

- 1 oz. Canadian whisky
- ½ oz. dry vermouth
- ¾ oz. Campari aperitif
- 3 to 4 ice cubes

Combine all ingredients in mixing glass, and stir well. Strain into glass.

YELLOWKNIFE

A 4-oz. cocktail glass, chilled

- 1½ oz. Canadian whisky
- 2 tbs. orange juice
- 1 tsp. yellow Chartreuse
- 3 to 4 ice cubes

Combine all ingredients in shaker, and shake vigorously. Strain into glass.

IRISH WHISKEY RECIPES

BLACK and TAN
A 10- to 14-oz. tall glass

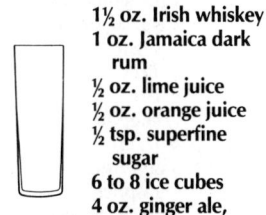

1½ oz. Irish whiskey
1 oz. Jamaica dark rum
½ oz. lime juice
½ oz. orange juice
½ tsp. superfine sugar
6 to 8 ice cubes
4 oz. ginger ale, chilled

Combine Irish whiskey, rum, lime and orange juice, sugar, and 3 to 4 ice cubes in shaker, and shake vigorously. Put remaining ice in glass. Strain mixture into glass, and fill with ginger ale.

CAMERON'S KICK
A 4-oz. cocktail glass, chilled

1¼ oz. Irish whiskey
1 oz. Scotch whisky
2 tsp. lemon juice
2 to 3 dashes orange bitters
4 to 5 ice cubes

Combine all ingredients in mixing glass, and stir well. Strain into glass.

COMMANDO FIX
A whiskey sour glass, chilled

Crushed ice to fill whiskey sour glass
2 oz. Irish whiskey
¼ oz. Cointreau
½ oz. lime juice
1 to 2 dashes raspberry liqueur

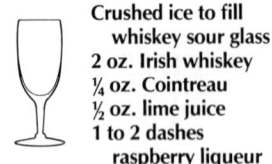

Fill glass with ice. Add Irish whiskey, Cointreau, and lime juice, and stir slowly. Dot surface of drink with raspberry liqueur.

GEORGE BUSH

Crushed ice to fill glass to ¾ level
1½ oz. Old Bushmills Irish whiskey
1 strip lemon peel
3 to 4 oz. ginger ale, chilled

Fill glass with crushed ice to ¾ level. Add Irish whiskey. Twist lemon peel over drink to release oil, and drop it in. Top with ginger ale. *Old Bushmills Irish Whiskey, The Jos. Garneau Co., New York, N.Y.*

GREEN DEVIL
A whiskey sour glass, chilled

2 oz. Irish whiskey
2 oz. clam juice
1 to 2 dashes green crème de menthe
½ tsp. lemon juice
3 to 4 ice cubes

Combine all ingredients in shaker, and shake vigorously. Strain into glass.

IRISH SHILLELAGH
An old-fashioned glass, chilled

1 oz. Irish whiskey
½ oz. sloe gin
1 tbs. light rum
1 oz. lemon juice
1 tsp. superfine sugar
2 slices peach, crushed or chopped
4 oz. crushed ice
3 or 4 fresh raspberries
1 black cherry

Combine all ingredients except raspberries and cherry in shaker, and shake vigorously (or these ingredients can be processed in blender at low speed for 10 to 15 seconds). Strain into glass. Garnish with raspberries and cherry.

L'IL ORPHAN ANNIE

A 4-oz. cocktail glass, chilled

1½ oz. Irish whiskey
1 oz. Bailey's Irish Cream
2 tbs. chocolate-flavored Ovaltine powder (or 1 tbs. chocolate syrup)
3 to 4 ice cubes
1 tsp. shaved chocolate

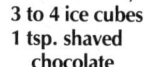

Combine all ingredients except shaved chocolate in shaker, and shake vigorously. Strain into glass. Garnish with shaved chocolate.

PADDY'S WAGON

An old-fashioned glass, chilled

1½ oz. Irish whiskey
1½ oz. sweet vermouth
1 to 2 dashes Angostura bitters
1 to 2 dashes Southern Comfort
5 to 7 ice cubes

Combine all ingredients except 2 to 3 ice cubes in shaker, and shake vigorously. Place remaining ice in glass, and strain drink into glass.

RUDDY McDOWELL

An old-fashioned glass, chilled

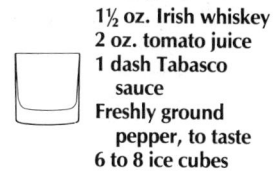

1½ oz. Irish whiskey
2 oz. tomato juice
1 dash Tabasco sauce
Freshly ground pepper, to taste
6 to 8 ice cubes

Combine all ingredients except 3 to 4 ice cubes in shaker, and shake vigorously. Place remaining ice in glass, and strain drink into glass.

SERPENT'S SMILE

An old-fashioned glass, chilled

¾ oz. Irish whiskey
1½ oz. sweet vermouth
¾ oz. lemon juice
1 tbs. kummel
2 dashes Angostura bitters
5 to 7 ice cubes
1 strip lemon peel

Combine all ingredients except 2 to 3 ice cubes and lemon peel in shaker, and shake vigorously. Place remaining ice in glass, and strain drink into glass. Twist lemon peel over drink to release oil, and drop it in.

SHAMROCK

An old-fashioned glass, chilled

1½ oz. Irish whiskey
1½ oz. dry vermouth
2 to 3 dashes green Chartreuse
2 to 3 dashes green crème de menthe
5 to 7 ice cubes
1 green maraschino cherry

Combine all ingredients except 2 to 3 ice cubes and cherry in mixing glass, and stir well. Place remaining ice in glass, and strain drink into glass. Garnish with cherry.

TIPPERARY

A 4-oz. cocktail glass, chilled

1 oz. Irish whiskey
1 oz. sweet vermouth
¾ oz. green Chartreuse
4 to 5 ice cubes

Combine all ingredients in mixing glass, and stir well. Strain into glass.

SCOTCH WHISKY RECIPES

Scotch Syndrome

My first trip to Scotland many years ago taught me that the drinking Scotsman is of a heroic mold. Never could I get one to agree that Scotch whisky should be mixed or combined with other spirits. It was agreed only that "good water to mix with" was permissible, but only "cold." It is tradition alone that has kept the mixed drink explosion from penetrating Scotch as much as it has gin, rum, and vodka.

Recipes for Scotch drinks are usually less contrived. Scotch whisky more than any other spirit is like a wine, and it must be savored as a civilized spirit.

AFFINITY
A 4-oz. cocktail glass, chilled

- ¾ oz. dry vermouth
- ¾ oz. sweet vermouth
- 1½ oz. Scotch whisky
- 2 dashes Angostura bitters
- 3 to 4 ice cubes
- 1 strip lemon or orange peel
- 1 maraschino cherry

Combine all ingredients except peel and cherry in mixing glass, and stir well. Strain into cocktail glass. Twist lemon or orange peel over drink to release oil, and drop it in. Garnish with cherry.

WHISPERING ITALIAN
Follow recipe for Affinity (above), using J & B Scotch whisky, and *shake* ingredients in shaker (instead of stirring).

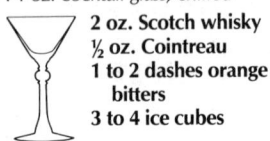

BAIRN
A 4-oz. cocktail glass, chilled

2 oz. Scotch whisky
½ oz. Cointreau
1 to 2 dashes orange bitters
3 to 4 ice cubes

Combine all ingredients in shaker, and shake vigorously. Strain into glass.

BARBARY COAST
An old-fashioned glass, chilled

1 oz. Scotch whisky
1 oz. gin
1 oz. light rum
¾ oz. white crème de cacao
4 to 5 ice cubes

Combine all ingredients except 1 or 2 ice cubes in shaker, and shake vigorously. Place extra ice in glass, and strain into glass.

BALMORAL
A 4-oz. cocktail glass, chilled

1¼ oz. gin
1¼ oz. Scotch whisky
½ oz. Ricard (anise-flavored liqueur)
3 to 4 ice cubes

Combine all ingredients in shaker, and shake vigorously. Strain into glass.

BARN DOOR
A 4-oz. cocktail glass, chilled

1 oz. Cointreau
1½ oz. Scotch whisky
2 dashes orange bitters
3 to 4 ice cubes

Combine all ingredients in shaker, and shake vigorously. Strain into glass. *Cointreau Ltd., Lawrenceville, N.J.*

BEADLESTONE

A 4-oz. cocktail glass, chilled

2 oz. Scotch whisky
1 oz. sweet vermouth
2 dashes Angostura bitters
3 to 4 ice cubes

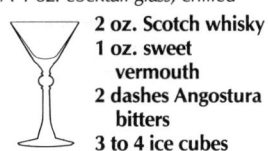

Combine all ingredients in shaker, and shake vigorously. Strain into glass.

THISTLE

Follow recipe for Beadlestone (above), but omit 2 dashes Angostura bitters.

BLOODY SCOT

Follow recipe for Blood and Sand (above), with following changes: Use *1 oz.* (instead of ¾ oz.) Scotch whisky. Use *1 oz.* (instead of ½ oz.) Cherry Marnier.

BOBBY BURNS

A 4-oz. cocktail glass, chilled

1½ oz. Scotch whisky
½ oz. dry vermouth
½ oz. sweet vermouth
1 dash Benedictine
3 to 4 ice cubes

Combine all ingredients in mixing glass, and stir well. Strain into glass.

BONNIE DOON

Follow recipe for Bobby Burns (above), with following changes: Omit dry vermouth. Use 2 tsp. (instead of 1 dash) Benedictine.

DAILY MAIL

A 4-oz. cocktail glass, chilled

2½ oz. Scotch whisky
½ tsp. superfine sugar
2 tsp. lemon juice
2 dashes curaçao
1 dash amaretto
3 to 4 ice cubes
Crushed ice to fill cocktail glass

Combine all ingredients except crushed ice in mixing glass, and stir well. Fill cocktail glass with crushed ice. Strain into glass.

GIBRALTAR

A 4-oz. cocktail glass, chilled

1 oz. Scotch whisky
1 oz. dry sherry
2 tsp. lemon juice
2 tsp. passion fruit syrup
3 to 4 ice cubes

Combine all ingredients in shaker, and shake vigorously. Strain into glass.

GOLDENBERG'S FOLLY

An old-fashioned glass, chilled

3 to 4 ice cubes
1½ oz. Pinch 12-year-old Scotch whisky
6 oz. cola, chilled

Place ice in glass. Add Scotch. Top with cola. Stir 1 turn. *Haig & Haig Pinch 12-year-old Scotch, Renfield Importers Ltd., New York, N.Y.*

HEATHER on the HILL
A 4-oz. cocktail glass, chilled

1½ oz. Scotch whisky
1 tsp. dry vermouth
½ oz. Drambuie
1 dash orange bitters
3 to 4 ice cubes

Combine all ingredients in mixing glass, and stir well. Strain into cocktail glass.

IRON LADY
A 4-oz. cocktail glass, chilled

1½ oz. Scotch whisky
½ oz. dry vermouth
½ oz. port
1 dash orange bitters
3 to 4 ice cubes

Combine all ingredients in mixing glass, and stir well. Strain into cocktail glass.

HIGHLAND FLING
An old-fashioned glass, chilled

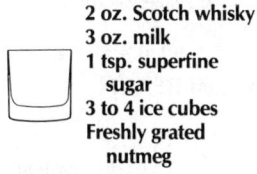

2 oz. Scotch whisky
3 oz. milk
1 tsp. superfine sugar
3 to 4 ice cubes
Freshly grated nutmeg

Combine all ingredients except nutmeg in shaker, and shake vigorously. Strain into glass. Sprinkle nutmeg on top.

JAPANESE FIZZ No. 2
An old-fashioned glass, chilled

2 oz. Suntory Scotch whisky
2 oz. dry red wine
2 tsp. lemon juice
1 tsp. sugar syrup
3 to 4 ice cubes
2 oz. club soda, chilled
1 pineapple spear

Combine whisky, wine, lemon juice, sugar syrup, and ice in shaker, and shake well. Pour, unstrained, into glass. Add soda. Garnish with pineapple spear.

KERRY BLUE

A 4-oz. cocktail glass, chilled

1½ oz. Scotch whisky
1 dash orange bitters
1 dash dry vermouth
½ oz. blue curaçao
3 to 4 ice cubes

Combine all ingredients in shaker, and shake vigorously. Strain into glass.

LOCH LOMOND

A 4-oz. cocktail glass, chilled

1½ to 2 oz. Scotch whisky
1 tsp. Falernum syrup
2 dashes Angostura bitters
3 to 4 ice cubes

Combine all ingredients in shaker, and shake vigorously. Strain into glass.

LOCH NESS MONSTER

An old-fashioned glass, chilled

1½ oz. Scotch whisky
1 tsp. peppermint schnapps
3 to 4 ice cubes
3 oz. club soda, chilled
1 twig of Scotch pine (or any fir tree), about 6-inch length

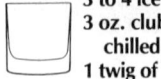

In shaker, combine Scotch whisky, peppermint schnapps, and ice, and shake vigorously. Strain into glass. Add soda and stir slowly. Garnish with twig.

MIAMI BEACH

A 4-oz. cocktail glass, chilled

1½ oz. Scotch whisky
1½ oz. dry vermouth
2 tbs. grapefruit juice
3 to 4 ice cubes

Combine all ingredients in mixing glass, and stir well. Strain into glass.

ROB ROY
A 4-oz. cocktail glass, chilled

2 oz. Scotch whisky
½ oz. dry vermouth
5 to 6 ice cubes
1 strip lemon peel

Combine all ingredients except 2 or 3 ice cubes in mixing glass, and stir well. Place extra ice in glass, and strain into glass. *The Waldorf-Astoria, New York, N.Y.*

SCOTCH MIST
An old-fashioned glass, chilled

6 to 8 oz. crushed ice
1½ to 2 oz. Scotch Glenlivet
1 strip lemon peel

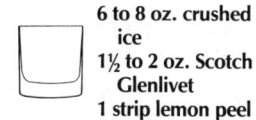

Put ice in glass. Add Scotch. Twist lemon peel over drink to release oil, and drop it in. Serve with short straw. *Courtesy of "Seagram's Complete Party Guide"*

SCOTCH SOUR

Follow recipe for Whiskey Sour, using 2 oz. Scotch whisky instead of American blended whiskey.

SCOT'S BREAKFAST
An old-fashioned glass, chilled

2 oz. Scotch whisky
6 oz. milk
1 tsp. superfine sugar
3 to 4 ice cubes
1 2-inch square shortbread or Lorna Doone biscuit
1 dash freshly grated nutmeg plus extra for topping

Combine all ingredients except shortbread and dash of nutmeg in shaker, and shake vigorously. Strain into glass. Crumble shortbread and sprinkle on top. Add sprinkle of nutmeg.

CHOCOLATE FLING

Follow recipe for Scot's Breakfast, with following changes: Use 6 oz. chocolate milk instead of plain milk. Use pinch of freshly grated chocolate instead of nutmeg.

TILT the KILT
A 4-oz. cocktail glass, chilled

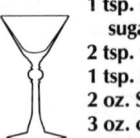

- 1 tsp. superfine sugar
- 2 tsp. water
- 1 tsp. lemon juice
- 2 oz. Scotch whisky
- 3 oz. crushed ice
- 1 tsp. triple sec

In mixing glass, combine sugar and water, and stir until sugar is dissolved. Add lemon juice and Scotch, and stir. Put ice in cocktail glass. Strain drink into glass. Float triple sec on top.

QUEEN of SCOTS

Follow recipe for Tilt the Kilt, with following changes: Omit triple sec. Top drink with ½ tsp. green Chartreuse and ½ tsp. blue curaçao, giving green/blue plaid effect.

WALKMAN
A 4-oz. cocktail glass, chilled

- ¾ oz. Scotch whisky
- ½ oz. Cherry Marnier
- ¾ oz. sweet vermouth
- ½ oz. orange juice
- 3 to 4 ice cubes

Combine all ingredients in mixing glass, and stir well. Strain into glass.

WALTER MITTY
A 4-oz. cocktail glass, chilled

- 1½ oz. Scotch whisky
- 1 egg white
- 1 tsp. Falernum syrup
- 1 tsp. curaçao
- 3 to 4 ice cubes

Combine all ingredients in shaker, and shake vigorously. Strain into glass.

OTHER SPIRIT RECIPES

ARABIAN NIGHT
(Bedouin's Revenge)
A highball glass, chilled

Ice cubes to fill glass to ¾ level
1½ oz. arak
3 to 4 dashes Angostura bitters
4 to 6 oz. tonic water, chilled
1 thin orange slice

Fill glass to ¾ level with ice. Add arak and bitters. Fill glass with tonic, and stir 2 to 3 turns. Garnish with orange slice.

ARABIAN 'NYET'
A highball glass, chilled

Ice cubes to fill glass to ¾ level
1½ oz. arak
3 to 4 dashes Angostura bitters
½ oz. Cointreau
4 to 6 oz. Russian tea, chilled
1 thin orange slice

Fill glass to ¾ level with ice. Add arak, bitters, and Cointreau. Fill glass with tea, and stir 2 to 3 turns. Garnish with orange slice.

Beer, Ale, and Sake

ABOUT BEER, ALE, AND SAKE

People used to drink beer because they thought it was cheap. However, on an alcoholic basis, it can be quite expensive. Most beers marketed in America, domestic and imported brands, average 3.6 percent alcohol by volume as compared to an average of 14 percent in wine and 40 percent (80 proof) in spirits.

Many foreign beers contain a higher alcoholic content in their own countries, up to 12 to 14 percent but adjust the content for sale in the American market. According to federal regulation, beer, or any other malt beverage, must be a minimum of 0.5 percent alcohol by volume, and there is no upward limit, although some states set a limit of 4 or 5 percent. Some state laws also distinguish a lower alcohol beer at 3.2 percent.

Beer is made by cooking and fermenting grains, usually germinated (malted) barley, and flavored with the flower of the hop plant to give it a bitter taste.

Serving Beer

Bottle or can, poured into glass: Beer tastes best when it is served at its ideal temperature, and this varies. American lager beer (light-bodied) should be served at 42°F.; full-bodied ale at 55°F.; and most imported beers at 48°F. to 50°F.

To correctly pour a glass of beer from a bottle or can, pry off cap or pull tab quickly. Tilt glass at a 45-degree angle and pour beer down side of glass until it is three fourths full. Then straighten glass and pour down the center. This procedure should result in a three-quarter-inch head of foam. For no head, keep glass tilted all the way.

Draught beer—from the barrel: The pleasure of bulk beer from the barrel is the fresh brewery taste. But this rich, fragrant flavor is fleeting unless certain precautions in dispensing draught beer are carefully observed:

Barrel beer must be maintained at a temperature of 38°F. to 42°F. Its natural carbonation must be held at a constant pressure from barrel, through the coils, through the dispenser, and into the glass. (This system can be checked by the beer distributors.) Also, to preserve this special barrel flavor, every aspect of equipment must be clean and odorless: faucets, tubing, hose, coils, taps, vents, direct draw systems, serving glasses, bar area.

To draw a glass of draught beer, hold glass at a 45° angle close to the tap. Pour beer into glass, lowering and straightening glass as it fills with beer to half an inch from top, and close tap. About one fifth of the glass should be head foam.

Types of Beer

Lager: A brew that has been aged to settle, resulting in a light, clear-bodied beer; representative of most American beers. (Lager is the German word meaning to age or store.)

Ale: Fuller bodied and more bitter than lager; favored by the English.

Porter: More sweet, less bitter hop than ale.

Stout: In every sense an expression of its name—dark, with strong flavors of malt, sugar, and hops.

Pilsner: Any light lager beer; originally developed by Pilsner Urquell in Czechoslovakia. Today there are many imitations.

Bock: Traditionally prepared in winter and available during a period of about six weeks in early spring; dark and sweetish in taste compared to regular beer.

The Beer World

Malt beverages don't encourage mixability. There are some combinations, however, that have been around for a long time. One that is enjoying a revival is the Boilermaker, which is one's favorite brew preceded by one's favorite spirit (aquavit, vodka, schnapps).

Beer, which was the G.I.'s staple alcoholic beverage, became the base for other mixed drinks created during World War II. It was during this era that many of us got our first taste of non-American brews, i.e., English, Mexican, Canadian, Dutch, Filipino, Australian, etc. Perhaps most of it was consumed warm, but many who were in the U.S. Air Force, flew a few cases up into the wild blue yonder to chill it! It was during these thirty-minute excursions of "cooling off" that ideas such as Wild Brew Yonder, Brew Beard, and Am I Brew were sired.

There is no way to bring into focus in this book the 5,000 or so brands of beer produced worldwide, but we can review a few of the better-known styles of beers—American and imports from countries of high per capita consumption, whose labels appear in the U.S. market:

Australia: The city of Darwin lets it be known that per capita consumption there is 55-plus gallons. Most brews from Australia are strong and "hoppy" like the kangaroo. The best known exports are Black Swan, Foster's, and Tooth.

Austria: Perhaps only 35 to 40 brewers remain in this once great brewing center, but Austria still exports two outstanding lagers—Puntigam and Gooser, both typically German style.

Belgium: The Belgians brew with imagination. There is wonderful red ale from Flanders as well as Cristal Alken, Jupiter, and its most famous—Stella Artois. There are beers made like champagne—which go through secondary fermentation—and a type of beer using wild yeasts (naturally floating) instead of brewer's yeast, which is the Lambic beer method. One unusual variety of this production method is Kirek, which consists of steeping whole blackberries in the beer (as a sweetening agent) for four or more months.

Canada: Canadian brewers seem to treat the U.S.A. the way American winemakers deal with European importers of American wines: We are getting only a "bit of the taste." We do import the ales from Molson, Labatt, VS "50," and O'Keefe, but relatively few brews from north of the border get here compared to many more from Germany. Yukon Gold will soon be available throughout the U.S., thanks to Jules Berman & Co., Los Angeles. This Canadian brew is somewhat heartier and has a higher alcohol content that is much appreciated by American beer drinkers. But why can't we also enjoy India Pale Ale from Labatt?

Czechoslovakia: Pilsner Urquell is internationally known and is one of the two national brands in the country. The other is Budvar which has its origins in the German name Budweis from whence also comes American Budweiser. Beer popularity here is mainly regional, with great style and variety; the country is not a prime exporter.

Denmark: Tuborg and Carlsberg are best known, but today they are also made in this country. Unfortunately, the better brands such as Oden, Thor, or unpasteurized FAD remain in Copenhagen.

England: A hundred years ago there were more than 15,000 brewers in Great Britain; today the figure is, perhaps, 10 percent of that. Since the early sixties English brewers encouraged inroads to be made through promotion and big investment from "international" brands, which further undercut English tradition. But the tide of internationals petered out, and the beer-drinking Englishman remained with his ale—which is unpasteurized, unfiltered, and served at cellar temperature. The English beer is flavorful because of top fermentation, relatively low alcoholic content, and mild hoppy taste.

Germany: Germany produces 75 percent of the brews in the European economic community. Munich brewings are a malty style, whereas those from Dortmund have a more even balance of hops and malt. From the south, the beers usually are higher in alcohol—up to 13 percent for beer from Kulmsbach. Beers from Cologne are usually pale. Dusseldorf beer is probably similar to British ale in finish. Average annual beer consumption in Germany is about equivalent to 17 cases (24-count) for every man, woman, and child.

Holland: What has happened to the once enviable Heineken's quality? I still can't pronounce Grolsch (the sound begins back in the throat like you are clearing it), but this beer with an old-fashioned porcelain stopper is real beer. Frankly, I enjoy Amstel Light, now controlled by Heineken and a head above its parent. Also, you may find some Royal Holland on the West Coast.

Japan: As sushi and sashimi bars are becoming part of our fast-food scene, Americans are also enjoying the compatible beer. Today Japan's Kirin beer is the largest producer in the world outside the U.S.

Mexico: Beer is a national drink, cooling sweating brows from the tropical heat and soothing palates burned from the love of chiles. Mexican beer is smartly light and refreshing. Good brands available in the United States are Bohemia, Carta Blanca, Superior, Dos Equis (XX, Tecate).

United States: Local beers are the ones worth knowing, even if America has become a land of big TV brands. Look for them and try them when you find them or travel to their regions—such as Eagle of Pottsville, Pennsylvania (America's oldest brewery—since 1829); Rolling Rock and Straub, also of Pennsylvania; Genesee of Rochester, N.Y.; Coors of Denver; Lone Star of San Antonio. The feeling of discovery is still there when I can find Anchor Steam beer on the West Coast or De Bakker and Leinenkugel when I get to Wisconsin. For a taste tour of the beer world, you need go no further than our nation's capital. Should you visit the White House or embark on other usual sightseeing, set aside time for a stop at the Brickskeller Saloon, where, during my last stop, I could only count as far as 397 different beers, and there were many more to go!

Sake (Beer or Wine?)

With the rising popularity of Japanese cuisine in America, Japanese beer—and sake—are most compatible libations. Although sake is often referred to as "rice wine," it is technically a beer-type of beverage because it is fermented from a grain mash (rice) versus the fermentation of fruit for wine.

To serve, sake is usually heated in the bottle, then poured warm into small porcelain cups, and sipped. It is drunk before and with the meal. Sake can be a rather strong potion, ranging from 12 to 18 percent alcohol. It is rarely the base for a mixed drink but it is also often added to the stock in Japanese cooking.

BEER, ALE, AND SAKE RECIPES

AUGUST MOON
A 4-oz. cocktail glass, chilled

1½ oz. Bourbon
1 oz. sake
1 tsp. orgeat syrup
1 tsp. lemon juice
3 to 4 ice cubes

Combine all ingredients in shaker, and shake vigorously. Strain into glass.

BEER MEXICAN STYLE
A beer glass, chilled

1 12 oz. bottle or
 can of beer, cold
Pinch of coarse
 salt
Small wedge of
 lemon or lime

Pour beer into glass. Add pinch of salt. Squeeze a few drops of lemon or lime over drink, and dicard wedge. Do not stir. (When drinking beer out of can, Mexicans drop salt and lemon or lime juice through opening in can and discard wedge.)

BLACK VELVET
A highball glass, chilled

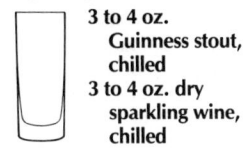

3 to 4 oz. Guinness stout, chilled
3 to 4 oz. dry sparkling wine, chilled

Pour stout into glass. Add wine.
Note: This idea of mixing a malt beverage with sparkling wine seems intimidating at first. Actually, the wine cuts the thickness of the stout and offers a surprisingly pleasant libation.

FAITH, HOPE and GARRITY
A 12- to 14-oz. tall glass, chilled

1 oz. Irish whiskey
3 to 4 oz. V-8 juice
1 tsp. smoky barbecue sauce
1 tsp. lemon juice
4 to 5 ice cubes
6 oz. beer, chilled

Combine all ingredients except beer in mixing glass, and stir well. Strain into tall glass, and fill with beer.

GOLDEN GEISHA
A 4-oz. cocktail glass, chilled

1½ oz. gold rum
1 oz. Gekkeikan sake
1 tsp. Falernum syrup
1 tsp. lime juice
4 oz. crushed ice
1 tsp. pineapple juice
1 maraschino cherry

Combine rum, sake, Falernum syrup, lime juice, and 2 oz. ice in shaker, and shake vigorously. Put remaining ice in glass, and strain drink into glass. Spoon pineapple juice on top. Garnish with cherry. *Gekkeikan Sake, Sidney Frank Importing Co., Inc., New York, N.Y.*

SAKETINI
(Sock-It-to-Me)
A 4-oz. cocktail glass, chilled

1 oz. gin
1 oz. vodka
½ oz. Gekkeikan sake
3 to 4 ice cubes

Combine all ingredients in mixing glass, and stir well. Strain into glass. *Gekkekian Sake, Sidney Frank Importing Co., Inc., New York, N.Y.*

SEMICONDUCTOR
A 4-oz. cocktail glass, chilled

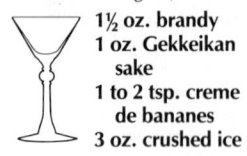

1½ oz. brandy
1 oz. Gekkeikan sake
1 to 2 tsp. creme de bananes
3 oz. crushed ice

Combine all ingredients in shaker, and shake vigorously. Strain into glass.

SHANDYGAFF
A 12- to 14-oz. tall glass, chilled

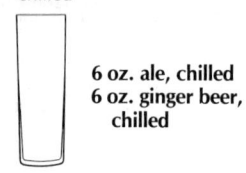

6 oz. ale, chilled
6 oz. ginger beer, chilled

Simultaneously pour ale and ginger ale into glass. Stir 2 to 3 turns.

WILD BREW YONDER
A highball glass, chilled

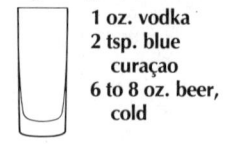

1 oz. vodka
2 tsp. blue curaçao
6 to 8 oz. beer, cold

Combine vodka and blue curaçao in glass, and stir. Top with cold beer.

PUNCHES

ARTILLERY PUNCH
A 6- to 7-gal. tub or drum

- 1 qt. fresh strawberries, stemmed
- 12 oz. unsweetened pineapple juice, chilled
- 1 qt. orange juice, chilled
- 1 500 ml. bottle Jamaica dark rum
- 1 750 ml. bottle Bourbon
- 4 qt. hard cider (or strong Irish tea), chilled
- 1 large block ice, or several small ones
- 10 750 ml. bottle dry sparkling wine

This recipe should be started a day ahead of serving. The day before, puree strawberries in blender or food processor. In 6-qt. container, combine strawberry puree, pineapple juice, and orange juice, and stir vigorously. Add rum, Bourbon, and cider or tea, and stir briefly. Let mixture stand overnight.

At serving time, place ice in tub. Pour mixture over ice. Add wine, and stir briefly.

Note: There are many versions of this classic. Gin or brandy can replace Bourbon, or 1 bottle dry red wine can be added to any version.

Approx. 100 servings

BACARDI CONFETTI PUNCH
An 8-qt punch bowl, chilled

- 40 to 60 ice cubes, or large block of ice
- 1 6-oz. can frozen lemonade concentrate, thawed
- 1 6-oz. can frozen grapefruit juice concentrate, thawed
- 1 6-oz. can fruit cocktail, drained
- 1 750 ml. bottle Bacardi light rum, chilled
- 2 qt. club soda, chilled

Place ice in bowl. Add two concentrates, drained fruit cocktail, rum, and soda, and stir gently until mixed. *Bacardi Imports, Inc., Miami, Fla.*
16 to 20 servings

BREW BEARD
A 2-qt pitcher

- 1 12-oz. bottle of beer, chilled
- 6 oz. grapefruit juice, chilled
- 2 tbs. lime juice
- 2 tbs. blue curaçao
- 4 tsp. superfine sugar
- 6 oz. ginger ale, chilled
- 15 to 20 ice cubes for pitcher, plus extra for glasses

Combine all ingredients except extra ice in pitcher, and stir well. Put 2 or 3 ice cubes in each glass, and fill with mixture.
For 4 servings

CASSIS PUNCH
A 4-gal. punch bowl

- 4 cups fresh strawberries, stemmed
- 4 oz. crème de cassis
- 1 block ice
- 10 750 ml. bottles dry white wine, chilled

Coat strawberries with crème de cassis in mixing bowl, and let stand in refrigerator 1 to 2 hours. Place ice block in bowl. Drain crème de cassis from strawberries, and pour over ice. Add wine. Float strawberries.
For 60 servings

C.C. the EGGNOG
A 6-qt. punch bowl, chilled

12 eggs, separated
1½ c. superfine sugar
¼ tsp. salt
1 qt. light cream
¼ c. light rum
¼ c. brandy
1 750 ml. bottle Canadian Club whisky
1 pt. heavy whipping cream, whipped
Freshly grated nutmeg

In a large bowl (at least 6-qt. size), beat egg yolks until light. Gradually beat in 1 cup sugar and continue beating until mixture is light and fluffy. Add salt, light cream, rum, brandy, and whisky, and stir well. Beat egg whites until frothy. Gradually add remaining sugar and beat until soft peaks are formed. Fold egg whites and whipped cream into mixture and chill thoroughly. Before serving, stir and sprinkle with nutmeg. *Canadian Club, Hiram Walker Incorporated, Detroit, Mich.*

COCO LOPEZ PONCHE COLADA
A 2- to 3-gal. punch bowl, chilled

1 qt. fresh strawberries, stemmed
1 qt. orange juice, chilled
2 qt. apple juice
3 750 ml. bottles Coco Lopez Piña Colada, chilled
1 block ice
4 pineapples, peeled and cut into cubes
Cocktail picks
6 750 ml. bottles chilled Montserrat sparkling wine

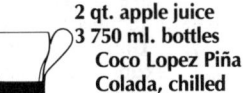

Puree strawberries in blender. Combine strawberry puree, orange juice, apple juice, and Coco Lopez Piña Colada in bowl, and stir well. Add ice.

To serve, arrange a drink center composed of punch bowl with its mixture, bowl of pineapple cubes, cocktail picks, bottle of chilled wine, and punch cups. For 1 serving, ladle about 4 oz. mixture into cup. Fill with wine. Garnish with 2 pineapple cubes on cocktail pick. *Coco Lopez, San Juan, P.R.*
For 60 to 75 servings

COPLEY CHRISTMAS PUNCH

A 5- to 6-qt. tureen, rinsed in hot water

- 1 750 ml. New England rum
- 8 oz. superfine sugar
- 6 to 8 oz. brandy
- 1 qt. brewed Major Grey tea, strained
- 2 cups fresh lemon juice
- 4 oz. maraschino liqueur
- 1 qt. ginger ale, chilled

Set aside 2 oz. rum and 4 oz. sugar. Combine remaining rum and sugar, brandy, tea, lemon juice, maraschino liqueur, and ginger ale in large saucepan, and stir over low heat until mixture is warm but not boiling. Transfer mixture to large warm tureen. Combine reserved rum and sugar in small saucepan, and warm. Pour into ladle. Hold ladle over tureen, ignite, and slowly lower flaming ladle into tureen. *The Copley plaza Hotel, Boston, Mass.*

For 20 to 24 servings

CREOLE RED WINE PUNCH

An 8-qt. punch bowl, chilled

- 2½ 750 ml. bottles dry red wine
- 2 cups lemon juice
- 2 cups superfine sugar
- 2 lemons, thinly sliced
- 1 block ice
- 1½ qt. club soda, chilled

Combine wine, lemon juice and sugar in large refrigerator container, and mix well—until sugar is dissolved. Add lemon slices, and refrigerate until chilled. At serving time, place ice in punch bowl. Add chilled mixture. Add club soda, and stir briefly.

For 24 to 30 servings

FISH HOUSE PUNCH
(Original Recipe)

An 8-qt. punch bowl, chilled

2 cups lemon juice
6 oz. superfine sugar
2 750 ml. Jamaica gold rum
1 750 ml. Cognac or brandy
1 cup peach brandy
1 block ice
1 pt. club soda, chilled

The day before, combine lemon juice and sugar in mixing bowl, and stir until sugar is dissolved. In 4-qt. container, combine lemon juice and sugar mixture, rum, Cognac or brandy, and peach brandy, stir, and store in refrigerator until chilled, ideally overnight.

At serving time, place ice in punch bowl, and add mixture. Add club soda and stir gently.

Frank C. Baker, New York, N.Y.

Note: This is undoubtedly the most famous punch in America. It has always been the standard-bearer of The Fish House, a men's club founded in 1732 in Philadelphia. Originally The Fish House was a fishing club located on the Schuylkill River. Today it is a cooking and eating club whose members are a select group of bankers, lawyers, brokers, and executives.

The original recipe is still used and carries considerable authority. (It is said that the only days George Washington failed to record in his lifelong diary are those he spent at The Fish House.)

Ideally, this recipe should be started a day ahead.

For approximately 30 servings

FRENCH PUNCH
A 6-qt. punch bowl

1 lb. peaches, peeled and sliced
6 tbs. superfine sugar
3 750 ml. bottles dry white wine, chilled
1 qt. club soda, chilled
2 oz. cognac
2 oz. triple sec
1 block ice

Toss peaches with sugar in punch bowl. Add wine and let mixture stand at room temperature approximately 1 hour. At serving time, add soda, cognac, and triple sec, and stir briefly. Add ice.

For 20 to 24 servings

GIN BOWL
An 8-qt. punch bowl, chilled

4 750 ml. bottles dry white wine, chilled
12 oz. gin
1 cup brewed green tea, chilled
Optional: 1 cup light rum
1 block ice
20 thin slices lemon

Combine wine, gin, tea, and lemon slices in punch bowl. For stronger mixture, add rum. At serving time, add ice.

HAPPY HOUR PUNCH

An 8- to 12-qt. punch bowl, chilled

- 1 750 ml. bottle Southern Comfort
- 8 oz. pineapple juice
- 8 oz. grapefruit juice
- 4 oz. lemon juice
- 1 block ice
- 4 750 ml. bottles dry sparkling wine, chilled
- 12 to 16 thin slices orange

Combine Southern Comfort, pineapple juice, grapefruit juice, and lemon juice in punch bowl, and stir. Add ice. Then add wine and stir briefly. Garnish with orange slices. *Southern Comfort Corp., St. Louis, Mo.*
For 30 to 36 servings

HAWAIIAN SPARKLING WINE PUNCH

A 3- to 4-gal. punch bowl, chilled

- 3 pineapples
- 3 cups superfine sugar
- 1 500 ml. bottle light rum
- 1 500 ml. bottle brandy
- 4 oz. curaçao
- 4 oz. maraschino liqueur
- 1 block ice
- 3 750 ml. bottles dry sparkling wine, chilled

This recipe should be started a day ahead. The day before punch is to be served, peel and core pineapples, and puree pulp in blender. Combine puree and sugar in large mixing bowl or pot (about 6-qt.), mix well, and let mixture stand 3 to 4 hours. Add rum, brandy, curaçao, and maraschino liqueur, stir, and let mixture stand overnight.

At serving time, transfer mixture to punch bowl. Add ice and wine. Stir briefly to mix.
For 24 to 30 servings

HONOLULU PUNCH

A 2½- to 3-gal. punch bowl, chilled

- 2 pineapples
- ¾ cup superfine sugar
- 2 cups pineapple juice
- ½ cup lemon juice
- 1 500 ml. bottle brandy
- 1 500 ml. bottle Hawaiian rum
- 1 block ice
- 4 750 ml. bottles dry sparkling wine, chilled

This recipe should be started a day ahead. The day before serving, peel and core pineapples. Puree pulp of 1 pineapple in blender and transfer to 3- to 4-qt. container. Cut pulp of second pineapple into bite-size cubes, place in separate container, and refrigerate. Add sugar to pureed pineapple, mix, and let stand at least 1 hour. Add pineapple juice, lemon juice, brandy, and rum, and let stand overnight.

At serving time, transfer mixture to punch bowl. Add ice, wine, and pineapple cubes, and stir gently.

For 30 to 36 servings

JEFFERSON DAVIS PUNCH

A 10- 12-gal. tub or drum

- 12 750 ml. dry red wine
- 1 750 ml. dry sherry
- 1 500 ml. brandy
- 8 oz. dark rum
- 8 oz. maraschino liqueur
- 2 cups fresh lemon juice
- 6 lemons, thinly sliced
- 4 oranges, thinly sliced
- Several blocks ice
- 3 qt. tonic water, chilled
- 6 qt. club soda, chilled

Combine wine, sherry, brandy, rum, lemon juice, and maraschino liqueur in tub or drum, and stir well. Add lemon and orange slices. Let mixture stand overnight. At serving time, add ice, tonic and soda, and stir briefly.

For 125 to 150 servings

MONTSERRAT PONCHE

A 2- to 3-qt. pitcher or punch bowl, chilled

> 6 oz. seedless black raspberry jam
> 1 tbs. lemon juice
> 1 tbs. lime juice
> 1 750 ml. bottle Montserrat dry sparkling wine
> 2 oz. gin
> 2 oz. orange juice
> 12 to 18 ice cubes

Combine black raspberry jam, lemon juice, and lime juice in small saucepan, and stir over low heat until jam is dissolved. Cool jam syrup. Combine all ingredients in pitcher and mix well.
For 6 to 10 servings

NAVY PUNCH

An 8- to 12-qt. punch bowl, chilled

> 1 500 ml. dark rum
> 1 500 ml. Cognac
> 1 500 ml. Southern Comfort
> 2 cups pineapple cubes
> 3 oz. lemon juice
> 1½ tsp. superfine sugar
> 1 block ice
> 4 750 ml. dry sparkling wine, chilled

Combine rum, Cognac, Southern Comfort, pineapple cubes, lemon juice, and sugar in punch bowl, and stir well. Add ice. Add wine, and stir briefly.

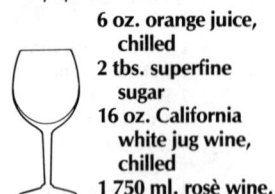

ORANGE OASIS
A 1-qt. pitcher

6 oz. orange juice, chilled
2 tbs. superfine sugar
16 oz. California white jug wine, chilled
1 750 ml. rosè wine, chilled
24 to 30 ice cubes

Combine orange juice, sugar, and white wine in pitcher, and stir until sugar is dissolved. For each serving, place 4 to 5 ice cubes in wine glass, and add 3½ to 4 oz. pitcher mixture. Top with about 4 oz. rosé wine.
For 6 servings

PARK AVENUE ORANGE BLOSSOM
An 8- to 12-qt. punch bowl, chilled

1 block ice
2 qt. orange juice (preferably fresh-squeezed), chilled
1 cup maraschino cherries, drained
3 750 ml. dry sparkling wine, chilled

Place ice in bowl. Add juice, cherries, and sparkling wine, and stir gently.
For 24 to 30 servings

PEPPERY PUNCH
A 4-qt. pitcher or punch bowl, chilled

> 1 750 ml. Paul Masson dry sparkling wine, chilled
> 1 750 ml. Paul Masson dry white wine, chilled
> 12 oz. lemon soda, chilled
> 8 fresh ripe strawberries
> Freshly ground black pepper

Sugar-frost rims of wine glasses. Combine sparkling wine, white wine, and lemon soda in pitcher or punch bowl, and stir. Pour mixture into prepared glasses. Garnish each serving with 1 strawberry and sprinkle of pepper. *Paul Masson Vineyards, Saratoga, Calif.*
For 8 servings

PINK COCO WINE PUNCH
An 8-qt. punch bowl, chilled

> 1 cup coconut milk (fresh or canned), chilled
> 1 oz. lime juice
> 2 tbs. light brown sugar
> 20 to 24 ice cubes
> 2 750 ml. Paul Masson pink sparkling wine, chilled
> 6 to 8 curls of lemon or lime peel

Combine coconut milk, lime juice, and sugar in blender, and blend. Place ice in bowl. Add blended mixture. Add wine, and stir gently. Garnish with curls of lemon or lime peel. *Paul Masson Vineyards, Saratoga, Calif.*
For 12 to 16 servings

PRINCETON REUNION RECOVERY PUNCH

A 6-qt. punch bowl, chilled

> 1 750 ml. Bourbon, rum, or brandy
> 2 cups peach brandy
> 1 qt. milk
> 1 qt. non-alcoholic eggnog mix
> 1 qt. vanilla ice cream
> Freshly grated nutmeg

A few hours to a day before serving, combine Bourbon (or rum or brandy), peach brandy, milk, and eggnog mix in large bowl or pot, and mix well. Cover and let mixture stand in refrigerator at least 6 hours or overnight. An hour or so before serving, let ice cream stand at room temperature to soften.

At serving time, combine mixture and ice cream in punch bowl and stir. (Taste for strength; if stronger punch is desired, add more spirit.) Serve in punch cups. Top each serving with sprinkle of nutmeg.

Note: If serving is to be prolonged so that punch would become warm, *do not* place ice in punch. To keep punch cold, place punch bowl in larger bowl filled with ice-cold water, or pour punch into pitchers and place them in ice water. *Frank C. Baker, New York, N.Y., for Princeton alumni reunions*

For 24 servings

PUNCINELLO
A 4-qt. punch bowl, chilled

- 12 oz. Sambuca Romana
- 1 qt. orange juice
- ¼ cup lemon juice
- 1 block ice
- 1 pt. bitter lemon soda
- 1 lemon, thinly sliced
- 1 orange, thinly sliced

In refrigerator container, combine Sambuca Romana, orange and lemon juice, and chill. At serving time, place ice in bowl. Pour chilled mixture over ice. Add bitter lemon and stir briefly. Float lemon and orange slices.
Sambuca Romana, Palmer & Lord Ltd., Syosset, N.Y.
For 12 to 15 servings

RED WINE FRUIT CUP
An 8-qt. punch bowl, chilled

- 1 750 ml. dry red wine, chilled
- 3 tbs. superfine sugar
- 3 oz. orange juice
- 1 tbs. lemon juice
- 2 oz. brandy
- 1 block ice
- 2 qt. club soda, chilled
- Strips of peel from 1 lemon
- 18 to 20 cucumber slices

Combine red wine and sugar in 2 qt. refrigerator container, and stir until sugar is dissolved. Add orange juice, lemon juice, and brandy, and refrigerate until chilled. At serving time, place ice in bowl. Pour mixture over ice. Add soda, and stir briefly. Garnish with strips of lemon rind and cucumber slices.
For 18 servings

SANGRIA

A 3-qt. pitcher or punch bowl, chilled

> 3 fresh peaches, peeled and pricked all over with fork
> 4 oz. Grand Marnier
> 1 orange, sliced
> 1 lemon, sliced
> 1 750 ml. dry red wine (usually Spanish or Italian), chilled
> 12 ice cubes
> 16 oz. club soda, chilled

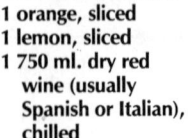

Place peaches in refrigerator container, sprinkle with Grand Marnier, and allow to marinate in refrigerator for 2 to 3 hours. At serving time, slice peaches and add reserved Grand Marnier. Combine peaches, Grand Marnier, orange and lemon slices, and wine in pitcher, and stir. Add ice and soda, and stir briefly. Each serving should contain some fruit in the glass.

For 4 to 6 servings

SPARKLING WINE BRUNCH PUNCH

A 6-qt. punch bowl, chilled

> 1 750 ml. Cognac or brandy
> 4 oz. curaçao
> 6 oz. orange juice
> 4 oz. lemon juice
> 4 oz. grenadine
> Superfine sugar, to taste
> 1 block ice, or 24 to 30 ice cubes
> 1 750 ml. dry sparkling wine, chilled
> Garnish: peels of 1 orange, in curls

Combine Cognac or brandy, curaçao, orange and lemon juice, and grenadine in bowl, and mix well. Add sugar to taste, and stir until sugar is dissolved. Add ice, wine, and orange peels, and stir briefly.

For 12 to 16 servings

SPARKLING WINE PUNCH
A 12-qt. punch bowl, chilled

16 oz. triple sec
1 500 ml brandy, rum, or Bourbon
8 oz. maraschino liqueur
3 cups unsweetened pineapple juice, chilled
1 block ice
1 qt. club soda or ginger ale, chilled
4 750 ml. dry sparkling wine, chilled

Combine triple sec, brandy (or rum or Bourbon), maraschino liqueur, and pineapple juice in punch bowl, and stir. Add ice, soda or ginger ale, and wine, and stir briefly.
For 40 to 48 servings

SPARKLING WINE SHERBET PUNCH
A 6-qt. punch bowl, well chilled

1 qt. orange sherbet, in 1 chunk—frozen firm
2 750 ml. dry sparkling wine, chilled
1 750 ml. Vouvray (medium-dry white wine), chilled

Place chunk of sherbet in center of punch bowl. Pour sparkling wine and Vouvray around it. Serve with scoop, filling each cup with half sherbet and half wine. Insert plastic stirrer in each cup to swirl and mix sherbet and wine.
For 12 to 16 servings

STRAWBERRY BOWL
An 8-qt. punch bowl, chilled

- ½ cup superfine sugar
- 2 cups dry red wine
- 2 qt. fresh strawberries, sliced
- 1 block ice, or 18 to 24 ice cubes
- 2 750 ml. dry sparkling wine, chilled

Combine sugar and red wine in mixing bowl, and stir until sugar is dissolved. Add strawberries, and refrigerate mixture at least 1 hour. At serving time, place ice in punch bowl. Add strawberry mixture. Add sparkling wine, and stir gently.
For 18 to 24 servings

SUMMER PUNCH
An 8-qt. punch bowl, chilled

- 4 750 ml. bottles dry white wine, chilled
- 8 oz. crème de cassis
- 1 block ice or 30 to 36 ice cubes
- 2 cups fresh strawberries, stemmed
- About 8 thin slices orange

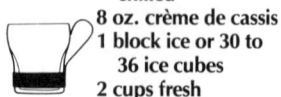

Combine wine and crème de cassis in bowl, and stir. Add ice and stir again. Float strawberries and orange slices.
For 16 to 24 servings

TAMPICO
An 8-qt. punch bowl, chilled

- 1 750 ml. vodka
- 1 46-oz. can tropical fruit punch
- 1 6-oz. can frozen lemonade concentrate
- 1 block ice, or 30 to 36 ice cubes
- 1 qt. ginger ale, chilled
- 12 slices lemon
- 12 slices lime

Combine vodka, tropical fruit punch, and lemonade concentrate in refrigerator container, stir, and chill thoroughly. At serving time, place ice in bowl, and add chilled mixture. Add ginger ale, and stir. Garnish with lemon and lime slices.
For 24 servings

VICTORIAN MINT SHRUB

An 8-qt. punch bowl, chilled

½ cup crushed mint leaves
2 tbs. superfine sugar
4 oz. apricot liqueur
4 oz. brandy
2 oz. peppermint schnapps
1 block ice
4 750 ml. Almadén dry sparkling wine, chilled

Combine mint leaves, sugar, apricot liqueur, brandy, and peppermint schnapps in mixing glass, mix well, and let mixture stand 1 to 2 hours—to fuse. At serving time, place ice in bowl. Add mint mixture. Add wine, and stir gently. *Almadén Vineyards, Inc., San José, Calif.*
For 20 to 24 servings

WHITE WINE CUP

A 4-qt. pitcher or punch bowl, chilled

1 750 ml. dry white wine, chilled
4 oz. dry sherry
2½ tbs. anisette
2½ tbs. brandy
6 strips lemon peel
6 pineapple spears, ¼-inch thick
Superfine sugar, to taste
16 to 20 ice cubes
1 qt. club soda, chilled
8 to 10 mint sprigs

Combine white wine, sherry, anisette, brandy, lemon-peel strips, and pineapple spears in pitcher. Add sugar to taste, and stir until sugar is dissolved. Add ice and club soda. Serve in wine glasses. Garnish each serving with pineapple spear and mint.
For 8 to 10 servings

HOT DRINKS

BLACKBEARD CAFÉ
An 8-oz. mug, rinsed in hot water

> 1 oz. brandy
> 2 to 2½ oz. Jamaica dark rum
> 2 tsp. superfine sugar
> 3 or 4 oz. strong coffee, hot
> 1 strip orange peel

Combine all ingredients except orange peel in warm mug, and stir until sugar is dissolved. Twist orange peel over drink to release oil, and drop it in.

BLOW TORCH
An 8-oz. mug, rinsed in hot water

> 6 oz. hot chocolate (or chocolate milk, heated)
> 1½ oz. Steel peppermint schnapps
> Optional: 1 or 2 tbs. whipped cream

Pour hot chocolate into warm mug. Add peppermint schnapps and stir. Top with whipped cream, if desired. *Steel Peppermint Schnapps, Heublein, Inc., Hartford, Conn.*

BURNT PAW

An 8-oz. mug, rinsed in hot water

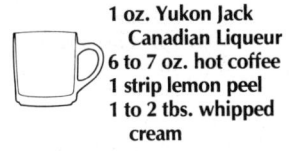

> 1 oz. Yukon Jack Canadian Liqueur
> 6 to 7 oz. hot coffee
> 1 strip lemon peel
> 1 to 2 tbs. whipped cream

Pour Canadian liqueur into warm mug. Top mug with hot coffee. Twist lemon peel over drink to release oil, and drop it in. Top with whipped cream. *Yukon Jack 100 proof Imported Canadian Liqueur, Heublein, Inc., Hartford, Conn.*

CAFÉ AMORE

An 8-oz. coffee cup, rinsed in hot water

> 6 oz. hot coffee
> 1 oz. Hiram Walker Amaretto & Cognac
> 1 to 2 tbs. whipped cream

Pour coffee into warm cup. Add Amaretto & Cognac, but do not stir. Top with whipped cream. *Hiram Walker Amaretto & Cognac, Hiram Walker, Inc., Detroit, Mich.*

CAFÉ BENITEZ

An 8-oz. mug, rinsed in hot water

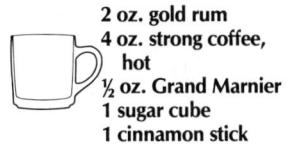

> 2 oz. gold rum
> 4 oz. strong coffee, hot
> ½ oz. Grand Marnier
> 1 sugar cube
> 1 cinnamon stick

In warm mug, combine rum and all but 1 tsp. Grand Marnier. Slowly add hot coffee while stirring. Place sugar cube in spoon with reserved Grand Marnier. Hold spoon over drink and ignite sugar cube. Allow sugar to flame for 2 or 3 seconds and slide it into drink.

CAFÉ GRANDE

A 6-oz. coffee cup, rinsed in hot water

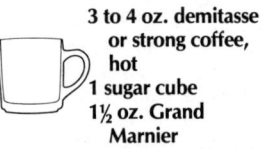

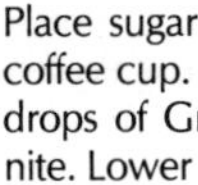

> 3 to 4 oz. demitasse or strong coffee, hot
> 1 sugar cube
> 1½ oz. Grand Marnier

Pour hot coffee into warm cup. Place sugar cube in spoon over coffee cup. Wet cube with a few drops of Grand Marnier and ignite. Lower flaming cube into hot coffee. Add remaining Grand Marnier and stir gently.

CAFÉ ROYALE

An 8-oz. coffee cup, rinsed in hot water

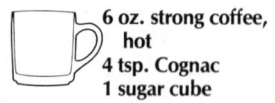

- 6 oz. strong coffee, hot
- 4 tsp. Cognac
- 1 sugar cube

Pour coffee into warm cup. Float 2 tsp. Cognac on hot coffee. Put remaining Cognac in tablespoon with sugar cube. Warm spoon over coffee. Ignite Cognac in spoon and slowly lower into coffee, which will ignite floating Cognac.

CRUZAN APPLE SIZZLE

An 8-oz. mug, rinsed in hot water

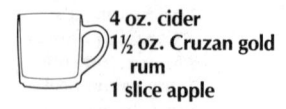

- 4 oz. cider
- 1½ oz. Cruzan gold rum
- 1 slice apple

Warm cider in small saucepan and pour it into warm mug. Add rum and stir. Garnish with apple slice. *Cruzan Virgin Islands Rum, Schenley's, Dreyfus, Ashby & Co.*

COCOA ROYAL

An 8-oz. cup, rinsed in hot water

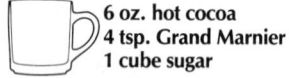

- 6 oz. hot cocoa
- 4 tsp. Grand Marnier
- 1 cube sugar

Pour cocoa into warm cup. Float 2 teaspoons Grand Marnier on hot cocoa. Put remaining Grand Marnier in tablespoon with sugar cube. Warm spoon over hot cocoa. Ignite Grand Marnier in spoon and slowly lower into cocoa, which will ignite floating Grand Marnier.

EAST INDIAN COMPANY TEA PUNCH

An 8-oz. mug, rinsed in hot water

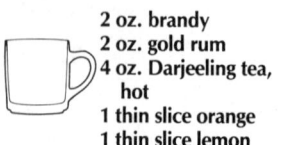

- 2 oz. brandy
- 2 oz. gold rum
- 4 oz. Darjeeling tea, hot
- 1 thin slice orange
- 1 thin slice lemon

Combine brandy, rum, and hot tea in warm mug, and stir. Garnish with orange and lemon slices.

ESKIMO CIDER

An 8-oz. mug, rinsed in hot water

> 1½ oz. Yukon Jack Canadian liqueur
> About 6 oz. cider
> 1 cinnamon stick
> ¼ lime (wedge cut)
> 1 tsp. (pat) butter

Pour Canadian liqueur into warm mug. Warm cider in small saucepan and add cider to mug. Add cinnamon stick, lime wedge, and pat of butter. (Butter floats and gradually melts.). *Yukon Jack 100 proof Imported Canadian Liqueur, Heublein, Inc., Hartford, Conn.*

FINNISH GLOGG

8-oz. mugs, rinsed in hot water

> 1 750 ml Finlandia vodka
> 6 oz. superfine sugar
> 1 750 ml. dry red wine
> ½ cup blanched roasted almonds
> ½ cup currants
> 2 tbs. grated orange rind
> 6 cinnamon sticks
> 16 to 18 whole cloves

Combine 2 oz. vodka and 2 oz. sugar in small container, and set aside. Combine all remaining ingredients in large chafing dish or saucepan and stir over low heat until boiling. Simmer 3 to 4 minutes. Pour reserved vodka and sugar mixture into large ladle. Hold ladle over flame, ignite, and slowly lower into drink mixture. Ladle into warm mugs. *Ilka Polari, Helsinki, Finland.*
For 14 to 16 servings

FLAMING GLOGG

8-oz. mugs, rinsed in hot water

> 1 750 ml. bottle dry red wine
> 1 500 ml. aquavit
> Grated rind of 2 oranges
> 8 oz. orange juice
> 15 to 20 whole cloves
> 1 tbs. superfine sugar
> 1 oz. Grand Marnier
> 10 to 12 whole blanched almonds
> 1 tsp. sesame seeds

Combine red wine, 8 oz. aquavit, grated orange rind, orange juice, cloves, sugar, and Grand Marnier in large saucepan or chafing dish. Warm mixture over low heat, but do not boil. Remove from heat. Add remaining aquavit, and stir. Add almonds and sesame seeds. Ladle drink into warm mugs.

For 6 to 8 servings

GINGER TODDY

An 8-oz. mug, rinsed in hot water

> 1½ oz. De Kuyper ginger-flavored brandy
> 1 tsp. butter
> 1 tsp. superfine sugar
> 6 oz. boiling water

Combine brandy, butter, sugar, and boiling water in warm mug, and stir until sugar is dissolved.

De Kuyper Ginger-flavored Brandy, National Distillers Products Co., New York, N.Y.

GLOWWORM WINE PUNCH
8-oz. mugs, rinsed in hot water

> 2 750 ml. dry red wine
> ¾ cup superfine sugar
> 6 whole cloves
> Strips of peel from ½ lemon
> ½ tsp. ground cinnamon
> 8 to 10 thin slices orange

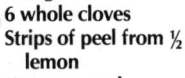

Combine wine, sugar, cloves, lemon peels, and ground cinnamon in large saucepan over low heat. Stir and bring slowly to boil. Pour hot mixture into warm mugs. Garnish each serving with orange slice.
For 8 to 10 servings

GLUEWEIN
An 8-oz. mug, rinsed in hot water

> 6 oz. dry red wine (or cider)
> 1½ tsp. superfine sugar
> 1 cinnamon stick
> 1 whole clove
> Dash of rum or calvados (if desired)

Combine first 4 ingredients in small saucepan and bring slowly to boil. Serve hot in mug. Add dash of rum or calvados if desired.

GORILLA SWEAT
An 8-oz. mug, rinsed in hot water

> 2 oz. white or gold tequila
> 1 tsp. (pat) butter
> 1 whole clove
> About 6 oz. boiling water
> 1 cinnamon stick

Combine all ingredients except cinnamon stick in warm mug. Stir briskly with cinnamon stick.
José Cuervo Tequila, Heublein, Inc., Hartford, Conn.

HOT BRANDY FLIP

An 8-oz. mug, rinsed in hot water

1 egg
1 tsp. superfine sugar
1½ oz. brandy
4 oz. hot milk
Freshly grated nutmeg

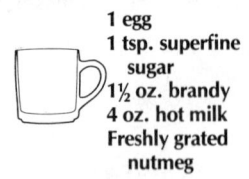

Combine egg, sugar, and brandy in blender, and blend until frothy. Pour mixture into warm mug. Add hot milk and stir. Sprinkle nutmeg on top.

HOT BUTTERED COMFORT

An 8-oz. mug, rinsed in hot water

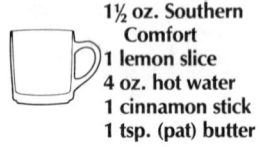

1½ oz. Southern Comfort
1 lemon slice
4 oz. hot water
1 cinnamon stick
1 tsp. (pat) butter

In warm mug, combine Southern Comfort, lemon slice, and hot water, and stir with cinnamon stick. Float pat of butter on top of drink. *Southern Comfort Corp., St. Louis, Mo.*

HOT BUTTERED RUM

An 8-oz. mug, rinsed in hot water

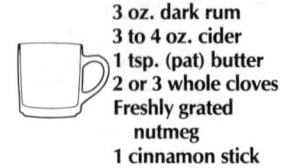

3 oz. dark rum
3 to 4 oz. cider
1 tsp. (pat) butter
2 or 3 whole cloves
Freshly grated nutmeg
1 cinnamon stick

Put rum in warm mug. In small saucepan, heat cider over low heat until it simmers, and add to mug. Add cloves. Sprinkle with nutmeg. Float pat of butter on top of drink, and stir with cinnamon stick.

HOT CREOLE

An 8-oz. mug, rinsed in hot water

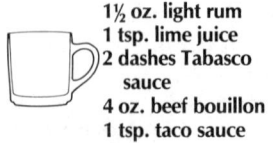

1½ oz. light rum
1 tsp. lime juice
2 dashes Tabasco sauce
4 oz. beef bouillon
1 tsp. taco sauce

Combine all ingredients except taco sauce in small saucepan, and stir over low heat until mixture simmers. Pour into warm mug. Add taco sauce and stir.

HOT and HEAVY GROG

An 8-oz. mug, rinsed in hot water

- 4 oz. boiling water
- 2 oz. Jamaica dark rum
- 1 tsp. superfine sugar
- 1 oz. over-proof rum (151-proof)
- 3 to 4 whole cloves
- 1 thin slice orange

Put boiling water in warm mug. Add dark rum, sugar, and over-proof rum, and stir. Add cloves and orange slice. Let drink steep for 1 or 2 minutes before serving.

Note: For spicier grog, add pinch of ground clove and pinch of ground cinnamon to hot mixture.

HOTSY TOTSY

An 8-oz. mug, rinsed in hot water

- 1 egg yolk
- 1 oz. superfine sugar
- 1 tsp. dark crème de cacao
- 4 to 6 oz. milk
- 2 oz. Jamaica dark rum
- Freshly grated nutmeg

Combine egg yolk and sugar in small bowl, and mix. Add crème de cacao and milk. Transfer mixture to small saucepan. Stir over low heat until mixture is warm. (Do not boil, or mixture will curdle.) Pour rum into warm mug, add mixture, and stir. Sprinkle nutmeg on top.

HOT TUB

An 8-oz. mug, rinsed in hot water

- 1 750 ml. bottle California dry red wine
- 3 to 4 oz. honey
- 1 tsp. ground clove
- 4 thin slices orange
- 4 cinnamon sticks

Pour wine into medium saucepan, and warm over low heat (do not boil). Remove from heat, add honey, and stir until honey dissolves. Add ground clove, and stir again. Pour into warm mugs. Garnish each drink with orange slice and cinnamon stick. *Jas. Cooper, Bedford-Westco, South San Francisco, Calif.*
For 4 servings

IRISH COFFEE (BUSHMILLS)

A 6-oz. or larger wine glass, rinsed in hot water

4 oz. hot black coffee
1 to 2 tsp. superfine sugar
1½ oz. Old Bushmills Irish whiskey
1 to 2 tbs. whipped cream

Fill glass with hot water and allow to stand a few seconds; then empty. Add hot coffee. Add sugar according to taste and stir until dissolved. Add Irish whiskey. Top with whipped cream; do not stir. (Drink through cream.) *Old Bushmills Irish Whiskey, The Jos. Garneau Co., New York, N.Y.*

DOUBLE IRISH COFFEE

Follow recipe for Irish Coffee (Bushmills), adding ½ oz. Emmet's Irish Cream before topping with whipped cream.

ISLAND RUM TEA

8-oz. mugs, rinsed in hot water

24 oz. hot tea, in teapot
2 cinnamon sticks
3 oz. Jamaica dark rum
6 to 8 whole cloves
1 tsp. Minttu Peppermint Schnaapps

Add cinnamon sticks and cloves to fresh pot of hot tea, and steep 5 minutes. When ready to serve, add rum and peppermint schnapps. Pour into mugs.
For 3 to 4 servings

JAMOCHA STOKER

An 8-oz. mug, rinsed in hot water

1½ oz. dark rum
1 tsp. sugar syrup
4 oz. strong coffee, hot
1 tbs. vanilla ice cream
Ground cinnamon

In warm mug, combine rum, sugar syrup, and coffee, and stir. Add ice cream and stir again. Sprinkle cinnamon on top.

LOCOMOTIVE

An 8-oz. mug, rinsed in hot water

> 1 egg yolk
> 1 tsp. superfine sugar
> 1 oz. De Kuyper curaçao
> 4 oz. dry white wine
> Ground cinnamon
> 1 slice lemon

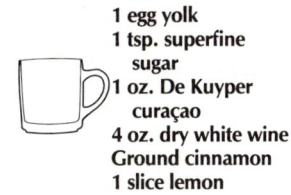

In small saucepan, combine yolk and sugar, and stir well. Add curaçao and wine. Stir over low heat, but do not boil (or yolk will curdle). Pour into warm mug. Sprinkle with cinnamon. Garnish with lemon slice. *De Kuyper Curaçao, National Distillers Products Co., New York, N.Y.*

HOT MATADOR

An 8-oz. mug, rinsed in hot water

> 1 oz. De Kuyper blackberry brandy
> 6 oz. beef bouillon, hot
> 1 slice lemon

Combine brandy and beef bouillon in warm mug, and stir. Garnish with lemon slice. *De Kuyper Blackberry Brandy, National Distillers Products Co., New York, N.Y.*

MULLED CIDER

An 8-oz. mug, rinsed in hot water

> 3 oz. superfine sugar
> 1 qt. hard cider
> 4 oz. light rum
> Pinch of ground allspice
> 6 cinnamon sticks

Combine sugar, cider, rum, and allspice in medium saucepan, and stir over low heat until mixture simmers and sugar is dissolved. Strain into mugs. Place cinnamon stick in each drink.
For 6 servings

MULLED RED WINE

An 8-oz. mug, rinsed in hot water, metal skewer, red-hot

> 1 tsp. superfine sugar
> ¼ cup water
> 5 oz. dry red wine
> 1½ tsp. lemon juice
> 1 to 2 dashes orange bitters
> 1 pinch ground cinnamon

Combine sugar and water in a small saucepan, and stir over low heat until sugar dissolves. Remove from heat and add wine, lemon juice, bitters, and cinnamon, and stir. Pour drink into warm mug, and mull with red-hot metal skewer.

NINOTCHKA'S NIGHT
An 8-oz. mug rinsed in hot water

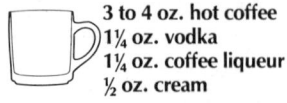

3 to 4 oz. hot coffee
1¼ oz. vodka
1¼ oz. coffee liqueur
½ oz. cream

Pour coffee into warm mug; combine remaining ingredients in mixing glass and stir. Add to coffee; do not stir.

POET'S PUNCH
An 8-oz. mug, rinsed in hot water

6 oz. milk
1 cinnamon stick
1 strip lemon peel
1 strip orange peel
1 egg yolk
½ tsp. vanilla extract
1 oz. Irish Mist liqueur
Freshly grated nutmeg

Combine milk, cinnamon stick, and strips of lemon and orange peel in small saucepan. Warm slowly over low heat (do not boil). Place yolk in mixing glass, add 2 to 3 tbs. hot milk, and mix. Add remaining milk, and stir. Add vanilla extract and Irish Mist. Strain into warm mug. Sprinkle with nutmeg. Add cinnamon stick for stirrer. *Imported Irish Mist Liqueur, Heublein, Inc., Hartford, Conn.*

RUSSIAN TEA
An 8-oz. tea cup, rinsed in hot water

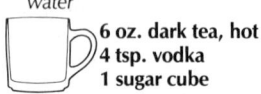

6 oz. dark tea, hot
4 tsp. vodka
1 sugar cube

Pour tea into warm cup. Float 2 tsp. vodka on hot tea. Put remaining vodka in tablespoon with sugar cube. Warm spoon over hot tea. Ignite vodka in spoon and slowly lower into tea, which will ignite floating vodka.

RUSTLER'S BREAKFAST
A highball glass, rinsed in hot water

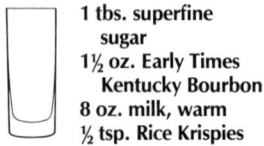

1 tbs. superfine sugar
1½ oz. Early Times Kentucky Bourbon
8 oz. milk, warm
½ tsp. Rice Krispies

Combine sugar and Bourbon in warm glass, and stir until sugar is dissolved. Add warm milk, and stir again. Top with Rice Krispies. *Early Times Kentucky Bourbon, Brown-Fouman Distillers Corp., Louisville, Ky.*

SEAN SWEENEY

An 8-oz. mug, rinsed in hot water

    6 oz. hot coffee
    1 oz. Jeremiah Weed Bourbon liqueur
    Garnish: 1 strip lemon peel, or 1 to 2 tbs. whipped cream

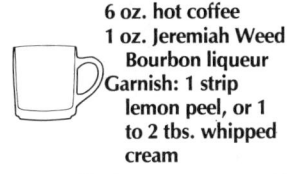

Pour coffee into warm mug. Add Bourbon liqueur. Garnish with twist of lemon peel or dollop of whipped cream. *Jeremiah Weed 100 proof Bourbon Liqueur, Heublein, Inc., Hartford, Conn.*

SILENT MAJORITY

An 8-oz. mug, rinsed in hot water

    1 oz. Majorska vodka
    6 oz. hot tea
    Superfine sugar, to taste
    1 lemon wedge stuck with 2 whole cloves
    1 cinnamon stick

Combine vodka and tea in warm mug. Add sugar to taste, and stir. Add lemon wedge with 2 whole cloves. Stir again, with cinnamon stick, and drop it in. *Majorska Vodka, Palmer & Lord Ltd., Syosset, N.Y.*

SOUPERMAN

An 8-oz. mug, rinsed in hot water

    1¼ oz. Majorska vodka
    1 lemon slice
    6 oz. bouillon, hot
    Salt and pepper, if desired

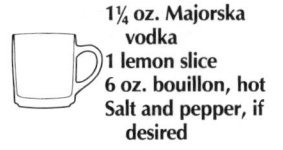

Combine vodka, lemon slice, and bouillon in warm mug, and stir. Season with salt and pepper, if desired. *Majorska Vodka, Palmer & Lord Ltd., Syosset, N.Y.*

SPUMONI COFFEE

An 8-oz. mug, rinsed in hot water

    ½ oz. Tuaca coffee liqueur
    ½ oz. Galliano
    ½ oz. dark crème de cacao
    4 to 5 oz. strong coffee or espresso, hot
    2 tbs. whipped cream
    1 tsp. shaved chocolate

Combine coffee liqueur, Galliano, and crème de cacao in warm mug, and stir. Add coffee and stir. Top with whipped cream and sprinkle with shaved chocolate. *Panorama Restaurant, Hilton Hotel, Portland, Ore.*

TOM & JERRY
8-oz. mugs, rinsed in hot water

> 2 eggs, separated
> 1½ oz. gold rum
> ⅛ tsp. baking soda
> 2 tsp. superfine sugar
> 1½ oz. brandy
> 3 to 4 oz. milk, hot
> Freshly grated nutmeg

Put egg whites in small bowl and beat with rotary beater until they form soft peaks. Place yolks in separate small bowl and beat until foamy. Add yolks to whites and, using rubber scraper, fold together lightly and evenly. Sprinkle ½ oz. rum, baking soda, and sugar on top of egg mixture, and blend with small whisk. Divide mixture into 2 mugs. Divide remaining rum and brandy in each mug. Then divide hot milk in each mug, and stir. Sprinkle nutmeg on top.
For 2 servings

TWO FINGERS MARIACHI
An 8-oz. coffee cup, rinsed in hot water

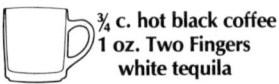

> ¾ c. hot black coffee
> 1 oz. Two Fingers white tequila
> ½ oz. Hiram Walker Chocolate Mint liqueur
> 1 to 2 tbs. whipped cream
> Red and green decorative sugar crystals

Pour coffee into warm cup and add tequila and chocolate mint liqueur. Top with whipped cream. Sprinkle red and green sugar crystals on top for festive touch. *Two Fingers Tequila, Hiram Walker Incorporated, Detroit, Mich.*

VESUVIO
An 8-oz. mug, rinsed in hot water

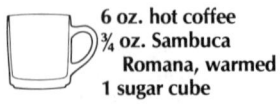

> 6 oz. hot coffee
> ¾ oz. Sambuca Romana, warmed
> 1 sugar cube

Pour hot coffee into warm coffee cup. Pour half of Sambuca Romana over inverted spoon so that Sambuca Romana floats on top of coffee. Place sugar cube in spoon and hold directly over cup. Fill with rest of warm Sambuca Romana, ignite, and dip spoon into cup. *Sambuca Romana, Palmer & Lord Ltd., Syosset, N.Y.*

YARD of FLANNEL

A 1-qt. pitcher, rinsed in hot water
8-oz. mugs, rinsed in hot water

> 1 qt. ale
> 4 oz. gold rum
> 3 oz. superfine sugar
> 4 eggs
> ½ tsp. freshly grated nutmeg
> ½ tsp. ground cinnamon

In large saucepan, warm (but do not boil) ale over low heat. In mixing bowl, combine eggs, sugar, cinnamon, nutmeg, and rum, and beat well with rotary beater. Pour mixture into pitcher. Add warm ale slowly, stirring constantly. Continue to stir vigorously until mixture is creamy. Pour into warm mugs.

For 6 servings

NON-ALCOHOLIC DRINKS

BANANA FROSTED
A 12- to 14-oz. tall glass, chilled

½ ripe banana, peeled and sliced
4 oz. milk, chilled
1 oz. pineapple juice
1 tsp. coconut extract
4 oz. crushed ice

Combine all ingredients in blender, and blend until smooth (15 to 20 seconds). Pour into glass.

BLACK COW
A 14-oz. or larger tall glass, chilled

10 oz. root beer, chilled
1 scoop vanilla ice cream

Pour 3 to 4 oz. root beer in glass. Add 1 to 2 tsp. ice cream, and stir until creamy. Add remaining ice cream. Pour in remaining root beer.

CAFÉ au LAIT

An 8-oz. coffee cup, rinsed in hot water

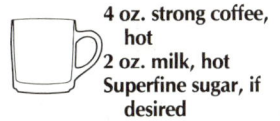

> 4 oz. strong coffee, hot
> 2 oz. milk, hot
> Superfine sugar, if desired

Simultaneously pour hot coffee and hot milk into warm coffee cup. Sweeten with sugar, if desired.

CAFÉ TOULOUSE

8-oz. coffee cups, rinsed in hot water

> 8 oz. heavy cream
> 2 tbs. superfine sugar
> 1 tsp. vanilla extract
> 2 egg whites
> 4¼ cups brewed French-roast coffee, hot

In mixing bowl, beat heavy cream until almost stiff. Add sugar and vanilla extract, and beat until cream holds its shape. In another bowl, beat egg whites to soft peaks. Fold whipped cream and egg whites together. Divide mixture into 6 warm coffee cups. Fill each cup with hot coffee.
Christian Gardet, Gardet Frères, Marseilles, France
For 6 servings

CHRISTMAS CIDER

A 10- to 14-oz. tall glass, chilled

> 2 oz. half and half cream
> 1 egg
> ½ tsp. superfine sugar
> 3 oz. crushed ice
> 6 oz. cider
> Freshly grated nutmeg

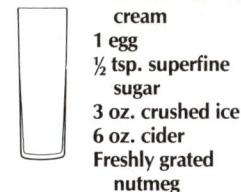

Combine half and half, egg, sugar, and crushed ice in shaker, and shake vigorously. Strain mixture into glass. Add cider. Top with sprinkle of nutmeg.

CRANBERRY JERRY

A 14-oz. tall glass, chilled

> 4 oz. Ocean Spray cranberry cocktail, chilled
> 2 oz. unsweetened pineapple juice
> 2 to 3 ice cubes
> 4 oz. club soda, chilled
> 1 slice lemon

Combine cranberry cocktail, pineapple juice, and ice in glass, and stir slowly while adding soda. Garnish with lemon slice.

FROSTED FRUIT BUTTERMILK (or YOGURT)

A 14-oz. tall glass or wine glass, chilled

1 cup sliced or diced fresh ripe fruit, (e.g. apricot, banana, melon, mango, peach, papaya, pineapple, strawberry)
4 oz. buttermilk or plain yogurt
1 tsp. honey
½ tsp. lemon juice
¼ tsp. grated lemon rind
4 oz. crushed ice
1 mint sprig

Combine all ingredients except mint in blender, and blend at high speed until smooth. Pour drink into glass and garnish with mint.

GRAPEFRUIT GORGEOUS

A highball glass, chilled

4 oz. frozen grapefruit concentrate
1 tsp. honey
4 oz. ginger ale, chilled
1 dash grenadine

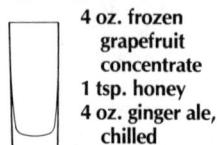

Combine grapefruit concentrate ad honey in blender, and blend 20 to 25 seconds. Pour mixture into glass. Add ginger ale, and stir 2 turns. Add grenadine.

MOCK JULEP

A highball glass, chilled

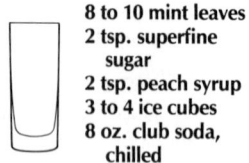

8 to 10 mint leaves
2 tsp. superfine sugar
2 tsp. peach syrup
3 to 4 ice cubes
8 oz. club soda, chilled

Place mint leaves and sugar in glass, and muddle with spoon or stirrer. Add peach syrup and ice, and top with club soda.

ORANGE TINKLE
Highball glasses, chilled

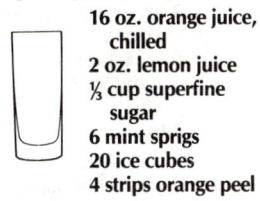

16 oz. orange juice, chilled
2 oz. lemon juice
⅓ cup superfine sugar
6 mint sprigs
20 ice cubes
4 strips orange peel

Combine 8 oz. orange juice, sugar, and mint sprigs in enamel pan, and stir over low heat until mixture boils. Simmer 3 or 4 minutes. Add remaining orange juice and lemon juice to mixture. *To serve,* place 5 ice cubes in each highball glass, and divide drink mixture among 4 glasses. Light match, twist orange peel over glass next to flame, and drop in peel.
For 4 servings

PINEAPPLE TINKLE

Follow recipe for Orange Tinkle, using 16 oz. pineapple juice instead of orange juice.

ROSEANNA BANANA
10- to 14-oz. tall glasses, chilled

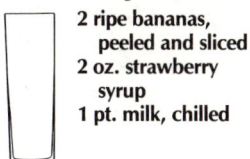

2 ripe bananas, peeled and sliced
2 oz. strawberry syrup
1 pt. milk, chilled

Combine all ingredients in blender, and blend until smooth (20 to 25 seconds). Pour into glasses.
For 2 servings

SNAPPY YOGURT
Old-fashioned glasses, chilled

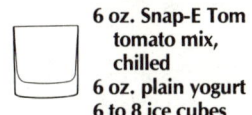

6 oz. Snap-E Tom tomato mix, chilled
6 oz. plain yogurt
6 to 8 ice cubes

Combine tomato mix and yogurt in shaker, and shake well. Place 3 or 4 ice cubes in each glass, and pour drink into glasses.
For 2 servings

WEDDING NIGHT NOG
4 old-fashioned glasses, chilled

- **1 pt. milk, chilled**
- **2 eggs**
- **8 oz. fresh orange juice, chilled**
- **⅓ cup superfine sugar**
- **4 oz. crushed ice**
- **Ground cinnamon**

Combine milk, eggs, orange juice, sugar, and ice in blender, and blend until smooth. Strain mixture into 4 glasses. Top each drink with sprinkle of cinnamon. *For 4 servings*

YOGI BITTER
A highball glass, chilled

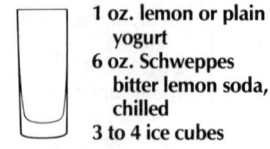

- **1 oz. lemon or plain yogurt**
- **6 oz. Schweppes bitter lemon soda, chilled**
- **3 to 4 ice cubes**

Combine yogurt and 2 oz. bitter lemon soda in glass, and stir until blended. Add ice and remaining bitter lemon soda. Stir 1 to 2 turns.

THE DRINK DIRECTORY

Index By Marilyn Delson

Abbey, 130
Abbot's Delight, 168
Absinthe, 103
Absinthe-flavored drinks (anise/licorice):
   Balmoral (Ricard), 316
   Cocatoo (Pernod), 222
   Whiskey TNT (Ricard), 295
   White Shadow (Pernod), 295
Acapulco No. 1, 211
Acapulco No. 2, 211
Ace of Spades, 130
Addington, 78
Adios, Muchachos, 212
Adonis, 78
Advocaat (Eggnog Liqueur) drinks:
   Butterfly, 173
   Casablanca, 174
   Fast Tango, 178
Affinity, 315
After-Dinner Mint, 168
A. J. Cocktail, 108
Alabama, 108
Alaska, 131
Alcoholic Administration Act, Federal, 101
Alcoholic volume, 24, 324
Ale (see also Beer, Sake), 325-328
   Shandygaff, 332
Alexander, 109
Alexander's Sister, 131
Alfonso Special, 131
Algonquin, 79
Alliance, 79
Almond Cocktail, 79
Almond Cookie, 71
Almond Fizz, 169
Althea Gibson, 144
Alto Parlare, 62
Amaretto & Cognac Continental Stinger, 169
Amaretto drinks (Almond-flavor liqueur):
   Almond Fizz, 169
   Amaretto & Cognac Continental Stinger, 169
   Amaretto Ice, 169
   Bolseye, 173
   Cafe Amore, 351
   Crown Jewel, 223
   Halifax, 308
   H. Walker's Sparkplug, 183
   Lady Luck, 186
   Orgasm, 194
   Pavarotti, 195
   Pittsburgh Spirit, The, 275
   Plaza Pleaser, 236
   Swinger's Cocktail, 242

Tawny Russian, 205
Toasted Almond, 206
Amaretto Ice, 169
Ambrosia for Two, 62
Americana, 63
American Beauty, 109
American Beauty Rose, 79
Americano, 80
Andalusia, 212
Anisette drinks:
   Baltimore Bracer, 111
   Barbarella, 171
   Crema Cafe, 177
   Ermine Tail, 178
   Foreign Affair, 180
   Lady Luck, 186
   Puncinello, 345
   Roman Snowball, 200
   Roman Stinger, 200
   Santa Ana's Bandana, 201
   Slalom, 279
   Suissese, 204
   Vesuvio, 362
   White Cloud, 208
   White Sale, 167
   White Velvet, 209
   White Way, 129
Ankle Breaker, 212
Aperitifs (see also Bitters, Vermouths), 74-77
   Addington, 78
   Adonis, 78
   Algonquin, 79
   Alliance, 79
   Almond Cocktail, 79
   American Beauty Rose, 79
   Apple Lillet, 110
   Betsy Rosso, 112
   Brazil, 82
   Bushranger, 219
   Cabaret, 137
   Campobello, 137
   Cinzano, 82
   Diplomat, 82
   Dry Dock, 83
   Dubonnet Manhattan, 287
   Duchess of Denver, 83
   Favorite Blonde, 142
   First Strike, 83
   Green Room, 84
   Harper's Ferry, 84
   Hoopla, 84
   Italian, 84
   Kingdom Come, 85
   Lemon Cooler, 85
   Lillet Cocktail, 85
   Louisiana Lullaby, 232
   Morning Becomes Electric, 85
   Negroni, 86
   Nightmare Alley, 158
   Oom Paul, 123
   Pale Moon, 86
   Party Girl, 86
   Perpetual, 87
   Phoebe Snow, 123
   Pink Pussy, 87
   Puntigroni, 87
   Rosita, 252
   Rubino, 87
   Silence Is Golden, 165

Sour Bowl, 88
Tango of Love, 88
Toronto Cocktail, 310
Up the Academy, 88
Vermouth Cassis, 88
Weep No More, 129
Whip, 88
Aphrodite's Love Potion, 109
Apple Blow, 110
Apple Brandy Cocktail, 109
Apple Brandy Liqueur drinks:
   A. J. Cocktail, 62
   Ambrosia for Two, 62
   Apricot Lady, 213
   French Lieutenant's Woman, 118
   Kiss 'n' Tell, 120
   Klondike, 309
   Liberty, 121
   Peugeot a Paris, 197
   Prince's Smile, 162
   Special Rough, 126
   Star, 162
Apple Cart, 110
Applejack drinks:
   Apple Blow, 110
   Apple Brandy Cocktail, 109
   Apple Cart, 110
   Apple Lillet, 110
   Apple Sour, 110
   Big Apple, 116
   Bolero, 218
   Dempsey, 116
   Flintlock, 299
   Jackrabbit, 120

   Moonlight Serenade, 122
   Mule Shoe, 218
   Polaris, 241
   Star Daisy, 127
   Stone Fence, 127
   Zero Option, 281
Apple Knocker, 260
Apple Lillet, 110
Apple Pie, 212
Apple Sour, 110
Apres Ski, 169
Apricot Brandy, 111
Apricot Brandy Liqueur drinks:
   Apricot Brandy, 111
   Apricot Sour, 111
   Barnum, 132
   Coney, 220
   Costa del Sol, 115
   Cuanta Costa, 139
   Dry Hole, 224
   French Flag, 59
   Golda Major, 268
   Paradise Island, 160
   Prince's Smile, 162
   Ron Coco, 238
   Sourball, 126
   Star of Brazil, 206
Apricot Lady, 213
Apricot Pie, 213
Apricot Sour, 111
April in Paris Ball, 63
Aquavit (see also Spirits), 90
   Arctic Trick, 105
   Cherry Danish, 105
   Danish Mary, 106

Fjord, 106
Flamingo Grogg, 354
Great Dane, 106
Last Dansk, 106
Midnight Sun, 107
Swedish Secret, 107
Viking, 107
Aqueduct, 260
Arabian Night, 323
Arabian 'Nyet,' 323
Arak, 104
Arctic Trick, 105
Arriba, 213
Artillery, 131
Artillery Punch, 333
Assassins, 282
August Moon, 330
Aunt Agatha, 213
Aunt Jemima, 111

Bacardi American Flyer, 214
Bacardi Ancient Mariner, 214
Bacardi Banana Daiquiri, 214
Bacardi Cocktail, 214
Bacardi Confetti Punch, 334
Bacardi Driver, 215
Bacardi Frio, 215
Bacardi Monkey Wrench, 215
Bacardi Original Daiquiri, 215
Bacardi Strawberry Daiquiri, 216
Bachelor and Bobby Soxer, 132
Baggy Pants, 307
Bailey's Irish Cream drinks:
   B-52, 170
   Barnum & Bailey, 171

Brown Calf Belt, 173
Golden Dream, 182
L'il Orphan Annie, 313
Orgasm, 194
Super Bowl Cocktail, 205
Bailey's Shillelagh, 170
Bairn, 316
Balmoral, 316
Baltimore Bracer, 111
Baltimore Oriole, 296
Banana Boat, 261
Banana Daiquiri No. 2, 170
Banana Frosted, 364
Banana Liqueur drinks:
   Bacardi Frio, 215
   Banshee, 171
   Cabana Frappe, 173
   Cockatoo, 222
   Cool Banana, 176
   Golden Dream, 182
   Green Machine, 183
   Hollywood and Wine, 56
   Jolly Roger, 230
   La Jolla, 120
   Pacific Pacifier, 195
   Polar Bear, 197
   Velvet Kiss, 166
Bananago, 170
Banff Cocktail, 306
Banshee, 171
Barbarella, 171
Barbary Coast (gin/scotch), 316
Barbary Coast (rum/scotch), 132
Barclay, 171
Barnacle Bill, 261

Barn Door, 316
Barnum, 132
Barnum & Bailey, 171
Bartending techniques, 19-23
Batida de Pina, 216
Beach Blanket, 216
Beach Bum, 216
Beadlestone, 317
Beaufort Blast, 306
Beauty and the Beach, 216
Beauty Mark, 80
Beauty Spot, 132
Beer (see also Ale, Sake):
   Beer Mexican Style, 330
   Black Velvet, 331
   Brew Beard, 334
   by country, 326-328
   Depth Charge, 248
   Faith, Hope and Garrity, 331
   serving, 324-325
   types, 325
   Wild Brew Yonder, 332
   Yard of Flannel, 363
Beer Mexican Style, 330
Bee's Kiss, 217
Belize City, 59
Bellini Punch, 63
Benedictine drinks:
   Aunt Jemima, 201
   Chinchilla, 175
   Frisco Valley, 287
   Gypsy Moth, 268
   Kentucky Colonel, 302
   Savoy Hotel, 201
   Widow's Dream, 210

   Widow's Kiss, 129
Bennett, 133
Bermuda Rose, 133
Bertha, 245
Betsy Ross, 112
Betsy Rosso, 112
Between the Sheets, 112
B-52, 170
Big Apple, 112
Bishop's Benediction, 133
Bishop's Cocktail, 134
Bitch on Wheels, 134
Bitter Bikini, 80
Bitters (see also Aperitifs;
   Vermouth), 21, 74-77
   Adonis, 78
   Americano, 80
   Bitter Bikini, 80
   Blue Denim, 81
   Blue Moon, 81
   Brazil, 82
   Cinzano, 82
   Fernet Branca, 142
   Gold Stripe, 83
   Italian, 84
   Negroni, 86
   Pink Pussy, 87
   Puntigroni, 87
   Rubino, 87
   Sour Bowl, 88
Black & Tan, 311
Blackbeard Cafe, 350
Blackberry Brandy Liqueur
   drinks:
   Ace of Spades, 130

373

    Canadian Blackberry, 307
    Dark Eyes, 267
    Hot Matador, 359
    Lady Luck, 186
    Solidarity, 279
Black Bird, 296
Black Cow, 364
Black Hawk, 282
Blacklady, 209
Black Magic, 217
Black Marble, 261
Black Maria, 217
Black Sapphire, 217
Black Stripe, 218
Black Tie, 80
Black Velvet (stout), 331
Black Velvet (sparkling wine), 63
Blazing Saddle, 283
Blended Comfort, 283
Blended Whiskey, 102
    Assassins, 282
    Black Hawk, 282
    Blazing Saddle, 283
    Blended Comfort, 283
    Boot Hill, 283
    Boston Sour, 284
    Brassy Blonde, 284
    Cablegram, 284
    California Girl, 285
    California Street, 288
    Chapel Hill, 285
    Cold Kiss, 285
    Copperhead, 293
    Cotton Bale, 286
    Creole, 285

    Dark Shadow, 286
    Dear John, 286
    Derby, 286
    De Riquerer, 286
    Dinah, 286
    Dixie Darling, 287
    Double Standard, 287
    Dubonnet Manhattan, 287
    Five-O'Clock Shadow, 295
    Frisco Trolley, 287
    Fu Man-Chu, 289
    Ginger Fizz, 289
    Gloom Lifter, 288
    Horse Car, 288
    Horse's Neck, 288
    Japanese Fizz No. 1, 289
    Lady Day, 289
    Lady in Red, 289
    Lip Balm, 290
    Manhasset, 290
    Manhattan (dry; medium),
        290, (sweet), 291
    Narragansett, 291
    New York Cocktail, 291
    New York Sour, 291
    Opening Nite, 292
    Palm Reader, 292
    Pear Bottom, 284
    Preakness, 292
    Rattlesnake, 293
    Santa Anita, 292
    7 & 7, 293
    Soul Kiss, 293
    Stick Shift, 294
    T.L.C., 294

Wheeler Dealer, 294
Whiskey Sour, 294
Whiskey T.N.T., 295
White Shadow, 295
Bloodhound (gin), 134
Bloodhound (vermouth), 81
Bloodstone, 81
Bloody Bull, 261
Bloody French Dragon, 113
Bloody Maria, 245
Bloody Mary, 263
Bloody Scot, 317
Blow Torch, 350
Blueberry Liqueur drinks:
  Blueberry Sombrero, 172
  Bluebird of Happiness, 172
Blueberry Sombrero, 172
Bluebird, 134
Bluebird of Happiness, 172
Blue Chimney Smoke, 246
Blue Denim, 81
Blue Devil, 135
Blue Heaven, The, 172
Blue Lagoon, 263
Blue Monday, 263
Blue Moon (gin), 135
Blue Moon (vermouth), 81
Blue Mountain, 218
Blushin' Russian, 264
Bobby Burns, 317
Boggy Bay, 264
Bolero, 218
Bolseye, 173
Bombay, 82
Bonjour Tristesse, 135

Bonnie Doon, 318
Boomerang (gin), 135
Boomerang (vodka), 271
Boot Hill, 283
Bosom's Caress, 113
Boston Sour, 284
Bottled in Bond, 103
Bourbon, 102
Bourbon drinks:
  August Moon, 330
  Baltimore Oriole, 296
  Black Bird, 296
  Blue Denim, 296
  Bourbon and Branch, 296
  Bourbon Cowboy, 297
  Bourbon Daisy, 297
  Bourbon Italian, 297
  Brennan's Milk Punch, 297
  Busted Brownie, 298
  Chateau Julip, 298
  Cool Colonel, 298
  Delta Flight, 299
  Double Derby, 59
  El Rancho Brandy, 299
  Ewing, J. R., 299
  Fancy Turkey, 299
  Flintlock, 299
  Forester, 300
  Glowworm, 300
  Golden Glow, 300
  Golden Nugget, 300
  Grand Central Station, 301
  Great Divide, 301
  Ground Zero, 183
  Julep I, 301

Julep II, 302
Kentucky Colonel, 302
Las Vegas, 302
Mason-Dixon, 302
Midnight Cowboy, 303
Millionaire, 303
Mother 'n' Calf, 303
Old Devil Moon, 303
Original Kentucky Mint Julep, 29
Praline Bourbon Street, 197
Presbyterian, 304
Reindeer Milk, 199
Richelieu, 304
Rodeo Rider, 304
Rustler's Breakfast, 360
San Francisco Trolley, 304
Scarlet Lady, 305
Spaghetti Western, 297
Stone Age Sour, 305
Sub-Bourbon, 305
Bourbon and Branch, 296
Bourbon Cowboy, 297
Bourbon Daisy, 297
Bourbon Italian, 297
Bourbon Liqueur drinks:
  Bright Feather, 172
  Pappy McCoy, The, 195
  Sean Sweeny, 361
Boxcar No. 1, 136
Boxcar No. 2, 136
Brandy drinks:
  A. J. Cocktail, 108
  Adios, Muchachos, 212
  Alabama, 108
  Alexander, 109
  Ambrosia for Two, 62
  American Beauty, 109
  Andalusia, 212
  Aphrodite's Love Potion, 109
  Apple Blow, 110
  Apple Brandy Cocktail, 109
  Apple Cart, 110
  Apple Lillet, 110
  Apple Sour, 110
  Apricot Brandy, 111
  Apricot Sour, 111
  Aunt Jemima, 111
  Baltimore Bracer, 111
  Barclay, 171
  Barnum, 132
  Betsy Ross, 112
  Betsy Rosso, 112
  Between the Sheets, 112
  Big Apple, 112
  Bloody French Dragon, 113
  Bombay, 82
  Bosom's Caress, 113
  Brandy Blazer, 113
  Brandy Gump, 113
  Brandy Old-Fashioned, 114
  Cafe Royal, 352
  Cavalieri, 114
  Champs Elysees, 114
  Cherry Blossom, 114
  Chicago, 64
  City Slicker, 115
  Classic, 115
  Cold Deck, 115
  Da Vinci, 116

Dante's Inferno, 116
Delos Greek Fire, 116
Dempsey, 116
Dream Cocktail, 117
Dry Dock, 83
East Indian Tea Co. Punch, 352
Egg Sour, 117
El Rancho Brandy, 299
Falkland Island Crusta, 140
Fancy Brandy, 117
Father Sherman, 117
Fish House Punch, 337
Foreign Affair, 180
Foxhound, 118
French Lieutenant's Woman, 118
Gazette, 118
Ginger Toddy, 354
Granada, 118
Grand Central Station, 301
Great Divide, 301
Hail Caesar!, 228
Hot Brandy Flip, 356
Hot Mikado, 119
Hungarian Martini, 119
Ibiza, 72
Il Paradiso, 119
Italian Dream, 184
Jackrabbit, 120
Japanese, 120
Juarez Cocktail, 123
Kiss 'n' Tell, 120
La Jolla, 120
Lanson Cocktail, 66

Liberty, 121
Maneater, 121
Messalina, 121
Metaxa Sunrise, 121
Metropolitan, 122
Midnight Delight, 122
Mississippi Mud, 122
Moonlight Serenade, 122
Morning Becomes Electric, 85
Oom Paul, 123
Pancho Villa, 123
Pavarotti, 195
Peach Velvet, 123
Pepe Lamoka, 196
Phoebe Snow, 123
Pisco Sour, 124
Polaris, 124
Prince's Smile, 162
Rimini, 124
Roman Stinger, 200
San Juan, 239
Saratoga, 124
Scorpion, 240
Semiconductor, 332
Sicilian Kiss, 125
Sidecar, 125
Sink or Swim, 125
Sleepyhead, 125-126
Sloe Brandy, 126
Sourball, 126
South Pacific, 126
Sparkling Wine Branch Punch, 346
Special Rough, 126
Stab in the Back, 57

Star, 127
Star Daisy, 127
Stinger, 127
Stone Fence, 127
Tom & Jerry, 362
Tre Scalini, 128
Unicycle, 128
Via Veneto, 128
Washington, 128
Weep No More, 129
Whip, 88
White Way, 129
Widow's Kiss, 129
Zoom, 129
Brandy Blazer, 113
Brandy Gump, 113
Brandy Old Fashioned, 114
Brassy Blonde, 284
Brazil, 82
Brennan's Milk Punch, 297
Brew Beard, 334
Bright Feather, 172
Bronx Cocktail, 136
Bronx Golden, 136
Bronx Silver, 136
Brown Calf Belt, 173
Brown Derby, 218
Brunch, drinks with, 2
Buenas Noches, 219
Buffalo Sour, 58
Bullfrog, 264
Bull Shot, 262
Burnt Paw, 351
Bushranger, 219
Busted Brownie, 298
Butterfly, 173

Cabana Frappe, 173
Cabaret, 137
Cablegram, 284
Cafe Amore, 351
Cafe au Lait, 365
Cafe Benitez, 351
Cafe de Paris, 137
Cafe Grande, 351
Cafe Royale, 352
Cafetal, 219
Cafe Toulouse, 365
California Girl, 285
California Street, 288
Calorie measures, 18
Cameron's Kick, 311
Campobello, 137
Canadian Blackberry, 307
Canadian McIntosh, 307
Canadian Misty Morning, 307
Canadian Redcoat, 308
Canadian Whisky Liqueur
  drinks, 102
  Baggy Pants, 307
  Banff Cocktail, 306
  Beaufort Blast, 306
  Burnt Paw, 351
  Canadian Blackberry, 307
  Canadian McIntosh, 307
  Canadian Misty Morning, 307
  Canadian Redcoat, 308
  Cherry Picker, 307
  Dominion, 308
  Eskimo Cider, 353
  Fur Trapper, 308
  Halifax, 308
  Jackhammer, 185

378

Jack 'n' Juice, 185
Jack O'Hara, 185
Klondike, 309
MacKenzie Gold, 188
Northern Light, 309
Northern Lights, 192
Renfrew, 309
Snakebite, 202
Toronto Cocktail, 310
Walrus, 202
Western Martini, The, 310
Yellowknife, 310
Candy Cane, 174
Caney, 220
Cape Codder, 264
Cape Grape, 265
Carmen Miranda, 265
Caruso, 138
Casa Blanca, 220
Casablanca, 174
Casino, 138
Casino Cooler, 220
Cassis Punch, 334
Catnip, 265
Cat's Meow, 174
Cavalieri, 114
C. C. the Eggnog, 335
Chablis Cooler, 55
Cha-Cha-Cha, 221
Chambord Liqueur Royale drinks:
 French Summer, 180
Champagne (see Sparkling Wine)
Champs Elysees, 114
Changuirongo, 246
Chapel Hill, 285
Charro, 246
Chartreuse drinks:
 Alaska, 131
 Finnian's Rainbow, 178
 Jewel, 150
 Tipperary, 314
 Widow's Kiss, 129
Chartreuse Sparkling Wine, 64
Chaser, 24-25
Chateau Julep, 298
Chelsea Morning, 138
Chemistry, of drinks, 23-24
Cherry Blossom, 114
Cherry Chase, 138
Cherry Cola, 174
Cherry Danish, 105
Cherry Liqueur Brandy drinks:
 Ankle Breaker, 212
 Bloody Scot, 317
 Candy Cane, 174
 Cherry Blossom, 114
 Cherry Chase, 138
 Cherry Cola, 174
 Cherry Picker, 307
 Cherry Rum Daiquiri, 221
 Cherry Sparkler, 175
 Danish Snowball, 177
 Easy Piece, 266
 Finnian's Rainbow, 178
 French Lieutenant's Woman, 118
 Great Dane, The, 182
 Kiss Off, 151

379

Open Sesame, 266
Red Russian, 182
Singapore Sling, 165
Sunshine Special, The, 182
Unicycle, 128
Volga Boatman, 280
Cherry Picker, 307
Cherry Rum Daiquiri, 221
Cherry Sparkler, 175
Chicago, 64
Chilling glasses, 19
China, 221
Chinchilla, 175
Chocolate Fling, 321
Chocolate Liqueur drinks:
   Chocolate Mint Smoothie, 175
   Kiss, The, 271
   Last Mango in Texas, 186
   M & M Cocktail, 187
   Nueces Amigo, 233
Chocolate Mint Smoothie, 175
Christmas Cider, 365
Christopher Columbus, 222
Cinzano, 82
City Slicker, 115
Claire's Delight, 176
Clamdigger, 265
Classic, 115
Clock and Dagger, 222
Cloudberry Liqueur (Lakka) drinks:
   First Snow, 179
Cobbler:
   basic recipe, 25

fix, 27
Red Wine Cobbler, 60
Cockatoo, 222
Cock 'n' Bull, 262
Cocktail, 1, 25
Cocktail Mixes, prepared, 13
Cocoa Royal, 352
Coco Loco, 247
Coco Lopez Poncho Colada, 335
Coconut/Rum Liqueur drinks:
   Banana Daiquiri No. 2, 170
   Malibu Beach, 188
   Old Forge Punch, 193
   Palm Sundae, 195
   Welsh Connexion, 208
Coffee Brandy Liqueur drinks:
   After-Dinner Mint, 168
   Apres Ski, 169
   Arriba, 213
   B-52, 170
   Barclay, 171
   Black Magic, 217
   Black Maria, 217
   Blue Mountain, 218
   Brown Calf Belt, 173
   Buenas Noches, 219
   Cabana Frappe, 173
   Cafetal, 219
   Crema Cafe, 177
   Fan-Tan, 267
   Gentle Bull, 249
   Hawaiian Eye, 269
   Holy Moley, 228
   Italian Dream, 184

Kahlua Hummer, 186
Melon Jamaican, 189
Nuthouse Delight, 192
Pete's Banana, 197
Russian Coffee, 277
Spumoni Coffee, 361
Thirsty Camel, 206
Toasted Almond, 206
Cognac, 90
Cointreau drinks:
  Apple Cart, 110
  Bairn, 316
  Barbarella, 171
  Barn Door, 316
  Beach Bum, 216
  Between the Sheets, 112
  Black Lady, 209
  Blue Monday, 263
  Boxcar No. 1, 136
  Chelsea Morning, 138
  Costa del Sol, 115
  Cuanta Costa, 139
  Dry Hole, 224
  Jesse White, 270
  Maiden's Prayer, 153
  Old Devil Moon, 303
  Opal, 158
  Pacific Pacifier, 195
  Panzer, 275
  Peugeot a Paris, 197
  Velvet Hammer, 207
  White Lady, 208
  White Lily, 209
  White-Out, 209
Cole Porter, 139

Collins:
  basic recipe, 25-26
  Delos Greek Fire, 116
Columbia, 222
Commando Fix, 312
Compadre, 247
Conchita, 247
Cool Banana, 176
Cool Colonel, 298
Cooler, 26
  Chablis Cooler, 55
  Midori Cooler, 190
  O'Tooles Cooler, 72
  Red Wine Cooler, 60
  Red Wine Rum Cooler, 61
  Sparkling Wine Cooler, 69
Copley Christmas Punch, 336
Copperhead, 293
Cordial (see Liqueur)
Cordial Medoc Cup, 64
Corkscrew, 223
Corn Whiskey, 103
Costa del Sol, 115
Cotton Bale, 286
Cranberry Jerry, 365
Cranberry Liqueur drinks:
  Baggy Pants, 307
  Boggy Bay, 264
  Cape Grape, 265
  Midnight Sauna, 190
  Scarlet Lady, 305
  Stirrup Cup, 203
Cream Liqueur drinks:
  B-52, 170
  Barnum & Bailey, 171

Brown Calf Belt, 173
Cat's Meow, 174
Golden Dream, 182
Indian Dream, 184
L'il Orphan Annie, 313
Orgasm, 194
Super Bowl Cocktail, 205
Venetian Blind, 207
Cream of Melon, 176
Creamsicle, 176
Creamy Thighs, 71
Crema Cafe, 177
Creme de Cacao drinks:
Alexander (white), 109
Aunt Jemima (brown), 111
Barbary Coast (white), 316
Busted Brownie (dark), 298
Cavalieri (white), 114
Chocolate Rum, 221
Finnian's Rainbow (dark), 178
Frostbite (white), 181
Grasshopper (white), 182
Holy Moley, 228
Icehopper, 182
Jelly Bean Fix, 231
Kretchma (white), 272
Minttu Schnaappsicle, 191
Mississippi Mud (dark), 122
Pavarotti, 195
Russian Bear (dark), 277
Savoy Hotel (white), 201
Slalom (white), 279
Spumoni Coffee (dark), 361
Velvet Hammer, 207
White Mouse, 209

Creme de Cassis (Currant Liqueur):
Cassis Punch, 334
Finnish Flyer, 179
Kir, 56
Kir Royale, 66
M & M Cocktail, 187
Minttu Parfait, 191
Parisian, 160
Party Girl, 86
Sour Bowl, 88
Vermouth Cassis, 88
Creme de Menthe (green & white):
Alexander's Sister, 131
Caruso (green), 138
Chocolate Rum, 221
Emerald Isle (green), 140
Grasshopper (green), 182
Nutty Stinger, 193
Stinger (white), 127
Creme Yvette drinks:
Union Jack, 166
Creole, 285
Creole Red Wine Punch, 336
Creole Woman, 223
Crimson Tide, 139
Crown Jewel, 223
Crusta, 26
Falkland Island Crusta, 140
Polynesian Crusta, 162
Cruzan Apple Sizzle, 352
Cuanta Costa?, 139
Cuba Libre, 223
Cuba Libre Cocktail, 224

Cuban Cocktail Special, 224
Cucumber Sparkling Wine, 64
Cup, 26
Curacao drinks:
   Blue Devil, 135
   Blue Heaven, The, 172
   Cool Banana, 176
   Egg Sour, 117
   Golden Margarita, 249
   Kerry Blue, 320
   Orange Tonic, 194
   Welsh Connexion, 208

Daily Mail, 318
Daiquiri:
   Bacardi Banana Daiquiri, 214
   Bacardi Original Daiquiri, 215
   Bacardi Strawberry Daiquiri, 216
   Cherry Rum Daiquiri, 221
   Frozen Mint Daiquiri, 227
   Gin Daiquiri, 146
   Rose Wine Daiquiri, 61
   Strega Daiquiri, 204
Daisy, 26
   Bourbon Daisy, 297
   Gin Daisy, 146
Dandelion, 177
Danish Mary, 106
Danish Snowball, 177
Dante's Inferno, 116
Dark Eyes, 266
Dark Shadow, 286
Da Vinci, 116
Dear John, 286

Deep Six, 139
Delos Greek Fire, 116
Delta Flight, 299
Dempsey, 116
Depth Charge, 248
Derby (gin), 140
Derby (whiskey), 286
De Rigueur, 286
Dinah, 286
Diplomat, 82
Distillation process, 89
Dixie Darling (gin), 140
Dixie Darling (whiskey), 287
Dominion, 308
Double Derby, 59
Double Irish Coffee, 358
Double Standard, 287
Drambuie (Scotch whiskey liqueur):
   Heather on the Hill, 319
   Renfrew, 309
   Russian Nail, 278
   Rusty Nail, 200
Dream Cocktail, 117
Dry Deck, 83
Dry Hole, 224
Dublin Delight, 266
Dubonnet drinks:
   Bushranger (rouge), 219
   Cabaret (blanc), 137
   Dubonnet Manhattan (rouge), 287
   Favorite Blonde (blanc), 142
   Louisiana Lullaby (rouge), 232
   Nightmare Alley (blanc), 158

Oom Paul (rouge), 123
Richelieu (blanc), 304
Rubino (rouge), 87
Weep No More (rouge), 129
Dubonnet Manhattan, 287
Duc d'Aix en Provence, 61
Duchess of Denver, 83
Duke's Daisy, 248

East Indian Company Tea Punch, 352
Easy Piece, 266
Eau de Vie (water of life), 90, 92
Eclipse, 177
Egghead, 266
Eggnog, 26-27
    C. C. the Eggnog, 335
    Princeton Reunion Recovery Punch, 344
Eggs, adding to drinks, 21
Egg sour, 117
El Conejo, 248
El Coqui, 225
Elke Summer, 65
El Presidente, 225
El Rancho Brandy, 299
Emerald Isle, 140
Equipment, drink preparation, 8
Ermine Tail, 178
Eskimo Cider, 353
Eve, 65
Ewing, J. R., 299
Exorcist, 148
Eye Opener, 225

Fair and Warmer, 226
Faith, Hope and Garrity, 331
Falernum Sour, 226
Falkland Islands Crusta, 140
Fallen Angel, 141
Fancy Brandy, 117
Fancy Gin, 141
Fancy Turkey, 299
Fan-Tan, 267
Farmer's Almanac, 141
Farmer's Daughter, 71
Fast Tango, 178
Father Sherman, 117
Favorite, 142
Favorite Blonde, 142
Fernet Branca, 142
Fiesta, 248
50-50, 143
Fig Leaf, 226
Fine and Dandy, 141
Finnian's Rainbow, 178
Finnish Flyer, 179
Finnish Glogg, 353
Finnish Minttini, 179
Fire 'N' Ice, 179
First Lady, 226
First Nighter, 143
First Snow, 179
First Strike, 83
Fish House Punch (Original Recipe), 337
Five-O'Clock Shadow, 295
Fix:
    basic recipe, 27
    Gin Fix, 146
Fizz, 27
    Exorcist, 148

Fizzoletto, 147
Gin Fizz, 147
Gin Mint Fizz, 147
Golden Fizz, 148
Hungarian Cream Fizz, 184
Japanese Fizz No. 1, 289
Japanese Fizz No. 2, 319
Orange Fizz, 159
Ramos Gin Fizz, 163
Silver Fizz, 148
Sloe Gin Fizz, 202
Strawberry Blow Fizz, 166
Fizzoletto, 147
Fjord, 106
Flame of Love, 267
Flaming Glogg, 354
Flamingo Road, 180
Flintlock, 299
Flip, 27
  basic recipe, 28
  Cold Wine Flip, 58
  Hot Brandy Flip, 356
Float, 22-23
Foreign Affair, 180
Forester, 300
43 Liqueur (Vanilla-flavor) drinks:
  Creamsicle, 176
  143 Percent, 193
Foxhound, 118
Frangelico (hazelnut) Liqueur drinks:
  Abbot's Delight, 168
  Friar Tuck, 180
  Puro's Palace, 239
  Super Bowl Cocktail, 205
Frankensteen, 143
Frappe, 28
  Bacardi Frio, 215
  Cabana Frappe, 173
  Duc d'Aix en Provence, 61
  Frosted Vines, 59
  Frozen Sommeliere, 55
  Slalom Frappe, 202
  Sommeliere Frappe, 61
Free Silver, 227
French Flag, 59
French Foam, 65
French Lieutenant's Woman, 118
French Lift, 65
French Punch, 338
French Summer, 180
Friar Tuck, 180
Frisco Trolley, 287
Frithco Blower, 144
Frobisher, 66
Front-Page Dynamite, 267
Frostbite, 181
Frosted Fruit Buttermilk (or yogurt), 366
Frosted Vines, 59
Frosting glasses, 19-20
Frozen Mint Daiquiri, 227
Frozen Sommeliere, 5
Frozen Tequila, 249
Fruit Garnish, 22
Fruity Wine Cooler, 59
Fu Man-Chu, 289
Fur Trapper, 308

Galliano Liqueur drinks:
  Harvey Sly Banger, 183
  Harvey Wallbanger, 269
  Orange Galliant, 193
  Spumoni Coffee, 361
  Vegas Smile, 206
Garden of Sweden, 181
Gauguin, 27
Gavilan .45, 249
Gazette, 118
Geisha Girl, 262
Gentle Bull, 249
George Bush, 312
Gibraltar, 318
Gibson, 144, 154
Gilded Cage, 227
Gimlet, 144
Gin drinks:
  Abbey, 130
  Ace of Spades, 130
  Alaska, 131
  Alexander's Sister, 131
  Alfonso Special, 131
  Alliance, 79
  Almond Cocktail, 79
  Althea Gibson, 144
  Artillery, 131
  B.V.D., 137
  Bachelor and Bobby Soxer, 132
  Balmoral, 316
  Barbary Coast, 132
  Barbary Coast, 316
  Barnum, 132
  Beauty Mark, 79

Beauty Spot, 132
Bee's Knees, 133
Bennet, 133
Bermuda Rose, 133
Bishop's Benediction, 133
Bishop's Cocktail, 134
Bitch on Wheels, 134
Bloodhound, 134
Bloodhound, 81
Bloodstone, 81
Blue Devil, 135
Blue Moon, 135
Blue Moon, 81
Bluebird, 134
Bonjour Tristesse, 135
Boomerang, 135
Boxcar No. 1, 136
Boxcar No. 2, 136
Bronx Cocktail, 136
Bronx Golden, 136
Bronx Silver, 136
Cabaret, 137
Cafe de Paris, 137
Campobello, 137
Caruso, 138
Casino, 138
Chelsea Morning, 138
Cherry Chase, 138
Christopher Columbus, 222
Coco Loco, 247
Cole Porter, 139
Costa del Sol, 115
Crimson Tide, 139
Cuanta Costa, 139
Deep Six, 139

386

Dempsey, 116
Derby, 140
Dixie Darling, 140
Double Standard, 287
Eclipse, 177
Emerald Isle, 140
Exorcist, 148
Falkland Islands Crusta, 140
Fallen Angel, 141
Fancy Gin, 141
Farmer's Almanac, 141
Favorite, 142
Favorite Blonde, 142
Fernet Branca, 142
50-50, 158
Fine and Dandy, 141
Finnish Minttini, 179
First-Nighter, 143
Fizzoletto, 147
Frankenstein, 143
Frithco Blower, 144
Frobisher, 66
Gibson, 144
Gimlet, 144
Gin & It, 145
Gin & Sin, 145
Gin & Tonic, 145
Gin 'n' Bitters, 145
Gin Bowl, 338
Gin Daiquiri, 146
Gin Daisy, 146
Gin Fix, 146
Gin Fizz, 147
Gin Mint Fizz, 147
Gin Swizzle, 147

Gin Zoom, 148
Ginny-Gin Southern, 181
Golden Fizz, 148
Golden Pond, 149
Gopher Ball, 143
Great Dane, The, 182
Gypsy, 149
Haarlem, 149
Hasty Pudding, 149
Hit & Miss, 150
I.R.S., 150
Invisible Man, 150
Jamaica Glory, 230
Jewel, 150
Jeweler's Rouge, 151
Jockey Club, 151
KGB, 151
Kiss Off, 142
Ladyfinger, 152
Landon, 152
Leap Year, 152
Mahattan South, 153
Maiden's Blush, 152
Maiden's Prayer, 153
Martini, 153-154
Merry Widow, 155
Mississippi Mule, 155
Monkey Gland, 155
Montmartre, 156
Moonshot, 156
Morning "Minute Maid," 156
Morro Castle, 156
Moulin Rouge, 157
Mule Shoe, 157
Napoleon, 157

387

Napoleon III, 157
Nightmare Alley, 158
Nineteen, 158
1984, 143
Oasis, 158
Opal, 158
Opera, 159
Orange Blossom, 159
Orange Fizz, 159
Orchid, 160
Palm Beach, 160
Panzer, 275
Paradise Island, 160
Parisian, 160
Park & 59th, 160
Perfect Cocktail, 86
Peter Seller's Minky, 155
Pink Gin, 160
Pink Lady, 161
Pink Panther, 161
Pink Pussycat, 161
Pink Rose, 161
Pirate of Penzance, 236
Polynesian Crusta, 162
Poodle TV Special, 162
Prince's Smile, 162
Princeton, 162
Puntegroni, 87
Q.E. 2, 163
Racquet Club, 163
Ramos Gin Fizz, 163
Red Lion, 199
Red Snapper, 164
Rolls-Royce, 164
Rose Cocktail, 164

Rosetta Stone, 164
Saketini, 331
Salty Dog, 164
Seville, 165
Silence Is Golden, 165
Silver Fizz, 148
Singapore Sling, 165
Snowball, 165
South Pacific, 126
Star Daisy, 127
Star of Brazil, 203
Stick Shift, 294
Strawberry Blow Fizz, 166
Union Jack, 166
Velvet Kiss, 166
Weekend, 207
White Sale, 167
Gin & It, 145
Gin & Sin, 145
Gin & Tonic, 145
Gin Bowl, 338
Gin Daiquiri, 146
Gin Daisy, 146
Gin Fix, 146
Gin Fizz, 147
Ginger Snap, 268
Ginger Toddy, 354
Gin Mint Fizz, 147
Gin 'n' Bitters, 145
Ginny-Gin Southern, 181
Gin Swizzle, 147
Gin Zoom, 148
Ginzu Fizz, 289
Glassware, 4-7, 154
Gloom Lifter, 288

388

Glowworm, 300
Glowworm Wine Punch, 355
Gluewein, 355
Golda Major, 268
Goldenberg's Folly, 318
Golden Dream, 182
Golden Fizz, 148
Golden Geisha, 331
Golden Glow, 300
Golden Margarita, 249
Golden Nugget, 300
Golden Pond, 149
Gold Stripe, 83
Gopher Ball, 143
Gordita, 250
Gorilla Sweat, 355
Gorky Park, 267
Granada, 118
Grand Central Station, 301
Grand Margarita, 251
Grand Marnier drinks:
  Alfonso Special, 131
  April in Paris Ball, 63
  Bacardi Ancient Mariner, 214
  Banff Cocktail, 306
  B-52, 170
  Cafe Grande, 351
  Cocoa Royal, 352
  Dominion, 308
  Front-Page Dynamite, 267
  High Roller, 270
  Il Paradiso, 119
  Imperial Czar, 270
  Jelly Bean Fix, 231
  Last Mango in Texas, 186
  Orange Galliant, 193
  Weekend, 207
  Red Lion, 199
Grapefruit Gorgeous, 366
Grasshopper, 182
Grass Skirt, 268
Great Dane, 106
Great Dane, The, 182
Great Divide, 301
Green Demon, 182
Green Devil, 312
Green Hornet, 72
Green Machine, 183
Green Room, 84
Ground Zero, 183
Gypsy, 149
Gypsy Moth, 268

Haarlem, 149
Hail Caesar!, 228
Halifax, 308
Hand Grenade, 250
Happy Hour Punch, 339
Harper's Ferry, 84
Hart Breaker, 228
Harvey Sly Banger, 183
Harvey Wallbanger, 269
Hasty Pudding, 149
Havana Club, 228
Hawaiian Eye, 269
Hawaiian Mint Limeade, 269
Hawaiian Sparkling Wine
  Punch, 339
Hayride, 269
Heather on the Hill, 319

Highball, 28
Highland Fling, 319
High Roller, 270
Hit and Miss, 150
Holiday drinks, 3-4
Holly Golightly, 301
Hollywood and Wine, 56
Holy Moley, 228
Honey Bee, 229
Honeysuckle, 229
Honolulu Punch, 340
Hoopla, 84
Horny Bull, 250
Horse Car, 288
Horse's Neck, 288
Hot and Heavy Grog, 357
Hot Brandy Flip, 356
Hot Buttered Comfort, 356
Hot Buttered Rum, 356
Hot Creole, 356
Hot drinks, 28
   Blackbeard Cafe, 350
   Blow Torch, 350
   Burnt Paw, 351
   Cafe Amore, 351
   Cafe Benitez, 351
   Cafe Grande, 351
   Cafe Royale, 352
   Cocoa Royal, 352
   Cruzan Apple Sizzle, 352
   Double Irish Coffee, 358
   East Indian Company Tea Punch, 352
   Eskimo Cider, 353
   Finnish Glogg, 353
   Flaming Glogg, 354
   Ginger Toddy, 354
   Glowworm Wine Punch, 355
   Gluewein, 355
   Gorilla Sweat, 355
   Hot and Heavy Grog, 357
   Hot Brandy Flip, 356
   Hot Buttered Comfort, 356
   Hot Buttered Rum, 356
   Hot Creole, 356
   Hot Matador, 359
   Hotsy Totsy, 357
   Hot Tub, 357
   Irish Coffee (Bushmills), 358
   Island Rum Tea, 358
   Jamocha Stoker, 358
   Locomotive, 359
   Mulled Cider, 359
   Mulled Red Wine, 359
   Ninotchka's Night, 360
   Poet's Punch, 360
   Russian Tea, 360
   Rustler's Breakfast, 360
   Sean Sweeney, 361
   Silent Majority, 361
   Souperman, 361
   Spumoni Coffee, 361
   Tom & Jerry, 362
   Two Fingers Mariachi, 362
   Vesuvio, 362
   Yard of Flannel, 363
Hot Matador, 359
Hot Mikado, 119
Hotsy Totsy, 357
Hot Tub, 357

Hungarian Cream Fizz, 184
Hungarian Martini, 119
Hurricane, 229
H. Walker's Sparkplug, 183

Ibiza, 72
Ice, 19
Icebreaker, 184
Ice Cream Colada, 229
Icehopper, 182
Il Paradiso, 119
Imperial Czar, 270
Indian Paintbrush, 230
Invisible Man, 150
Irish Coffee (Bushmills), 358
Irish Mist Liqueur drinks:
    Niagara Falls, 309
    Poet's Punch, 360
Irish Shillelagh, 312
Irish Whiskey drinks, 102
    Black & Tan, 311
    Cameron's Kick, 311
    Commando Fix, 312
    Faith, Hope & Garrity, 331
    George Bush, 312
    Green Devil, 312
    Irish Shillelagh, 312
    L'il Orphan Annie, 313
    O'Toole's Cooler, 72
    Paddy's Wagon, 313
    Ruddy McDowell, 313
    Serpent's Smile, 313
    Shamrock, 314
    Tipperary, 314
Iron Lady, 319

I.R.S., 150
Island Rum Tea, 358
Italian, 84
Italian Dream, 184
Italian Red Wine Cocktail, 60

Jackhammer, 185
Jack 'N' Juice, 185
Jack O'Hara, 185
Jackrabbit, 120
Jamaica Farewell, 230
Jamaica Glory, 230
Jamocha Stoker, 358
Japanese, 120
Japanese Fizz No. 1, 289
Japanese Fizz No. 2, 319
Jefferson Davis Punch, 340
Jelly Bean, 185
Jelly Bean Fix, 231
Jesse White, 270
Jewel, 150
Jeweler's Rouge, 151
Jockey Club, 151
Jolly Roger, 230
Juarez Cocktail, 123
Judgment Day, 270
Julep, 28
    basic recipe, 29
    Chateau Julep, 69
    Julep I, 301
    Julep II, 302
    Smash, 29
    Sparkling Wine Julep, 69
Julep I, 301
Julep II, 302

Junta, 231
Kahlua Hummer, 186
Kangaroo, 271
Kentucky Colonel, 302
Kerry Blue, 320
KGB, 151
Kingdom Come, 85
Kir, 56
Kir Royal, 66
Kirsch/Kirschwasser drinks:
    Nineteen, 158
Kiss, The, 271
Kiss 'n' Tell, 120
Kiss Off, 151
Kiwi Liqueur drinks:
    Boomerang, 271
Klondike, 309
Knockout, 142
Kremlin Colonel, 271
Kretchma, 272
Kummel drinks:
    Foxhound, 118

La Belle Liza, 272
Lady Day, 289
Ladyfinger, 152
Lady in Red, 289
Lady Luck, 186
La Jolla, 120
Lanson Cocktail, 66
Last Dansk, 106
Last Mango in Texas, 186
Las Vegas, 302
Latango, 186
Leap Year, 152

Lemonier Liqueur drinks:
    Lemon Drops, 187
Le Coq Hardy, 66
Lemon Cooler, 85
Lemon Drops, 187
Lemon Montserrat, 67
Liberty, 121
Lichine, Alexis, 75
Light Fantastic, 187
Lillet Cocktail, 85
L'il Orphan Annie, 313
Lime Daiquiri, 231
Limey, 231
Lip Balm, 290
Liqueur drinks:
    Abbot's Delight, 168
    After-Dinner Mint, 168
    Alexander, 109
    Almond Fizz, 169
    Amaretto Ice, 169
    Amaretto & Cognac
        Continental Stinger, 169
    Apple Cart, 110
    Apres Ski, 169
    Aunt Jemima, 111
    B-52, 170
    Bailey's Shillelagh, 170
    Baltimore Bracer, 111
    Banana Daiquiri No. 2, 170
    Bananago, 170
    Banshee, 171
    Barbarella, 171
    Barclay, 171
    Between the Sheets, 112
    Bishop's Benediction, 133

Bishop's Cocktail, 134
Blacklady, 209
Blowtorch, 350
Blue Heaven, The, 172
Blueberry Sombrero, 172
Bluebird of Happiness, 172
Bolseye, 173
Boxcar No. 1, 136
Boxcar No. 2, 136
Bright Feather, 172
Brown Calf Belt, 173
Butterfly, 173
Cabana Frappe, 173
Candy Cane, 174
Casablanca, 174
Cat's Meow, 174
Cavalieri, 114
Chapel Hill, 285
Cherry Blossom, 114
Cherry Cola, 174
Cherry Sparkler, 175
Chinchilla, 175
Chocolate Mint Smoothie, 175
City Slicker, 115
Claire's Delight, 176
Coed Kiss, 285
Cold Feet, 175
Cool Banana, 176
Cream of Melon, 176
Creamsicle, 176
Crema Cafe, 177
Cuanta Costa?, 139
Dandelion, 177
Danish Snowball, 177
Dream Cocktail, 117
Eclipse, 177
Egg Sour, 117
Ermine Tail, 178
Fast Tango, 178
Finnian's Rainbow, 178
Finnish Flyer, 179
Finnish Minttini, 179
Fire 'n' Ice, 179
First Snow, 179
Flamingo Road, 180
Foreign Affair, 180
French Lieutenant's Woman, 118
French Summer, 180
Friar Tuck, 180
Frostbite, 181
Garden of Sweden, 181
Ginny-Gin Southern, 181
Golden Dream, 182
Grasshopper, 182
Great Dane, The, 182
Green Demon, 182
Green Hornet, 72
Green Machine, 183
Ground Zero, 183
H. Walker's Sparkplug, 183
Harvey Sly Banger, 183
Hot Mikado, 119
Hungarian Cream Fizz, 184
Icebreaker, 184
Icehopper, 182
Imperial Czar, 270
Italian Dream, 184
Jack 'n' Juice, 185

Jack O'Hara, 185
Jackhammer, 185
Jelly Bean, 185
Kahlua Hummer, 186
Kiss Off, 151
Lady Luck, 186
Last Mango in Texas, 186
Latango, 186
Lemon Drops, 187
Light Fantastic, 187
M & M Cocktail, 187
Mackenzie Gold, 188
Man in the Moon, 188
Mardi Gras Float, 189
Melon Ball, 189
Melon Jamaican, 189
Melon Lady, 189
Melon Patch, 190
Meloncholy Baby, 188
Midnight Sauna, 190
Midori Cooler, 190
Midori Sour, 190
Minttu Parfait, 191
Minttu Schnaappsicle, 191
Minttu Shooter, 191
Minty Moose, 192
Northern Light, 309
Northern Lights, 192
Nuthouse Delight, 192
Nutty Stinger, 193
Old Forge Punch, 193
143 Percent, 193
Orange Galliant, 193
Orange Tonic, 194
Orangecicle, 194

Orgasm, 194
Oxbend Bend, 194
Pacific Pacifier, 195
Palm Sundae, 195
Pappy McCoy, The, 195
Pavarotti, 195
Pear Sour, 196
Pearls of Praline, 196
Pepe Lamoka, 196
Persian Melon, 196
Pete's Banana, 197
Peugeot a Paris, 197
Polar Bear, 197
Pousse Cafe, 198
Praline Bourbon Street, 197
Red Lion, 199
Red Russian, 199
Reindeer Milk, 199
Rhett Butler, 199
Rivet, 200
Roman Snowball, 200
Roman Stinger, 200
Russian Bear, 277
Russian Coffee, 277
Russian Nail, 278
Rusty Nail, 200
Santa Ana's Bandana, 201
Savoy Hotel, 201
Scarlett O'Hara, 201
Slalom Frappe, 202
Slalom, 279
Sloe Gin Fizz, 202
Slow Comfortable Screw, 202
Slow Screw, 202
Snakebite, 202

Snowbird, 202
Sombrero, 203
Star of Brazil, 203
Stirrup Cup, 203
Strawberry Fields, 204
Strega Daiquiri, 204
Strega Freeze, 204
Suissese, 204
Sunshine Special, The, 205
Super Bowl Cocktail, 205
Swedish Lullaby, 205
Tawny Russian, 205
Thirsty Camel, 206
Toasted Almond, 206
Tre Scalini, 128
Uncle Minty, 206
Vegas Smile, 206
Velvet Hammer, 207
Venetian Blind, 207
Volga Boatman, 280
Walrus, 207
Weekend, 207
Welsh Connexion, 208
Whiskey TNT, 295
White Cloud, 208
White Gloves, 208
White Lady, 208
White Lily, 209
White Mouse, 209
White-Out, 209
White Shadow, 295
White Velvet, 209
White Way, 129
White Whisker, 210
Widow's Dream, 210

Widow's Kiss, 129
Loch Lomond, 320
Loch Ness Monster, 320
Locomotive, 359
London, 152
London Special, 67
Louisiana Lullaby, 232
Low Ball, 28

MacKenzie Gold, 188
Maiden's Blush, 152
Maiden's Prayer, 153
Main Chance, 235
Mai Tai, 232
Malibu Beach, 188
Malinky Malchik, 272
M & M Cocktail, 187
Mandeville, 232
Maneater, 121
Manhasset, 290
Manhattan (dry; medium), 290, (sweet), 291
Manhattan South, 153
Man in the Moon, 188
Mardi Gras Float, 189
Margarita No. 1, 250
Margarita No. 2, 251
Maria Sanger, 262
Marquise, 56
Martini, 153-154
Mary Pickford, 232
Mason-Dixon, 302
Matador, 251
Meals, drinks with, 3
Measurements, 15-16

395

Meloncholy Baby, 188
Melon Ball, 189
Melon Jamaican, 189
Melon Lady, 189
Melon Liqueur drinks:
   Claire's Delight, 176
   Cream of Melon, 176
   Dublin Delight, 266
   Finnian's Rainbow, 178
   Green Hornet, 72
   Green Machine, 183
   Hot Mikado, 119
   Melon Ball, 189
   Melon Jamaican, 189
   Melon Patch, 190
   Midori Cooler, 190
   Midori Sour, 190
   Park & 59th, 160
   Persian Melon, 196
Melon Patch, 190
Merry Widow, 155
Messalina, 121
Metaxa Brandy drinks:
   Aphrodite's Love Potion, 109
   Delos Greek Fire, 116
   Metaxa Sunrise, 121
Metropolitan, 122
Mexican Brandy drinks:
   Adios, Muchachos, 212
   Midnight Delight, 122
   Pancho Villa, 123
Mexican Sunrise, 251
Miami Beach, 320
Miami Whammy, 233
Midnight Cowboy, 303

Midnight Delight, 122
Midnight Sauna, 190
Midnight Sun (aquavit), 107
Midnight Sun (vodka), 272
Midori Cooler, 190
Midori Sour, 190
Millionaire, 303
Minttu Parfait, 191
Minttu Schnaappsicle, 191
Minttu Shooter, 191
Minty Moose, 192
Mississippi Mud, 122
Mississippi Mule, 155
Mist drinks, 29
   Scotch Mist, 321
Mr. Lucky, 273
Mistress Mary, 232
Mixology, 1-4
Mockingbird, 251
Mocha Liqueur drinks:
   Bananago, 170
   Latango, 186
   Pepe Lamoka, 196
Mock Julep, 366
Monkey Gland, 155
Montmartre, 156
Montserrat Ponche, 341
Moonlight Serenade, 122
Moon over Moscow, 273
Moonshot, 156
Morning-after drinks, 2
Morning Becomes Electric, 85
Morning "Minute Maid," 156
Morro Castle, 156
Moscow Mule, 273

Mother & Calf, 303
Moulin Rouge, 157
Mule Shoe, 157
Mulled Cider, 359
Mulled Red Wine, 359
Mystic Cooler, 274

Naked Maja, 274
Napoleon, 157
Napoleon III, 157
Narragansett, 291
Navy Grog, 233
Navy Punch, 341
Neat, 29
Negroni, 86
New Encyclopedia of Wine and Spirits, 75
New York Cocktail, 291
New York Sour, 291
Niagara Falls, 309
Nightcap, 4
Nightmare Alley, 158
Nineteen, 158
1984, 158
Ninotchka, 274
Ninotchka's Night, 360
Non-alcoholic drinks:
   Banana Frosted, 364
   Black Cow, 364
   Cafe au Lait, 365
   Cafe Toulouse, 365
   Christmas Cider, 365
   Cranberry Jery, 365
   Frosted Fruit Buttermilk (or yogurt), 366
   Grapefruit Gorgeous, 366
   Mock Julep, 366
   Orange Tinkle, 367
   Pineapple Tinkle, 367
   Roseanna Banana, 367
   Snappy Yogurt, 367
   Wedding Night Nog, 368
   Yogi Bitter, 368
Northern Light, 309
Northern Lights, 192
Nueces Amigo, 233
Nuthouse Delight, 192
Nutty Stinger, 193

Oasis, 158
Odessa File, 274
Ojos Verdes, 233
Okoleayo, 104
Old Devil Moon, 303
Old Forge Punch, 193
143 Percent, 193
On-The-Rocks, 30
Oom Paul, 123
Opal, 158
Opening Nite, 292
Open Sesame, 275
Opera, 159
Orange Blossom, 159
Orangecicle, 194
Orange Fizz, 159
Orange Galliant, 193
Orange Oasis, 342
Orange Tinkle, 367
Orange Tonic, 194
Orchid, 160

Orgasm, 194
Original Kentucky Mint Julep, 29
O'Toole's Cooler, 72
Oxbend Bend, 194

Pacific Pacifier, 195
Paddy's Wagon, 313
Pago Pago, 234
Pale Moon, 86
Palm Beach, 160
Palm Reader, 292
Palm Sundae, 195
Panama, 234
Pancho Villa, 123
Panzer, 275
Pappy McCoy, The, 195
Paradise Island, 160
Paradise Lost, 234
Parisian, 160
Parisian Blonde, 234
Park & 59th, 160
Park Avenue Orange Blossom, 342
Party drinks, 3-4
Party Girl, 86
Patriarca, 67
Pavaroti, 195
Peacharino, 275
Peach Brandy Liqueur drinks:
  Alabama, 108
  Corkscrew, 223
  Fish House Punch, 337
  Peach Velvet, 123
  Princeton Reunion Recovery Punch, 344

Peach Velvet, 123
Pear Cordial Liqueur drinks:
  Hungarian Cream Fizz, 184
  Pear Sour, 196
Pear Bottom, 284
Pearls of Praline, 196
Pear Sour, 196
Pepe Lamoka, 196
Peppermint Schnapps Liqueur drinks:
  Apres Ski, 169
  Beaufort Blast, 306
  Blowtorch, 350
  Brown Calf Belt, 173
  Candy Cane, 174
  Chocolate Mint Smoothie, 175
  Cold Feet, 175
  Cold Kiss, 285
  Dry Deck, 83
  Finnian's Rainbow, 178
  Finnish Flyer, 179
  Finnish Minttini, 179
  First Lady, 226
  Ground Zero, 183
  Ice Breaker, 184
  Ice Hopper, 182
  Jackhammer, 185
  Light Finntastic, 187
  M & M Cocktail, 187
  Man in the Moon, 188
  Midnight Sauna, 190
  Minttu Parfait, 191
  Minttu Schnaappsicle, 191
  Minty Moose, 192

Moon Over Moscow, 273
Polar Bear, 197
Reindeer Milk, 199
Rivet, 200
Slalom Frappe, 202
Uncle Minty, 206
White Gloves, 208
White Mouse, 209
White-Out, 209
White Whisker, 210
Peppery Punch, 343
Perfect Cocktail, 86
Perpetual, 87
Persian Melon, 196
Peter Seller's Minky, 155
Pete's Banana, 197
Peugeot a Paris, 197
Phoebe Snow, 123
Pina, 252
Pina Colada, 234
Pinata, 252
Pineapple Tinkle, 367
Pink California Sunshine, 67
Pink Coco Wine Punch, 343
Pink Creole, 235
Pink Gin, 160
Pink Lady, 161
Pink Mink, 275
Pink Panther, 161
Pink Pussy, 87
Pink Pussycat, 161
Pink Rose, 161
Pink Veranda, 235
Pirate of Penzance, 236
Pisco Sour, 124

Pistacha Liqueur drinks:
   Green Demon, 182
   Jelly Bean, 185
   Nutty Stinger, 193
   Persian Melon, 196
Pittsburgh, Spirit, the, 275
Planter's Cocktail, 236
Planter's Punch, 236
Plaza Pleaser, 236
Poet's Punch, 360
Poinsettia, 68
Poker, 240
Polar Bear, 197
Polaris, 124
Polish Sidecar, 276
Polynesian Crusta, 162
Ponce de Leon, 236
Poodle TV Special, 162
Pousse Cafe, 22-23
   combinations, 198
   Finnian's Rainbow, 178
   Savoy Hotel, 201
Prairie Oyster, 276
Praline Bourbon Street, 197
Praline Liqueur drinks:
   Mardi Gras Float, 189
   Pearls of Praline, 196
   Praline Bourbon Street, 197
Preakness, 292
Precious Lady, 236
Presbyterian, 304
Prince's Smile, 162
Princeton, 162
Princeton Reunion Recovery Punch, 344

Proof, 24, 89, 324
Puff, 30
Punches:
 Artillery Punch, 333
 Bacardi Confetti Punch, 334
 Brew Beard, 334
 Cassis Punch, 334
 C. C. the Eggnog, 335
 Coco Lopez Ponche Colada, 335
 Copley Christmas Punch, 336
 Creole Red Wine Punch, 336
 Cup, 26
 Fish House Punch (Original Recipe), 337
 French Punch, 338
 Gin Bowl, 338
 Happy Hour Punch, 339
 Hawaiian Sparkling Wine Punch, 339
 Honolulu Punch, 340
 Jefferson Davis Punch, 340
 Montserrat Ponche, 341
 Navy Punch, 341
 Orange Oasis, 342
 Park Avenue Orange Blossom, 342
 Peppery Punch, 343
 Pink Coco Wine Punch, 343
 Princeton Reunion Recovery Punch, 344
 Puncinello, 345
 Red Wine Fruit Cup, 345
 Sangria, 346
 Sparkling Wine Punch, 347
 Sparkling Wine Sherbet Punch, 347
 Strawberry Bowl, 348
 Summer Punch, 348
 Syllabub, 32
 Tampico, 348
 Victorian Mint Shrub, 349
 White Wine Cup, 349
Puncinello, 345
Puntegroni, 87
Pure Food Act, 75
Puro's Palace, 239
Purple Passion, 276
Pusser's Pain Killer, 237

Q. E. 2, 163
Quarter Deck, 237
Queen of Scots, 322

Racquet Club, 163
Ramos Gin Fizz, 163
Raspberry Cocktail, 56
Raspberry Liqueur Brandy drinks:
 Blushin' Russian, 264
 Columbia, 222
 Holly Golightly, 301
Rattlesnake, 293
Red Baron, 276
Red Flannels, 263
Red Lion, 199
Red Rock Canyon, 277
Red Russian, 199

Red Snapper, 164
Red Wine drinks (see also
　Wine), 41-43, 47-48
　Betsy Ross, 112
　Buffalo Sour, 58
　Cold Wine Flip, 58
　Creole Red Wine Punch, 336
　Crimson Tide, 139
　Double Derby, 59
　Dux d'Aix en Provence, 61
　Finnish Glogg, 353
　Flaming Glogg, 354
　French Flag, 59
　Frosted Vines, 59
　Fruity Wine Cooler, 59
　Glowworm Wine Punch, 35
　Gluewein, 35
　Iron Lady, 319
　Italian Red Wine Cocktail, 60
　Japanese Fizz No. 1, 289
　Jefferson Davis Punch, 340
　Mulled Red Wine, 359
　Red Wine Cobbler, 60
　Red Wine Cooler, 60
　Red Wine Fruit Cup, 345
　Red Wine Rum Cooler, 61
　Rose Wine Daiquiri, 61
　Sangria, 346
　Sommeliere Frappe, 61
Red Wine Cobbler, 60
Red Wine Cooler, 60
Red Wine Fruit Cup, 345
Red Wine Rum Cooler, 61
Refresco, 237
Reindeer Milk, 199

Renaissance Man, 72
Renfrew, 309
Revolution, 252
Rhett Butler, 199
Richelieu, 304
Rickey, 30
Rimini, 124
Rivet, 200
Rob Roy, 321
Rodeo Rider, 304
Rolls-Royce, 164
Roman Snowball, 200
Roman Stinger, 200
Ron Coco, 238
Roseanna Banana, 367
Rose Cocktail, 164
Rosetta Stone, 164
Rose Wine Daiquiri, 61
Rosita, 252
Rubino, 87
Ruby Hunter, 238
Ruddy McDowell, 313
Rum drinks (see also Spirits), 98-
　100
　Acapulco No. 1, 211
　Acapulco No. 2, 211
　Adios, Muchachos, 212
　Andalusia, 212
　Ankle Breaker, 212
　Apple Pie, 212
　Apricot Lady, 213
　Apricot Pie, 213
　Arriba, 213
　BVD, 137
　Bacardi American Flyer, 214

Bacardi Ancient Mariner, 214
Bacardi Banana Daiquiri, 214
Bacardi Cocktail, 214
Bacardi Confetti Punch, 334
Bacardi Driver, 215
Bacardi Frio, 215
Bacardi Monkey Wrench, 215
Bacardi Original Daiquiri, 215
Bacardi Strawberry Daiquiri, 216
Barbary Coast, 132
Barbary Coast, 316
Batida de Pina, 216
Beach Blanket, 216
Beach Bum, 216
Beauty and the Beach, 216
Bee's Kiss, 217
Between the Sheets, 12
Black & Tan, 311
Black Magic, 217
Black Maria, 217
Black Sapphire, 217
Black Stripe, 218
Blackbeard Cafe, 350
Blue Heaven, The, 172
Blue Mountain, 218
Bolero, 218
Brown Derby, 218
Buenas Noches, 219
Bushranger, 219
Cafe Benitez, 351
Cafetal, 219
Caney, 220
Carmen Miranda, 265
Casa Blanca, 220

Casino Cooler, 220
Cha-Cha-Cha, 221
Cherry Rum Daiquiri, 221
China, 221
Chocolate Rum, 221
Christopher Columbus, 222
Clock and Dagger, 222
Cockatoo, 222
Coco Loco, 247
Columbia, 222
Copley Christmas Punch, 336
Corkscrew, 223
Creole Woman, 223
Crown Jewel, 223
Cruzan Apple Sizzle, 352
Cuba Libre, 223
Cuba Libre Cocktail, 224
Cuban Cocktail Special, 224
Dry Hole, 224
East Indian Tea Company Punch, 352
Eggnog, 26-27
El Coqui, 225
El Presidente, 225
Eye Opener, 225
Fair and Warmer, 226
Falernum Sour, 226
Falkland Islands Crusta, 140
Fig Leaf, 226
First Lady, 226
Fish House Punch, 337
Free Silver, 227
Frozen Mint Daiquiri, 227
Garden of Sweden, 181
Gauguin, 227

Gilded Cage, 227
Gin Daiquiri, 146
Glowworm, 300
Golden Geisha, 331
Golden Glow, 300
Grand Central Station, 301
Green Machine, 183
Hail Caesar!, 228
Hart Breaker, 228
Havana Club, 228
Holy Moley, 228
Honey Bee, 229
Honeysuckle, 229
Hot Buttered Rum, 356
Hot Creole, 356
Hot and Heavy Grog, 357
Hotsy Totsy, 357
Hurricane, 229
Ice Cream Colada, 229
Indian Paintbrush, 230
Island Rum Tea, 358
Jamaica Farewell, 230
Jamaica Glory, 230
Jamocha Stoker, 358
Jelly Bean Fix, 231
Jesse White, 270
Jolly Roger, 230
Junta, 231
Kahlua Hummer, 186
Latango, 186
Lime Daiquiri, 231
Louisiana Lullaby, 232
Mai Tai, 232
Main Chance, 235
Mandeville, 232

Mary Pickford, 232
Mason-Dixon, 302
Melon Jamaican, 189
Metaxa Sunrise, 121
Miami Whammy, 233
Mississippi Mud, 122
Mistress Mary, 232
Morro Castle, 156
Mulled Cider, 359
Navy Grog, 233
Nueces Amigo, 233
Ojos Verdes, 233
Pago Pago, 234
Panama, 234
Paradise Lost, 234
Parisian Blonde, 234
Pina Colada, 234
Pink Creole, 235
Pink Veranda, 235
Pirate of Penzance, 236
Planter's Cocktail, 236
Planter's Punch, 236
Plaza Pleaser, 236
Poker, 240
Ponce de Leon, 236
Precious Lady, 236
Princeton Reunion Recovery
    Punch, 344
Puro's Palace, 239
Pusser's Pain Killer, 237
Quarter Deck, 237
Refresco, 237
Renaissance Man, 72
Ron Coco, 238
Ruby Hunter, 238

Rum Dandy, 238
Rum Oasis, 238
Rumpelstiltskin, 239
San Juan, 239
San Juan's Bolero, 239
Saxon Lord, 239
Scorpion, 240
September Morn, 240
Sevilla, 240
Shanghai, 240
Shark's Tooth, 241
Sledgehammer, 241
Spiritual Rubescence, 241
Star of Brazil, 203
Stiletto, 241
Strega Daiquiri, 204
Sun Worshipper, 242
Sutter's Mill, 242
Swinger's Cocktail, 242
Tahiti Club, 242
Thirsty Camel, 206
Tom & Jerry, 362
Torrid Zone, 243
Vegas Smile, 206
Venetian Blind, 207
White Lily, 209
White Lion, 243
Witch's Twitch, 243
Yard of Flannel, 363
Zombie, 244
Rum Dodge, 238
Rum Oasis, 238
Rumpelstiltskin, 239
Russian Bear, 277
Russian Cocktail, 277

Russian Coffee, 277
Russian Lady, 278
Russian Nail, 278
Russian Pipeline, 278
Russian Tea, 360
Rustler's Breakfast, 360
Rusty Nail, 200
Rye, 103

Sake (see also Ale, Beer), 328-329
   August Moon, 330
   Geisha Girl, 262
   Golden Geisha, 331
   Saketini, 331
   Semiconductor, 332
Saketini, 331
Salt Lick, 278
Salty Dog, 164
San Francisco Trolley, 304
Sangaree, 30
   basic recipe, 31
Sangria, 346
Sangrita Highball, 253
San Juan, 239
San Juan's Bolero, 239
Santa Ana's Bandana, 201
Santa Anita, 292
Saratoga, 124
Sauterne Cocktail, 57
Sauza Cocktail, 253
Savoy Hotel, 201
Saxon Lord, 239
Scarlet Lady, 305
Scarlett O'Hara, 201

Schnapps, 104
Scorpion, 240
Scotch Mist, 321
Scotch Sour, 321
Scotch Whiskey drinks, 102
   Affinity, 315
   Bairn, 316
   Balmoral, 316
   Barbary Coast, 132
   Barbary Coast, 316
   Barndoor, 316
   Beadlestone, 317
   Bloody Scot, 317
   Bobby Burns, 317
   Bonnie Dune, 318
   Canadian Redcoat, 308
   Cameron's Kick, 311
   Chocolate Fling, 321
   Daily Mail, 318
   Gibraltar, 318
   Goldenberg's Folly, 318
   Heather on the Hill, 319
   Highland Fling, 319
   Iron Lady, 319
   Japanese Fizz No. 2, 319
   Kerry Blue, 320
   Loch Lomond, 320
   Loch Ness Monster, 320
   Miami Beach, 320
   Queen of Scots, 322
   Rob Roy, 321
   Rusty Nail, 200
   Scotch Mist, 321
   Scotch Sour, 321
   Scot's Breakfast, 321
   Thistle, 317
   Tilt the Kilt, 322
   Walkman, 322
   Walter Mitty, 322
   Whispering Italian, 315
Scot's Breakfast, 321
Screwdriver, 279
Sean Sweeney, 361
Semiconductor, 332
September Morn, 240
Serpent's Smile, 313
7 & 7, 293
Sevilla, 240
Seville, 165
Shaking, 21-22
Shamrock, 314
Shandygaff, 332
Shanghai, 240
Shark's Tooth, 241
Sherry (see also Wine), 51
   Almond Cookie, 71
   Andalusia, 212
   Brazil, 82
   Creamy Thighs, 71
   Gibraltar, 318
   Granada, 118
   Green Hornet, 72
   Ibiza, 72
   O'Toole's Cooler, 72
   Quarter Deck, 237
   Renaissance Man, 72
   Seville, 240
   Spanish Milk Maid, 73
   Straight Law, 73
   Tuxedo, 73

Shooter, 31
Shrub, 31
Si!, 253
Sicilian Kiss, 125
Sidecar, 125
Silence Is Golden, 165
Silent Majority, 361
Silk Stockings, 254
Silver Fizz, 148
Singapore Sling, 165
Sink or Swim, 125
Sir Walter, 125
Slalom, 279
Slalom Frappe, 202
Sledgehammer, 241
Sleepyhead, 125-126
Slim Jim, 279
Sling:
   Singapore Sling, 165
Sloe Brandy, 126
Sloe Gin drinks:
   Black Bird, 296
   Eclipse, 177
   Irish Shillelagh, 312
   Kiss 'n' Tell, 120
   Sloe Brandy, 126
   Sloe Gin Fizz, 202
   Slow Comfortable Screw, 202
   Slow Screw, 202
Sloe Gin Fizz, 202
Slow Comfortable Screw, 202
Slow Screw, 202
Smash, 31
Snacks, with drinks, 14
Snakebite, 202

Snake River Stinger, 254
Snappy Yogurt, 367
Snowball, 165
Snowbird, 202
Solidarity, 279
Sombrero, 203
Sommeliere Frappe, 61
Soul Kiss, 293
Souperman, 361
Sour, 31
   Apple Sour, 110
   Apricot Sour, 111
   basic recipe, 32
   Boston Sour, 284
   Buffalo Sour, 58
   Egg Sour, 117
   Midori Sour, 190
   New York Sour, 291
   Pear Sour, 196
   Pisco Sour, 124
   Scotch Sour, 321
   Sourball, 126
Sourball, 126
Sour Bowl, 88
Sour Mash, 103
Southern Comfort drinks:
   Beach Blanket, 216
   Blazing Saddle, 283
   Blended Comfort, 283
   Cool Colonel, 298
   Dear John, 286
   Delta Flight, 299
   Ginny-Gin Southern, 181
   Happy Hour Punch, 339
   Hot Buttered Comfort, 356

Junta, 231
Maneater, 121
Mule Shoe, 157
1984, 158
Oxbend Bend, 194
Rhett Butler, 199
Scarlet O'Hara, 201
Stirrup Cup, 203
South Pacific, 126
Soyer au Champagne, 68
Spaghetti Western, 297
Spanish Dancer, 68
Spanish Milkmaid, 73
Spanish Moss, 254
Sparkling Carib Cocktail, 68
Sparkling Wines drinks (see also Wine), 48, 54
  Alto Parlare, 62
  Ambrosia for Two, 62
  Americana, 63
  April in Paris Ball, 63
  Bellini Punch, 63
  Black Velvet, 63
  Bloody French Dragon, 113
  Chartreuse Sparkling Wine, 64
  Chateau Julep, 298
  Chicago, 64
  Coco Lopez Ponche Colada, 335
  Cordial Medoc Cup, 64
  Cucumber Sparkling Wine, 64
  Elke Summer, 65
  Eve, 65
  Fizzoletto, 147
  French Foam, 65
  French Lift, 65
  Frobisher, 66
  Happy Hour Punch, 339
  Hawaiian Sparkling Wine Punch, 339
  Honolulu Punch, 340
  Imperial Czar, 270
  Kir Royale, 66
  Lanson Cocktail, 66
  Le Coq Hardy, 66
  Lemon Montserrat, 67
  London Special, 67
  Montserrat Ponche, 341
  Navy Punch, 341
  Park Avenue Orange Blossom, 342
  Patriarca, 67
  Pink California Sunshine, 67
  Pink Coco Wine Punch, 343
  Poinsettia, 68
  Soyer au Champagne, 68
  Spanish Dancer, 68
  Sparkling Carib Cocktail, 68
  Sparkling Wine Brunch Punch, 346
  Sparkling Wine Cooler, 69
  Sparkling Wine Julep, 69
  Sparkling Wine Polonaise, 69
  Sparkling Wine Punch, 347
  Sparkling Wine Sherbet Punch, 347
  Spiaggia Privata, 69
  Spinning Peach, 70
  Spumanti Granade, 70

Strawberry Bowl, 348
Vero, Vero Verde, 70
Victorian Mint Shrub, 349
Sparkling Wine Brunch Punch, 346
Sparkling Wine Cooler, 69
Sparkling Wine Julep, 69
Sparkling Wine Polonaise, 69
Sparkling Wine Punch, 347
Sparkling Wine Sherbet Punch, 347
Special Rough, 126
Spiaggia Privata, 69
Spinning Peach, 70
Spirits, 89
   absinthe, 103
   aquavit, 90, 105-107
   arak, 104, 323
   brandy, 90-92, 108-129
   gin, 92-93, 130-167
   liqueur (cordial), 93-98, 168-210
   okoleayo, 104
   rum, 98-100, 211-244
   schnapps, 104
   tequila, 100-101, 245-259
   vodka, 101-102, 260-281
   whiskey, 102-103
      American blended, 282-295
      bourbon, 296-305
      Canadian, 306-310
      Irish, 311-314
      Scotch, 315-322
Spiritual Rubescence, 241
Spritzer, 57

Spumanti Granade, 70
Spumoni Coffee, 361
Stab in the Back, 57
Star, 127
Star Daisy, 127
Star of Brazil, 203
Starters, 2
Stick Shift, 294
Stiletto, 241
Stinger:
   Amaretto Cognac Continental Stinger, 169
   basic recipe, 127
   Nutty Stinger, 193
   Roman Stinger, 200
Stirring, 21-22
Stirrup Cup, 203
Stoli Freeze, 280
Stone Age Sour, 305
Stone Fence, 127
Storage, of alcoholic beverages, 9-10
Straight, 32
Straight Law, 73
Strawberry Blow Fizz, 166
Strawberry Bowl, 348
Strawberry Fields, 204
Strawberry Liqueur drinks:
   Pink Mink, 275
   Strawberry Blow Fizz, 166
   Strawberry Fields, 204
Strega Daiquiri, 204
Strega drinks:
   Exorcist, 148
   Strega Daiquiri, 204

Strega Freeze, 204
Strega Freeze, 204
Sub-Bourbon, 305
Sugar, 20
Sugar syrup recipe, 20
Suissese, 204
Summer Punch, 348
Sunrise, 254
Sunset, 255
Sunshine Special, The, 205
Sun Worshipper, 242
Super Bowl Cocktail, 205
Supplies, ingredient, 9-13
Sutter's Mill, 242
Swedish Lullaby, 205
Swedish Punch Liqueur drinks:
    Garden of Sweden, 181
    143 Percent, 193
    Swedish Lullaby
Swedish Secret, 107
Swinger's Cocktail, 242
Swizzle:
    basic recipe, 32
    Gin Swizzle, 147
Syllabub, 32
Syrups, flavored, 20-21

Tahiti Club, 242
Tampico, 348
Tango of Love, 88
Tawny Russian, 205
Tapatio, 255
Taxco Fizz, 255
Tequila drinks:
    Acapulco I, 211

Bertha, 245
Bloody Maria, 245
Blue Chimney Smoke, 246
Changuirongo, 246
Charro, 246
Coco Loco, 247
Compadre, 247
Conchita, 247
Depth Charge, 248
Duke's Daisy, 248
El Conejo, 248
Fiesta, 248
Frozen Tequila, 249
Gavilan .45, 249
Gentle Bull, 249
Golden Margarita, 249
Gordita, 250
Gorilla Sweat, 355
Grand Margarita, 251
Hand Grenade, 250
Horny Bull, 250
Juarez Cocktail, 123
Margarita No. 1, 250
Margarita No. 2, 251
Matador, 251
Mexican Sunrise, 251
Mockingbird, 251
Oxbend Bend, 194
Pappy McCoy, The, 195
Pina, 252
Pinata, 252
Revolution, 252
Rosita, 252
Sangrita Highball, 253
Sauza Cocktail, 253

Si!, 253
Silk Stockings, 254
Snake River Stinger, 254
Spanish Moss, 254
Sunrise, 254
Sunset, 255
Tapatio, 255
Taxco Fizz, 255
Tequila Bloody Bull, 255
Tequila Collins, 256
Tequila Julep, 256
Tequila Martini, 256
Tequila 'n' Coke, 256
Tequila Neat, 257
Tequila with Sangrita Chaser, 257
Tequila Tropical, 258
TNT, 258
Toreador, 258
Trombone, 259
Two Fingers Mariachi, 362
Villa Villa, 259
Walrus, 207
Tequila Bloody Bull, 255
Tequila Collins, 256
Tequila Julep, 256
Tequila Martini, 256
Tequila 'n' Coke, 256
Tequila Neat, 257
Tequila with Sangrita Chaser, 257
Tequila Tropical, 258
Thirsty Camel, 206
Thistle, 317
Tilt the Kilt, 322

Tingle, 280
Tipperary, 314
T.L.C., 294
TNT, 258
Toasted Almond, 206
Toddy:
    basic recipe, 32-33
    Ginger Toddy, 354
Tom & Jerry, 362
Tonic:
    Arabian Night, 323
    basic recipe, 33
    Gin & Tonic, 145
    Orange Tonic, 194
    TNT, 258
Toreador, 258
Toronto Cocktail, 310
Torrid Zone, 243
Tre Scalini, 128
Triple Sec drinks:
    Boxcar No. 2, 136
    Chapel Hill, 285
    Chinchilla, 175
    City Slicker, 115
    Holly Golightly, 301
    Margarita No. 1, 250
    Melon Patch, 190
    Orangecicle, 194
    Paradise Lost, 234
    Parisian Blonde, 234
    Refresco, 234
Tuaca Liqueur drinks:
    Dandelion, 177
Tuxedo, 73
Twist, citrus, 22

Two Fingers Mariachi, 362

Uncle Minty, 206
Unicycle, 128
Union Jack, 166
Up the Academy, 88

Vegas Smile, 206
Velvet Hammer, 207
Velvet Kiss, 166
Venetian Blind, 207
Vermouth Cassis, 88
Vermouth (see also Aperitifs;
  Bitters), 51, 74-77
  Addington, 78
  Adonis, 78
  Affinity, 315
  Algonquin, 79
  Alliance, 79
  Almond Cocktail, 79
  American Beauty, 109
  American Beauty Rose, 79
  Americano, 80
  Apple Pie, 212
  Artillery, 132
  Assassins, 282
  BVD, 137
  Beadlestone, 317
  Beauty Mark, 80
  Bitter Bikini, 80
  Bloodhound, 81
  Blue Denim, 81
  Blue Moon, 81
  Bobby Burns, 317
  Bombay, 82
  Bourbon Italian, 297
  Brazil, 82
  Campobello, 137
  Caruso, 138
  Cinzano, 82
  Creole, 285
  Deep Six, 139
  Diplomat, 82
  Dry Dock, 83
  Duchess of Denver, 83
  Favorite, 142
  Fiesta, 248
  50-50, 143
  First Strike, 83
  Frankensteen, 143
  Gazette, 118
  Gin & It, 145
  Gold Stripe, 83
  Green Room, 84
  Gypsy, 149
  Harper's Ferry, 84
  Horse Car, 288
  I.R.S., 150
  Iron Lady, 319
  Italian, 84
  Jewel, 150
  Kangaroo, 271
  Kingdom Come, 85
  Knockout, 142
  Lemon Cooler, 85
  Martini, 153-154
  Merry Widow, 155
  Metropolitan, 122
  Miami Beach, 320
  Morning Becomes Electric, 85

Negroni, 86
Nineteen, 158
Odessa File, 274
Paddy's Wagon, 313
Pale Moon, 86
Parisian, 160
Park & 59th, 160
Party Girl, 86
Perfect Cocktail, 86
Perpetual, 87
Pink Panther, 161
Pirate of Penzance, 236
Puntegroni, 87
Rolls-Royce, 164
Rosita, 252
Serpent's Smile, 313
Sevilla, 240
Shamrock, 314
Soul Kiss, 293
Star, 127
Stick Shift, 294
Tango of Love, 88
Tipperary, 314
Toronto Cocktail, 310
Unicycle, 128
Up the Academy, 88
Vermouth Cassis, 88
Walkman, 322
Washington, 128
Wheeler Dealer, 294
Whip, 88
Vero, Vero Verde, 70
Vesuvio, 362
Via Veneto, 128
Victorian Mint Shrub, 349

Viking, 107
Viva Villa, 259
Vodka drinks:
  Apple Knocker, 260
  Aqueduct, 260
  Banana Boat, 261
  Banshee, 171
  Barnacle Bill, 261
  Black Marble, 261
  Bloody Bull, 261
  Bloody Mary, 261
  Blue Lagoon, 263
  Blue Monday, 263
  Blue Mountain, 218
  Blushin' Russian, 264
  Boggy Bay, 264
  Boomerang, 271
  Bull Shot, 262
  Bullfrog, 264
  Cape Codder, 264
  Cape Grape, 265
  Carmen Miranda, 265
  Casablanca, 174
  Catnip, 265
  Clamdigger, 265
  Cock 'n' Bull, 262
  Cold Feet, 175
  Cole Porter, 139
  Dark Eyes, 266
  Dublin Delight, 266
  Easy Piece, 266
  Egghead, 266
  Fan-Tan, 267
  Finnish Glogg, 353
  Fjord, 106

Flame of Love, 267
Front-Page Dynamite, 267
Geisha Girl, 262
Ginger Snap, 268
Golda Major, 268
Gorky Park, 267
Grass Skirt, 268
Ground Zero, 183
Gypsy Moth, 268
Harvey Sly Banger, 183
Harvey Wallbanger, 269
Hawaiian Eye, 269
Hawaiian Mint Limeade, 269
Hayride, 269
High Roller, 270
I.R.S., 150
Imperial Czar, 270
Jesse White, 270
Judgement Day, 270
KGB, 151
Kangaroo, 271
Kiss, The, 271
Kremlin Colonel, 271
Kretchma, 272
La Belle Liza, 272
Malibu Beach, 188
Malinky Malchick, 272
Maria Sangre, 262
Melon Ball, 189
Melon Patch, 190
Midnight Sun, 272
Moon over Moscow, 273
Moscow Mule, 273
Mr. Lucky, 273
Mystic Cooler, 274

Naked Maja, 274
Ninotchka, 274
Odessa File, 274
Open Sesame, 275
Panzer, 275
Peacharino, 275
Pink Mink, 275
Pittsburgh Spirit, The, 275
Polish Sidecar, 276
Prairie Oyster, 276
Purple Passion, 276
Red Baron, 276
Red Flannels, 263
Red Rock Canyon, 277
Red Russian, 199
Rubino, 87
Russian Bear, 277
Russian Cocktail, 277
Russian Coffee, 277
Russian Lady, 278
Russian Nail, 278
Russian Pipeline, 278
Russian Tea, 360
Saketini, 331
Salt Lick, 278
Screwdriver, 279
Silent Majority, 361
Slalom, 279
Slim Jim, 279
Snowbird, 202
Solidarity, 279
Souperman, 361
South Pacific, 126
Stoli Freeze, 280
Swinger's Cocktail, 242

413

Tampico, 348
Tawny Russian, 205
Tingle, 280
Vodka Martini, 280
Volga Boatman, 280
Warsaw, 280
Whistler's Mother, 281
White Whisker, 210
Wild Brew Yonder, 332
Wombat, 281
Yellow Fever, 281
Zero Option, 281
Vodka Martini, 280
Volga Boatman, 280

Walkman, 322
Walrus, 207
Walter Mitty, 322
Warming, cups & mugs, 20
Warsaw, 280
Washing glasses, 19
Washington, 128
Wedding Night Nog, 368
Weekend, 207
Weep No More, 129
Welsh Connexion, 208
Western Martini, The, 310
Wheeler Dealer, 294
Whip, 88
Whiskey (see Spirits)
Whiskey Sour, 294
Whiskey TNT, 295
Whispering Italian, 315
Whistler's Mother, 281

White Cloud, 208
White Gloves, 208
White Lady, 208
White Lily, 209
White Lion, 243
White Mouse, 209
White-Out, 209
White Sale, 167
White Shadow, 295
White Velvet, 209
White Way, 129
White Whisker, 210
White wine (see also Wine), 38-41, 45-46
  Cassis Punch, 334
  Chablis Cooler, 55
  French Punch, 338
  Hollywood & Wine, 56
  Kir, 56
  Locomotive, 359
  Marquise, 56
  Mr. Lucky, 273
  Orange Oasis, 342
  Peppery Punch, 343
  Raspberry Cocktail, 56
  Sauterne Cocktail, 57
  Spritzer, 57
  Stab in the Back, 57
  Summer Punch, 348
  White Wine Cup, 349
  Wine Chiller, 57
White Wine Cup, 349
Widow's Dream, 210
Widow's Kiss, 129
Wild Brew Yonder, 332

Wine, 34
- bottles, 17
- character chart, 45-48
- choosing, 35-36
- dessert wine, 50-51
- food and, 52-53
- labels, 37-38
- opening, pouring & serving, 53-54
- red, 41-43, 58-61
- sherry, 51, 71-73
- sparkling, 48, 62-70
- table wine, 44
- white, 38-41, 55-57
- vintage chart, 49

Wine Chiller, 57
Witch's Twitch, 243
Wombat, 281

Yard of Flannel, 363
Yellow Fever, 281
Yellowknife, 310
Yogi Bitter, 368

Zero Option, 281
Zombie, 244
Zoom, 129

AS THE DRINK WORLD CHANGES . . . YOU ARE INVITED TO SEND US RECIPES OF NEW DRINKS WHICH YOU HAVE CREATED OR DISCOVERED

THE DRINK DIRECTORY will continue to collect authentic recipes of new drinks which become popular as well as on-going classics for future editions. You are invited to contribute recipes for new drinks which you have created or discovered, which have become popular in your establishment or area. Please send your recipe(s), containing precise ingredients (including type of glass and amount of ice) and preparation instructions, with your name, address, and signature to:

THE DRINK DIRECTORY
P.O. BOX 5221
F.D.R. Station
New York, NY 10150

Submission of your recipe(s) with your signature constitutes your full permission to the author to use your recipe(s) in future editions and promotion of *THE DRINK DIRECTORY*, without charge or obligation. If your recipe is used, you will have your contribution duly credited, and will receive a complimentary copy of that edition.

THANK YOU VERY MUCH!   CHEERS!